AF556431

MARATHAS AND THEIR ADMINISTRATION

Encyclopaedic History of Indian Freedom Movement Series

MARATHAS AND THEIR ADMINISTRATION

Edited by

OM PRAKASH

ANMOL PUBLICATIONS PVT. LTD.

NEW DELHI - 110 002 (INDIA)

ANMOL PUBLICATIONS PVT. LTD.
4374/4B, Ansari Road, Daryaganj
New Delhi - 110 002
Ph.: 23261597, 23278000
Visit us at: www.anmolpublications.com

Marathas and Their Administration

First Edition, 2004

ISBN 81-261-1510-6

PRINTED IN INDIA

Published by J.L. Kumar for Anmol Publications Pvt. Ltd., New Delhi - 110 002 and Printed at Mehra Offset Press, Delhi.

Contents

Preface

'Golden bird' as India was known in yore days, rich in natural resources and well-developed cottage industries it was considered an affluent country. Indian spices, fabrics and other handicrafts were in great demand the world over. In the lure of having these goods and riches, many European powers made adventurous voyages to locate India.

The story of European expansions in Asia forms one of the great epics of modern times. India was the cornerstone of European imperialism in Asia. It was the lure of the lucrative 'Indian trade' which incited European adventurers to seek a new route to India, thus inaugurating a new era of contact between these two distant lands. Among the European empires in Asia, the British empire was the most enduring and prosperous one. And India was the finest jewel of the British dominion. It is worthwhile to remember that European exploration and adventure in the east were encouraged by the great demand in Europe for the products from Malabar like spices and calicoe cloth. Symbolically, the European age in Indian and indeed Asian history began with the landing of Vasco-de-Gama at Calicut on the 27th of May 1498. During this period, there was a continuous struggle between European traders and their native rivals and among the Europeans themselves. By the end of the eighteenth century this struggle for supremacy had been resolved in favour of the English.

The European traders were originally in the position of supplicants before the native rulers in India. For example, when William Hawkins arrived at the court of Jehangir with a letter from King James I asking for trade facilities, he had brought with him, a gift of 25,000 Gold pieces. As Lane Poole observes,

"There was nothing to suggest the most distant dream that in two centuries and a half the slight introduction Hawkins was then effecting between England and India would culminate in the sovereignty of a British Queen over the whole empire."

But unlike their European rivals like the Portuguese and the Dutch, the English made their bid for power in India only when the powerful Mughal empire had begun to decline. In any case the Portuguese and the Dutch had only small coastal settlements in India even at the height of their power and influence in this country.

By the end of the seventh Century, the Portuguese had been displaced by their Dutch rivals in Malabar and in the islands, of the East Indies. As for the Dutch, they were compelled by force of circumstances to regard the factories "which they established on the main land merely as marketing points for the products of an Empire which had its capital at Batavia in the East Indies."

Moreover, the Dutch power in India was largely jeopardised on European battle fields.

The wars with England and France drained the resources of this nation. Thus, it was left to the French to provide real opposition to the English in India.

The same pattern can be detected in the story of European activity in Malabar. Here the intensity of their rivalry was greater because of three main reasons. Malabar with its many fine harbours and backwaters was more accessible from the sea, increasing the scope for European interference.

Thus, European powers who came to India with the intention of trade snatched the political power and sovereignty from the local states, principalities and feudal lords. And established complete control over India. After over hundred years colonial rule, the feeling of national integration and freedom from the clutches of foreign power developed among the Indians. Thus, began the saga of freedom movement.

This encyclopaedic study is phased into two most significant and historic diversions having deep bearing on varied kinds of events which moulded the destiny of millions of people of Indian sub-continent. These events having complete political overtones, became a glaring phenomenon with the downfall of the Mughal Empire almost with the commencement of the 18th century. The ambitious piercing eyes of four European powers — the British, the French, the Portuguese and the Dutch—did cast upon several gainful economic successes in India.

Of these powers, the East India Company's government, with well organised force, bureaucracy and diplomats achieved phenomenal successes against their adversaries. The first phase,—therefore has been marked from Plassey to the Mutiny of 1857 (The First War of Independence) when the Company's role came to an end.

The second phase, naturally, came very much in the hands of the British Government functioning under the Whitehall and ended with the dawn of Swaraj on 15 August 1947.

This multi-volumes study would take up several themes, viz. political, socio-economic, religious, constitutional, educational, press, revolutionaries, local pioneers, legislation, revenues and judicial policy, on-going process of reaction — violent and non-violent, moderates and extremists, local and all India movements, reaction of the British Raj, efforts for conciliation, significant Acts passed by the Central Legislature, the impact of two global wars, 1914-1919 and 1939-1945; Congress, Muslim League, Hindu Mahasabha and the British Policy, a significant change in Britain soon after 1945, the Labour Government of Clement Attlee and Partition of India in August 1947.

In the first lot eleven volumes have appeared while in the present second lot ten volumes are being brought out namely the Marathas and their administration; Lord William Bentinck and Metcalf era of reforms; Raja Rammohun Roy: the reformer; Mutiny and its aftermath; History of Anglo-Sikh wars;

Emergence of Maharaja Ranjit Singh; Lord Hastings and his administrative measures; Ranjit Singh administration and British policy; British policy of intervention and expansion; and Lord Wellesley and policy of expansion.

This prestigious project is arranged, managed and looked after by a team of most dedicated and long experienced scholars of modern Indian history.

In gathering the authentic information, we have taken liberty to draw the material from the learned works of many great scholars in the field. We are deeply beholden to all those whose works are partially cited or substantially made use of in the project. I am indebted to Mr. J.L. Kumar, Managing Director, Anmol Publications Pvt. Ltd., New Delhi for his constant inspiration and moral support and finally to bring out this work. Last but not the least I am thankful to all those who have assisted me one way or other while preparing the manuscript.

—Om Prakash

1

Central Government

I

1. Disorder and Anarchy a Heritage

"Shivaji Raja was famous for his forts", says Lokahitavadi.[1] He had captured and built no less than two hundred and forty forts and strongholds.[2] He used to prize them highly and large sums were usually granted for their up-keep and repair.[3] The importance of these forts in a defensive war had been amply demonstrated in his lifelong struggle against the Mughals, yet no one will concede for a moment that fortification of inaccessible hills and rocky isles formed Shivaji's best claim to the reverence of posterity. His greatness as a military leader has never been contested, but his greatness as a civil administrator is perhaps still more undoubted. The Marathas have been well known for their military prowess from time immemorial. The old Rashtrikas, their ancestors, were soldiers of no mean reputation. They had fought under the banner of the Chalukya prince Palakeshin and beaten back the victorious army of the great Harshavardhan. Ferishta tells us how difficult the Bahmani kings found it to tackle the mountain chiefs of Maharashtra. They had again won fresh laurels under the celebrated Malik Amber, when the Mughal forces of the great Akbar had to beat an ignominious retreat before them. Shivaji, therefore, found the materials for an efficient army ready made. The rocks and hills, the mountain passes of his native land, offered him suit, able sites for impregnable forts. But neither the nature of the country nor the character of its inhabitants was in favour of the establishment of an orderly government.

Shivaji had to evolve order out of chaos. The Nizamshahi dynasty had been overthrown by the Mughal arms while Shivaji was still a little child. The Bijapur government was not strong enough to maintain peace and order. The country was devastated by war, and even the neighbourhood of Poona was depopulated. Dadaji Konddev had to offer rewards for killing wolves[4] that infested the uncultivated fields and deserted homesteads and the people who lived in the Mawal valley were in many respects worse than wild beasts. Blood feud was the order of the day, and plunder and rapine formed the normal state of things. Almost every watan had two or more claimants and they fought to the bitter end. In his blind fury the Maratha watandar felt no pity for his rival's widow and orphan children. But even the apparent destruction of the family would not bring the feud to an end. The loyalty of an old adherent would often save a pregnant lady or an infant heir in some village or mountain fastness far away from their native hamlet. The child would never be allowed to forget the wrongs of his family. When grown up he was sure to avenge his dead relations, and plundered house.[5] The anarchy of the time has left its marks on the family papers of the old Deshmukhs, and nowhere do we get a more terrible account of these feuds in all their horrors and bloodshed than in the papers of the *Jagdales* of *Masur* and the Jedhes of Rohidkhore. The Jagdales could not even count on the fidelity of their own servants. Their family history runs as follows:

"The Desai of Karhad was Jagde Rau Rajgardal Deshmukh. He had two wives, they had four sons; Babaji Rau was the son of the first wife. The sons of the second were three, the eldest Ramaji Rau, the second Vithoji Rau, and the youngest, Dayaji Rau. Such were the four (sons). Then the father became old, and they began to quarrel. The father said, "You should not quarrel. I shall divide among you what is yours" so he said. Then he gave to the eldest. Babaji Rau the Patilship and the Deshmukhi of Masur and the villages under its jurisdiction. To Ramaji Rau (and others) he gave four villages, Karhad, Aud and two other villages under the jurisdiction of Karhad. Then Ramaji Rau stationed two barbers of Aud as his agents at Karhad and two clerks. Raghunath Pant and another, for the work of management. At that time the barber, the clerk and the Mokasi had united. Then these three decided to murder the three brothers Ramaji Rau, Vithoji Rau and Dayaji Rau. They shut the two brothers Ramaji and Dayaji Rau in a room and murdered (them). Then the remaining brother Vithoji Rau fled and came to Masur. At that time the Patilship of Targaon also was ours. A Brahman was stationed there as an agent. The Brahman engaged two servants Kaligade and Khochre and he and his son proceeded to Benares; on the way they were murdered by Kaligade and Khochre. Then these two began to quarrel about the Patilship. And Babaji Rau became very old. He had two sons—the elder Vithoji and the younger Kumaji. A *mali* (gardener) was in his service. Every day five maunds of flowers were strewn on his bedstead for Babaji Rau's enjoyment. Then he became very old and the *mujavar* (sweepers of the mosque) waxed strong in the village. The sons of his old age (being very young) were 4 and 1½ years of age. So he engaged the mali for the management of his household, and for the management of the fields was engaged a *ḍhangar* who tended (his) sheep. Mangi dhangarin was his mother. The mujavar, the mali and the dhangarin made a common cause and decided to murder Babaji Rau and his children. And then the murderers came. They wrapped the younger son in a rug and threw him below the cot and murdered Babaji Rau in his bed. Then the elder son said, "I have recognised you. You are the sweepers of the village mosque and you have murdered my father." Thus he spoke, and they murdered him. Babaji's wife had concealed herself in a corner. She fled to Chitli with the younger son Kumaji. These are by no means the only murders in the bloody annals of the Jagdale family. The mujavars did not escape unpunished. Young Kumaji wreaked a terrible vengeance and decapitated three of them.[6] Shahaji, the father of Shivaji, took the Patilship of Masur with the life of its owner, an uncle of Mahadji Jagdale Deshmukh.[7] The revenge of those irreconcilable spirits knew no awe or respect for power, and the Jagdales sought a strong ally to assert their claim against Shahaji's son Shivaji. But their connection with the Mughals brought fresh disasters on them and at length these turbulent Deshmukhs had to forget their pride and seek Shivaji's protection and patronage.

If the Jagdale annal is a savage one, no less gruesome is that of the Jedhes. One of the two Jedhe brothers, while returning from the Adilshahi capital with a *farman* for their watan, was waylaid and murdered by one Khore, a rival claimant. The surviving brother Baji fled to the sea coast, assembled a few adherents, purchased the assistance of twelve good swordsmen at the cost of a portion of his ancestral property, and calmly waited for a suitable opportunity. Such an opportunity came, when Khopre, off his guard, was celebrating his marriage. Hardly were the nuptials over, then Baji Jedhe with his followers fell upon Khopre and murdered him with sixty of his attendants. Kanhoji, a descendant of Bai, became so powerful that he defied the authority of the Adilshahi king. He left seven sons; the youngest of whom Naikji was won over by the Sultan; two of his elder brothers killed him in their anger, and were in their turn murdered by Naikji's widow Ansaba, who afterwards gave birth to a posthumous son. Her infuriated brothers-in-law had no mercy either for the widow or for her baby. Ansaba was soon after murdered, but the devotion of a nurse saved the child who took shelter with Baji Pasalkar. Hardly was the family dissension over then Kanhoji, son of Naikji, began to quarrel with the Bandal Deshmukh and a bloody battle was fought. Their differences were settled when Kanhoji entered the service of Shivaji.[8] But the Khopres, though humbled, had not been rendered altogether harmless. They joined Afzal Khan against their rivals' master, Shivaji.[9]

Such were the men whom Shivaji had to deal with and the times in which he had to work.

2. Further Difficulties

He was further handicapped in his work of reorganisation and reform by the ignorant indifference of his subordinates and lack of comprehension on their part. The art of war, as a source of honour and emolument appealed to them more than the art of peace. If they had been allowed to follow their individual inclination, they would have gladly renounced the work of consolidation for a campaign of conquest. No less a man than Nilo Pant Mazumdar had earnestly prayed to be relieved of his civil duties so that he might "render military service, like other men and capture forts when necessary." Nor was he reconciled to his duties until Shivaji had assured him that his services in his civil capacity were as important as those of a commanding officer and would be appreciated in the same manner as the military exploits of the Peshwa.[10]

But Shivaji never tried to achieve the impossible. A practical statesman, he wisely rejected all unworkable ideals. He knew that the difficulties in his way were great, but he also knew that without an orderly government his kingdom would not be worth a moment's purchase, and so long as private war and blood feuds continued, he would not be able to introduce in his young army that strict discipline which was essentially required for his very existence. Peace and order were absolutely necessary. But unless he could unite under his banner the numerous chiefs who exercised petty sovereignty in Maharashtra, a strong orderly government would be an idle dream. Once his aim was defined, he refused to be hampered by ordinary scruples. Policy required that he should try conciliation first. He was frequently unsuccessful, but whenever conciliation failed he did not hesitate to take stronger measures. One by one, the Deshmukhs of Mawal submitted to his authority and a considerable portion of the Bijapur territory was conquered.

It was now that Shivaji had to frame a working scheme of government; but he was confronted with a very difficult problem. He had to decide how far the old system should be continued and to what extent reformed. Wholesale conservation and wholesale reform were equally out of question. The first would grant a fresh lease of life to feudalism with its concomitant evils of private war, blood feud, anarchy and oppression. A keen observer, he did not fail to notice the evil effects of the feudal system in the tottering kingdoms of Bijapur and Golkonda. But the total abolition of feudalism would alienate most of his countrymen, some of whom had submitted to him but reluctantly. He knew that the great defect of the Maratha character was its selfish individualism. The Maratha watandar thought of his watan first and of his country afterwards. Shivaji had, therefore, to strike a mean between the two extremes that would at the same time reconcile the watandars and ensure comparative order and peace.

3. General Structure of Government

The village communities in Southern India flourished from the dawn of history. When these democratic institutions first came into existence none can tell.[11] But in the absence of a highly developed central government, as we now have, the village communities served the needs of the time admirably. Shivaji decided to leave them undisturbed in their internal organisation. It fact the village republics exercised almost the same powers, enjoyed the same privileges and underwent the same responsibilities from the time of their origin down to the establishment of the British Government in India, when many of their immunities and privileges were found incompatible with a highly centralised modern government. Over a group of these self-contained units had formerly been placed the Deshmukhs and the Deshpandes. Originally appointed for revenue collection, they gradually made their office hereditary and assumed and exercised almost sovereign authority. The circumstances of the times, and the geographical features of the country, helped this feudal evolution. But Shivaji, therefore, appointed his own revenue officers, but the Deshmukhs and the Deshpandes were left in the enjoyment of their old rights and perquisites. They were on no account to exercise their old tyranny. Rayats were given to understand that henceforth they would have nothing to do with the Desais and the Deshmukhs. To render them altogether harmless Shivaji further prohibited them to build any walled or bastioned castle, and like Henry II of England, demolished some of the strongholds of these local tyrants.[12] "In the provinces", Sabhasad says, "the rayats were not to be subjected to the jurisdiction and regulations of the Zamindar, such as the Deshmukh and the Desai. If they offer to plunder the rayats, by assuming authority (over them), it does not lie in their power. The Adilshahi, the Nizamshahi and the Mughlai Desh were conquered (by Shivaji). In the Desh all the rayats used to be under the Patil and the Kulkarni of those places, and the Deshmukhs. They used to make the collection and to pay an unspecified sum (as tribute). For a village, where the Mirasdars took one to two thousand (Hons or Rupees?), (they) used to render two hundred to three hundred to the Government as quit-rent. Therefore the Mirasdar grew wealthy and strengthened (himself) by building bastions, castles and strongholds in the village and enlisting footmen and musketeers. They did not care to wait on the revenue officers. If the revenue officers said that they could pay more revenue (the Mirasdars) stood up to quarrel with them. In this way (they grew) unruly and forcibly misappropriated the (lands in the) Desh. On this account did the Raja demolish the bastions, the castles and the strongholds after conquering the Desh. Where there were important forts, he posted his own garrison. And nothing was left in the hands of the Mirasdars. This, done, (he) prohibited all that the Mirasdars used to take at their sweet will, by inam (right) or revenue farming, and fixed the rates of due in cash and grains for the Zamindars, as well as of the rights and the perquisites of the Deshmukh, the Deshkulkarni, and the Patil (and) the Kulkarni, according to the yield of the village. The Zamindars were prohibited to build bastioned castles. (They were to) build houses (and) live (therein). Such were the regulations for the provinces". In this manner the danger of feudal anarchy was to some extent averted.

4. Astha-Pradhan Council

Like the Kamavisdars and the Subhedars of the Peshwa period, the Karkuns, the Tarafdars, the Havaldars and the Subhedars of Shivaji had to look after all the branches of Civil administration. At the head of the government was the king himself, assisted by a council of state. It was known as the Ashta Pradhan Council, as eight ministers had seats in it. These were:

1. The Peshwa or the Mukhya Pradhan.
2. The Mazumdar or the Amatya.
3. The Wakins or the Mantri.
4. The Dabir or the Sumanta.
5. The Surnis or the Sachiv.
6. The Pandit Rao, or the Royal Priest.
7. The Senapati or the Commander-in-Chief.
8. The Nyayadhish or the Chief Justice.

When this council was first organised, we do not precisely know. At the time of the coronation the eight[13] 'pradhans' (ministers) had stood on either side of the throne to pour holy water from gold and silver jars and basins, over the king's head.[14] Malhar Ram Rao Chitnis tells us that it was then that the council came into being.[15] These offices, however, were by no means new. Though the Mukhya Pradhan, the Amatya, the Mantri, the Sumanta, the Sachiv and the Senapati were unknown, people were quite familiar with the Peshwa, the Mazumdar, the Wakins, the Dabir, the Surnis, and the Sarnobat. What Shivaji did, was to retain the old posts with new Sanskrit designations. But whether these new designations meant any new power or new responsibility, is not certain. It is, however, significant that an official paper (kanujabta) was drawn in the first year of the *Abhisheka* era to enumerate the duties of the eight Councillors (pradhans) and other heads of departments.[16] But it is quite possible that this paper was drawn up simply to enforce a stricter method in the existing organisation. Sabhasad tells us that the following officers had enjoyed the privilege of taking part in the coronation ceremony as members of the Astha Pradhan Council:

1. Moro Pant, son of Trimbak Pant, as Mukhya Pradhan.
2. Naro Nilkantha and Ramchandra Nilkantha as joint Amatya.
3. The son of Raghunath Rao as Pandit Rao.
4. Hambir Rao Mohite as Senapati.
6. Ramchandra Pant, son of Trimbakji Sondev Dabir as Sumanta.
7. Annaji Pant (Datto) as Sachiv.
8. Niraji Rauji as Nyayadhish.[17]

These men had already held these offices for some time past. Sabhasad, while describing the coronation, refers simply to their new Sanskrit designations, but does not say that these posts were newly created. It is quite possible that Chitnis also had in his mind the introduction of Sanskrit designations when he wrote of the Raja's decision of appointing a council of eight. Both Sabhasad and Chitnis make frequent mention of the past incumbents of these offices. Sabhasad, for example, says that one Sham Rao Nilkanth was Moro Trimbak Pingle's[18] predecessor in the Peshwarship.[19] Shivaji's first Sarnobat was one Tukoji Chor Maratha.[20] He was succeeded by Mankoji Dahatonde.[21] We do not know why Tukoji lost his master's confidence, but after the conquest of Jawli, the Chief command of the army was conferred on Netaji Palkar[22] as Mankoji had in the meantime died. Netaji was dismissed for his failure to succour Panhala,[23] and an enterprising cavalry officer, Kadtaji Gujar, obtained the Sarnobatship with the title of Pratap Rao. Finally after Pratap Rao's heroic death in a hard-fought battle, his lieutenant Hasaji Mohite was promoted to be Commander-in-Chief.[24] It was this Hasaji or Hambir Rao, the fifth or according to another account, the sixth Sarnobat,[25] who stood with a silver jar filled with milk at the time of the ceremonial bath, during Shivaji's coronation.[26] Similarly Nilo Sondev and Gangaji Mangaji had served as Surnis and Wakins respectively, before Annaji Datto and Dattaji Trimbak.[27] It is also certain that both before and after his coronation, Shivaji held a council of these and other officers. To cite only one instance, when Afzal Khan invaded his infant kingdom, Shivaji called a council of his principal ministers, among whom figured not only Moro Pant, Gangaji Mangaji, Netaji Palkar and Raghunath Ballal (most of them afterwards members of the Ashtha Pradhan Council), but also men like Gomaji Naik, Krishnaji Naik and Subhanji Naik.[28] It does not appear, therefore, that the council was first organised at the time of the coronation. Nor can it be maintained that the Ashtha Pradhan Council owed its origin to the creative genius of Shivaji. The Persian designation of such officers as the Dabir, the Surnis, the Wakins, and the Mazumdar clearly shows that analogous offices did exist under the Muhammadan governments of the south. Mention has also been made of such councils in old Hindu works on polity. In the Shukraniti, for example, we find that the chief Priest and the Chief Justice should have seats in the cabinet, and this was a special feature of Shivaji's council.[29]

When the Peshwas rose to power, most of these offices had become hereditary, but in Shivaji's time, the pradhans (councillors) were not appointed for life. They were liable to be dismissed at the king's pleasure and could not transmit their office to their sons of brothers. In the Peshwa period principal officers generally became founders of new families. This was impossible in Shivaji's time. First, because he took good care to keep all offices, both high and low, free from a hereditary character. We have seen how six Commanders-in-Chief had been in succession appointed by Shivaji, but not in a single case had he selected for the post a near relative of the last incumbent. Suryaji Malsure was no doubt appointed Subhedar of the Mawali forces, after the death of his brother Tanaji; but in this case the officer in question had rendered such distinguished service as fully deserved public recognition.[30] Secondly, because Shivaji made it a rule not to assign any Jagir to any office, civil or military. It was strictly laid down that no soldier or military officer should have anything to do with the revenue collection of the country and there was, in those days of anarchy and war, hardly any officer who was not required to take up arms. In Sabhasad's account we find that, "the balance of their dues (was paid by) `varats' (orders) either on the Huzur (central government) or on the district (establishments). In this manner were their annual accounts punctually settled. Mokasa mahals or villages with absolute rights should on no account be granted to the (men in the) army, the militia and the garrisons of the fort. Every payment should be made by `varats' or with cash from the treasury. None but the Karkuns had authority over the lands. All payments to the army, the militia, and the garrison, should be made by the Karkuns."[31] These wise regulations had their desired effect, and arrested for the time being the growth of feudalism in Maharashtra. In the words of Ranade, "None of the great men, who distinguished themselves in Shivaji's time, were able to hand over to their descendants large landed estates. Neither Moropant Pingle nor Abaji Sondev, nor Ragho Ballal or Datto Annaji or Niraji Raoji, among the Brahmans, nor the Malusares or Kanks, or Pratap Rao Gujar, Netaji Palkar, Hambirrao Mohite or the Maratha *Sardars*, were able to find ancient families such as those which Shahu's ministers in the early part of the eighteenth century succeeded in doing".[32]

Though we do not know precisely when the Ashta Pradhan Council came into being, yet we have a fairly accurate knowledge of what was expected of the pradhans.

In a paper[33] already referred to, their duties have been clearly defined. From this and other state papers, it does not appear that Shivaji aimed at a bureaucratic from of government. A great Maharashtra scholar, the late Justice Ranade, has thrown clear hints that the Ashta Pradhan Council, in its essential characteristics, bore a striking resemblance to the Viceroy's Executive Council. Says the great savant, "The *Peshwa* was Prime Minister, next to the king and was at the head of both the civil and military administrations, and sat first on the right hand below the throne. The *Senapati* was in charge of the military administration, and sat first on the left side. *Amatya* and *Sachiv* sat next to the *Peshwa,* while the *Mantri* sat next below the *Sachiv* and was in charge of the king's private affairs. The *Sumant* was Foreign Secretary, and sat below the *Senapati* on the left. Next came *Panditrao,* who had charge of the ecclesiastical department,, and below him on the left side sat the Chief Justice. It will be seen from these details that the *Astha Pradhan* system has its counterpart in the present constitution of the Government of India. The Governor-General and Viceroy occupies the place of the *Peshwa;* next comes the Commander-in-Chief of the army. The Finance and Foreign Minister come next. In the Government of India, the Executive Council makes no room for the head of the ecclesiastical department, or for the Chief Justice on one side and the Private Secretary on the other, and in their place sit the Member in Charge of the Home Department, the Legal Member, and the Public Works Minister. These variations are due to the difference of circumstances, but the conception which lies at the bottom of both systems is the same of having a council of the highest officers of the State, sitting together to assist the king in the proper discharge of his duties."[34]

Although there seems to be some apparent resemblance between the Astha Pradhan Council of Shivaji and the Executive Council of the Viceroy and the Governor-General of India, the principles underlying the two are by no means identical. The Government in India is widely known to be a bureaucracy. The subordinate officers are responsible to the heads of their departments and these departmental heads are mainly responsible for initiating the policy in the particular branches of administration entrusted to them. Although they can and do deliberate upon grave questions affecting departments other than theirs, there is a clear-cut division of duties. The Law Member is never called upon to lead a military expedition, nor is the Commander-in-Chief required to hear a title suit. But six out of the eight members of Shivaji's council had to perform military duties whenever necessary, and all the eight had, as occasions arose, to attend a Hazir Majalasi to hear appeals in both civil and criminal cases. The first Pandit Rao[35] had to render diplomatic service, when he was sent an an emissary to Jai Singh. This is not, however, the only difference. The Viceroy, though he can in theory override the decisions of his Executive Council, is in practice expected to be guided by it. But neither his subjects, nor his officers ever expected that Shivaji should always be guided by the wisdom of the Councillors. He was not bound to consult them, unless he felt inclined to do so. The ministers were frequently absent on distant expeditions and some of them were further encumbered with the heavy work of provincial governments. Shivaji's ministers cannot, therefore, be regarded as heads of departments and his Government was by no means a bureaucracy. It was, if anything, an autocracy. But the autocrat, fortunately for his people was a practical statesman and acted as a "Benevolent Despot". His ministers were his servants, proud to carry out his instructions and his government had more resemblance with those of his Hindu and Muhammadan predecessors than with the British Government of today.

5. The Duties of the Pradhans

A detailed statement of the duties of the eight pradhans will further confirm the above conclusion. And nothing will serve our purpose better than the kanujabta (memorandum) drawn up in the first year of the coronation (Abhisheka) era and published by Rao Bahadur Kashinath Narayan Sane. All that is required here is to reproduce the paper in full.

SHRI

"The Kanu Jabta of the year 1 of the coronation era, the Sambatsar being Ananda by name, Tuesday, the thirteenth day of Jestha.

The Mukhya Pradhan should perform all works of administration. He should put his seal on official letters and documents. He should make expeditions with the army and wage war and make necessary arrangements for the preservation of the districts that may come into (our) possession and act according to the orders of the king. All military officers should go with him and he should proceed with them all.

The Senapati should maintain the army and make war and expeditions. He should preserve the (newly) acquired territories, render an account of (the spoils), and act according to the orders (of the king). He should make known (to the king) what the men of the army had to say. All military officers should go with him.

The Amatya should look after the account of income and expenditure of the whole kingdom. The Daftardar and the Fadnis should be under him. He should carefully estimate the writing work (to be done). He should put his sign (or seal) on the letters from the Fadnis's and the Chitnis's office. He should (render) military service in (times of) war. He should look after the districts and be guided by (our) orders.

The Sachiv should carefully look into the royal correspondence and make (necessary) correction of the contents, whenever a letter is omitted. He should serve in war, preserve the (newly) annexed districts, and behave according to (our) orders. On royal letters (and official documents) he should put his seal as a sign of his approval.

The Pandit Rao should have jurisdiction over all religious questions. He should punish (all offences) after judging what is right and what is wrong. He should put his sign of approval on all papers relating to custom, conduct and penance. He should receive good scholars of reputation. He should perform, when occasion arises, charity and shanti (performances to appease offended deities) and celebrate other religious performances.[36]

The Nayadhish should have jurisdiction over all suits in the kingdom and try them righteously after finding out what is right and what is wrong. On the judgement paper, he should put his sign of approval.

The Mantri should carefully conduct the political and diplomatic affairs of the kingdom. The invitation and the intelligence departments are under him. He should look after the districts and serve in war. He should put his sign of approval on official documents.

The Sumanta should have the charge of foreign affairs. He should receive and entertain ambassadors from other kingdoms when they come. He should serve in war and put his sign of approval on state documents and letters".

Besides the duties enumerated above, three of the eight pradhans were in charge of extensive provinces.[37] When they were away from the metropolis, their agents resided at the court. Sabhasad says that this apparently clumsy arrangement was made in response to the demand for good government. "The kingdom was extended on four sides. How to carry on the governance of the kingdom? Then in Moro Pant Peshwa's charge were placed the country from Kalyan and Bhivandi, including Kolawan up to Salheri, the country above the Ghats and the Konkan. Lohagad and Junnar with the twelve Mawals from the pass of Haralya (were placed) under the Peshwa. The Konkan from Chaul to Kopal, including Dabhol, Rajapur, Kudal, Bande, and Phond, was placed under Annaji Datto. The Warghat (country above the ghats) from Wai to Kopal on the Tungabhadra (was) the province placed under Dattaji Pant Waknis. Dattaji Pant was stationed at Panhala. In this manner was the kingdom placed under three Sarkarkuns. Besides these, a few (five to seven) Brahman Subhedars were stationed in the Mughal provinces. They were kept under the orders of the Peshwa. The Sarkarkuns were to enquire into the needs and welfare of the forts and strongholds. But what Killedar and Karkuns were to be appointed, the Raja himself should appoint after personal scrutiny. If the Sarkarkuns found any serviceable soldier, they should enlist him in excess of the fixed number of the quota (tainat). The agents of the Sarkarkuns should remain with the Raja. The Sarkarkuns should come to see the Raja (once) every year with the accounts and the revenue of their provinces".[38] When Shivaji made this division of his territories and placed them under three of his principal ministers, we do not know, for Sabhasad does not give any date. But that the pradhans had still some districts under their charge and had to leave their agents or mutaliks at court during their absence in their respective provinces or on a distant expedition, even after the coronation and the reorganisation of the council, can be proved by the following entry in the memorandum already quoted. "The darakhdars appointed for (the management of) districts and market cities placed under the eight pradhans, and to assist them when on a military expedition, should all work in the name of the Huzur and carry on their correspondence in the same manner (as the pradhans) when they would go on an expedition; the mutaliks appointed for them should continue all their work. They should stay at the court."[39]

Before we take leave of the eight pradhans it should be noted here that they could not select their own subordinates. These were invariably appointed, as in the Peshwa period, by the supreme head of the state. Even the mutaliks, who were apparently expected to act on behalf and in the interests of an absent minister, were not appointed by him, but by the king. We do not know whether on such occasions the approval of the officer affected was sought or not. This practice was evidently borrowed from the Muhammadans. The Muhammadan rulers of Delhi required the provincial Governors and Generals on active service to leave their agents or wakils at the imperial court during their absence on duty. These agents acted in the same manner as the mutaliks of Shivaji's pradhans, but they generally considered it their first duty to safeguard the interests of their immediate masters.

The number of councillors was by no means fixed. From Sabhasad's list already quoted, it appears that there were nine of them at the time of Shivaji's coronation as the Amatya's office was jointly held by two brothers, Naro and Ramchandra. Sambhaji dismissed, decapitated and imprisoned many of his father's old servants. Sambhaji had a council in name only, he ruled as he liked, and did not care to consult any one except his notorious favourite Kavi Kalush or Kavji, a Kanojia Brahman. He has been styled as Chhandogyamatya in contemporary papers. The Pandit Rao in Shivaji's time was entitled to the additional designation of Chhandogyamatya. It has been suggested that Kavi Kalush was not Sambhaji's Pandit Rao.[40] Kalush enjoyed so much influence and so much power that he was for all practical purposes the prime minister of Sambhaji. When the Rajmandal was revived under Rajaram, a new member was added, who superseded all others both in status and in pay. Pralhad Niraji was appointed Pratinidhi or the king's vicegerent at Jinji during the struggle for national existence.[41] Henceforth the Pratinidhi always held the first seat in the council, until the rise of the Peshwas revolutionised the constitution of the Maratha empire.

6. Secretaries

Outside the council but in no way inferior to the eight ministers was the Chitnis or Secretary. Just below the pradhans had stood Bal Prabhu Chitnis, and Nil prabhu Parasins,[42] at the time of Shivaji's coronation. The Private Secretary of an autocratic king naturally enjoys great influence and is a power behind the throne. Balaji Avji, Shivaji's chitnis was a man of exceptional ability. Not only did he perform the ordinary duties of his office, but he had been further entrusted with the exceedingly delicate task of taking down the behests of the great goddess Bhavani communicated through Shivaji's mouth.[43] It is said that Shivaji had actually offered him a seat in the council, but the modesty of the great Prabhu statesman stood in his way.[44] The duties of his office are thus enumerated by Malhar Ram

Rao Chitnis. "The Chitnis Patralekhak will write all royal letters and diplomatic correspondence. Divining what is in the king's heart he should at once cleverly put it into writing discussing the various aspects of the case. He should write in such a manner that what is generally accomplished by war and great exertion, should be achieved by means of letters only. He should write answers to the letters that may come".[45] In the memorandum published by Rao Bahadur Sane we come across the following entry under Chitnis: "He should write all official letters and papers of the State. He should write answers to diplomatic letters. Sanads, deeds of grant and other orders to be issued (to the officers in the districts) should be written according to the regulations framed for the Fadnis's papers. On hand notes and letters of special importance there should be a seal or the king's signature only, and no seal of other officers. The Chitnis alone should put his sign".[46] Such were the duties that the Chitnis had to perform.

Although in the above regulations the Chitnis is required to write all correspondence and draw up all state documents, in practice he was to a considerable extent relieved by others. Chitragupta tells us that the Fadnis alone and no other official could issue deeds of royal grant. All letters to the provincial and district officers were written by the Chitnis, while answers to the letters from commanders of forts had to be written by an officer called Gadnis. Letters to foreign courts were sent from the Dabir's office, and the Parasnis had to carry on all correspondence with the Emperor of Delhi, his wazir and Muhammadan potentates.[46a]

Chitragupta was not a contemporary of Shivaji. Mr. V. K. Rajwade has described his work as a mere elaboration of Sabhasad's chronicle. We do not get a complete list of the Chitnis's official duties in Chitragupta. This want,[47] however, has fortunately been removed by a jabta of the first year of the coronation era. In that document the Fadnis also has been mentioned with the Chitnis in their official relation. A subordinate secretariat officer of no great importance in

Shivaji's time, the Fadnis rose to great power and authority during the Peshwa regime. The Potnis was responsible for the account of income and expenditure of the metropolitan treasury, while the Potdar was only an assay officer. The eight pradhans had under them, besides their staff, the officers in charge of the eighteen *karkhanas* and twelve *mahals*. What precisely their duties were we do not know. The eighteen *karkhanas* and the twelve *mahals* were as follows:[48]

The Eighteen Karkhanas:[49]

1.	Khajina	...	Cash
2.	Jawahir Khana	...	Jewel store
3.	Ambar Khana	...	Granary
4.	Sharbat Khana	...	Medicines
5.	Top Khana	...	Artillery
6.	Daftar Khana	...	Record Department
7.	Jamdar Khana	...	Public treasury containing all sorts of things.[50]
8.	Jirat Khana	...	Corn Depot, according to Molesworth, Armoury, according to R. V. Kosh.
9.	Mutbak Khana	...	Kitchen
10.	Ushtar Khana	...	Camels and their trappings.
11.	Nagar Khana	...	Band
12.	Talim Khana	...	Gymnasim[51]
13.	Pil Khana	...	Elephant shades, etc.
14.	Faras Khana	...	Carpets, tents and accessories.
15.	Abdar Khana	...	Drink
16.	Shikar Khana	...	Game, aviary, chase and allied materials.
17.	Daru Khana	...	Magazine
18.	Shahat Khana	...	Conservancy Department.

The Twelve Mahals:

1.	Pote	...	Treasury
2.	Saudagir	...	Merchandise
3.	Palkhi	...	Palanquins
4.	Kothi	...	Warehouse and granaries.
5.	Imarat	...	Building
6.	Bahili	...	Chariots
7.	Paga	...	Stables
8.	Seri	...	Comforts
9.	Daruni	...	The Zenana
10.	Thatti	...	Cowsheds
11.	Tanksal	...	Mints
12.	Sabina	...	Guards[52]

It is clear from the name of the departments that most of these officers were concerned more with the king's household than with any work of imperial or public interest. A few of them, on the other hand, like those in charge of the Artillery, the mint, and the public treasury, fall under a different category. Shivaji's division of his government and household affairs into eighteen karkhanas and twelve mahals was, therefore, not a scientific one. But we cannot expect from a man surrounded on all sides by enemies, and ever engaged in a war of defence as well as of conquest, a scientific division of departments on modern lines. He had evidently copied from the existing system and found little leisure in his eventful career to improve upon it.

In his departmental duties each of the eight pradhans was assisted by a staff of eight clerks. They were:

1. The Dewan.
2. The Mazumdar or Auditor and Accountant.
3. The Fadnis or Deputy Auditor.

4. The Sabnis or the Daftardar.
5. The Karkhanis or Commissary.
6. The Chitnis or Correspondence Clerk.
7. The Jamdar or Treasure.
8. The Points or Cash-Keeper.[53]

7. The King

The king formed the great pivot on which rested this stupendous structure. His was the hand that worked this gigantic but by no means easy machine. Not only the officers in charge of the eighteen karkhanas and the twelve mahals, not only secretariat officers as the Fadnis, Sabnis and Potnis, but also their official superiors, the eight pradhans and the Chitnis, formed a vast array of clerks and military commanders to carry out the orders of the king and to execute his great designs. They were but so many machines, not inanimate it is true, not unconscious of the great part they were playing, but at the same time hardly having any independent existence. Even the Pandit Rao, the officer in charge of the ecclesiastical branch of the administration, whose Brahman birth and learning might have given him some advantage over his non-Brahman master, could hardly take any step without the cognisance and sanction of the king. Even Kalush, the all-powerful minister of Sambhaji, deemed it necessary to consult the king's pleasure before he could authorise the re-admission of a repentant renegade into his former caste after the necessary penance.[54] Everything depended on the personal ability and qualities of the sovereign. There was nothing to check him except his own good sense and of course the constant fear of a formidable Muhammadan invasion. It was for this reason alone that Sambhaji found it so easy to subvert his father's system, the day after his accession to the throne. It is this very reason again that impelled Rajaram, while sorely pressed by the victorious imperial army, to revive some of the old institutions his father had found so useful. The system required a strong and good ruler. After Shahu, there was none among Shivaji's descendants who possessed the requisite qualities, and that is why the Peshwas found it so easy to do away with the central government. The eight pradhans still continued, but the hereditary councillors found themselves in an anomalous situation. They enjoyed great fiefs, but were never in practice called upon to perform their civil duties. The Peshwa, in theory their equal, become in reality their superior. The king, their master, was a state prisoner. The Peshwa's Fadnis, originally an officer of no importance, gradually rose to very great power, and the central government was transferred from Satara to Poona. But through all these changes and revolutions, both bloody and bloodless, the village communities survived unaffected, and the Peshwas also found it convenient to continue the provincial governments as they existed in Shivaji's time.

REFERENCES

1. Lokahitavadi, *Aitihasik Goshti*.
2. Sabhasad, pp. 98-101 and Sen, Sivachhatrapti, pp. 140-148.
3. Rajwade, *M.I.S.*, Vol. VIII, pp. 17-19.
4. See *Bombay Gazetteer*.
5. He would often seek the assistance of a powerful neighbour, generally at the price of a portion of the disputed watan, and this man would take up the quarrel as if it was his own. See Rajwade, *M.I.S.*, Vol. XV, pp. 117-118.
6. Rajwade, *M.I.S.*, Vol. XV, p. 9.
7. Rajwade, *M.I.S.*, Vol. XV, p. 1.
8. Sardesai, pp. 173-174.
9. Rajwade, *M.I.S.*, Vol. XV, p. 394.
10. Rajwade, *M.I.S.*, Vol. VIII, pp. 8-9. The document is very important, but an English translation is not necessary as the sense has been given above.
11. The Maratha village system will be fully described in Book II.
12. Sabhasad, pp. 32-33, and Sen, Sivachhatrapati, pp. 37-38.

13. Sabhasad, p. 82; Chitnis, p. 162. Sen, Shivachhatrapati, p. 115.
14. Chitnis, p. 161.
15. But all these offices, existed long before the coronation. By the word Astha Pradhan here, Chitnis, therefore, does not mean the mere offices but the council. In the next sentence he mentions the appointment of the two Secretaries. These were also by no means new appointments. It is quite possible that the old officers were formally reappointed, according to the rites prescribed by the *Shastras* for the coronation ceremony. See also Lokahitavadi, Aitihasik Goshti, p. 7.
16. Sabhasad, p. 83. Sen, Shivachhatrapati, p. 116.
17. Sane, Patre Yadi Bagaire, p. 357. Also see Sanads and Letters edited by P. V. Mawji and D. V. Parasnis, pp. 123-24.
18. I do not call him Moro Trimal as he is described as *Trimbak suta Moreshwar*, Moreshwar son of Trimbak, in the couplet inscribed on his seal.
19. Sabhasad, pp. 7, 8, 11, Peshwas' Diaries, Vol. I., p. 41.
20. Sabhasad, p. 8.
21. *Ibid*, 9.
22. *Ibid*, 11.
23. Shabhasad, p. 59.
24. *Ibid*., p. 79.
25. J. N. Sarkar says that according to Narain Shenvi Anand Rao succeeded Pratap Rao Gujar.
26. Chitnis, p. 162.
27. Sabhasad, p. 11., Sen, Sivachhatrapati, pp. 7-8.
28. Sabhasad, p. 14., Sen, Sivachhatrapati, p. 11.
29. A more detailed discussion is reserved for Book III.
30. Sabhasad, pp. 56-57., Sen, Sivchhatrapati, pp. 72-74.
31. Sabhasad, p. 30., Sen, Sivachhatrapati, pp. 33-34.
32. Ranade, R.M.P., pp. 129-130.
33. Sane, Patre Yadi Bagaire, p. 357.
34. Ranade, R. M. P., pp. 126-127.
35. Sabhasad, p. 41., Sen, Sivachhatrapati, pp. 50-51.

36. The late Justice Telang, summarised the duties of the Pandit Rao in the following manner: - "It states that the Pandit Rao's duties are to exercise all the ecclesiastical powers of the State, and to order punishment to be inflicted after investigating into what is and is not in accordance with the religious law. He is to receive learned persons on behalf of the State, and countersign all documents that may be issued from the Sovereign relating to *Achara, Vyavahara,* and *Prayaschitta,* that is to say, rules of conduct, civil and criminal law, and penances, the three departments of the *Dharmasashtras.* He is also to look after the performance of *Shantis* and other ceremonials, and the distribution of the royal bounty". Ranade, R.M.P., p. 261.

37. Annaji Datto, for instance, is styled in a Portuguese letter as Subedar-mor or Governor General of Konkan. (Reis Visinhos, Vol. I, fol. 2).

38. Sabhasad, pp. 77-78., Sen, Sivachhatrapati, pp. 106-107.

39. Sane, P. Y. B., p. 359., The Portuguese letter, already mentioned in a previous note also proves that the Sachiv held the office of Governor General of Konkan in January, 1678 when the letter was written.

40. Bharat Itihas Sanshodhak Mandal—Varshik Itivrita (1837), III-13.

41. The Ashta Pradhan Council was certainly not a cabinet as a detailed examination of its constitution (in the text) shows. Prof. Sarkar, however, seems to hold a different view when he writes "Pralhad Niraji, on whom the high title of Regent (Pratinidhi) was conferred and who thus stood *outside and above the cabinet* of eight ministers (Ashta Pradhan)" (History of Aurangzib, Vol. V, p. 26). The opinion of so distinguished a scholar certainly deserves more than a passing notice, but we have been spared the task of refuting him, as he seems to have reconsidered the question and changed his view when he wrote at another place. "To provide posts for all his most influential servants, the normal *council* of eight ministers was expanded by *adding two more men.* The *Hakumat Panah* and the *Pratinidhi*" (History of Aurangzib, Vol. V, p. 195). Thus he admits that it was a council and the number of councillors was by no means rigidly fixed.

42. Sabhasad, p. 84; Chitnis, p. 162., Sen, Sivachhatrapati, p. 117.

43. Sabhasad, Chitnis, Chitragupta and all old chroniclers tell us that whenever Shivaji had to face any exceptional difficulty, the goddess Bhavani used to take possession of his body and tell

him what he should do. As the king lay unconscious all the time, the behest of the deity was taken down by Balaji Avji. See also History of the Maratha People by Kincaid and Parasnis.

44. Chitnis, p. 170.

45. Chitnis, p. 168.

46. Sane, P. Y. B., p. 358.

46a. Chitragupta Bakhar (in the Kavyetihas Sangraha), pp. 104-105.

47. For the jabta see Appendix.

48. The eighteen Karkhanas are referred to in the *Peshwanchi Bakhar* (p. 80) but the names given by Rao Bahadur Sane in the footnote are somewhat different.

49. It should be noted that Chitnis's division of these departments is not exactly similar; for instance Jamdar Khana is placed by him under the heading mahal. For his list see Chitnis, pp. 75-76 and Appendix B.

50. Jamdar Khana was Vasanagar or royal wardrobe according to the *Raj Vyavahar Kosh*, p. 6.

51. Prof, Sarkar translates *talimkhana* as school (Mughal Administration. 2nd edition, p. 194), and adds that in Firuz Shah's time it was called *ilmkhana.* I have, however, relied on the *Raj Vyavahar Kosh.* Raghunath Pandit, the Lexicographer, had a first-hand knowledge of these *Karkhanas* and the translated *talimkhana* as *malalashala* (p. 13) and the word is mentioned under the heading *Shastra Vargah*. The Marathi historian, referred to by Prof. Sarkar, is therefore perfectly right when he calls it a wrestling school. The Marathas did not blindly copy the Muslim institutions, though Shivaji was quite willing to borrow good institutions from all his neighbours. For instance Shivaji's *daru-khana* had no Muhammadan prototype, (Sarkar, Mughal Administration, p. 193) but the word is a literal translation of the Portuguese word *casa de polbora,* and Shivaji knew that he was not bringing a new thing into existence when in addition to *Topkhana* he decided to have a *daru-khana* as well.

52. Sabhasad, pp. 94-95.

53. Grant Duff, Vol. I, p. 191.

54. Rajwade, M.I.S., Vol. VIII, p. 36.

For a further treatment of the subject, the reader is referred to Book II.

APPENDIX A

A memorandum (enumerating) the writing duties of the Chitnis of Kshatriya Kulavatansa Shri Raja Shivachhatrapati, dated the first of Jeshtha of the year 1 of the coronation era, the Sambatsar being Ananda by name.

Of the letters and grant deeds to be issued when a new *inam* is granted to any one:

Letters to the grantee Do to the Mokdams	should be written by the Fadnis.
Letters to the Talukdars Do to the Subha and Mamla officers. present and future. Do to the Deshmukh, the Deshpande and the Zamindars	should be written by the Chitnis.

Of the letters to be issued when a village in mokasa, or land as a stipend, is granted to any one:

Letters to the Mokdams Do to the Talukdars	should be written by the Fadnis.
Do to the Kamavisdars Do to the Zamindars	should be written by the Chitnis.

Excepting the above, all letters of grant to any one should be written by the Chitnis. All answers, orders and diplomatic letters should be written by the Chitnis. The Chitnis should also write reminders or notes about:

1. Saranjams
2. Sanads relating to lands
3. Professional rights
4. Inams
5. Assignments (Varats).

The rules about the Chitnis's duties and a memoradum about them all, including those relating to customs duties:

All *kauls* to be issued about lands to villages and provinces should be written by the Chitnis.

The Fadnis should write the kauls or agreements about the contribution fixed (by the proper authorities) to be levied (in a foreign country). Of the sanads of new officers, Kamavis, etc., those addressed to the officer should be written by the Fadnis, those addressed to the Zamindars and others should be written by the Chitnis. All notes to be issued about Ghasdana with notes about Fadfarmas should be written by the Chitnis.

Letters for sending cash advance and presents for marriage ceremonies (in the Raja's house) should be written by the Chitnis. Of these, if the Chitnis has written letters about sanads for recovery of the sum advanced from the Mahals, the Fadnis should mention in his letters that the said sanad has been recorded. If the balance of revenue, considered unrecoverable, has been realised, letters regarding it should be addressed by the Chitnis, and the remittance transfer of the shortage should be granted by the Fadnis. All notes of remission (with regard to the following) should be written by the Chitnis:

1. Land (revenue).
2. When a remission of the due (balance) is granted.
3. When revenue is (conditionally) remitted for failure of crops and the revenue is to be realised after inspection.

All letters of (warning) about any right to and possession of old inams, watans, and varshasanas that may be in force in home dominions and foreign territories, should be written by the Chitnis, enumerating the villages and the names of the parties (interested).

When an old watan is confirmed after a due enquiry about its (proprietorship), all letters, whether addressed to the watandar or Jilhedars and Subhedars, should be written by the Chitnis. Space should be left for any *harki* or *sherni* that may have been promised. These gaps should be filled up by the Fadnis with his own hands, stating the amount.

If a new watan or inam is granted to any one, the letter addressed to the grantee should be written by the Fadnis stating the sum (or rupees) taken. All other letters (in this connection) should be written by the Chitnis.

When a *Prayashchitta* is prescribed, or a man is to be (re) admitted into his caste, orders to the Joshis and letters to the Upadhyas and Brahmans or Shudras, or to any body else, should be written by the Chitnis. Harki and Shela should be taken by the government for the Prayashchitta. The Fadnis should make an entry that so much has been realised (specifying the sum). All letters, if the transaction is to be made without any stipulation about money, should be the Chitnis's business; the Fadnis will have nothing to do with them.

If parties after quarrelling with each other, come for a decision to the court, all letters according to the decision (of the court) about the harki to be paid by the winning and *gunhegari* to be paid by the losing party, should be written by the Chitnis. The total of harki and gunhegari should be stated by the Fadnis.

Letters about contribution, fines, harkis and incomes (arising from) adultery cases, should be written by the Chitnis.

If an assignment or carat is made in any one's favour and there is any delay in making it good, the Chitnis should write reminders, (requesting) the officers (concerned) to pay the money in accordance with the terms of the assignment. If an assignment is made of one hundred rupees and there is a shortage of money in the Mahal (concerned), and a fresh assignment of fifty rupees out of the entire sum has to be made, it will be done by the Fadnis. If an assignment of one hundred rupees is once made, and if it is returned, and a fresh grant has to be made, the document is to be drawn up by the Chitnis. If any correction is to be made about the sum, (literally if the sum is either more or less), the letters will be written by the Fadnis.

All passports for travelling and permission for establishing warehouses should be written by the Chitnis. Summons should be written by the Chitnis. Memoranda enumerating regulations for watani Mahals, ports, and forts, etc., should be written by the Chitnis.

Letters about ammunition and clothes to be sent each year to forts, strongholds or military outposts, or to be brought to the headquarters from those places, should be written by the Chitnis. If any objection is to be raised about these works, it is to be done by the Fadnis.

The Chitnis is to open envelopes and read (to the king) the letters that may come, and to enclose and despatch letters.

The memorandum of rules for regulating the price of things should be drawn up by the Chitnis.

If officers are sent from the head quarters to a village or a warehouse or a Pargana, all letters to the District officer should be written by the Chitnis.

All orders of confiscation of property and restoration of property to its owner, should be written by the Chitnis.

Letters for conferring (the command of) forts, and strongholds, , etc., for setting a boundary, for imprisoning or releasing any one, should be written by the Chitnis.

Letters of political intelligence should be written by the Chitnis.

All letters in which royal signature is to be inserted, hand-notes, and documents with seals, should be written by the Chitnis. All letters about the appointment to the command of forts and strongholds, grants of saramjam, inam, or watans, or communication about any assignment accompanied by the customary clothes of honour, should be written by the Chitnis, as well as letters specifying contribution, fine, harki or subscription and nazar (to be paid by the addressee). He should also frame a list of these and send it to the Daftar. The officers there will accordingly make their accounts of income and expenditure. Closed letters and handnotes should be written by the Chitnis, no one but the Chitnis should put his sign in the handnotes.

Kauls for settling (new inhabitants in any place) and interim kauls or assurance deeds should be drawn by the Chitnis.

Letters for attaching or conferring a house or homestead, fuels, or rice lands, should be written by the Chitnis.[1]

Besides the duties enumerated above, the Chitnis was in charge of the Abdar khana and Saraf Khana also.[2]

REFERENCES

1. Sanads and Letters edited by Mawji and Parasnis, pp. 127-130.
2. *Ibid*, p. 125.

APPENDIX B

A List of Karkhanas compiled from the Raj Vyavahar Kosh

KHAJINA—Treasury, where the cash is kept, the officer in charge is the Jamdar or the *Kosharakshaka* (treasurer). The second officer is designated *Koshapala* or Havaldar.

POTE—Treasury, where from payment is made. The chief officer is Havaldar. The second officer is Jamdar, an accountant and the Potdar or assay master were also attached to this department.

JAWAHIR KHANA—Jewel store;the officer in charge, Havaldar, his assistant Jamdar, and a jewel expert styled *johari* were employed by this department.

JAR KHANA—or Gold store, but no officer is mentioned, probably it was a sub-department of jawahir khana.

JAMDAR KHANA—Wardrobe, chief officer, Havaldar; his assistant Jamdar; a *Vastra Lekhaka* or clerk for keeping account of the department is mentioned.

MUDBAKH KHANA—Kitchen, the Mudbakhi or cook and taster, *Ruchigraha,* are mentioned in this connection.

ABDAR KHANA—Jalasthana—literally water department, not only drinks but intoxicants like tobacco and opium on the one hand, and musk, otto, essence of flowers and scented oils on the other, are mentioned under this department.

SHARAB KHANA—Wine store, the officer in charge was the Sharabdar, *tambul* or betel leaf and its accessories are mentioned in this connection.

DAWA KHANA—Dispensary.

SHIKAR KHANA—Aviary.

FARAS KHANA—The department of carpets, tents etc. The officer incharge was designated Havaldar.

JIRAT KHANA—Armoury—The chief officer—Havaldar, the second officer Havalgir and a clerk for keeping accounts of the departments. No separate Toph Khana or Daru Khana is mentioned;but in the list of arms and armours, given in connection with this department *top* (artillery) and *daru* (gum powder) are mentioned.

TALIM KHANA—Gymnasium.

PHIL KHANA—Elephant stables, Mahavats or elephant drivers, elephant trainers and elephant keepers are mentioned under this department.

PAGA—Stables.

BAHILL—Chariots, it is styled a mahal.

SHUTAR KHANA—Camel stables.

ALAM KHANA—Band and music.

AMBAR KHANA—Granary. This department is mentioned under *durgavargah* or forts and herein probably lies the distinction between *Kothi* and *Ambar Khana.*

IMARATI—Buildings—this department is also mentioned under the forts.

DAFTAR KHANA—Secretariat or records department. The chief officer is called Daftardar.

KOTHI—Granary. This is styled a *mahal* and comes under *Janpadavargah* or the provinces. As rent was paid in kind, it was necessary for the revenue collectors in the provinces to have *Kothis* or store houses for grains. The officer in charge of Kothi is designated *Havaldar.* He was assisted by the accountant (Dhanyalekhaka) and another subordinate styled Kothival who probably measured grains.

Chitnis's list of Mahals and Karkhanas:

1. Mahals

1. Daruni—Zenana
2. Pote—Stores
3. Kothi—Granary
4. Paga-Stables
5. Thati—Cowsheds
6. Sheribag—Comforts
7. Tankshala—Mint
8. Palanquins etc.
9. Imarat—Buildings
10. Saudagiri—Merchandise
11. Chaubina—Guards
12. Jamdarkhana—Wardrobe

The Karkhanas

1. Pil khana—Elephant stables
2. Ambar khana—Granary
3. Nagar khana—Band
4. Toph khana—Artillery
5. Sharbat khana—Medicines
6. Abdar khana—Drinks
7. Shutar khana—Camel stables
8. Faras khana—Tents
9. Shikar khana—Shields
10. Talim khana—Gymnasium
11. Jawahir khana—Jewel store
12. Mudbakh khana—Kitchen
13. Shile khana—Armoury

14. Sharab khana—Betel leaves etc.
15. Gadi khana—Conveyance
16. Jinnas khana—Stores
17. Daftar khana—Secretariat
18. Nat khana—Music etc.

Chitnis says that Shivaji had about three hundred (300 to 350) elephants, about one thousand (1000 to 1500) camels, from two to four thousand cows and five thousand buffaloes. A glance at the lists given above will show that the Maratha Karkhanas and Mahals were really speaking state departments and establishments and not state owned or state controlled factories.

II

IMPERIAL SECRETARIAT

The Secretariat, called by the Marathas the *Huzur Daftar*, was a very big establishment, employing more than two hundred Karkuns, where records of all branches of the Peshwa's administration were preserved with the utmost care and order. An enquirer could confidently turn to the daftar-records for any information concerning the Peshwa's government, and in fact the materials of the present work are drawn mostly from the same source. "The general contents of the Daftar under the Peshwas", says Mr. J. Macleod, "may be described as follows; *viz.*, all accounts rendered to the Government of the revenue and expenditure of the districts, with the settlements of them by Government; the accounts of districts rendered by the hereditary district officers; and those of villages by village officers, of farms, of customs, etc., accounts of all alienations of public revenue, whether Surinjam, Inam or otherwise, of the pay, rights, and privileges of the Government and village officers; accounts of the strength and pay of troops and the expenses of all civil, military and religious establishments. The Rozkirds (daily registers) were registers of all revenue transactions generally, together with all grants and payments, and more particularly the accounts of all contributions and exactions, levied on foreign state. The whole of which were considered and exhibited in one comprehensive view in the Turjamas." It is said that Nana Fadnavis introduced many improvements in the working of the daftar as well as in the accounts department in general; and it is no small tribute to the ability of the Maratha officers and the Maratha Karkuns that after the English occupation of Poona, documents concerning government transactions of all kinds for a period of eighty-eight years were found tolerably complete in this vast storehouse of information. At the head of this great establishment was the Huzur Fadnavis, and it is needless to say that the very nature of of this office required a man of the highest ability.

For convenience the Daftar was divided into several departments, the chief of which were the Chatle Daftar and the Ek Beriz Daftar. The latter department had to deal with accounts of all sorts, and was, therefore, permanently fixed at Poona; while the Chatle Daftar was always under the direct supervision of the Fadnavis.

The Chatle Daftar was again subdivided into several branches, namely, the Fad, Beheda, Saranjam, etc. The Fad was the Fadnavis's own office. All sanads and orders were issued from this office. Here the Fadnavis checked and passed all accounts, and received informations from other departments. In the Fad were made and kept Rozkirds or daily transactions of all sorts. The Beheda department made the *Taebands, Ajamas* (estimate), and *Beheda* (budget) for the Fadnavis's information out of the accounts of income and expenditure annually submitted by the village and district officers. In the Talebands were shown in a small space a complete abstract of the actual receipt and expenditure of the revenue during the past year, the Ajamas or the estimate of possible income and expenditure for the revenue during the past year, the Ajamas or the estimate of possible income and expenditure for the current year was based on the

Taleband, and from the information thus carefully collected and classified was framed the Beheda or the authorised budget for the guidance of the Kamavisdars and the Mamlatdars. These Behedas were framed with so much care and accuracy that the district officers found it very difficult to find any fault with them, and had to find out an excuse of exceptional nature for the smallest extra expenditure or remission of revenue. In the Saranjam department were kept accounts of Saranjam or military Jagris and all *Dumalla* lands (land under double authority--where more than one person had different rights). Separate departments were entrusted with military accounts and contribution, etc. "But these arrangements, however, varied with the pleasure of the Furnavees, or the business that might occur."

In the Ek Beriz Daftar at Poona were kept classified accounts from all other departments and here were framed the Tarjuma—showing the total receipt, expenditure and balance of the government income for the year, and Khataunis or "abstracts of all expenditure arranged alphabetically under their proper heads." It is therefore no wonder that armed with the knowledge supplied by their department the daftar-officers successfully supervised the work of the village and district establishments.

It will not be out of place here to add a sentence or two about the reliability of the daftar-officers, specially because Mr. Macleod has some doubt upon that point. In all cases of proprietorship the Maratha watandar, if he failed to produce his sanad, referred the government official to the daftar. The British officers were on several occasion referred to the Poona daftar for copies of the original grants by the Maratha Jagirdars. Unless they had complete confidence in the authenticity of the papers in the daftar and the honesty of the daftar-officers, they would certainly have not relied so much on the Secretariat for copies of their family papers. Thus writes the then representative of the Parasnis family to Henry Brown "papers relating to our property are in the Marathi Daftar of the Peshwa." The descendant of Visaji Krishna

Biniwale wrote to the same officer "of the old papers we have got copies only which we send for your inspection. The originals will be found in the daftar."

The Daftar, however, was neglected during the administration of that bad prince Baji Rao II and it fell into complete disorder. "The Daftar was not only much neglected," says Macleod, "but its establishment was almost entirely done away and people were even permitted to carry away the records, or do with them what they pleased."

2
Revenue Administration

I

The revenue policy of the Peshwas was based on the principle of securing the prosperity of the tax-payer. The Maratha financier never forgot that the government can after all only share the wealth of the country with the governed, and although the income of the government can be temporarily raised by exacting a large share, its permanent increase can only be secured by encouraging the people to produce more wealth. True to this principle they often preferred to postpone present enjoyment for future gain. They would watch and help the growth of a new suburb or a new market town without exacting a single pie for *hashil* or customs duties for six or seven years, and then draw a tariff list (with utmost attention to minute details of which the Maratha officer was a master) on the *istawa* principle (that of annual increment). Thus the maximum taxation would again be postponed for another five or seven years. They would pursue the same policy for bringing fallow and waste lands into cultivation, for encouraging profitable industries, and they tried to counteract the evil influences of perpetual disorder and insecurity by making the assessment flexible. As a result of this policy Wellington found the Maratha country highly cultivated and Fitzclarence writing in 1819 described the Peshwa's territory as "one of the finest in India returning richly to his treasury."[1] Captain William Gordon, who was deputed to the Poona court in 1739, was favourably impressed with the revenue policy of the Peshwa He wrote,—"Bajirao has a great extent of country, appearing more fertile and valuable than any other I had passed through. His territories are well peopled, and the poorer sort, in the farming way, are rendered easy in their rents, which causes his extent of dominion to be in a very flourishing condition, more so than any other in the possession of the Marathas."[1a] Even the Jagirdars or feudal Barons, who exercised sovereign authority within their fiefs were not always indifferent to the welfare of their subjects. On the 28th August, 1818, General Munro wrote to Mountstuart Elphinstone,—"All the branches of the Putwurdhu family are popular in the country. They treat the inhabitants with great kindness, and their lands are well cultivated."[1b]

The sources of the Peshwa's income can be classified as follows:

(1) Land Revenue and the Demesne land.

(2) Customer duties and income-tax in some form.

(3) Forest.

(4) Mints.

(5) Courts of Law.

1. Land Revenue

We shall discuss the land revenue first, as the most important of these items. The Demense lands were divided into *sheri* (cultivated fields), *kurans* (grass lands), *bag* (garden), and *ambarai* (orchards). These were, as we have already seen, under the direct management of the district officer, Mamlatdar or the Kamavisdar as the case might be, and were often sublet to Upri tenants or leaseholders.

The Patil, as we know, was responsible for revenue collection. When the time for collection came, the Mahar called the rent-payers to the village *Chawdi* where the Patil held his office. The Kulkarni or the village account-keeper was present there with his records to assist the Patil in his work and so were the Potdars. The latter assayed and stamped the money when paid, for which the rent-payer got a receipt from the Kulkarni. When the collection was over, the money was sent to the Kamavisdar with a letter under the charge of the Chaugula, and a similar letter, often a duplicate copy, was sent to the Deshmukh under the charge of the Mahar. The Chaugula got a receipt from the Mamlatdar for the sum paid, which was carefully preserved in the Kulkarni's bundle of village accounts. Sometimes a Shibandi was sent by the officer in charge of the district or Tarf to help the Patil in his work of collection. The revenue was generally paid in four instalments and sometimes in three.

2. Mokasa Babti and Sahotra

Here we may also explain some terms which will often appear unintelligible to the reader of the old records.[2] The Marathas, unlike the modern European nations, did not extend their empire by peaceful penetration. Their victims had no reason to misunderstand their method. Shivaji invaded the territories of his enemies and offered them the option of purchasing security or submitting to plunder. The price that he first demanded was the Sardeshmukhi or Rs. 10 for every 100 levied by the Government. To the Sardeshmukhi was subsequently added another claim, that of the Chauth or 25 per cent of the total Government collection. The whole of the Chauth was reserved for the Government treasury. The *Babti* or 25 per cent of the Chauth was collected for the Raja by his principal officers, *viz.*, the Pratinidhi, the Peshawa, and the Pant Sachiv,—the rest was called the *Mokasa* and was partitioned among the Sardars for maintaining troops. Six per cent of the whole Chauth was, however, reserved for the Pant Sachiv and was called the *Sahotra* and three per cent was reserved as *Nadgaunda* to be granted at different times to different persons according to the pleasure of the King. Thus only sixty-six per cent of the *Chauth* could be available for other *Mokasa*-holders. The Sardeshmukhi also came to be similarly divided afterwards.

When the territories paying the Chauth and the Sardeshmukhi were finally annexed to the Maratha dominions, the remaining three-fourth of the revenue were styled as *Jagir* in contradistinction to the Chauth. It is needless to add that the Jagir also was granted in *inama*. As a result of this complex division, and complicated arrangement different individuals might have different claims over the same village. One might claim the *Sahotra,* a second, half the *Mokasa,* a third the other half, while to a fourth might have been granted some percentage of the *Jagir*. If all these, claimants had sent different collectors, as they sometimes did, the rayat would have been subjected to unnecessary inconvenience. The duty of collection in such cases was, therefore, for common convenience entrusted to one of the grantees only.[3]

3. Principle and Method of Assessment

Now to turn to the method of assessment, its merits and demerits. Agriculture was then, as it is now, the principal industry of the country. Consistently with their policy of increasing the total wealth of the country, the Maratha revenue officer had to pay full attention to the improvement of agriculture. The Peshwas never forgot to remind their officers that their principal duty was to encourage agriculture, and to keep the rayats contented. They were also asked to base their assessment on actual inspection of the condition of cultivation and careful survey of the cultivated area. To illustrate this we may here quote several documents containing instructions to Kamavisdars and the Mamlatdars at the time of their appointment.

When Bahiro Ram was put in charge of the Mamla Revdanda in 1747, he was instructed among other things to take steps to plant coconut trees at the rate of five trees per year, for every hundred trees then existing[4]. Among the instructions issued to Naro Trimbak of Prant Rajpri (1748-49) occurs the following significant sentence—"bullocks and buffaloes purchased for agricultural purposes by the rayats should be exempted from octroi for five years."[5] In 1760-61 Lakshman Bhikaji Mamlatdar of Wan and Dindori was told that the villages should be surveyed. The lands should be classed as superior ordinary and inferior and also as *jirayat* and *bagayat* as well as *patshal* and *motsthal* (watered by canals and watered by Mot) and should be measured. The result should be reported to the Amin, who would fix the rate to be charged. The land should be assessed accordingly.[6] That waste lands in these two Parganas should be brought under cultivation within two or three years. In case of failure in this respect, the Kamavisdar would not be continued in his office. That in case of failure of crops or disturbance in the country, remission would be granted according to the usual practice.

In fact the Peshwas were so much bent upon the improvement of agriculture that they took almost all the means known to modern governments for that purpose, the most remarkable being their attempt to create for the cultivators a permanent interest in their land by giving them long lease of five to seven years, and by forbidding sale and mortgage of land. The last measure was specially enforced during the administration of the second Madhava Rao, as will be proved by the following documents:

In 1774-75, the Mamlat of Pargana Amod in Prant Gujrat was given to Madhava Nana Shet, Raghunath Hari the former incumbent being dismissed. The following are some of the instructions issued for the guidance of the new Mamlatdar:

(1) Waste lands should be brought under cultivation and a detailed report of cultivation should be submitted to the Sarsubha annually. *Tagai* should be given in the sowing season and you should behave according to the guidance of the Sarsubha and not otherwise.

(2) The Zamindars of the aforesaid Pargana exact from the rayats more than their customary dues, you should enquire into the matter and report to the Huzir the amount of the extra exaction.

(3) Land mortgaged or sold in the above Pargana should be taken back and restored to the rayat. No mortgage or sale should in future be allowed.[7]

A similar set of instructions was issued in 1784-85, when the Mamlat of Pargana Hasot in Prant Gujrat was transferred from Sakharam Sheshadri to Balaji Ram.[8] The new officer was told that he should see that the cultivation of the said Pargana be made according to the *istawa* and the details of the cultivation be submitted every year to the Sarsubha. If however the amount of the cultivation fell short of the *istawa* contact, the Government loss should be compensated by the Kamavisdars.

(1) The Zamindars of the aforesaid Pargana take from the rayats more than their customary dues. You should enquire into the matter and report to the Sarsubha.

(2) Lands sold or mortgaged in the said Pargana should be restored to the rayats and no such mortgage of sale should in future be allowed.

It is noteworthy that the Punjab Government have also recently made attempts to stop the alienation of agricultural lands by the prohibition of sale and mortgage of such land by the poor peasant. The second item of the instructions enumerated in the last document also demands our notice, as it requires the Kamavisdar to compensate any loss that the government might incur from decrease in cultivation. Thus it was not merely the duty of these revenue officers to pay their best attention to the improvement of agriculture, but also their interest to do so, as the increase or decrease of cultivation in their districts affected their purse so much.

The Peshwa's government had good reasons to encourage cultivation, as the assessment was always based on *'pahani'* or actual inspection. We have numerous documents enumerating the names as well as the remuneration of the *'Pahanidars'* or survey and inspection officers sent to different Parganas in different years. One dated 1742-43 runs as follows:

"Inspecting officers sent for inspecting Jirayat lands:

Officers sent to Tarft Nagothne should get at the following rate, alter one month till the work or inspection was over, Ragho Ballal Amin Rs. 8, Hari Balaji Karkun Rs. 8, Rs. 16 in total, over and above these two sepoys and one measurer (parwari), three in all. Given from Honaji Balkavade's establishment. Blank sheets of papers for writing and a piece of rough cotton cloth." Similar remuneration and establishment were granted to Naro Ballal Amino sent to Tarf Pal, but his Karkun got a salary of Rs. 7 per month. Pahanidars were also sent to Tarf Nane Mawal.[9] Bagyayat lands were also assessed after inspection and we have already seen in connection with the village system that the Patil as the guardian of the cultivators' interest could demand a pahani whenever he thought that his village had been over-assessed. It seems that the principle of 'no pahani no extra 'assessment was generally recognised by the government. A letter of the time of the second Madhava Rao may be quoted here for illustration.

The officer of Prant Kalyan Bhiwandi represented that the *jamabandi* of the province could not be fixed without inspection of the lands and asked sanction to the expenditure of Rs. 700 or 800 on account of diet-money to officers making the inspection. He was ordered to make the inspection, if it was calculated to raise the revenue, and to take care that the inspection was honestly made, and that no oppression was caused to the rayats. Rs. 400 to 500 were sanctioned for expenditure as diet money" (summary by K. B. Marathe.)[10]

4. Classification of Lands

In fact, assessment without inspection was impossible. For not only were the lands divided into three classes superior, ordinary and inferior, for revenue purposes, but the condition of irrigation and the nature of the crops had to be taken into consideration at the time of fixing the land tax.

Old cultivated lands were taxed at a rate higher than those recently brought under the plough. Thus, the scale of land-tax as well as the manner of payment differed indifferent parts of the country. We get the following rate for Tarf Haveli Pal[11] for the year 1740-41, from a document of the time of Balaji Baji Rao Peshwa.

(1) Rice lands should be assessed as before at 10 maunds per bigha including the levy on account of Babti but excluding the levies of Hakkdars.

(2) Lands producing sugar-cane should be assessed at Rs. 5 per bigha as before.

(3) Vegetable-producing lands should pay Rs. 2 per bigha as before.

(4) Lands under summer crops should be assessed at Rs. 1-8 per bigha as before.

During the administration of the same Peshwa in the same year a kaul was granted to the village of Kathapur in Samat Koregaon of Prant Wai fixing the rate of assessment as follows:[12]

Class of land	*Maunds*	*Payli per Bigha*
Superior	3¼	1
Ordinary	2½	2
Inferior	1¼	1

A third document from the daftar of the same Peshwa (1749-50) shows the difference in the rate of assessment for black and rocky soils, as well as for old cultivated lands and that brought recently under cultivation. The terms of a kaul granted to the village of Pimpalagon/Baswant in Pargana Chandwad were as follows:

(1) Jirayat land having black soil, already under cultivation should be assessed at Rs. 2 per bigha: land of a rocky description, already under cultivation, should be assessed at Re. 1 per bigha. In regard to land newly brought

under cultivation the following rates should be applied:

	Black soil per bigha			*Rocky soil per bigha*		
	Rs.	A.	P.	Rs.	A.	P.
1st year	0	4	0	0	2	0
2nd year	0	8	0	0	4	0
3rd year	1	0	0	0	8	2
4th year	1	8	0	0	12	0
5th year	2	0	0	1	0	0

(2) Bagayat lands already under cultivation including lands bearing sugar-cane and other crops should be assessed at Rs. 10 per bigha. Waste lands newly brought under cultivation, and irrigated by canal, should be assessed as under:

1st year	Rs. 5	per bigha.
2nd year	Rs. 6	per bigha.
3rd year	Rs. 7	per bigha.
4th year	Rs. 8	per bigha.
5th year	Rs. 10	per bigha.

In the case of the jirayat land turned into bagayat by the sinking of new wells the following assessment should be imposed:

1st year	Re. 1	per bigha
2nd year	Rs. 2	per bigha
3rd year	Rs. 3	per bigha
4rd year	Rs. 4	per bigha
5th year	Rs. 5	per bigha

Mango trees in bagayat lands should not be separately taxed. Mango trees belonging to Patils and others should, when they begin to bear fruit, be inspected and taxed at the rate of Re. 1 per thousand fruits. Mango trees belonging to the government should be protected, and the proceeds of the fruit thereof be credited to the government.[13] Finally the document wound up with the instruction that only about a tenth part of the village was under cultivation. The remaining portion should be brought under cultivation within five years. This document clearly shows how the Maratha financiers managed to secure for the government a due share of the unearned increment, without however diminishing the cultivator's zeal for further improvement of his farm land. We will quote only one more document to show the difference of rates for different crops. The villages in Taluka Neral held under the Mokasis were assessed at the following rates after the usual pahani in the year 1772-73. (Administration of the first Madhava Rao):

	Rs	*A.*	*P.*	
1st class land	5	0	0	per bigha
2nd class land	4	0	0	per bigha
3rd class land	3	0	0	per bigha
Rabi lands	1	8	0	per bigha
Warkas lands	1	8	0	per bigha
Hemp lands	.5	0	0	per bigha
Sugar-cane lands	5	0	0	per bigha
Palm trees	0	4	0	for every tree.
Cocoanut trees	0	8	0	for every tree.

"A further addition of half the above rates was levied on account of the Mokasis except on waste land."[14]

It is evident from these documents that payment was made both in kind and cash, probably according to the convenience of the rayats. The rayat was often permitted to commute rent in kind into rent in cash, although it seems that the Peshwa sometimes felt disinclined to encourage such commutation. In 1743-44 Naro Ramchandra, of Jila Mawal, was directed not to commute the land revenue in kind, into a money payment but the Peshwa's order was by no means absolute.[15] For the officer was not only permitted to use his discretion but was also furnished with a complete price list for his use in granting commutation. The list is interesting as probably it gives us the then prevailing market rates, and is therefore, quoted below:

	Rs.	*A.*	*P.*
Rice per maund	1	4	0
Nagli per maund	1	8	0
Wari Sawa per maund	1	4	0
Til four Paylis, Kaili	1	0	0
Jawari per Khandi	35	0	0
Gram per Khandi	40	0	0
Wheat per Khandi	40	0	0
Ghi, two seers by weight	per rupee.		

The following year a similar letter was addressed to the officer in charge of Raipuri, asking him to realise in kind as far as possible the arrears of the preceding year. But in case the rayats did not possess any grain the officer was instructed to allow money payment at the rate of Rs. 15 per khandi.[16]

(One payli=4 seers and one khandi=20 maunds).

It seems that the rayats preferred to pay in cash, and their prayer for such commutation, so far as we can infer from the documents at our disposal, was favourably considered. In the year 1745-46 at the prayer of Sadashiv Lakshman another price list was drawn up for commutation of rent in kind into that in cash for the benefit of the rayats of Prant Mawal who had fallen in arrears.[17] This price list is also qûoted here, for a cursory glance as it will show that the price differed from that of the previous list. The arrears of land revenue in kind in Prant Mawal were ordered to be realised in cash at the following rates:

Rice	Rs.	30 per Khandi.
Nagli[18]	Rs.	35 per Khandi.
Sawa wari[19]	Rs.	30 per Khandi.
Sesamum	Rs.	70 per Khandi.
Jowri and Bajri	Rs.	45 per Khandi.
Kathan (Wheat, grain, etc.)	Rs.	70 per Khandi.
Ghi at 2 seers by weight per Rupee.		

Two years later the rayats of Tarf Nane Mawal and Paun Mawal, were at the request of Naro Keshav permitted to pay in cash part of their arrears of land revenue in kind.

5. Payment in Cash Usually Permitted

"A letter of Naro Ramchandra: There is an arrear of seventy khandis of grain out of the land revenue of the years San Sit and San Saba in Tarfs Nane Mawal and Paun Mawal. Rajshri Naro Keshav came to the Huzur and prayed that part of the arrears might be commuted into money payment and the realisation of the rest might be postponed. Therefore commutation of twenty khandis out of the total due has been permitted. Take cash for rabi crops at the rate of three paylis per Rupee, and for cereals, nachna, wari and rice at the rate of six paylis per Rupee. The remainder is to be postponed for the present and to be realised at the coming season."[19a] The price list drawn up in this case is worth quoting for comparison with the previous list. Rabi crops are quoted here at the rate of three paylis per Rupee and cereals like nachna (*Eleusine Corocana*) and wari (*Coix Barbata*) and rice are valued at six paylis per Rupee.

6. Special Treatment of Brahmans

During the administration of the next Peshwa, the first Madhava Rao, we find the Brahmans claiming commutation for money payment as a customary favour shown to them. In 1767-68, a Brahman of Chambharli, in Tarf Tungartan of Prant Karnalà, Balambhat Godbole by name, prayed for commutation and the land revenue payable by him was fixed at the rate of Rs. 5-2-6 per bigha.[19b]

The assessment may appear quite impartial on the face of it if we compare it with our table of money-rent already quoted, but that it was an undue favour can be proved beyond doubt by a document of the time of Balaji Baji Rao. It shows how the Brahmans of Tarf tungartan, who used to pay at the rate of ten maunds of rice per bigha when the Tarf was under the Angria, got their rent in kind converted into a cash payment of Rs. 5-2-3 per bigha. Even at the most liberal calculation they could not expect such a low assessment if the market price of the grains had been taken into consideration.

A Sand to Ramaji Mahadev, officer in charge of Salsette: "The Brahmans of Tarf Tungartan have represented that when the aforesaid Tarf was under the Angria, rent was exacted at the rate of ten maunds of rice per bigha. At present the aforesaid Mahal has come under the Sarkar; it has been therefore, prayed that the Brahmans should be assessed at the rate prevalent in Prant Kalyan. So rent has been fixed at the rate of Rs. 5-2-3 per bigha. Realise accordingly. Brahmans in Kalyan Prant are not called upon to render forced service or to pay any tax on purchases; accordingly, do not make those demands on the above mentioned Brahmans too."[20] This partiality towards the Brahmans imposed, as Justice Ranade has pointed out, an unnecessary burden on the finances of the land, and contributed not a little to the breakdown of the Peshwa's power.

7. Cocoanut and Other Plantations

Among the instructions drawn up for the guidance of district officers we have seen one drawing their attention towards the planting of cocoanut trees. In one of our tables of land revenue, we have also seen that every cocoanut tree meant for the Peshwa's treasury an additional income of eight annas. Evidently cocoanut plantation was, therefore, very profitable for the government. But, as I have pointed out, the government knew how to wait, and was in no indecent haste to exact a share of the Rayat's hard-won profits. As we all know, cocoanut plantations do not immediately pay; consequently, labour and capital, invested in them, lay idle for a considerably long period, and the planters required special inducements and concessions. The Peshwa's government, therefore, refrained from taxing these costly plants until they were twenty years old.

"Should any person plant the following trees no tax shall be levied on their account for the number of years specified below:

Cocoanut trees	18 or 20 years according to the nature of the land.
Betelnut trees	15 years.
Undani tree	12 years.

After the lapse of the above period the following levies shall be made:

For each cocoanut tree annas four and a load of loppings. For each cocoanut tree used by Bhandaris (liquor manufacturers) Rupee one and a load of loppings. For each betelnut tree, anna 1. For each Undani tree, annas 3."[21]

Similarly in a kaul granted to the Taluka Suvarnadurg for the better cultivation of bagayat lands, we read—"According to custom, cocoanut trees, on sandy soil, should be exempted from taxation until they are eighteen, and on red soil until twenty years old. Betelnut trees, jack trees, and Undani trees should not be taxed until they are fifteen and twelve years of age, respectively." Then each cocoanut tree should pay at the rate of 4 annas, Bhandari cocoanut at the rate of Re. 1, betelnut tree one anna and Undani and jack tree three annas respectively per year.[22]

The cultivation of the specially profitable crops was encouraged by the adoption of special measures and special concessions.

8. Waste Lands

We have already seen how specially lenient assessment was made for bringing waste lands into cultivation. During the administration of the second Madhava Rao, the government went further. It seems that the rocky parts of Talukas Anjanvel and Suvarnadurg were specially unsuitable for farming purposes. The documents say that even trees and grass did not grow there. The Maratha peasants and the Peshwa's government were not, however, daunted by the niggardliness of nature, and the peasants offered to level the hill tops and fill up the *nalas* with newly-brought earth and thereby convert nature's wilderness into teeming fields if suitable terms were offered them. The Peshwa's government was equally prompt in coming forward, and the following well acceptable terms were offered:

"1. Should any person bring an entirely rocky ground under cultivation by covering it with earth, and by providing embankments around it, half the land shall be given him as Inam, and the remaining half shall be continued rent-free for twenty years, and at reduced rates for five years more, and shall, after that period, be subjected to full assessment.

2. Should any person reclaim cultivable land on the seacoast by providing embankments, one-fourth of the land shall be given to him as Inam and the remaining portion shall be continued rent-free and at reduced rates, for such period as, upon a consideration of the money and labour spent, may seem fit."[23]

Naro Anant Parchure, Mahajan of Kasba Guhagar, came to the Huzur at the Mukkam of fort Purandhar, and represented that, formerly, there were bagayat lands in the Taluka Anjanvel. Lately, however, the crop did not grow so well, and the government tax, therefore, was felt to be heavy; the Rayats, therefore, became disheartened, and every year the cultivation of bagayat lands became less. If the Swami, however, granted a kaul of remission and a rate of cash payment, the Rayats will regain hope and will renew cultivation. The Rayats expected to convert rocky places, where trees and grass did not grow at all, into new fields by spreading earth (brought from elsewhere) over the area and to level the rocks by breaking stone, and to convert them into new fields by filling *nalas* and *odhas* with earth. Therefore, if half the land, so reclaimed, was allowed rent-free for twenty years, and at reduced rent for five years more to the cultivator who might reclaim it, cultivation of these lands would be undertaken. Therefore taking the question of the improvement (literally abundance) of cultivation into consideration, a kaul of remission (mafi) and an istawa rate (gradual increase) to the following purport is granted to those who will undertake bagayat cultivation and reclamation of land in the aforesaid manner.

1. The Rayats expect to convert the rocky soil of the Taluka into new fields by bringing earth from elsewhere and by breaking the stones of the rocks and filling the natural ditches and depressions (*nala* and *odha*) with earth. He who will do so, will get as inam half the land reclaimed by him, and will be permitted to enjoy the other half rent-free for twenty years, at a reduced rate for five years more, and the usual rate afterwards.
2. Rayats expect to reclaim cultivable lands, in the aforesaid Taluka, now engrossed in the sea water, by constructing dams. If any one does so, he will get as Inam one-fourth of the land reclaimed, and the terms and periods of remission of rent and Istawa for the remaining three-fourths will be settled according to the amount of labour and money spent for the reclamation.

9. Remission of Rent

Though the Peshwas tried so much to encourage reclamation of waste lands, they did not neglect the lands already under cultivation or the cultivators who worked them. Whenever any famine raged, or the village was plundered, or rain fell short, or the crops failed for some other reason, the Peshwa's government never hesitated to grant a remission of rent, either partial or full, and sometimes for two years or more. When the village of Kanu in Tarf Nane was burnt in the year 1745-46, land revenue to the extent of one khandi and twelve maunds was remitted.[24]

In the year 1747-48, Ramchandra Ballal, officer in charge of the Parganas Bakvada and Jalalabad in Sarkar Bijyagad, represented that his districts were visited by a terrible famine, and in spite of his attempts at relief made in the shape of tagai advancement, several people had already succumbed to the effects of the scarcity of food. He therefore requested a reduction of the assessment for four years and his prayer was granted.[25]

In the year 1750-51, the villagers of Pachora, Pargana Wan, went to Poona and prayed for a remission of rent for the failure of crops and a remission of Rs. 1,313 out of Rs. 2,613 was granted. The Rayats were further permitted to pay off the remaining Rs. 1,300 in four annual installments.[26]

During the administration of the First Madhava Rao, the village of Alandi in Tarf Chakan of Prant Junnar had been plundered in the year 1770-71, and on the representations of the Deshpande of the Tarf, the Peshwa granted full remission of rent for two years.[27]

One thing, in these kauls, is worth noticing as it leaves no doubt about the motive of the Peshwa in granting such remissions. It is always clearly stated that the kaul is granted in view of the improvement of cultivation. Although the Peshwa's government was always ready to help the Rayat in his distress, it did not forget the common prudence of enquiring into the genuineness of the alleged cases of difficulty and their extent. The following case may be cited as typical.[28]

"In 1763-64., Bhikaji Vishwanath, Havaldar of Tarf Khed Chakan and the Deshmukh and the Deshpande of Sarkar Junnar represented that the villages of Prant Junnar had been plundered and burnt by the Mughals; that it was therefore necessary that the Subhedar should offer some concessions to the cultivators, that the Subhedar, however, had not come and the sowing season was passing away. They asked permission to issue kauls to the Rayats. The following concessions were consequently granted:

1. Villages which had been totally burnt down and robbed of cattle, forage and grain to be exempt from assessment for one year.
2. Villages partially burnt and partially plundered, to be subject to half the assessment for one year.
3. Villages which had been plundered but not burnt, to be subject to one-third assessment for one year.
4. Villages which saved themselves by paying a subsidy to be subject to half the assessment for one year.
5. Villages which have received no harm, to be subject to full assessment.
6. The assessment for the following years to be fixed afterwards according to the circumstances of each village."

10. Policy of Taxation

The last sentence in the above document strikes the key-note of the Maratha Policy of taxation. Every man was to be taxed in proportion, to his resources; not a pie more, not a pie less; this was the instruction that the Peshwas gave to revenue officers and this was the prayer that the Rayat made when he applied for a revision of assessment.

We have, in the foregoing pages, tried to show the measures adopted in connection with cases of general distress which affected villages and sometimes Tarfs and Parganas, but there were instances of individual distress. These arose specially from the misconduct of the Peshwa's own soldiers. We find in several documents, complaints of plunder and consequent loss, because the Peshwa or some of his high officers had encamped in the neighbourhod. In such cases the amount of loss was ascertained generally in the presence of the District Officer, and the affected parties were duly compensated. In the year 1768-69, the Peshwa Madhava Rao I had encamped at Garpir, Kasba Puna. The damage in this case was done in pitching the Peshwa's tent in some cultivated fields and also in erecting a temporary stable for his elephants. The villagers got Rs. 162 as compensation.[29] In the year 1773-74, some crops were injured in Kasba Supe in course of the Peshwa Madhava Rao H's state tour. Ananda Rao Trimbak, Subhedar of the Pargana, enquired into the amount of loss and the Rayats got a suitable compensation.[30]

11. Irrigation

The remission of rent in times of difficulty, and payment of compensation in case of damage done by the government, were no doubt good measures; but these were by no means all that the Peshwas did for their subjects. The question of irrigation and tagai grant did not escape their attention. In fact the Hindu kings had taken good care for effectual irrigation of cultivated areas from the earliest times of Indian history, as can be proved by Kautilya's *Arthashastra*, Kalhana's *Raja Tarangini* and the Girnar rock inscription of the Shaka Satrap Rudradamana. The Peshwas also followed this traditional Hindu method for improving agriculture. Irrigation by aqueduct was very common and this gave origin to the word 'patsthal' (from *pat*, and elevated water-course to convey water to a plantation or field), and that well was also used for irrigation purposes may be proved by the word 'motsthal'. But generally rain and river water was stored up for future use by the construction of dams. Sometimes the entire expense for building a new dam or of repairing an old one was granted by the government while the government frequently gave a part of the necessary expenses while the remainder was levied by public subscription.

"A letter to Govind Rao Yadava Kamavisdar of Pargana Kopal in Taluka Dharwar: The rice lands of the Pargana were irrigated by means of a dam in a canal in the Tungabhadra; the dam was damaged by rain. Two thousands Hons have recently been granted for repairing the dam, therefore, get it carefully required and the above-mentioned sum shall be deducted from the revenue of your Pargana."[31]

"A letter to the Mokadam of Mauja-Nasrapur, Tarf Khedebare: Lakshman Krishna has been ordered to construct a dam near Shri baneshwar in the aforesaid Mauja at an expense of Rs. 800. It has been settled that half of the sanctioned expenditure, Rs. 400, should be given by the government and the other half should be realised from those whose lands were to be irrigated. The owners of such lands should, therefore, pay according to their share of half the sanctioned expenditure and you should also pay the share due to your land without making any objection."[32]

12. Tagai

The tagai served two purposes. It supplied the Rayats with necessary capital at a time of scarcity and famine, and at the same time saved them from the clutches of the money-lenders (Shahukars). The Peshwas were a century ago as much conscious of the imporverishing effect of a high rate of interest at the British Government is today. The Co-operative Credit Societies were still undreamt of, but the Peshwas tried their best to undo the evil in their own way. The economic theory of *Laissez Faire,* once popular and now practically rejected in Europe, was still unknown; and the Peshwa, as the father of his people, effectually interfered with the industrial organisation of the country. Such intervention was often beneficial, and there is not doubt that it was so, when he tried to save his Rayats from the cruel exactions of the unscrupulous. Although it will sound shocking to the worshippers of law, the Peshwas frequently excused emburdened tenants from paying interest and compelled the money-lenders to grant their victims easy terms of payment. At another place we have seen how the Zamindars and Patils of Taluka Shivner, unable to make their grievances know in any other way, had seceded to Kasba Ale; one of these grievances was that the Rayats were over-burdened with debt and an enquiry was demanded as to the justice of the money-lender's claims. Their demand and the government order have been summed up in the document in question as follows: "You represent that in *different* villages the Rayats are in debt to the Sawkars (money-lenders). If the just claim is settled after examining the accounts, and if we find that an adequate sum in cash is wanting for payment you will repay the debt from the produce of the villages (grains etc.). An enquiry about the justice of the claims will be made and when you find the interest too high you should not pay that, but a reasonable rate of interest should be fixed and the debt should be liquidated by instalments out of the real produce of the village (grains, etc.)."[33]

It is needless to point out that mere legal suppression of usury is useless. So long as there is a need for capital, men in want will borrow at any interest when money is not available on reasonable terms. The tagai removes this need. It was practically a state loan although the Mamlatdar had to provide for it out of his own resources. The Rayat was not oppressed for interest. Sometimes he got the loan without any interest and frequently easy terms of payment were granted. In the year 1750-51, Ragho Govinda was desired to advance Rs. 1,500 as tagai loan to Kasba Mukhde, in Pargana Patode and he was told that the money was to be recovered in two years.[34] No mention of interest is made in the letter. But in another document we find that while the current rate of interest was 75 per cent the government reduced the interest to 25 per cent on tagai advanced to the Rayats of Prant Rajpur.

"A letter to Khandoji Mankar: You represented that about five or six hundred khandis of grain have been given as tagai during the present year as well as during the last year. An order has been issued to realise it with the usual compensation. The present rate of interest is fifty or seventy-five p.c. The Rayats cannot pay so much. You have, therefore, prayed that some remission may be granted for the welfare of the Rayats. Taking into consideration the welfare of the Rayats it is now settled that the five or six hundred khandis of grain given as tagai should be fully realised with an interest twenty-five p.c. before the month of Magh. Not a seer should be permitted to remain unpaid."[35]

A third document directs an officer, Lakshman Hari, not to dun Ibhramji Nadkar, Khot of Kasba Govale of the same Tarf, for the repayment of tagai as the crops had failed that year (1743-44).[36]

The tagai was advanced in both cash and kind, and generally by the Kamavisdar or the Mamlatdar out of his own purse, and in case of his dismissal before the recovery of the tagai loan, it was repaid by his successor in office.[37] Thus we see that the Peshwas did almost everything necessary and possible for the improvements of cultivation. Grants were made for irrigation works, special terms were offered for the reclamation of waste lands, tagai loan on reasonable interest and easy terms of payment was advanced to the Rayats to save them from the oppression of the money-lenders and finally to create interest in the permanent improvement of their land, kauls were granted for three to seven years and alienation by sale or mortgage was prohibited. Mr. Ranade remarks, "The system of revenue management under Balaji Baijirao, Madhavrao and Nana Fadnavis was, on the whole, careful. New sources of revenue were developed, and the old improved. The land settlements made by the Peshwas during this period show that, while anxious not to oppress the rayats, every care was taken to insist on the rights of the government. Whenever the country needed that relief, leases varying from three to seven years were granted on the terms of Istawas, *i.e.*, gradually increasing assessments."[38]

The result of this liberal policy was that Wellington during his first campaign in the Maratha country found it "highly cultivated" and Elphinstone recommended the continuation of the Maratha system after the conquest of the Peshwa's territories by the English. The land revenue system of the Peshwas will not suffer by comparison with that of contemporary Ireland. The Maratha peasant was certainly better off than his Irish brother and he had practically gained the fixity of tenure and a fair rent for which the Irish were vainly crying even in the first decade of the 19th century. The Maratha peasants had been relieved of forced labour by Peshwa Madhava Rao I, while the French were still labouring under similar disadvantages until the red flood of the Revolution washed away all inequities. But theirs were not rights fought for and bought by blood. The gifts of a paternal despot could be taken away by another less benevolent, and the whole system was upset by that infamous prince Baji Rao II "born of the weakness of Raghunath Rao and wickedness of Anandi Bai." He reintroduced the old Muhammadan system of revenue-farming abolished by Shivaji so long ago. Mahals and Mamlats were sold to the highest bidder and the Peshwa's favourites were induced to bid high. The result was that Districts changed hands every year, and Mamlatdars no longer felt any interest in the welfare of the Rayats. If the Patil refused to assist the revenue-farmers, collection was made without his agency. So even the excellent village system of Maharashtra failed to be a remedy against the misrule of a wicked man.

Before concluding this chapter we shall take a short notice of the Batai system here. As we have seen, the Maratha Peasant and the Maratha government preferred a fixed rent either in cash or in kind. Their collection was always flexible, as "large remissions were made, whenever the seasons were found to be unfavourable. Under the old revenue system, cultivated lands alone paid revenue; and in bad years the revenue fell, and remissions had to be constantly made in the State accounts."[39] The Batai arrangement was, therefore, made where the soil was very poor and the produce extremely variable "Whenever the Batai system of crop division obtained, the Government, after deducting for seeds and other necessary charges paid by the rayats, left 1/2 or 1/3 of the crop to the cultivator, and took the rest for the State. In Shivaji's time, the proportions are stated to have been 2/5 and 3/5. The Batai system was not much in favour."[40]

II

Ranade was not the only scholar to point out that "Like the first Napoleon, Shivaji in his time was a great organiser, and a builder of civil institutions."[41] Scott-Warning, writing in the first decade of the 19th century, observes "while Sevajee carried on his predatory warfare, he was not inattentive to his predatory warfare to the growing interests of his state. The lands in the Kokun were secured and defended."[42] That was not all. The lands were secured and defended and suitable measures were taken for the extension of cultivation and improvement of agriculture. Jervis tells us that according to the popular traditions, Shivaji's subjects enjoyed plenty though not peace. "In the midst of all this confusion, warfare, and general disloyalty, the state of the revenue and population is said to have prospered."[43] The reason is not hard to find out; Shivaji introduced a flexible system that long survived his dynasty's overthrow, and as Mr. Pringle Kennedy says "The peasant knew what he had to pay and he seems to have been able to pay this without any great oppression."[44]

It is certainly creditable to the great Maratha soldier that his subjects, in spite of his constant wars, should have enjoyed plenty and increased in number. But all that Shivaji had to do was to follow in the foot-steps of another great man. It is true that Shivaji cannot claim originality. But originality is not an indispensable factor in statesmanship. All that is expected of a practical statesman is that he should discern the needs of his time and adopt suitable measures to meet them. Whether these measures are his own or not does not matter. Akbar, one of the greatest of Indian rulers, frequently revived the long forgotten measures of some of his less known predecessors and with what effect is known to us all. Shivaji also had the keen discernment of a statesman and he could appreciate the good points, as she was fully aware of the defects of the existing government. He found that Malik Ambar's revenue system with a few slight modifications, would suit his country best and he revived it without any hesitation.[45] What Todar Mall did for the north, Malik Ambar did for the south. The great foreigner, who had served his adopted country so well, had to work almost under the same circumstances as Shivaji. While defending his master's tottering kingdom against the Mughal onslaughts, the great Abyssinian had to recognise its exhausted resources. He worked with an open mind and adopted the revenue system of his enemies. On the eve of its fall the Nizamshahi kingdom enjoyed a set of excellent regulations, but there was no one after Malik Ambar to work them out. Like Todar Mall he divided the arable lands into four separate classes according to fertility and ascertained their produce, roughly true, and fixed the assessment once for all. He, however, did not want the peasants to pay in kind. While a fixed permanent assessment was made, a commutation or money price was also fixed for ever. After fixing a money rent Malik Ambar turned his attention to the collecting agency. With one stroke of his pen he did away with the intermediate revenue agency which had been gradually assuming the character of a farming system. He then made the Patils and other revenue officers hereditary, but at the same time made them responsible for the full realisation of the government dues.[46] Such in short was Malik Ambar's revenue system and as some of Shahaji's jagirs had previously formed part of the Nizamshahi dominions, the people there were not unfamiliar with it. Nor was there any lack of officials who had seen it in its actual working. Dadaji Konddev, when he reclaimed the waste lands of his master's jagir, did nothing but revive the wise regulations of the great Abyssinian.[47]

But Shivaji was no blind imitator. He was, if anything, a lover of strict method; and Malik Ambar's system, in certain respects, lacked it. While therefore, accepting its principles, Shivaji did not commit himself to all its details. Malik Ambar had not carefully surveyed the land, and the survey work was fraught with many difficulties, more or less serious. There were different standards and units of measurement and Shivaji had to find out a standard unit before he could order a systematic survey.[48] Then again accurate measurement was impossible with a rope. The length of a rope was liable to slight variations in different seasons. So the measuring rope had to be rejected. Some Muhammadan rulers had substituted the rope by the *'tenab'* or measuring chain. But Shivaji replaced it by a *kathi* or a measuring rod.[49] The kathi was to be five cubits and five fists (*muthis*) in length. The length of the regulation rod was fixed in *tasus* also. Twenty rods square made a *bigha,* and one hundred and twenty bighas a *chavar*. The unit of measurement being thus fixed, Shivaji ordered a survey settlement and the work of surveying the Konkan was[50] entrusted to no less able an officer than the celebrated Annaji Datto, Shivaji's Sachiv.

Annaji's Survey

It can be safely asserted that the survey work was done with the utmost care. Annaji Datto refused to rely on irresponsible government officials, whose lack of local knowledge and necessary energy disqualified them for the work. He issued a circular letter to village officers urging them to undertake this important work with the co-operation of some of their co-villagers, whose interests were directly involved. A copy of this old circular[51] letter has come down to us, and has been deciphered and published by Mr. V.K. Rajwade. As this is the only document that tells us how the bighaoni survey of the Konkan was conducted by Annaji, it is a pity that this important paper has not escaped mutilation, and the sad ravages of time have made it impossible for Mr. Rajwade to decipher all the words. Many gaps have yet to be filled up mainly by conjecture. But it appears from what has been read, that the estimate of these village officers was not accepted without a proper examination. Annaji Datto himself revised their work. In every district, he visited at least one village of each description, estimated its yield, and then compared his own figure with that submitted by the village officers. It was the interest of these villagers not to over-estimate the possible revenue; consequently, the king alone was the only losing party if any error in these estimates remained undetected. This circular letter was issued in 1678, only two years before Shivaji's death. It is, therefore, clear that this survey settlement could not be finished in his life time and had, in all probability, commenced late in his reign.

Cesses and Abwabs

In those days people had to make numerous contributions to the state, to the village communities, and even to those criminal tribes whose protection or neutrality the commercial and agricultural classes considered necessary to purchase. An ordinary peasant, for instance, had to pay his share of the land revenue to the state, at the harvest time he had to give a certain measure of grain to the village officers including the artisans, and when he brought the green vegetables of his garden for sale at the market place, the Patil and the Kulkarni (the village headman and the village scribe) took a handful in pursuance of a very old practice. To appreciate properly the revenue reforms of Shivaji, it is essential to have a clear idea of the taxes and cesses that a peasant or an artisan had to pay. Elphinstone has given us a list of taxes and cesses that prevailed in the Peshwa period but unfortunately no such list is available for the preceding period. This deficiency can however be made up by a careful scrutiny of the Sanads or grant deeds published in Mr. V. K. Rajwade's *Marathyanchya Itihasanchi Sadhanen,* Mawji and Parasnis's *Sanads and Letter* and the Transactions of the Bharat Itihas Sanshodhak Mandal of Poona. These papers mention no less than fifty taxes, cesses and abwabs (extra duties), a formidable list indeed. But it should be remembered that some of these taxes were levied probably once in a lifetime, others were collected on special occasions, while some of them were undoubtedly confined to a particular locality.

About their nature and incidence the Sanads hardly enlighten us. They simply enumerate all customary cesses, taxes and obligations from which the grantee is exempted. It is clear that all the taxes mentioned below were not exacted by the state, nor did they all prevail in the same revenue area and never was the same man in any locality subjected to all the taxes, cesses and other financial obligations of his native Pargana:

1. *Beth Begari*—Forced labour.

2. *Farmasi*—"Fruit, vegetables, etc., furnished on occasions to Rajas and public officers, on the authority of their order upon the villages; any petty article or trifling work exacted from the ryots by Government or a public officer."—Molesworth.[52]

   "An occasional contribution in kind; often paid in commutation of service." Elphinstone.

3. *Belekati* — A tax exacted on the commencement of the harvest. (Balkati, cutting ears of corn) Thomas, *Revenue Resources of the Moghal Empire*, p. 19.

4. *Paiposi* — Cannot be positively identified; probably a tax paid in kind by the shoe-makers. The shoe-makers claimed the special right of paying their dues in kind.[53]

5. *Mejbani* — Literally dinner tax.[54]

6. *Mohimpati* —Expedition cess; a similar tax is mentioned by Kautilya, but we need not go to such a remote age, a tax like this was levied by the Portuguese in their Indian Estate.

7. *Karchapati* — Cannot be identified.

8. *Telpati* —Oil cess; perhaps levied for illumination on festive occasions.

9. *Tup* — A tax in kind levied perhaps on manufacturers of *ghi*.

10. *Faski* — A toll levied on green vegetable-sellers.
11. *Sadilvar* — A comprehensive term for any contingent charge.
12. *Tutpati* — Literally means a tax to cover losses. It might be similar to 'Kasar' charged from Khots in Janjira to cover the loss in any deficiency of measurement. Prof. Pissurlencar thinks that it was similar to *but patti* of Portuguese India.
13. *Idsubrati* — Jervis thinks it was a tax in kind paid by oilmen for illumination on the occasion of Id.
14. *Toraanbheti* — Arches for receiving distinguished guests.
15. *Ut* — A cess levied on transport camels.
16. *Ambe* — A tax levied on the produce of mango trees.
17. *Karujati* — Cannot be identified. Has it any relation to Karus, artisians?
18. *Hejib* — Probably means the perquisites of an insignificant village officer of the same name. Hejib is mentioned in an old document published in the *Itihas Sangraha, Aitihasik Charitren*, pp. 22-23.
19. *Pathevari* — The meaning is uncertain; is it Patwari, a tax levied for village officers?
20. *Ashvajakati* — A duty on sale of horse. This tax is mentioned by many Portuguese authors including Barros.
21. *Setsara* — A tax on arable land.
22. *Barhad Taka*[55] — Probably similar to *bharad* tax of Portuguese India.
23. *Sel Bail* — A duty on transport cattle.
24. *Jangampati* — A jingam is a lingayat. A tax on the Jangams or Saiva lingayats; see Book III.
25. *Peshkasi* — Same as the Paishkush of the Mughal period.

26. *Patisike Huhmayun* — Sike means a seal. This tax must be analogous to Batchhapai of the Peshwa period.

27. *Kar-i-Humayuni* — A tax levied for celebrating the royal birth day.

28. *Thanebhet* — In Portuguese India the villagers had to feed small bands of sepoys visiting the locality. Probably a similar obligation existed in some parts of Shivaji's kingdom.

29. *Dasrapati* — It is a cess levied on the occasion of Dasra? We know that under the Peshwa regime the Patil received some presents in kind, *e.g.*, a goat on the Dasra day. Sleeman noticed a somewhat similar practice in Central India. "In the first place, they (Thanadars) levy a fee of one rupee from every village at the festival of the Holi in February, another at that of the Dasehra in October," *Rambles and Recollections*, Vol. II, p. 217. The Ramoshi, Sarnaik also was entitled to the present of a goat from the neighbouring villages on the Dasra day. See Mackintosh, *Origin and present condition of the Tribe of Ramoossies*, p. 58.

30. *Huzur Bhet*

31. *Halpati*

32. *Ahisthan* —Cannot be identified.

33. *Virahisthan*

34. *Mohatarfa*—A tax on shop-keepers. Many cesses fall under this general heading.

35. *Thaljakati*—Custom duties levied on goods while in transit through land.

36. *Palbhara* — May be a tax on green vegetables.

37. *Ulphapati*[56] — A religious cess.

38. *Bakrid*[57] — Cannot be identified.

39. *Sardesmukhpati* — Same as Sardeshmukhi?
40. *Mashahira* — Same as Rasad of the Mughal Rulers.
41. *Caonkhandi* — Cannot be identified.
42. *Dani* — A tax in grain.
43. *Teji Bheti* — Cannot be identified.
44. *Jhadjhadoda* — A cess in kind levied on the fruits of village trees, generally collected at the rate of one per hundred mangoes or tamarinds.
45. *Bargujar* — "Tax on the fields near the city where Paun is cultivated." Jenkins, *Report on the Territories of Rajah of Nagpore,* p. 228.
46. *Inampati* — An occasional tax imposed in times of exigency on Inamdars.
47. *Akhduldivani* — Cannot be ascertained.
48. *Kar Imarati* — A tax to meet building expenses.
49. *Vihar huda* — An extra tax on lands watered from wells. Mention is made of another abwab, *Sinhasanpati* or coronation tax, levied on the watandars at the time of Shivaji's coronation.[58] Most of these taxes do not appear in *Elphinstone's* list and had been abolished in the interval.

Principle of Assessment

Annaji Datto had fixed the rent at 33% p.c. of the gross produce but Shivaji afterwards demanded a consolidated rent of 40% p.c.[59] when all the taxes and extra cesses had been abolished.[60] Neither *tagai* nor the *istawa* principle was unknown in his time. "Cattle should be given to the new rayats that may come Grain and money for (buying) seeds should be given. Grain and money should be given for their maintenance and the sum should be realised in two or four years according to the means of the debtor."[61] In this way, says Sabhasad, new settlers were encouraged to come and settle in Shivaji's dominions. Rent-free land was granted for founding a market town by Shivaji's minister Moro Pingle.[62] It is also certain that though extra cesses had been abolished, the customs duties were retained. No one could travel without a passport from a competent authority and Fryer mentions a customs officer stationed at Kalyan.[63]

We know, from many published documents, how much the peasant had to pay for each bigha he cultivated, during the Peshwa period. No such document of Shivaji's time has come down to us. Major Jervis has quoted exact figures in his work on the Konkan, but from what sources we do not know. It will not, however, be improper to quote these figures here, and the reader may accept them for what they are worth. Says Jervis, — "It is commonly believed indeed, that he (Shivaji) measured and classified all the lands, and then ascertained the amount of their produce from one or two villages in each Muhal of the Ouchitgurh, Rajpooree, Rygurh, Soowurndroog, Unjunvel, Rutnagiri and Veejydroog districts, for three successive years, from which data he established the rates, half in kind, half at a fixed commutation rate differing in each Talooka, to be paid by the beegah of each sort of land. The classification of the rice lands *mule* or *dhemp*, under 12 heads;the four first still retaining their former well-known distinctions. *Uwul,* first and best sort; *Doom* or *Dooyoom* second sort; *Seem* third sort; *Charoom* or *Charseem* fourth sort. The first was assessed at 12½ muns; the second at 10, the third at 8, the fourth at 6¼ muns...The remaining eight descriptions of land went by the following names, discriminating their respective qualities, and were assessed at the annexed rates. Ist, Raupal, on which small stunted brush wood grows; 2nd, Kharwut, lands in the neighbourhood of the sea or rivers, sometimes called salt bhatty lands; 3rd Bawul, rocky soil; 4th Khuree, stony soil; 5th Kuriyet or Toorwut, lands cultivated with pulse hemp, etc. 13 (sic) Manut, lands with the roots of large trees still uncleared, as near Indapur and Goregaon.

Raupal	8 maunds per beegah.
Kharwut	7½ maunds per beegah.
Bawul	6¼ maunds per beegah.
Khuree	6¼ maunds per beegah.
Kureyat Ist sort	6¼ maunds per beegah.
Ruho	5 maunds per beegah.
Toorwut or Katahnee	5 maunds per beegah.
Manut	5 maunds per beegah.

Subsequently the wretched cultivators have planted small spots on the most rocky eminences, wherever a little water lodged, and the least portion of soil favoured the growth of rice; this is frequent about Unijunvel and Rutnagiri Talookas, and have been classed under two heads, both called *sirwut*, the former assessed at 3¾ maunds, the latter the half of that; the produce of the first kind, would be about 16 bushels per beegah.[64]

Special rates were fixed for other harvests. Vijat jamin or uncultivable waste lands were generally excluded when a village was assessed.[65] But as cultivation spread, there was a great demand for arable plots, and waste lands of all sorts were gradually brought under the plough. At first they were exempt from assessment, but ultimately these were also taxed at a moderate scale. Jervis says that these *warkus* or dongur lands were assessed by the hal, mangar or plough and not by the bigha. In some instances six or seven bighas of such lands were counted as one for revenue purposes. The rent of such lands varied not only with their fertility but also with the nature of the crops raised. Major Jervis gives us the following scale:

Machni was assessed at 3¼ maunds per *nangar* in superior soil and 3 maunds in inferior soil.

Wari at 3 maunds and 2½ maunds.

Harik at 3 maunds.

Other kinds of inferior produce at 1¼ maunds.

Beside the principal harvest the peasants often raised a second crop on the first class lands. These second crops were also assessed at a special rate according to their nature and deteriorating effect on the land. Jervis gives the following figures:

Turmeric—Five maunds per bigha, each bigha being 3/4 actual measurement.

Hemp—Five maunds per bigha, each bigha being ¾ actual measurement.

Sugarcane—Cultivation assessed from 6¼ maunds to $3\frac{1}{3}$ of raw sugar per bigha.[66]

Special consideration was made by the Peshwa government for such costly plantations as those of sugarcane, cocoanut and betelnut. The planter had to wait long for any profit and so did the government. This was the common practice in the Deccan during the Peshwa regime, and I believe the principle existed also in Shivaji's time.

Revenue Divisions and Revenue Officers

The provinces under Shivaji's rule were styled Swarajya to distinguish them from Mughlai or provinces under other (generally Muhammadan) rulers. The Swarajya was, for revenue purposes, divided into a number of Prants consisting of two or more Districts. There were in all 16 provinces under Shivaji's government according to Ranade.[67] They were:

1. Maval.
2. Wai.
3. Satara.
4. Karad.
5. Panhala.
6. South Konkan.
7. Thana.

8. Trimbak.
9. Baglan.
10. Wanagad.
11. Bedmore.
12. Kolhar.
13. Srirangapatan.
14. Karnatik.
15. Vellore.
16. Tanjore.

But we get a larger number in a jabta[68] drawn in the earlier years of Chhatrapati Shahu. The document, written partly in Persian and partly in Marathi, is supposed to be in the hand-writing of Shankrajai Malhar. It gives the boundary and divisions of the Swarajya as understood in Shahu's time. The following are the provinces enumerated in Shahu's jabita Swarajya:

1. Subha Ramnagar including Ghandevi.
2. Subha Jawhar Prant.
3. Subha Prant Bhiwadi (12 Talukas).
4. Subha Kalyan (20 Talukas).
5. Subha Cheul (6 Talukas).
6. Subha Rajpuri (12 Talukas).
7. Subha Javali (18 Talukas).
8. Subha Dabhol (11 Talukas).
9. Subha Rajapoor (18 Talukas).
10. Subha Kudal (15 Talukas).
11. Subha Prant Bhimgad (5 Talukas).
12. Subha Prant Phonde (5 Talukas).
13. Subha Prant Akole (5 Talukas).

14. Subha Poona (6 Talukas).
15. Subha Baramati.
16. Subha Indapur.
17. Subha Prant Mawal (13 Talukas).
18. Subha Prant Wai (4 Talukas).
19. Subha Prant Satara (6 Talukas).
20. Subha Prant Kurhad (9 Talukas).
21. Subha Prant Khatao excluding Kasba Khatao (11 Talukas).
22. Subha Prant Man (4 Talukas).
23. Subha Prant Phaltan Mahal.
24. Subha Prant Belgaum.
25. Subha Sampgaon.
26. Subha Gadag.
27. Subha Laxmeshwar.
28. Subha Nawalghund.
29. Subha Kopal.
30. Subha Halyal.
31. Subha Betgiri.
32. Subha Malkapur (4 Talukas).
33. Subha Prant Panhala (10 Talukas).
34. Subha Tarle (5 Talukas).
35. Subha Ajera (51 Talukas).
36. Subha Prant Junnar (24 Talukas).
37. Subha Kolhapore.

Some of these may be later additions, but this list, we think, fairly represents the division of Shivaji's kingdom. Sambhaji had no mind to improve the administration and

Rajaram had no leisure. It is not, therefore, probable that many changes had been made in the territorial division of the kingdom before the accession of Chhatrapati Shahu.

Shivaji had done away with the agency of such old hereditary officers as the Patil and the Kulkarni in the village and the Deshmukh and the Deshpande in the district. They were left in the enjoyment of their old dues but the work of revenue collection was entrusted to new officers directly appointed by the king. The country had been divided by the Muhammadan government for revenue purpose into Mauja, Pargana, Sarkar, and Subhas; Shivaji abolished, or to be more accurate, modified these old divisions. In his time the country was divided into Maujas, Tarfs and Prants. The officer in charge of a Tarf was designated as Havaldar, Karkun or, in some rare instances, Paripatyagar. The officer in charge of a Prant was variously designated as Subhedar, Karkun or Mukhya Deshadhikari. Over several Prants was sometimes placed an officer called Sarsubhedar, to supervise the work of the Subhedars. These officers, like the Kamavisdars and the Mamlatdars of the Peshwa period, had to look after all the branches of the administration. The Subhedar's staff consisted of the usual complement of eight officers, *viz:*

1. The Dewan.
2. The Mazumdar.
3. The Fadnis.
4. The Sabnis.
5. The Karkanis.
6. The Chitnis.
7. The Jamadar.
8. The Potnis.

The Subheadar usually had an annual salary of four hundred Hons a year, including the palanquin allowance. while his Mazumdar's pay varied from one hundred to one hundred and twenty-five Hons a year. The Mazumdar also enjoyed the proud privilege of carrying a sun-shade[69] on public occasions and a small allowance was sanctioned by the government for its upkeep. A Havaldar in charge of a small village had often to be contented with a paltry allowance of three to five Hons only a year.[70]

The Kamavisdar and the Mamlatdar under the Peshwa regime, though appointed for a short term, were generally allowed to retain their office for life, and to transmit it to their heirs. No public office was hereditary under Shivaji's administration, and like the Magistrates and Commissioners of British India, his Karkuns, Havaldars, and Subhedars were, as a rule, transferred from district to district and province to province. This can be clearly proved by a list of officers carefully compiled by Mr. Bhashkar Vaman Bhat[71] from the official letters and documents published in the 15th, 16th, 17th, 18th and 20th volumes of Mr. Rajwade's *Marathyanchya Itihasanchi Sadhanen*.

In Mr. Bhat's list, we find that the following officers were in charge of the several districts for the years marked against their names:

	Havaldar	
Nimb	Yesaji Ram	1676 A.D.
Haveli	Amaji Kanho	1676 A.D.
Koregaon	Bhimaji Malhar	1676 A.D.
Tarf Satara	Kukaji Bayaji	1676 A.D.
Tarf Satara	Mahadaji Anant	1676 A.D.
Tarf Satara	Tukaji Rabhu	1677 A.D.

We are not in possession of a complete list of Havaldars, and we do not know whether in other districts also officers were changed so often as in Satara. Our information about Subhedars and Sarsubhedars is, however, more satisfactory and the working of the principle of a short term appointment and occasional transfer can be very conveniently proved by the following instances from Mr. Bhat's list:

	Subhedars	
Wai Prant	Yesaji Malhar	1676 A.D.
Wai Prant	Yesaji Malhar	1679 A.D.
Wai Prant	Yesaji Malhar	1687 A.D.
Wai Prant	Yesaji Malhar	1690 A.D.
Wai Prant	Yesaji Malhar	1696 A.D.
Wai Prant	Anaji Janardan	1697 A.D.
Jawali	Viroram	1664 A.D.
Jawali	Viththal Datto	1671-1672 A.D.
Jawali	Ambaji Mordeu	1676 A.D.
Jawali	Gopal Rayaji	1677 A.D.
Jawali	Kashi Rangnath	1680 A.D.
Prant Kol	Ganesh Jogdeu	1672 A.D.
Prant Kol	Venkaji Rudra	1677 A.D.
Prant Puna	Tryambak Gopal	1679 A.D.
Prant Puna	Vinayak Umaji	1681 A.D.

It is also certain that this principle survived Shivaji and continued down to the first decade of the 18th century so far as the appointment of Mudradharis was concerned. In support of this view, Mr. Bhat has produced the following list of Mudradharis or officers in charge of Sajjangad:

Jijoji Katkar	1676 A.D.
Jijoji Katkar	1682 A.D.
Makaji Katkar	1689 A.D.
Barhanji Mohite	1692 A.D.
Barhanji Mohite	1699 A.D.
Girjoji Bhonsle	1708 A.D.
Girjoji Bhonsle	1709 A.D.
Yesaji Jadhava, from 11th Falgun	1709 A.D.
Satbaji Daval	1712 A.D.

Mr. Bhat further points out that Ambaji Mordeu, who was Subhedar of Jawli in 1676, occupied the office of the

Subhedar of Satara from 1683-1685. Mahadji Shamraj, Subhedar of Jawli from 1706-1708, was formerly in charge of Prants Satara and Mawal.

From the multiplicity of their duties these officers were liable to corruption. Public opinion in those days was not offended if a Havaldar went out of his way to take a small present from a traveller for granting his passport, or from an aggrieved petitioner for redressing his grievances. Dr. Fryer, who visited the Maratha dominions towards the close of Shivaji's career, has left a quaint account of such an occasion. "When I came before the Governor," says the Doctor,[72] "I found him in State, though under an Hovel; where were many *Brachmins* with Account Books, writing at some distance; nearer, his Privy council, with whom he seemed to advise: I was placed on his left hand, desired my Interpreter to acquaint him my Errand withal in treating his favour for my secure passing the Hill: He made it a piece of difficulty, and told me I must return to *Bimly* for Orders, to whose *Havaldar* he was accountable not to him of *Gulleon;* which was within half a day's journey from whence I set forth. Hearing this I bore myself as sedately as I could, having been informed of the advantage they take of a disturbed Countenance; and sweetened him with his own Authority being sufficient, telling him of his Master's kindness of the *English,* and their friendship towards him: which worked him to a yielding temper; yet he scrupled my *Canister*, or Trunk, might be lined with Pearl, my Horse sold to the enemy, hoping to suck somewhat out of me; I replied, What I had brought were at his liberty to search, and that I went only on an amicable account to cure a sick person and should be as ready to serve him, if required, his fury was quite pawled but perceiving an hungry look to hang on them all, and suspecting lest they should serve me some Dog-trick, I made a small Present, and he signing the Pass, dismissed me with a Bundle of *Pawn* the usual Ceremony at Parting." "The hungry look' and the weakness for presents are perhaps pardonable, but another charge that the English Doctor brought against Shivaji's revenue officers is too serious to be overlooked.

Public officers in the 17th century whether Asiatic or European were not over scrupulous. But good kings, as a rule, exercised a strict control over them. Shivaji in particular was served by a very efficient intelligence department. It is an old practice in India to employ spies to watch over the conduct of government servants.[73] The work of District and Provincial officers was supervised by the Pant Amatya and the Pant Sachiv. Ranade tells us that "The district accounts had to be sent to these officers, and were there collated together, and irregularities detected and punished. These officers had power to depute men on their establishments to supervise the working of the district officers."[74] Shivaji, moreover, was very keen about the success of his government and wanted that his administration should compare favourably with that of his Muhammadan neighbours.[75] But all his cares and sound regulations were fruitless indeed if his revenue officers really worked as arbitrarily as Fryer says they did. "They are neither for Public Good nor Common Honesty, but their own private interest only: They refuse no Base Offices for their own Commodity, inviting merchants to come and trade among them, and then rob them, or else turmoil them on account of Customs; always in a Corner getting more for themselves than their Master, yet openly must seem mighty zealous for their Master's Dues: So that trade is unlikely to settle where he had anything to do; notwithstanding his Country lieing all along on the Sea-shore, and no, goods can be transported without his Permission; unless they go a great way about, as we are forced to do."

This is by no means the worst that the English traveller has to say against the Maratha officers. He continues—"It is a general calamity, and much to be deplored, to hear the complaints of the poor people that remain, or are rather compelled to endure the Slavery of *Seva Gi:* The *Desies* have land imposed upon them at double the former rates, and if they refuse to accept it on these hard conditions (if Monied Men) they are carried to Prison, there they are famished almost to death; racked and tortured most inhumanly till they confess where it is: They have now in Limbo several

Brachmins, whose Flesh they tear with pincers heated Red-hot, drub them on the shoulders to extreme Anguish (though according to their Law it is forbidden to strike a *Brachmin).* This is the accustomed Sawee all *India* over, the Princes doing the same by the Governors, when removed from their Offices, to squeeze their illgot estates out of them; which when they have done, it may be they may be employd again: And after this fashion the *Desies* deal with the *Combies;* so that the Great Fish prey on the Little, as well by Land as by Sea, bringing not only them, but their families into Eternal Bondage."[76] Fryer was of opinion that even Bijapore rule was milder than that of Shivaji.

If Fryer's account is borne out by facts, the state of the country was terrible indeed. But Fryer had made only a short trip through Shivaji's dominions and his stay there was by no means long. It does not appear probable that his account based on personal experience or first hand knowledge of any other kind. Shivaji is still adored as an ideal king, and people referred to his institutions with admiration in days of anarchy and misrule. Traditions may be exaggerated, but they are never entirely baseless. Traditions attribute all sorts of good institutions to such good rulers as Alfred and Elizabeth, but legends have not hitherto paid any tribute to the memory of such bad kings as John and James II. It is a very important point that the memory of Shivaji is still cherished by the people of Maharashtra as that of a great and good king. If he had really tortured his Brahman officers with red hot princers and they in their turn had dealt out similar treatment to the Desais, Shivaji would not have been revered as an incarnation of Shri Shambhu Mahadev. We have already seen how the great Maratha had striven to liberate the poor peasants from the tyranny of the Deshmukhs and Deshpandes. It, therefore, seems improbable that he should allow is officers to force lands on the Desais at an exorbitant rate. Far from molesting any Brahman, Shivaji never offered any insult to holy men and holy places of his Muhammadan enemies. Although many temples and idols were defile and desecrated by Muhammadan bigots, Shivaji never failed to send any copy of the Quran, he might come in possession of, to some of his Muslim officers. Even Khafi Khan, an inveterate enemy of the Maratha hero, paid him an unwilling compliment on that account.[77] Dellon a French Physician, who visited the Western coast about the same time as Fryer, remarks that "His (Shivaji's) subjects are pagans, like himself. But he tolerates all religions and is looked upon as one of the most politic princes in those parts."[78] Shivaji styled himself as *Go-Brahman Pratipalak,* `Protector of Brahmans and cows,' and could hardly with any consistency to his professed ambition, overlook the conduct of his officers, if they really tortured the Brahmans. Fryer's story, therefore, seems to be baseless. Corruption there certainly existed, and instances of tyranny and misrule doubtless occurred. Shivaji, in the midst of those wars of conquest and defence, could hardly get anytime for improving his government. But Fryer seems to have dipped his brush in the black dye too frequently while painting a picture of Shivaji's country. Grant Duff[79] says, "The Mahomedan writers, and one contemporary English traveller, described his country as in the worst possible state; and the former only mention him as a depredator and destroyer; but those districts taken by him from Beejaporek which had been under the management of farmers and direct agents of government, probably experienced great benefit by the change".

Mints and Coins

Besides land revenue and customs duties, a small income was derived from mints. The Peshwas did not permit free coining, but the goldsmith usually obtained licence for mints under certain restrictions. That must have been the practice in the pre-Peshwa period also. Shivaji never tried to control the currency and plainly told the English Ambassador, that "he forbids not the passing of any manner of Coins, nor on the other side, can he force his subjects to take those Monies whereby they shall be Losers; but if their Coin be as fine an

Allay, and as weighty as the *Mogul's,* and other Princes, he will not prohibit it."[80] The result was that all sorts of foreign coins were current in Shivaji's kingdom and even in his own treasury could be found few or no coins of the Rairi mint. Sabhasad says[81] that Shivaji had no less than 400,000 of Shivarai Hons at the time of his death, but these Shivarai Hons were in all probability of Vijayanagar origin, for only 2 or 3 Shivaji Hons have yet been discovered. Sabhasad enumerates no less than 32 different kinds of gold coins and 6 different kinds of silver coins while giving an account of Shivaji's treasurers. They were:

Gold Coins

1. Gambar.
2. Mohar.
3. Putli,
4. Padshahi Hon..
5. Satlamis or Satramis.
6. Ibhrami.
7. Shivarai Hon.
8. Kaveripak.
9. Sangari Hon.
10. Achyutrai Hon.
11. Devarai Hon.
12. Ramchandrarai Hon.
13. Guti Hon.
14. Dharwari Hon.
15. Falam (Fanam).
16. Pralkhati Hon.
17. Pav Naiki Hon.
18. Advani Hon.
19. Jadmal Hon.
20. Tadpatri Hon.
21. Afraji Hon.
22. Tribaluri Hon.
23. Trisuli Hon.
24. Chandavari (Tanjori) Hon.
25. Bildhari Hon.
26. Ulphakari Hon.
27. Muhammad Shahi Hon.
28. Veluri Hon.
29. Katerai Hon.
30. Devajvali Hon.
31. Ramnathpuri Hon.
32. Kungoti Hon.

Silver Coins

1. Rupees.
2. Asrafts.
3. Abashis.
4. Dabholi Kabri.
5. Chauli Kabri.
6. Basri Kabri.

Some of these coins were current in foreign countries: Ibhrami, for instance, was common in the market places of Bussorah.[82]

Shivaji had his mint at Raigad. His first coins were not probably issued before 1674. A large number of copper coins were issued, and no less than 25,000 of these were collected and examined by the Rev. Mr. Abbott.[83] But very few gold coins of Shivaji are known today, probably because only a few were struck.

Shivaji had no good mechanic to work his mint. The irregular shape of the coins and the mis-shapen alphabets of the legends show the crude method of their manufacture. The writer of the Bombary Gazetteer[84] gives the following account of the working of the Chandor mint closed in 1830. "A certain quantity of silver of the required test was handed over to each man who divided it into small pieces, rounded and weighed them, greater care being taken that the weights should be accurate and size should be uniform. For this purpose scales and weights were given to each of the 400 workmen, and the manager examined them every week. When the workmen were satisfied with the weight of the piece, they were forwarded to the manager who sent them to be stamped. In stamping the rupee an instrument like an anvil was used. It had a hole in the middle with letters inscribed on it. Piece after piece was thrown into the hole, the seal was held by a workman called *batekari;* and a third man gave a blow with a six pound hammer. Three men were able to strike 2,000 pieces an hour, or 20,000 in a working day of ten hours. As the seal was a little larger than the piece, all the letters were seldom inscribed." The Chandor mint was opened long after Shivaji's demise. But that the description holds good with respect to Shivaji's mint also, can be proved by a simple inspection of Shivarai coins. The small Shivai Hon in the museum of the Barat Itihas Sanshodhak Mandal, for example, lacks the compound letter "tra" in the word Chhatrapati, evidently because the little circular piece had originally been hammered on a seal of much larger size.

The goldsmith in charge of the mint could evidently boast of very little learning. In the copper coins alone we find no less than eight different spellings of the world Shri Raja Siva Chhatrapati. The Rev. Mr. Abbot gives the following eight variations in the spelling of this word on Shivarai pice:

1.	Ob	श्री राजाशिव छत्रपति	R.
2.	Ob	श्रीराजाशिव छत्रपती	R.
3.	Ob	श्रीराजाशीव छत्रपति	R.
4.	Ob	श्रीराजाशीव छत्रपती	R.
5.	Ob	श्रीराजासिब छत्रपति	R.
6.	Ob	श्रीराजासिवा छत्रपती	R.
7.	Ob	श्रीराजासीव छत्रपति	R.
8.	Ob	श्रीराजासीब छत्रपती	R.

The Small Shivarai Hon in the Bharat Itihas Sanshodhak Mandal's[85] museum has on the obverse the figures of Shiva and Bhavani seated side by side, and on the reverse the name of Shivaji inscribed in the following manner:

सीब

रा (modi) जछ (त्र)

पती

Chauth and Sardeshmukhi

But neither the land revenue, nor the customs duties and the income from mints, added so much to the treasury of Shivaji as the Chauth and the Sardeshmukhi. Even in normal times he depended more on his army than on his civil officers for the necessary finances. It is on this account that he has been branded as a robber chief both by his contemporaries and by posterity as well. But the great Maratha king had no other alternative. He had to brave the enmity of the Mughals and the sultan of Bijapore, not to count the pinpricks that he had often to bear from such minor powers as the Habshis of

Janjira, the Portuguese of Goa, and petty semi-independent chiefs like the Koli Rajas. He had to organise an army to defend his newly conquered territories, he had to build innumerable forts to fortify difficult passes, he had to fit out a fleet to prevent the piracy and the depredations of the Siddi's navy, he had to buy arms and ammunitions and needed money for these works. Nature was by no means munificent to the Maratha. The valleys yielded but a scanty return to the strenuous labour of the Mawali peasants. It would have been impossible for Shivaji to finance his army and navy from the limited resources of his native land alone, even if he had taxed all his ingenuity to enhance them. Consequently he had to make war furnish the means of war.

But Chauth and Sardeshmukhi were quite different from spoils of war. They were more or less permanent demands. Shivaji's claim to Sardeshmukhi was based on a legal fiction. He claimed to be the hereditary Sardeshmukh of his country and had put forth his claim early in his career. If his claim had been acknowledged, or if he had succeeded in obtaining a farman in its support, there would have been no legal flaw whatever in his demand. This imperial sanction, however, could not be obtained before Shahu's accession to his grandfather's throne, and in Shivaji's time at least, Sardeshmukhi was not recognised as his watan. Chauth was nothing but a tribute exacted from the weak by the strong. The Raja of Bednore and the Chief of Soonda agreed to pay Chauth in 1676, because they had no option in the matter. Shivaji had invaded their principalities with a strong army and any refusal would have been sternly punished. The Marathas obtained a legal right to levy Chauth, when the diplomacy of Balaji Vishwanath secured for Shahu an imperial recognition of that oft-repeated claim. This legal sanction would have been of little avail, if it had not been backed by the lance of the Maratha horseman. Nothing short of an expedition would make any chief or king, either Hindu or Muhammadan, admit Shivaji's claim to a quarter of his revenue and nothing but a strong army could enforce punctual payment. It was, therefore, a military contribution levied by a power without being in formal occupation of the country, and without observing the formalities specified by modern International Law. But the late Mr. Ranade does not admit that Chauth was a mere military contribution without any moral or legal obligation on the part of the Marathas to protect the Chauth-paying chiefs from the invasion of a third power or to restore peace and order in their country. He was of opinion that the policy underlying the exaction of Chauth was the same as that which impelled Lord Wellesley to enforce a subsidiary alliance on his weaker neighbours. "The demand for *chouth* was subsequently added with the consent of the powers whose protection was undertaken against foreign aggression, on payment of fixed sums for the support of the troops maintained for such service. This was the original idea as worked out by Shivaji, and it was this same idea which in the Marquis of Wellesley's hand bore such fruit a hundred and twenty five years later." Such is Ranade's interpretation of the Chauth policy.[86]

It is true that Shahu had, in return for the grant of Chauth, bound himself to maintain a body of 15,000 horse in the Emperor's service, to be placed at the disposal of the Subhedars, Faujdars and officers in the different districts "and to maintain peace and order." But neither Shahu nor the Peshwas ever cared to assist the Subhedars of the Deccan unless it served their own interest. Shivaji also had often offered his services to the Emperor of Delhi, but he had exacted Chauth at the point of his sword; the Emperor did not expect that Shivaji would ever look after the Mughal interests and Shivaji also knew that no treaty would serve him better than his own strong arms. It cannot, therefore, be denied that the Maratha kings exacted Chauth without undertaking the least responsibility for the country's welfare, and it should also be remembered that they never expected the Chauth-paying states to give up their diplomatic independence. Here lies the fundamental difference between the subsidiary system and the exaction of Chauth. The East India Company always held themselves responsible for the defence of the allied state, while they expected it to renounce all diplomatic relations with other powers. Moreover, the Marathas never care to maintain an extra Regiment when they received Chauth from a prince, nor had the amount of tribute any relation to the possible expense that might be incurred in the defence of the Chauth-paying territories. I do not, however, hold that the Maratha statesmen had no idea of a subsidiary arrangement.; such an arrangement was made with the Raja of Bundi by the Peshwas, but that was long after the demise of Shivaji.

The Chauth was therefore nothing but a contribution exacted by a military leader. But are such exactions sanctioned by International Law? The ancient Romans, while extending their empire, had set no limit to their rapacity. *"Bellum alit bellum"* war must pay for war, was their favourite maxim. But pillage has not ceased to be an inevitable characteristic of war with the dissolution of the Roman Empire. Even in the 19th century, so late as 1865, General Shermans campaign had been accompanied by the systematic pillage of the territories he marched through.[87] Requisition, which is only a variation of contribution, is also sanctioned by the most modern laws of war and was practised, though unwillingly, by no less a man than George Washington.[88] Shivaji also could plead as urgent a necessity as Washington. Both of them had been fighting for their country's liberation and both of them were sorely in need of money. Washington requisitioned the property of his unwilling fellow-citizens and Shivaji levied contribution on the enemy subjects. It served two ends at once. It not only weakened the enemy he was fighting, but at the same time added to his own resources.

Shivaji's kingdom was a military state if we are allowed to style it so. It was in a state of chronic warfare. Even for its finances, Shivaji depended more on war than on the processes of peace. The wealth amassed in the ports of his enemies by their commercial enterprise flowed into Shivaji's treasury, as a reward of his military prowess. The result of this policy was the inevitable ruin of trade and commerce. Surat, the premier port of Western India, lost its trade for ever. But while plundering his enemies' lands Shivaji took good care to protect his own country from a similar calamity. It was absolutely impossible that his attempts in this direction should be crowned with complete success. But he did all that was practicable. His statesmanship converted the hardy soldiers of Maharashtra into excellent civil administrators. Shivaji did not aspire to be an original legislator, indeed, he had no leisure for such work. But he revived some of the best regulations of his predecessors and made slight improvements upon them. It does not seem possible that he had been able to achieve much reform. We also do not know how far the spirit of these regulations was observed by Shivaji's officers. The public opinion of that time did not condemn bribery and corruption and we are afraid, Shivaji's officers were not much better, if not actually worse, than their successors of the Peshwa period. His country saw no peace till the overthrow of the Mughal power. Shivaji never had more than a couple of peaceful years at a time and even that not more than once in his life. It is futile to expect that commerce and agriculture should prosper under these circumstances. But Shivaji's regulations were well suited to the needs of the country. The assessment was flexible and varied from year to year. Whatever might have been the annual yield, a considerable share was left to the peasants. In the years of scarcity they could expect relief from the state. Consequently, they had good reasons to devote their attention to agricultural pursuits, but it is quite probable that the prospects and honour of a military career had stronger charms for the hardy peasant of the Ghat ranges.

APPENDIX C

"A Kaulnama from Rajashir Annaji Datto to the Deshmukh, and Deshkulkarni and Mokdam, Patil and the peasantry of Tarf Rohidkhore in the Subha of Mawal, dated Surasan Tisa Sabain Alaf (1678), — You came to the presence at camp Lakhevadi and (represented) that in the watani districts of His Majesty, the rayats should be encouraged by the confirmation of their kaul and fixing the rent of the lands. Having confidence... and taking into consideration the remissions made, we grant the following terms for the land. From the year San Saman (it is the practice to realise) half the produce, from the last year the lands were remeasured according to the *bighaoni* system and the rent was fixed from a calculation of the produce and it was settled that of the lands...the inspection (*pahani*) of what places had one year been made, and the produce was found to have decreased and a plot though originally a first class land had (now) deteriorated then...Such a settlement was not made after an understanding with the rayats. Therefore you petitioned that a settlement should be made (about the rent). Thereupon the following agreement is made that in the present year...is almost over and the last one month only remains...The agreement about the rent of San Sabaina...the (produce) should be estimated, such was the agreement made. If some Brahman or Prabhu Karkuns are appointed for this work, then what will those lethargic people do? Into how many blocks are village lands divided, what are the crops grown in the village, what rent should be realised, what (do those) poor men (know about that)...Therefore, as you are the people responsible for the revenue of your district. For this work, the Deshmukh and the Deshkulkarni and the Mokdam and officers...accompanied by a few rayats, should with one accord go from village to village and ascertain that the produce of such a village is so much, the land (in it)... is so much, of the (arable) land, the first, second, and third class (plots)... are so many. After carefully ascertaining (these things) and making an estimate of the crops grown...you should after a proper enquiry find out what may be the probable produce if (more) labour is applied, and put that amount (under that class of) lands... You should make your estimate after examining (proper) evidence, in the following manner—that at a certain place Malik Ambar's (estimated) produce was so much, of that autumnal or the first harvest of the first, second, third and the fourth class lands is so much, of the second or the vernal crop is so much. After determining the (produce of) the two harvests, you should state that in so many bighas is such and such crop (cultivated). After making these entries (under the heading) of each particular village, if there are few peasants...then according to the above order, you should make an estimate of produce of the whole Tape, and to do this work, time of a year from to-day, has been given to you. You must in the meantime, inspect the whole Tape, village by village, field by field, and carefully ascertain their yield and write to me. I shall thereafter come and inspect three villages of these (different) sorts in your Tape one...hilly, one marshy and one with black soil...and the villages near their boundary having been inspected according to the practice of the Karkuns,...having connected (and) (comparing that?)... Your total and what may be the produce of one village...and making it ready according to that...if the total under each item became 1¼, 1½ or double as much, then in that way... 1½, 1¼ and double...having been proved correct...and you are to (realise according)...should do if...do so then...it will be all right if it tallies...settlement...settlement...to be made...agree...to this effect has been made...we are agreeable...the cultivation of the district...Give such an assurance...from the Huzur.*

* Rajwade, H.I.S., Vol. XV, pp. 268-270.

APPENDIX D

Coins Mentioned by Sabhasad

I have not been able to identify all the gold coins mentioned by Sabhasad.

(1) Gambar is probably the same as Gubbur a coin current at Bombay in 1763. It was worth at that date 3 Rupees 12 annas and 6 pies. Hunter, *Annals of Rural Bengal,* Appendix O, p. 474.

(2 & 3) Mohar and Putlis are rather common coins, the value of a Putli is about 4 Rs.

Hon, Varaha and Pagoda are synonymous terms. The word Hon may be a corruption of Sanskrit Suvarna; Gerson da Cunha says that the original meaning of hun in Kanarese is gold (*Contribution to the Numismatics,* p. 10). Shivarai, Achyutrai, Devarai and Ramchandrarai Hons were Vijayanagar coins named after different kings who issued them, according to a custom prevalent in the country. The Portuguese chronicler Fernao Nuniz refers to this custom in the following words:-

"On the death of that king Bucarao there came to the throne his son called Pureoyre Deorao, which in Canara means `powerful lord' and he coined a money of *pardaos* which even now they call `*puroure deorao*'; and from that time forward it has become a custom to call coins by the names of the kings that made them; and it is because of this that there are so many names of *pardaos* in the kingdom of Bisnaga". Sewel. *A Forgotten Empire,* pp. 300-301. Kaveripak, Sangari, Guti, Dharwari, Advani, Chandavari (Tanjore), Veluri and Ramnathpuri Hons, I suppose, derive their names from mint towns. Ibhrami was current in coast towns of Persia and Western India. It has been mentioned by Fryer as Embraims and Dr. Crooke explains in a foot-note—"probably Ibrahimi of Abraham. See John Fryer's *East India and Persia,* Vol. II (Haklluyt Society's edition), p. 137 and also Bird's *History of Gujrat,* p. 109. Katerai Hon was the Mysore

Pagoda". For its weight and intrinsic value see Prinsep—*Useful Tables.* Forest says "Six Canterai pagodas are nearly equal to five star pagodas"—*Selection, Maratha Series,* p. 717. Ananda Ranga Pillai mentions Saiyid Muhammad, Amaldar of Tadpatri (see *The Private Diary of Ananda Ranga Pillai,* Vol. VII, p. 31 and p. 51) and we also read in his pages of Tadpatri *dupattis* (p. 208). Tadpatri Hon probably was a coin current in the district of that name.

Prinsep mentions in his *Useful Tables* a gold coin with the figure of a trident on it, probably in it we find the Trisuli Hon of Sabhasad. Is Afraji the same as Aftabi, a gold coin of Akbar, worth 10 Rs. or Aparanj of Princep?

Fanams were small gold coins current in Southern India. "The Fanam was originally worth about 1¼ Rupees; later it was coined of silver or base gold".—Crooke in Fryer, Vol. I, p. 106. Three silver Fanmas were equivalent to three halfpence when Heber wrote in 1825.

The silver coins mentioned by Sabhasad hardly present any difficulty.

The silver Asrafis were nothing but Portuguese Xerafins. A Xerafin was equal to 300 reis or pies. The word, Prof, Dalgado supposed, was derived from Perso Arabic Ashrafi. See Dalgado, *Glossario Luso Asiatico,* Vol. II, pp. 424-425.

Abashi must be Abasee of Fryer. Thevenot says that this coin was very common at Surat. The coin was of Persian origin and was named after Shah Abbas II according to Dr. Dalgado (*Glossario,* Vol. I, p. 4). Fryer says that in his time it was current at Calicut. "They (the people of Calicut) have yet a correspondence with Persia as may appear by their Abasees, a sixteen penny piece of silver, current among them" (*East India,* I, p. 143). According to Thevenot it was equivalent to 18 pence. *The Travels of Monseiur de Thevenot,* London, 1687, part III, p. 2. Dalgado says that Abassi was a silver coin of the value of about 300 reis (or 100 pice).

The word Kabir, I believe, is a misreading of Lari, a silver coin current in the coast towns of Persia and Western India.

Gerso da Canha dealt with the origin of Lari in a learned article contributed to the *Journal of the Bombay Branch of the Royal Asiatic Society*. The Portuguese called it "tanga Larim" and Emerson Tennent says that money in imitation of them, struck by the princes of Bijapur and by Sivaji, the founder of the Mahrattas, was in circulation in the Dekkan as late as the seventeenth century (Ceylon, Vol. I, p. 463). According to Dalgado (Glossario, Vol. I, p. 513) its value varied from sixty to hundred reis (or pies). In Sabhasad's list we read of Laris of Dabhol, Chaul and Bussora.

II

ORGANISATION OF THE MILITARY DEPARTMENT

1. Forts and Strongholds

In his military organisation Shivaji aimed at efficiency. Vastly inferior to his enemies in numerical strength, he tried to compensate by quality the lack of quantity. He, therefore, tried to enforce strict discipline in his army and appealed not only to the military instinct but also to the patriotism of his soldiers. His earliest adherents were the *Mawalis* a race of hardy hillmen, who came into prominence under Shivaji's leadership and have since then relapsed to their original obscurity. Shivaji depended mainly on these hillmen and the hills. The hills constituted an excellent defence, while the hillmen accompanied him in all his bold excursions and perilous raids. The ill clad and ill fed hillmen of Mawal captain, and he converted the bare rocks and mountains into impregnable forts to bar the enemy's progress through his country. At the time of his death, Shivaji possessed no less than two hundred and forty forts and strongholds, and in the jabita swarajya of Shahu[89] we find that not a single Taluka or Pargana was left without a protecting fort. Scott-Waring says that, "before his death he (Shivaji) had established his authority over an extent of country four hundred miles in length, and one hundred and twenty in breadth. His forts extended over the vast range of mountains which skirt the western shore of India. Regular fortification barred the open approaches: every pass was commanded by forts: every steep and overhanging rock was occupied as a station to roll down great masses of stone, which made their way to the bottom, and impeded the labouring march of cavalry, elephants, and carriages".[90] Chitnis pointedly remarked that forts were the very life of a kingdom,[91] and Lokahitavadi tells us that Shivaji was famous mainly for building forts.

Shivaji's hill forts, impregnable by nature, did not require a strong garrison. Five hundred was the normal strength, but in some[92] exceptional cases a stronger force was allowed. No single officer was ever placed in entire charge of the fort and its garrison. "In every fort", says Sabhasad, "there should be a Havaldar, a Sabnis (and) a Ṣarnobat; (and) these three officers should be of the same status. These three should conjointly carry on the administration. There should be kept a store of grain and war materials in the fort. An officer called Karkhanis was appointed for this work. Under his supervision should be written all accounts of income and expenditure. Where the fort was an important one and where forts were of extensive circuit, there should be kept five to seven Tat Sarnobats. The charge of the ramparts should be divided among them. They should be careful about keeping a vigilant watch. Of every ten men of the garrison to be stationed in the fort, one should be made a Naik; nine privates and the tenth a Naik. Men of good families should in this manner be recruited. Of the forces, the musketeers, the spearmen, the archers, and the lightarmed men should be appointed, after the Raja himself had carefully inspected each man individually and selected the brave and shrewd. The garrison in the fort, the Havaldar, and the Sarnobat should be Marathas of good families. They should be appointed after some one of the royal personal staff had agreed to stand surety (for them). A Brahman known to the king's personal staff should be appointed Sabnis and a Prabhu, Karkhanis. In this manner each officer retained should be dissimilar (in caste) to the others. The fort was not to be left in the hands of the Havaldar alone. No single officer could surrender the fort to any rebel or miscreant. In this manner was the administration of the forts carefully carried. A new system was introduced".[93]

The system was neither new nor unknown in Southern India. The regulations of Muhammad Adil Shah of Bijapur lay down clearly that the officers in charge of a fort should be three in number, neither less nor more. The Muhammadan ruler also says that these officers should be frequently transferred from one fort to another.[94] We have seen in the; preceding chapter that Shivaji also used to transfer the Mudradharis or officers in charge of forts and strongholds very often. He could not safely ignore the low standard of public morality that prevailed at the time while framing these regulations. It would have been sheer imprudence to leave a single officer entirely in charge of a fort in those days of disloyalty and treachery, when gold succeeded where policy and prowess failed. Shivaji himself frequently used the golden bait with success and it was but natural that he should take proper precaution against its repetition at his cost. It was also necessary that he should conciliate the three principal castes by distributing the responsible posts under his government equally among them. The Prabhus and the Brahmans were jealous of one another, may be for social reasons, but the state of their feeling could not be overlooked even in affairs administrative. Shivaji himself had reason to fear Brahman opposition when he assumed the sacred thread prior to his coronation. The Marathas of his time also eminently deserved high commands in the army. The different sections of the great Brahman caste were not in amity[95] and Chitnis tells us that the Sabnises were recruited from all classes of Brahmans, *viz.*, the Deshasthas, the Karhadas, the Konkanasthas and the Madhyandins.

2. The Three Chief Officers and Their Duties

The chief of the three officers was the Havaldar. He was to keep the keys with him. He was to shut the fort gates and lock them up with his own hands every evening. He was to draw the bolt and see whether the gates were properly secured. He was not to admit any one whether friend or foe, during night. Early in the morning he was to come and with his own hands open the principal gates.[96] Although he was to carry on other duties conjointly with his colleagues, the Havaldar was never allowed to relegate these to any one else. Shivaji tested the efficiency of his Havaldars mainly in their proper control of the gates. Chitnis gives an anecdote that will bear quotation here.[97] One night Shivaji went to Panhala and knocked at the gates of the fort. His attendants shouted out to the Havaldar that the Maharaja himself was seeking admission, hotly pursued by the enemy. The gates should be opened and the king taken in. The officer came and stood on the rampart with his colleagues. With due humility the Havaldar pointed out that the king's regulation did not permit the gates to be opened at that hour. He, however, offered to check the enemy till morning with the help of the guards of the out stations, while the Maharaja should wait near the gates. Then the king replied—"The regulations are mine and the order involving their breach is also mine. It is I who order you to open the gates". But the officer again submitted that he could not open the gates. Night was almost over. Till dawn the enemy would be kept off. Then Shivaji tried threats. "It is not proper, "said he, "that a servant like you should not obey my orders. I will make an example of you". But still the gates were not opened. Early in the morning the Havaldar unlocked and unbolted the gates and with clasped hands approached the king. "I have done wrong; Your Majesty should punish me according to my deads", said the officer. But the king applauded his sense of duty and promoted him on the spot. The chronicler of Shivadigvijaya informs us that those who failed this test were degraded or dismissed.

The Sabnis was in charge of the accounts in general and the muster roll in particular. The Karkhanis was mainly responsible for commissariat work. The kanujabta of the year 1, of the coronation era, thus enumerates their official duties:

The Sabnis should be in charge of accounts. On each order below the seal the Karkhanis should put his sign of approval. All orders of expenditure upon the cash and the treasury departments should be issued by the Sabnis, and under the seal of the Havaldar the Karkhanis should put his sign of approval. The daily account of these two departments should be drawn up under the supervision of both; the cash should be indicated on the account by the Sabnis, and below the Havaldar's seal, the Karkhanis should put his sign of approval.

If any order is to be issued from the fort to the district (under its jurisdiction), it should be issued by the Sabnis. The Havaldar should put his seal (on it), and below the seal the Karkhanis should put his sign of approval.

The muster roll of the men should be taken by the Sabnis. It should be verified by a clerk of the Karkhanis. In this manner was the work of the cash and treasury departments allotted.

If any order is made upon the district for either cash or clothes, it should be issued under the seal of the Sabnis with the Karkhanis's sign of approval. Besides this, all orders and requisitions should be made by the Karkhanis. Any tax (when necessary to meet the needs of the fort) should be levied by the Sabnis, and the Karkhanis should put his sign of approval under the seal.

All accounts, whether of his own or of the Karkhanis's department, should be explained by the Sabnis, whether to the Havaldar or to the district officer or to the central government. The Karkhanis should sit near the Sabnis, but all interrogations about their accounts should be made to the Sabnis.

All correspondence with the government or the district officers, or the Sardars, or the Subhedars or other Killedars, should be written by the Sabnis. The Sabnis should put his sign on them. After the Subhedar has sealed it, the Karkhanis should enter it in the daily ledger. He should not put his sign, but the letter should not be despatched without being recorded in the daily ledger.

All inspection and estimate of revenue of the province (under the jurisdiction of the fort) should be made by the Sabnis. This estimate should be entered into the accounts by the Karkhanis. The kaul and the order about the revenue should be issued by the Sabnis. After the Havaldar has put his seal on the papers, the Karkhanis should put his sign of approval.

All accounts of income and expenditure, either in weight or in approximate value (of commodities), should be daily made by the Karkhanis. After the Havaldar has put his seal (on the accounts), the Sabnis should put his sign of approval: The Karkhanis should write all orders of expenditure upon the granary. After the Havaldar has sealed (them), the Sabnis should put his sign of approval.

The distribution of stores, whether according to weight or according to approximate value, should be made by the Karkhanis. The Sabnis's Karkun should be present on the occasion for verification.

All orders for goods or commodities upon the province (under the jurisdiction of the fort) should be issued by the Karkhanis. The Sabnis should levy contribution (when necessary). He should put his sign of approval after the Havaldar has sealed the paper.

The Karkhanis should take charge of female slaves, boy servants, horses or cattle that may come. The Sabnis should put his sign of approval below the seal. If any loss occurs, the Karkhanis should put his sign below the seal.

The Karkhanis should supervise the work when a building is constructed. The Sabnis should inspect the work. Cash and clothes should be distributed among the Karkhanis's men when occasion arises. It should have the approval of the Karkhanis. The distribution of grain should be made by the Karkhanis with the approval of the Sabnis.

All accounts of the naval stores should be written by the Karkhanis's Karkuns. The work should be exacted by him under the supervision of the Sabnis".[98]

Thus did the three officers co-operate and serve as checks to one another. Not a single fort of Shivaji could, therefore, be betrayed to his enemies. But all these precautions could not absolutely prevent treason and corruption. When Shivaji was absent in the camp of Jai Singh, the entire charge of the fort of Rajgad had, for the time being, fallen on Keso Narayan Sabnis, as there was no Havaldar. Keso Narayan Sabnis, on that occasion, misappropriated a large sum from public funds.[99] In 1663 Shivaji postponed an expedition to the Konkan as disquieting information of a rebellion had come from Sinhgad. In a letter dated the 2nd April, 1663, Shivaji writes to Moro Trimbak Peshwa and Abaji Sondev that he was thinking of marching against Namdar Khan in the Konkan, but news arrived from Sinhgad that a revolt had lately taken place in the fort. He had, therefore, to give up his project of marching into the Konkan for the present The two officers were requested to march at once to Sinhgad with their troops and militia and take charge of the fort. They were further required to make an enquiry about the rebels and report their names to the king.[100]

Shivaji generally stored grains and provisions in large quantities in his forts for consumption during a siege. Towards the close of his career (in the year 1671-72), he decided to have a reserve fund to meet the extraordinary needs of forts beleaguered by the enemy. A paper under his seal drawn in the San Isanne say that Rajashri Chhatrapati Saheb has decided to raise money from each Mahal in his provinces and watans. This money should form a (reserve) fund, and should be spent only when war with Mughals would break out, and the Mughals lay siege to forts, and if money be not available from any other source; otherwise, this money should not be spent for any other government work. So has the Saheb decided and it has been settled that a sum of one lakh and seventy-five thousand Hons should constitute the reserve fund, and should be raised from the following Mahals and personages at the following rate:

Kudal	20,000
Rajapur	20,000
Kolen	20,000
Dabhol	15,000
Poona	13,000
Nagoji Govind	10,000
Jawli	5,000
Kalyan	5,000
Bhiwandi	5,000
Indapur	5,000
Supa	2,000
Krishnaji Bhaskar	5,000

It has been decided that the sum of one lakh and twenty-five thousand Hons (thus raised) should be set aside as a reserve fund.[101]

In the same year Shivaji granted a further sum of one lakh and seventy-five thousand Hons for repairing his principal forts. He observes that the workmen grew discontented as they did not get their wages in time. A considerable sum was on that account set aside for building and repair works alone. The sum of one hundred and seventy-five thousand was thus allotted:[102]

Sinhgad	10,000
Sindhudurg	10,000
Vijaidurg	10,000
Suvarnadurg	10,000
Pratapgad	10,000
Purandhar	10,000

Rajgad	10,000
Prachandgad	5,000
Prasiddhagad	5,000
Vishalgad	5,000
Mahipatgad	5,000
Sudhagad	5,000
Lohagad	5,000
Sabalgad	5,000
Shrivardhangad and Manaranjan	5,000
Korigad	3,000
Sarasgad	2,000
Mahidhargad	2,000
Manohargad	1,000
Miscellaneous	7,000
	1,75,000

What arms of defence were supplied to these forts we do not precisely know. Shivaji had an artillery department and Orme[103] tells us that, "He had previously purchased eighty pieces of cannons and left sufficient for all his matchlocks from the French Director at Surat." We find mention of matchlockmen and archers in Sabhasad's pages; we have there an account of at least one dashing rally by Murar Baji Prabhu when Diler Khan laid siege to Purandhar. The enemy was sometimes "assailed with rockets, musket-shots, bombs and stones".[104] Scott-Waring says that "his (Shivaji's) artillery was very contemptible, and he seems seldom to have used it but against the island of Gingerah".[105] But Shivaji's soldiers, in common with the Muhammadans of the Deccan, hurled a curious, but none the less, effective missile against their enemy while labouring up the steep sides of their inaccessible strongholds. Fryer saw "on the tops of the Mountains, several Fortresses of *Seva Gi's*, only defensible by Nature, needing no other Artillery but Stones, which they tumble down upon their Foes, carrying as certain destruction as Bullets where they alight."[106] Huge pieces of stone were for this purpose heaped at convenient stations and the Maratha soldiers rolled them down upon their enemy below. This could hardly check the progress of a determined foe; when this preliminary defence failed, the Marathas sallied out sword in hand and rushed upon the besiegers. But they did not always depend on their valour and gold was often used with very good results when steel failed.

The Havaldar of a fort usually enjoyed a remuneration of 125 Hons a year. Nagoji Bhonsle was appointed, Mudrahari of fort Utlur in 1680 on a salary of 150 Hons per year, out of which he had to pay 25 Hons to two servants attached to his office. Krishnaji Surevanshi was appointed Sarnovat of the above-mentioned fort in the same year on an annual salary of 100 Hons. The Havaldar in charge of the buildings in the fort got the same pay as the Mudradhari, and his Mazumdar was paid at the rate of 36 Hons per year. Four Tat Sarnobats were sent by Shivaji to take charge of the ramparts of Kot Utlur, and they were engaged on 4 Hons and 8 Kaveripak Hons (12 in all) a year. Along with them had been despatched seven *bargirs* on a yearly pay of 9 Hons (3 ordinary Hons and 6 Kaveripak) per head. In a document, dated the 26th July, 1677, we find that Timaji Narayan, a clerk, was appointed as an extra hand for the office work in Fort Valgudanar, on a monthly allowance of three Hons.[107] Besides the usual remuneration each officer got, according to his rank and the importance of his charge, an additional allowance for palanquin, torchbearers, personal attendants, sunshades and pages.[108]

The Ramoshis and Parwaris who kept watch lived outside the ramparts and got a very small remuneration.

4. Infantry and Cavalry

The Peshwa army consisted mainly of cavalry. The infantry was recruited from Hindustan and made but a poor impression on an Irish soldier, Col. W. H. Tone. Shivaji's military genius, however, had perceived early the necessity of light infantry and light cavalry in a guerrilla war and hill campaign. His Mawalis and Hetkaris have become famous in the military annals of India. Selected after personal examination by Shivaji himself, each man was trained into an excellent soldier, not by drilling in the parade ground but by the surer method of service in an actual war. "Shivaji had no idea of allowing his soldiers' swords to rust."[109] The result was that not only their weapons but the men who wielded them also gained in efficiency.

Shivaji's infantry was carefully divided into regiments, brigades and divisions. The smallest unit consisted of 9 men and the officer commanding it was called the Naik. The Havaldar of the infantry had five such units under him. Over two or three Havaldars was placed a Jumledar. The officer commanding ten jumlas was styled a Hazari and the Sarnobat of the infantry had seven Hazaris under him. The Jumledar had an annual salary of one hundred Hons and his Sabnis got forty. The Hazari got five hundred Hons per year, and his Sabnis's salary varied from one hundred to one hundred and twenty-five Hons.[110] Chitnis informs us that at the time of a marriage or any other ceremony of similar importance in the family, the officers could expect financial help.

The cavalry was divided into two classes, *viz.*, the bargirs and the shiledars. The bargir was equipped with horse and arms by the state, while the shiledar brought his own horse and sometimes came with a body of troops armed and equipped at his own expense. The bargir belonged to the *paga* proper, while the shiledar held a comparatively inferior position. "The strength of the paga", says Sabhasad, "was rendered superior (to that of the shiledar). Shiledars were placed under the jurisdiction of the paga. To none was left independence enough for rebelling. To every horse in the paga was appointed a trooper (bargir); over twenty-five such bargirs was appointed an expert Maratha Havaldar. Five Havaldars formed a jumla. The Jumledar had a salary of five hundred Hons and a palanquin, and his Majumdar a salary of one hundred to one hundred and twenty-five Hons. For every twenty-five horses were appointed a water-carrier and a farrier. A Hazari was a commander of ten such jumlas. To his office was attached a salary of one thousand Hons, a Mazumdar, a Maratha Karbhari and a Prabhu Kayastha Jamenis; for them was allotted a sum of five-hundred Hons. Salary and palanquin were given to each officer according to this scale. Accounts of income and expenditure were made up in the presence of all the four. Five such Hazaris were placed under a Panch Hazari. To him was given a salary of two thousand Hons. A Mazumdar, a Karbhari and a Jamenis were likewise attached to his office. These Panch Hazaris were under the command of the Sarnobat. The administration of the paga was of the same kind. Similarly the different brigadiers of the shiledars also were placed under the command of the Sarnobat".[111] Shivaji enlisted in his army not only Hindus but Muhammadans also. A body of seven hundred Pathans offered their services to the Maratha king and Shivaji enlisted them, it is said, in opposition to the majority of his officers. Shivaji pointed out that a king was a king first, and a Hindu or Muhammadan afterwards; and was supported in this wise resolution by an old officer Gomaji Naik Pansambal.[112] Shivaji knew quite well that an army, however efficient, could not be expected to operate with success in an enemy country, unless served by an efficient intelligence department. He organised a body of excellent spies, the chief of whom was Bahirji Naik Jadhav. Shivaji was so well served by these intelligent officers that he owed many of his most brilliant successes mainly to the information collected by them. On one occasion his army was saved from utter destruction by Bahirji's knowledge of unfrequented hill tracks.[113]

Shivaji could never expect to reach the numerical strength of his enemies. But he had detected the defects of the heavily armed Muhammadan soldiery and relied on speed for success against them. He, therefore, never allowed his soldiers to be encumbered with heavy arms or costly camp equipage. Dressed in tight-fitting breeches, cotton jackets and turbans,[114] armed mainly with swords both long and short, spears and lances, bows and arrows and match-locks, depending mainly on the spoils of war for their subsistence, Shivaji's soldiers were ready to march at a moment's notice. They were so quick both in mobilising and demoblising, that their enemies could hardly expect to get any information of their projects before their actual execution. Though the ordinary soldier was poorly dressed, Shivaji indulged in great expenditure in arming and equipping his body-guards. This regiment was divided into units of 20, 30, 40, 60, and 100 men. They were equipped at state expense and were given richly embroidered turbans and jackets of broad-cloth, gold and silver ear-rings and wristlets. Their sword-sheaths, guns and spears had silver rings and we may guess what a brilliant sight they offered when marching by the king's palanquin.[115]

Besides the regular forces Shivaji could in times of emergency call the feudal forces of the Maratha watandars. In a kaulnama, published in the Tritiya Sammelan Vritta of the Bharata Itihas Sanshodhak Mandal, two watandars. Mal Patil and Baji Patil of Birvadi, offered to serve Shivaji, when need arose, like the Mawali Deshmukhs, with ten of their attendants. For their subsistence the watandars expected six Rukas of half an anna per head per diem and they offered to serve in the army as long as the occasion demanded.[116] Unlike the later Peshwas, Shivaji never depended much upon these feudal levies, nor did he prefer the mercenary shieldars, who in certain respects resembled the *condottiere* of medieval Europe, to the bargirs of his paga. It is quite possible that when his power was firmly established, Shivaji did no longer summon these feudal forces.

Shivaji paid his soldiers either in cash or by an assignment on the district governments. He was entirely opposed to payment by jagir. But when any of his soldiers happened to be a cultivator as well, the rent payable by him was deducted from his salary. Their pay was never allowed to fall in arrears as in the Peshwa days. As Shivaji was strictly punctual in his payment, it was not necessary for him to offer very high salaries. "For the lower officers and men the pay varied from Rs. 9 to 3 for the infantry, and Rs. 20 to 6 in the cavalry, according to the higher or lower rank of the soldier or trooper".[117] Officers and privates of Shivaji's army were liberally rewarded for distinguished service in war. Wounded soldiers got a special allowance according to the nature of their wounds. Widows and orphans of soldiers who fell in active service were liberally pensioned by the state and the latter, if major, were enlisted in the royal army. In any case they could expect to enter Shivaji's army whenever they attained majority and in the mean time they were sure of a suitable maintenance.[118] Shivaji assembled all his soldiers after the destruction of Afzal's army and rewarded them in the usual manner. "The sons of the combatants, who had fallen in the action, were taken into his service. He directed that the widows of those who had no sons, should be maintained by (a pension of) half (husband's) pay. The wounded were given rewards of two hundred, one hundred, fifty or twenty-five Hons per man according to the nature of their wounds. Warriors of renown and commanders of brigades were given horses and elephants in reward. Some were sumptuously rewarded with (ornaments like) bracelets, necklace, crests, medallions, ear-rings and crests of pearl. Such were the present conferred on men. Some were rewarded with grants of villages in mokasa." This practice of rewarding soldiers for meritorious services, and maintaining their widow and orphans by adequate pensions, was continued throughout the Peshwa period.

5. Military Regulations

The Maratha camp during the Peshwa period presented a disreputable spectale. "Camp", says Elphinstone, "presents to a European the idea of long lines of white tents in the trimmest order. To a Mahratta it presents an assemblage of covering, of every shape and colour, spreading for miles in all directions, over hill and dale, mixed up with tents, flags, trees, and buildings. In Jones's `History' march means one or more columns of troops and ordnance moving along roads, perhaps, between two hedges; in the Mahratta history horse, foot and dragoons inundating the face of the earth for many miles on every side, here and there a few horses with a flag and a drum mixed with a loose and straggling mass of camels, elephants, bullocks, nautch-girls, fakeers, and buffoons: troops and followers, lancemen and matchlockmen, bunyans and mootasuddies".[119] Broughton gives a no less disparaging picture of Sindhia's camp. Wine was publicly sold and public women accompanied the army to the prejudice of discipline and order.[120] This was unthinkable in Shivaji's time. No one was allowed to keep in the camp a female slave or dancing girl and any breach of this rule was punished with death. Shivaji, a lover of discipline and method, had drawn up for his army a set of wise regulations. These have been summed up by Sabhasad in the following lines:

"The army should come to cantonments in the home dominions during the rainy seasons. There should be kept stored grains, fodder, medicines, houses for men and stables for horses thatched with grass. As soon as the *Dasra*[121] was over, the army should march out of their quarter. At the time of their departure, an inventory should be made, of the belongings of all the men, great or small, in the army and they should start on the expedition. For eight months, the forces should subsist (on their spoils) in the foreign territories. They should levy contribution. There should be no women, female slaves, or dancing girls in the army. He who would keep them, should be be-headed. In enemy territories, women and children should not be captured. Males, if found, should be captured. Cows should not be taken. Bullocks should be requistioned for transport purposes only. Brahmans should not be molested; where contribution had been laid, a Brahman should not be taken as a surety. No one should commit adultery. For eight months, they should be on expedition in foreign countries. On the way back to the barracks in the month of Vaishakh, the whole army should be searched at the frontier of the home dominions. The former inventory of the belongings should be produced. Whatever might be in excess, should be valued and deducted from the soldiers' salary. Things of very great value, if any, should be sent to the royal treasury. If any one secretly kept (any thing) and the Sardar came to know (of it), the Sardar should punish him. After the return of the army to their camp an account should be made and all the Sardars should come to see the Raja, with gold, jewels, clothes, and other commodities. There all the accounts should be explained and the things should be delivered to his Majesty. If any surplus should be found due to the contingents, it should be asked for in cash from His Majesty. Then they should return to the barrack. *Saranjam* should be given to the men who had worked hard in the late campaign. If any one had been guilty of violating the rules or of cowardice, an enquiry should be made and the truth ascertained with the consensus of many and (the offender) should be punished with dismissal. Investigation should be quickly made. For four months they should remain in the barracks, and on the Dasraday they should wait on the Raja. (Then) they should march out to the country, selected for the expedition, by the order of the Raja. Such were the rules of the army".[122]

These regulations were not designed merely to figure in the statute book, but were strictly enforced. While passing through the kingdom of Golkona on his way to Tanjore, Shivaji had ordered is soldiers not to harass the people in any way. Whatever they wanted was obtained by peaceful purchase and any breach of law was severely punished. Sabhasad tells us that Shivaji on this occasion had made examples of a few offenders to intimidate others, and his severity had the desired effect. But the spirit of the times was not favourable to strict discipline,[123] and although Shivaji's spies seldom failed to bring to his notice all cases of violence and fraud,[124] yet it was impossible for him to put a stop to military excesses. In a letter dated the 8th September, 1671, we read how a Maratha soldier had attacked the Sabnis of his regiment with a naked sword.[125] On the 23rd July of the next year Shivaji wrote to Dattaji Pant Waknis that the soldiers gave trouble to the pilgrims of the Chaphal fair.[126] At Chaphal lived Ramdas, Shivaji's spiritual guide. He was revered throughout Maharashtra as a great saint and an incarnation of the monkey-god Maruti. If soldiers did not behave properly in the precincts of Ramdas's temple, we may easily imagine to what extremes their insolence carried them at safer places. Shivaji, however, could not achieve the impossible. His countrymen had before them the example of the Bijapur army, where discipline was conspicuous by its absence. Shivaji placed before them a high ideal, but an ideal cannot always be forced on an unwilling people at the point of sword. Nonethe less, the great Maratha leader never failed to harangue his soldiers about their duties and responsibilities. In the year 1676 he came to learn that the regiment encamped at Chiplun had given great troubles to the people of the neighbourhood. The troops were short of provision and took by force what they wanted. Shivaji, therefore, issued a circular to the Jumledars, Havaldars, and Karkuns of the army reminding them that it was their duty to store sufficient provision in time. "If grain, bread, grass and vegetable were forcibly taken away from the peasant, they would desert the locality. Some of them would die of starvation and your presence would be more un-welcome than that of the Mughals". "Do not give the rayat the least trouble", continues Shivaji, "you have no need to stray out of your camping places. Money has been given to you from the government treasury. Whatever any soldier may want, either grain or vegetable or odder or the anmas should be purchased from the market. Violence should not be offered to any one on any account". The remarkable document fully illustrates Shivaji's anxiety for the welfare of his people and the god name of his soldiers. The last portion of the letter shows how the minutest details of the army administration did not escape his notice. He admonishes his officers to take special precaution against fire. Soldiers were not to smoke or cook near the haystacks and lamps were to be put out before the men went to bed lest mice dragged the burning wicks and set fire to the haystacks. "If the haystaks were burnt the necessary hay could not be procured even if the Kunbis were decapitated and the Karkuns harassed. The horses would die of hunger and the cavalry would be ruined".[127] Shivaji knew everything about his army, its needs and requirements. He was anxious to secure the welfare of his people and he tried his best to protect them from the violence of his soldiers. We should not be too severe with him if instances of tyranny or oppression took place in spite of his vigilance. We should judge him by what he attempted and not by what he achieved; although his achievements were by no means small.

In spite of his defects the Maratha soldier was a fine fellow. Of short stature and light built he was man for man inferior to the tall and stout Mughal and Deccani Mussulman. But his courage, hardihood, wonderful energy, presence of mind and agility more than compensated for his physical inferiority. Demoralised by the tactics of their elusive adversary, the Bijapuris and the Mughals at last failed to met him even in the open field on equal terms. Fryer's comparison of the two armies well illustrates the merits and demerits of the contending forces as they struck an intelligent foreign observer. Says the Doctor,[128] "*Seva Gi's* Men thereby being fitter for any Martial Exploit, having been accustomed to Fare Hard, Journey Fast, and take little Pleasure. But the other's will miss a Booty rather than a Dinner; must mount in state and have their Arms carried before them, and their Women not far behind them, with the Masters of Mirth and Jollity; will rather expect than pursue a Foe; but then they stand out better; for *Seva Gi's* Men care not much for a pitched Field, though they are good at Surprising and Ransacking; yet agree in this, that they are both of stirring Spirits." It is remarkable that the same love of luxury and comfort characterised the Maratha officers at Panipat. While Shivaji did not allow "Whores and Dancing Wenches in his army",[129] the Maratha army at Panipat was encumbered with a large number of women. Broughton says of Daulat Rao Sindhia's soldiers that, "such as think that life is bestowed for superior enjoyments and have a taste for more spirited modes of whiling it away, entire, at the approach of evening to the arrack shop, or the tent of the prostitute; and revel through the night in a state of low debauchery which could hardly be envied by the keenest votary of Comus and his beastly crew".[130] Shivaji's successors had for reasons best known to them suffered these salutary regulations to lapse and the result was disastrous for their army and themselves. The Maratha soldiers declined in morale, discipline and alertness that had made them so formidable under Shivaji's leadership.

REFERENCES

1. Fitzclarence, *Journal of a Route across India*, p. 286.

1a. Forrest, *Selections from State Papers* preserved in the Bombay Secretariat, Maratha Series, Vol. I, p. 79.

1b. Capt. West. *A Memoir of the States of the Southern Maratha Country*, p. 37. And Gleig, *The Life of Major General Sir Thomas Munro*, Vol. II, p. 276.

2. For this explanation, as for many other items of information, I am indebted to the valuable report of Elphinstone, one of the territories conquered from the Peshwa. (2nd Edition, pp. 22-23).

3. For a learned discussion of the policy of this distribution of revenue among the principal officers of the state, its origin, aim, merits, and demerits, see Sardesai's Marathi Ryasat, Vol. II, pp. 119-142.

4. P. D., Vol. III, pp. 259-261.

5. P. D., Vol. III, p. 265.

6. P. D., Vol. III, pp. 289-295.

7. P. D., Vol. VI, pp. 265-268.

8. P. D., Vol. VI, pp. 272-276.

9. P. D., Vol. III, pp. 205-206.

10. P. D., Vol. VI, p. 226

11. P. D., Vol. III, pp. 202-203

12. P. D., Vol. III, p. 203.

13. Parasnis's translation, P. D., Vol. III, pp. 211-212.

14. P. D., Vol. VII, pp. 5-12.

15. P. D., Vol. III, pp. 222-223.
16. P. D., Vol. III, p. 223.
17. P. D., Vol. III, p. 224.
18. *Cynosurus Corocanus.*
19. *Coix Barbata.*
19a. P. D., Vol. III, p. 230.
19b. P. D., Vol. III, p. 214.
20. P. D., Vol. III, p. 214.
21. P. D., Vol. III, pp. 242-245.
22. P. D., Vol. III, pp. 246-247.
23. P. D., Vol. VI, pp. 242-247.
24. P. D., Vol. III, p. 224.
25. P. D., Vol. III, pp. 226-227.
26. P.D., Vol. III, p. 231.
27. P. D., Vol. VII, pp. 18-19.
28. P. D., Vol. VII, pp. 19-20. (Joshi's translation)
29. P. D., Vol. VII, pp. 21-22.
30. P. D., Vol. VI, p. 253.
31. P. D., Vol. VII, p. 18.
32. P. D., Vol. VII, p. 18.
33. P. D., Vol. VI, pp. 227-228.
34. P. D., Vol. II, p. 237.
35. P. D., Vol. III, p. 237.
36. P. D., Vol. III, p. 236.
37. P. D., Vol. VI, p. 240. "Therefore encourage the cultivation of the aforesaid Pargana by advancing Tagai. If you are dismissed your money should be with interest paid by the next incumbent of the Mamlat."
38. Ranade, *The Miscellaneous Writings*, p. 358.
39. Ranade, *The Miscellaneous Writings*, p. 359.
40. Ranade, *The Miscellaneous Writings*, p. 358.
41. Ranade, *R. M.P.*, p. 115.
42. Scott-Waring, *History of the Mahrattas*, p. 96.

43. Jervis, p. 93.

44. Kennedy, *History of the Great Moghuls*, Vol. II, p. 125.

45. *Bombay Gazetteer*, Poona Volume.

46. See *Bombay Gazetteer*, Poona Volume and Jervis, pp. 66-68.

47. *Bombay Gazetteer*, Poona Volume.

48. Jervis enumerates the following—The gochurma or oxhide of land, the turub or plough land, secondly the khundee of land, the moora, the mun, the karika and so forth, that is lands requiring a khundee, moora, mun, karika and so forth of seed to sow them by which rule the produce was estimated and the government share fixed. Jervis, pp. 36-37.

49. See Sabhasad, p. 32. Sen, Sivachhatrapati, p. 36.

50. Whether a map was also prepared we do not know. Everything depends on the interpretation of *dhurang jhad* (Sabhasad, p. 32). The word is unintelligible and Rao Bhahadur Sane gives *durang jad* as an alternative reading. If we accept this second reading the sentence may mean that a bicolour map was drawn. But in those days paper was so scarce that it does not seem possible. I have no knowledge of any map or chart of Shivaji's time coming down to us. For a sensible suggestion about the meaning of the passage see *Vividha Dinanvistar*, p. 69 (1921).

51. V. K. Rajwade, M. I. S., Vol. XV, pp. 370-398. For an English translation of this letter see Appendix, C, pp. 119-122.

    It may be noted in this connection that Annaji was by no means the only officer charged with the work of survey settlement. Mention is made of similar work being done with regard to Shirval by Moro Pingle, the Peshwa. See, Rajwade, M.I.P., Vol. XX, pp. 94-96.

52. This tax is mentioned in a document dated 1675. See M. I. S., Vol. XV, p. 173. It therefore seems probable that all these cesses were not abolished and the state demands consolidated as Jervis asserts.

53. Rajwade, M.I.S., Vol. XX, p. 12.

54. It is not, however, clear who paid the cess and on what occasion.

55. Taka literally means an aggregate of sixteen Shivaraj pice: also an aggregate of four pice, an anna.—Molesworth. Barhadghan—The house in which wedding is celebrated, Molesworth. Is it a tax or cess on nuptials and analogous to Lagan pati?

56. *Ulpha* literally means unhusked grain given in alms to mendicants. It seems therefore probable that the cess was levied for charitable purposes.

57. May be one of the numerous cesses levied for the expense of popular festivals, either Hindu or Muhammadan.

58. Rajwade, M.I.S., Vol. XVI., p. 12.

59. This statement is based on Sabhasad Bakhar and Major Jervis's Konkan, but as I have already pointed out in a previous note, some of these dues continued to be levied till Shivaji's death and a few certainly survived him; but, as we do not know for certain whether they were state dues or perquisites of village officers or cesses levied by village communities, we cannot challenge the accuracy of this assertion without further investigation.

60. Jervis, p. 93

61. Sabhasad, p. 32, Sen, Sivachhatrapati, p. 37.

62. Rajwade, M.I.S., Vol. XX, p. 98.

63. "Till on the right, within a mile or more of *Gullean* they yield possession to the neighbouring *Seva Gi,* at which City (the key this way into that Rebel's Country) Wind and tide favouring we landed at about nine in the morning, and were civilly treated by the Customer in his *Choultry:* till the *Havaldar* could be acquainted of my arrival." Fryer, p. 123.

64. For these figures see Jervis, pp. 94-97

65. Rajwade, M.I.S., Vol. XX, p. 94.

66. Jervis, pp. 94-97.

67. Ranade, R.M.P., pp. 117-118.

68. Mawji, Jabita Swarayya, J.B. Br. R.A.S., Vol. XXII, pp. 36-39.

69. Abdagir.

70. Sabhasad, p. 31, Sen, Siva Chhatrapati, p. 35.

71. Bharat Itihas Sanshodhak Mandal, Tritiya Sammelan Vritta, pp. 128-131.

72. Fryer, p. 127.

73. See Kautilya. Arthashastra translated by R. Shama Shastry, p. 35.

74. Ranade, R.M.P., p. 125.

75. Rajwade. M.I.S., Vol. VIII, p. 24.

76. Fryer, pp. 146-147.

77. Elliot and Dowson, Vol. VII, p. 260.
78. Dellon, pp. 56-57.
79. Grant Duff, Vol. I, p. 188.
80. Fryer, p. 80.
81. Sabhasad, p. 95, Sen, Siva Chhatrapati, pp. 134-135.
82. Fryer, p. 210.
83. J.B. Br. R.A.S. Vol., XX, p. 109.
84. Bombay Gazetteer, Vol. XVI, p. 429.
85. Through the kindness of Prof. D. V. Potdar, the Joint Secretary of the B.I.S. Mandal, I obtained an opportunity of examining this really rare coin, but it has already been described by Mr. Bhave in the fifth Sammelan Vritta of the Mandal, p. 121.
86. Ranade, R.M.P., pp. 224-225.

    The Chauth was originally nothing but a black mail. The subjects of the Koli Raja of Ramnagar used to give considerable trouble to the Portuguese subjects of Daman by their robbery, depredation and plundering raids. At last the peaceful inhabitants of some villages in the District of Daman came to an amicable arrangement with the Raja of Ramnagar and agreed to pay him an annual tribute called the Chauth (Chouto) provided his people no longer caused them any loss or trouble. The Raja of Ramnagar was styled in the Portuguese records as the king Choutia as he used to receive Chauth. When this arrangement was made we do not exactly know, but it has been mentioned by Fr. Antonio de Gouveia as early as 1603. (*Jornada,* Fl. 125 quoted in Dalgado's *Glossario Luso Asiataico,* Vol. I, p. 280). The King Choutia and his claim to Chauth has been referred to in a royal letter in 1605. After the annexation of the Koli principalities of Jawhar and Ramnagar Shivaji asserted his claim to the Chauth of Daman. He demanded Chauth from his Muhammadan enemies for the first time in 1665 and it is noteworthy that he had passed through the principality of Ramnagar on his way to Surat in the previous year. It is therefore clear that Shivaji was not the originator of Chauth but he was certainly responsible for its wider application. For a more detailed discussion of this interesting question, the reader is referred to my *Historical Records at Goa,* pp. 12-24. The unpublished Portuguese records have been for the first time quoted there in extenso. The Raja of Ramnagar did not, it should be noted, offer to protect the people of Daman from foreign aggression but it was only the aggression of his own people that he undertook to prevent and Shivaji does not appear to have gone further than that.

87. Bentwitch, p. 28.
88. *Ibid,* p. 10.
89. J. B. Br. R. A. S., Vol. XXII, pp. 36-42.
90. Scott-Waring, pp. 96-97.
91. Chitnis, p. 80.
92. Fryer, p. 127.
93. Sabhasad, pp. 27-28. Sen. Siva Chhatrapati, pp. 29-30.
94. Itihas Sangraha, Aitihasik Sphuta Lekha, p. 27.
95. It may be incidentally mentioned here that the Konkanastha had not yet come to the forefront in Maratha politics and most of Shivaji's principal Brahman officers belonged to the Deshastha section. The keen intelligence of the Shenvis had already espied a bright prospect in another quarter and they had in large number entered the Portuguese service. With their characteristic literary aptitude, they mastered European tongues before long and acted as interpreters for European merchants of all nationalities. It is not clear whether their persecution had begun so early. In any case prudence demanded that Shivaji should recruit his officers from al the principal castes, and conciliate them all.
96. Chitnis, p. 79.
97. Chitnis p. 108. Sen, Siva Chhatrapati, pp. 220-221.
98. Mawji and Parasnis, Sanads and Letters, pp. 130-132.
99. Rajwade, M.I.S., Vol. VIII, p. 7.
100. Rajwade, M.I.S., Vol. VIII, p. 11.
101. Rajwade, M.I.S., Vol. VIII, pp. 16-17.
102. Rajwade, M.I.S., Vol. VIII, pp. 18-19.
103. Orme, Historical Fragments, p. 38.
104. Sarkar, Shivaji (Ist Ed.), p. 94.
105. Scott-Warning, p. 102.
106. Fryer, p. 123.
107. Rajwade, M.I.S., Vol. VIII, pp. 28-31.
108. Chitnis, p. 80.

109. Manucci ed. Irvine, Vol. II, p. 203
110. Sabhasad, p. 30. Sen, Siva Chhatrapati, p. 33.
111. Sabhasad, pp. 28-29. Sen, Siva Chhatrapati, pp. 30-31.
112. Chitnis, p. 33, Sen, Siva Chhatrapati., p. 164.
113. Sabhasad, p. 93. Sen, Siva Chhatrapati. p. 130.
114. Grant Duff, Vol. I. pp. 181-182.
115. Sabhasad, p. 58. Sen, Siva Chhatrapati, pp. 76-77.

    Among the weapons in the royal armoury or Jirat Khana Raghunath Pandit not only mentions swords, daggers, and spears of different descriptions but also shields, clubs (gurguza) and battle axes (parashu). The curious reader will find an excellent chapter on arms and armours of the Marathas in *"A des ription of Indian and Oriental Armour"*. By the Rt. Hon'ble Lord Egerton of Tattan, M.A., London, 1896.
116. B.I.S.M., Tritiya Sammelan Vritta, p. 163.

    The following account of Shivaji's camp from the pen of the celebrated French Governor Martin is certainly interesting. "His Camp is without any pomp and unembarrassed by baggage or women. There are only two tents in it, but of a thick simple stuff, and very small,—one for himself and the other for his minister. The horsemen of Shivaji ordinarily receive two pagodas per month as pay. All the horses belong to him and he entertains grooms for them . . . Ordinarily there are three horses for every two men, which contributes to the speed which he usually makes...This Chief pays his spies liberally, which has greatly helped his conquests by the correct information which they give him". *Indian Historical Records Commission, Proceeding of Meetings,* Vol. VI, p. 25
117. Ranade, R. M.P., 123.
118. Sabhasad, p. 25. Sen, Siva Chattrapati, p. 25.
119. Elphinstone to Grant Duff, quoted in Colebrooke's Life of Elphinstone, Vol. II, p. 137.
120. Broughton, Letters from a Maratha Camp, p. 21.
121. Scott-Waring wrongly supposes "The festival of the Dasra was instituted by Sivajee". It was an old practice of the Hindu kings to set on their expedition of conquest on the Dasra day.
122. Shabhasad, pp. 29-30. Sen, Sivachhatrapati, pp. 31-33.

123. From the preamble of a treaty it appears that Shivaji's men had carried away a number of men, women, children, cattle besides transport bullocks from Portuguese territories in contravention of Shivaji's military regulations. See Biker, *Colleccao de Tratados*, Tomo, IV, pp. 131-132 and Sen, *Historical Records at Goa*, p. 10.

124. He had numberless informers about his troops; so that if they kept back any money or goods from account. he forced them to give them up. Scott, Hist. of the Dekkan, Vol. II., p. 55.

125. Rajwade, M.I.S., Vol. VIII, p. 20.

126. Bhate, Sajjangad-wa Samartha Ramdas, p. 122.

127. Rajwade, M.I.S., Vol. VIII, pp. 23-25.

128. Fryer, p. 175.

129. Fryer, p. 174.

130. Broughton, p. 21.

3

Non-interference of Muslim Rulers

It has been fairly established that the Maratha administrative institutions had been evolved from their ancient Hindu prototypes. But the part played by the Muhammadan rulers of India in this interesting evolution was by no means insignificant. For centuries they had governed the land and had given the administration the shape in which the Marathas inherited it from them. The vast kingdom of Vijayanagar had come to an end before the rise of Shivaji, and although the Hindu system of administration still survived in many of the petty Hindu States of the South, it would have been altogether impossible for Shivaji and his successors to revive the old Hindu institutions had they been quite extinct in the hilly district, that formed the nucleus of the Maratha empire and had once been an integral part of the Bahmani Kingdom. Like the present rulers of the Bombay Presidency the Muhammadan conquerors of the Deccan did not aim at an administrative revolution. They kept the system they found in existence at the time of their conquest practically intact, but made a change here and an addition there to suit their taste and the theories they had inherited from Muslim theologians When, therefore, the Hindu Padashahi was founded by Shivaji he had to follow in the foot-steps of his Musulman predecessors and continue their policy of conservation and reform. So the evolution went on unchecked and people could hardly perceive any change in the main theories and principles of their Government. Maratha Subhedars replaced Muhammadan Subhedars, and the Maratha Chhatrapati occupied the position of the Muhammadan Sultan; but the revenue was still paid in Muhammadan coins, the revenue terms were still Persian, the sanads and instructions issued to Revenue collectors were mere translation of Persian farmans of the Muhammadan rulers.

We have before us the financial theories of old Hindu law-givers, but the principles laid down by them had been embodied by Muhammadan rulers in their instructions to Revenue officers. The Marathas simply continued the same form, the same terms and almost the same language in their appointment letters. Thus the survival of the old Hindu principles was due to the Muhammadans, and the Marathas in their turn helped the survival of the Muhammadan forms and practices.

1. Abul Fazl on the Duties of a Revenue Collector

The whole process will be evident from a comparison of a Persian farman and a Marathi sanad so far as the revenue principles were concerned. We have already seen how the old Hindu political philosophers had advocated concessions for cultivation of waste lands, financial help at the time of distress and humane and considerate treatment of the cultivators. These very principles had been strongly emphasised when Abul Fazl enumerated the duties of an ideal Revenue Collector. "The Collector of the Revenue," says he, "should be a friend of the agriculturist. Zeal and truthfulness should be his rule of conduct. He should not stop from punishing highway robbers, murderers and evil-doers, nor from heavily mulcting them, and so administer that the cry of complaint shall be stilled. He should assist the needy husbands with advances of money and recover them gradually. He should ascertain the extent of the soil in cultivation and weigh each portion in the scales of personal observation and be acquainted with its quality. The agricultural value of land varies in different districts and certain soils are adapted to certain crops. He should deal differently, therefore, with each agriculturist and take his case into consideration. He should take into account with discrimination the engagements of former collectors and remedy the procedure of ignorance or dishonesty. He should strive to bring waste lands into cultivation and take heed that what is in cultivation shall not be wasted. He should stimulate the increase of valuable produce and emit somewhat of the assessment with a view to its augmentation. He should be just and provident in his measurements. Let him increase the facilities of the husbands year by year, and under the pledge of his engagements, take nothing beyond the actual area under tillage.[1] Abul Fazl also recommends the employment of able and honest inspectors and surveyors to help the Revenue Collector in the work of assessment.[2]

2. Farmans and Sanads

These were the principles that the Muhammadan Emperors endeavoured to enforce; they were never tired of repeating them in every farman they issued to their Revenue officers. Two such farmans have been translated by Prof. Jadunath Sarkar in his *Studies in Mughal India*[3] and though the documents are very lengthy, their intrinsic interest and value will fully justify the quotation of some extracts from them. After the usual preamble, it is laid down — "That officers of the present and future and *amils* of the Empire of Hindustan from end to end, should collect the revenue and other [dues] from the *mahals* in the proportion and manner fixed in the luminous Law and shining orthodox Faith, and [according to] whatever has been meant and sanctioned in this gracious mandate in pursuance of the correct and trustworty Traditions—

And they should not demand new orders every year, and should consider delay and transgression as the cause of their disgrace in this world and the next.

First.—They should practise benevolence to the cultivators, inquire into their condition, and exert themselves judiciously and tactfully, so that [the cultivators] may joyfully and heartily try to increase the cultivation, and every arable tract may be brought under tillage.

Second.—At the beginning of the year inform yourself, as far as possible, about the condition of every ryot, as to whether they are engaged in cultivation or are abstaining from it. If they can cultivate, ply them with inducements and assurances of kindness; and if the desire favour in any matter show them that favour. But if after inquiry it is found that, in spite of their being able to till and having had rainfall, they are abstaining from cultivation, you should urge and threaten them and employ force and beating. Where the revenue is fixed proclaim to the peasants that it will be realised from them whether they cultivate the land or not. If you find that the peasants are unable to procure the implements of tillage, advance to them money from the State in the form of *taqavi* after taking security.

* * * * *

Sixth.—You fix such an amount that the ryots may not be ruined.

Seventh—You may change fixed revenue into share of crop, or *vice versa,* if the ryots desire it; otherwise not.

* * * * *

Ninth.—In lands subject to fixed revenues, if any non-preventable calamity overtakes a sown field, you ought to inquire carefully, and grant remission to the extent of the calamity, as required by the truth and the nature of the case. And in realising revenue in kind from the remnant, see that a net one-half [of the produce] is left to the ryots.

* * * * *

Fourteenth.—Concerning lands under fixed revenue: If a man builds a house on his land he should pay rent as fixed before;and the same thing if he plants on the land trees without fruits. If he turns an arable land, on which revenue was assessed, for cultivation into a garden, and plants fruit trees on the whole tract without leaving any open spaces [fit for cultivation], take Rs. 2¾, which is the highest revenue for gardens, although the trees are not yet bearing fruit. But in the case of grape and almond trees, while they do not bear fruit take the customary revenue only, and after they have begun to bear fruit, take Rs. 2¾, provided that the produce of one canonical *bigha*, which means 45 × 45 Shah Jahani yards, or 60 × 60 canonical yards, amounts to Rs. 5½ or more.

Fifteenth.—If any man turns his land into a cemetery or *serai* in endowment, regard its revenue as remitted.

* * * * *

Eighteenth. — In *muqasema* lands, if any calamity overtakes the crop, remit the revenue to the amount of the injury. And if the calamity happens after reaping the grain or before reaping, gather revenue on the portion that remains safe."

This farman was addressed to Muhammad Hashim, Dewan of Gujarat, in the 11th year of Emperor Aurangzib Alamgir. The document is so lengthy that it has not been possible to quote it in full with all the items and the commentaries. The second document translated by Prof. Sarkar was addressed to one Rasikdas. This officer is ordered to make a detailed inquiry about the condition of cultivation in the districts under his charge and the document reads almost like the concluding portion of Annaji Datto's circular letter quoted in Book I. The Emperor orders, "You should inquire into the real circumstances of every village in the *parganahs* under your *diwans* and *amins*, namely, what is the extent of the arable land in it? What proportion of this total is actually under cultivation, and what portion not? What is the amount of the full crop every year? What is the cause of those lands lying uncultivated? Also find out, what was the system of revenue collection in the reign of Akbar under the diwani administration of Tudar Mal? Is the amount of the *sair* cess the same as under the old regulations, or was it increased at His Majesty's accession? How many *mauzas* are cultivated and how many desolate? What is the cause of the desolation? After inquiring into all these matters, exert yourself to bring all arable lands under tillage, by giving correct agreements (*qaul*) and proper promises, and to increase the first-rate crops. Where there are disused wells, try to repair them, and also to dig new ones. And assess their revenue in such a way that the ryots at large may get their dues and the Government revenue may be collected at the right time and no ryot may be oppressed."

Rasikdas is further enjoined to make local enquiry through his *amils* as to the condition of the cultivation and to take a statistics of cultivators and ploughs, encourage the cultivator to increase the sowing and the extent of cultivation and to improve the quality of the produce, to make the amils work hard in order to induce the run away peasants to return, to gather cultivators from all sides by offering them various inducements and to devise means for the reclamation of waste lands.[4] The out standing arrears were to be realised by installments "according to the condition of the ryots".[5] The exaction of prohibited *abwabs* was to be checked and prevented.[6] And finally the papers of the records were to be gathered at the right time.[7]

The Marathas were no rivals of the Mughals in their literary achievements, and their language did not permit the flowery style and pompous grandiloquence for which Persian literature is famous. It will be therefore futile to expect that the terms of a Marathis appointment letter should in every detail and word for word tally with the revenue regulations quoted above. The Marathi document is terse ,succinct and brief and lacks the preamble and the ornate style of a Mughal, *farman*, but a close comparison of the two leaves no doubt that the one was inspired by the other so far as the general revenue principles were concerned. In the appointment letter of Lakshman Bhikaji, Mamlatdar of Wan and Dindori, for instance, we find the following instructions laid down for his guidance:

1. The village in the above-mentioned Parganas should be surveyed. The lands should be classed as superior, ordinary and interior and also as jirayat and bagayat, patsthal and motsthal, and their area should be ascertained and the result should be reported to the Amin. The Amin should fix the rates to be charged and the assessment should be made accordingly.
2. The waste and fallow lands should be brought under cultivation within two or three years from the current year. If you fail to bring waste lands under cultivation, you will lose your appointment.
3. If any serious disturbance or rebellion takes place, remission of rent will be made according to the custom of the land.
4. Fadfadmas will be fixed by the Government hereafter and paid accordingly.
5. Kauls of istawa have been granted to certain villages in these Parganas. You should make an enquiry about them and having ascertained which villages are unprofitable, report the result to the Amin. The Amin will consider the report and make necessary arrangements by which you should be guided.
6. Full information regarding the Parganas should be furnished to the Amin. He would then lay down the system of Jamabandi according to which collection should be made.[8]

Of course we do not come across all the instructions quoted from the farman addressed to Muhammad Hashim. But it should be remembered that while Muhammad Hashim was the Dewan of a province, Lakshman Bhikaji was in charge of a few Parganas only. Similarly the farman addressed to Rasikdas also differs in certain details from the addressed to Muhammad Hashim. But some of the revenue regulations that we miss in Lakshman Bhikaji's sanad will be found in other sanads granted by the Peshwas'

Government. Thus reference has already been made in Book II of Tagai or Taqavi loan mentioned in the Mughal farmans. In the same book mention has also been made of efforts made by the Peshwas' government to induce runaway peasants to return to their villages and resume the cultivation of their deserted fields. In Book I a quotation has been made from Sabhasad to show how Shivaji also wanted his revenue officers to use conciliation and reassurances in gathering together cultivators from all sides with praiseworthy diligence. And the surveyors and inspectors mentioned by Abul Fazl naturally reminds one of the Maratha Pahanidars. This establishes beyond doubt the close intimacy between the Maratha and the Mughal systems.

But it will be a mistake to suppose that the Muhammadans simply transmitted the old Hindu system and did not add to it anything of their own. It has not been possible to quote the two documents in full, but it is necessary to mention that in some of the omitted instructions of the Emperor Aurangzib makes distinction between the-paying and rent-paying lands which is certainly Islamic in origin. This distinction naturally did not find any place in the Maratha system which as we have already noticed (in Book II) recognised the claims of Brahmans to various concessions.

Item fourteenth of Muhammad Hashim's farman claims our special attention, as it deals with jirayat lands converted into bagayat and also with special concession and made for costly plantations which do not yield any immediate profit to the cultivator. The principle, as laid down here, is based on the orthodox Muhammadan theories of finance. Aghnides says that the rates for trees, palms and sugarcane plantations, according to al-Mawardi were ten, eight and six dirhams respectively. "The above taxes," says he, "concerning trees applied only in case they were closely planted in such a way that cultivation of the intervening space was impossible, for isolated trees growing in cultivated fields were exempt from tax for the land was then taxed as a cultivated land."[9] This principle the Marathas did not accept in *toto*. They laid special rates for the orchards and sugarcane plantations, while cocoanut palms as well as Undani and jack fruit trees were taxed as individual trees. But no tax ws levied until the palms and trees began to pay. Thus in this case the Marathas did not either reject or accept in full the principle of taxing palms and other trees, as enunciated by Muhammadan theologians and introduced in India by Musulman conquerors, but somewhat altered it to suit their purpose.

3. Paymalli Compensation

It was not infrequent that Marathas accepted the policy or principles, good, bad, or indifferent, as they had been transmitted by their Muhammadan predecessors One such instance is found in the Maratha custom of compensating aggrieved peasants and villagers for *paymalli* or loss caused by the Peshwas' forces when encamped near a village by treading on the crops in the neighbouring fields. Abdul Hamid Lahori, the author of *Badshah Nama,* tells us that such *paymalli* compensation was paid by Emperor Shah Jahan in the seventh year of his reign. "His Majesty's sense of justice and consideration, for his subjects," says Abdul Hamid, "induced him to order that the *Bakshi* of the *ahadis* with his archers should take charge of one side of the road, and the *Mir-atish* with his matchlock-men should guard the other, so that the growing crops should not be trampled under foot by the followers of the royal train. As, however, damage might be caused *daroghas, mushrifs* and *amins* were appointed to examine and report on the extent of the mischief, so that raiyats, and jagirdars under 1,000 might be compensated for the individual loss they had sustained."[10] It may however appear from the language of Abdul Hamid that this compensation was a pure act of kindness and grace on the part of ShahJahan, and not an obligation. Of course there is no obligation for an autocrat, but it was really a common practice of the Delhi Emperors and was continued by Shah Jahan's successors. Irvine says, "Even in the best time of the monarchy and under the strictest commanders the course of an army was marked by desolation. There were great destruction of growing crops when the army passed through a fairly cultivated country. Compensation under the name of *paemali* `foot treading', was certainly allowed, according to the rules, in the shape of a remission of revenue on the land injured, but this must have been a very incomplete indemnification for the loss of the crop."[11] It was "in the shape of a remission of revenue on the land injured" that the Peshwas' Government paid the *paemali* compensation, and there is reason to believe that in their case too the remission bore but a poor proportion to the loss sustained. It is, therefore, clear that in this instance at least the Marathas meekly followed the Mughal example which so far as the compensation itself was concerned was a laudable one. But the compensation naturally reminds one of the cause of the loss. It was as Irvine informs us the "great destruction of growing crops" by the Mughal forces, which could not be prevented by the strictest commander even in the best days of the monarchy.[12] So the Marathas were not the only offenders. Desolation was caused and growing crops had been destroyed by the Mughal forces too even while passing through the imperial territories in peaceful times, but the Maratha horseman has earned his unenviable notoriety as a plunderer and robber, because perhaps he was more thorough, more quick, more cunning and not because he was more ruthless, or less amenable to discipline than his Mughal brother.

In addition to the rent the Maratha government levied other taxes. It will not be possible to discuss all of them in detail here and I shall simply quote a list of these various taxes from Elphinstone's Report. We shall have to remember that these taxes called *Sivay Jama* or extra revenue varied in different places, and all of them were never simultaneously levied.

1. Extra Revenue

1. *Duluk Puttee*—a tax of one year's rent in ten on the lands of the Daishmookh and the Daishpande.

2. *Huk Choutaee*—a fourth of the fees levied every year.
3. *Mahar Mahillee*—a tax on the Inams of the Mahars.
4. *Mecras Puttee*—an additional tax once in three years on Meerasdars.
5. *Inam Tijaee*—a payment by Inamdars of 1/3 of the Government share of their lands annually.
6. *Inam Puttee*—an occasional tax imposed in time of exigency on the Inamdars.
7. *Pundee Gunna*—an additional levy equal to 12 p.c. on the Tunkha once in 12 years.
8. *Vihar Hoonda*—an extra tax on lands watered from wells.
9. *Ghur Puttee or Amber Saree*—a house tax levied from all but Brahmins and village officers.
10. *Bat Chappanee*—a fee on the annual examination of weights (this specially affected the retail traders but fell on others too) and measures.
11. *Tug*—a similar fee on examining the scale used for bulky articles.
12. *Luggun Tukka*—A tax on marriage.
13. *Pat-dam*—tax on widow re-marriage.
14. *Mhys Puttee*—a tax on she-buffaloes generally at the rate of one Rupee for a she-buffalo.
15. *Bakra Puttee*—a tax on sheep.
16. *Fudmash*—an occasional contribution in kind; often paid in commutation of service.

All these taxes were collected in the village by the Patil, although in the towns the government had a separate officer for that purpose. In addition to the levies enumerated above, the government also derived some income from other sources, those worth mentioning being:

1. *Beitul Maul*—or escheats.
2. *Wan Charaee*—paid by cattle grazing on Government lands.
3. *Ghatskuttanee*—on grass cut on Government lands.
4. *Dewastan Dubhee*—derived from offerings to idols.
5. *Khur-Boozwaree*—a tax on melon gardens on river beds.
6. *Watan Zapti*—produce of lands belonging to Zamindars sequestrated by Government.
7. *Succession Duty*—called *Nazar*. If a son suceeded his father he was exempted from this tax, unless he was a Jagirdar or a Government servant.
8. *Kotwalee* or town duty—which comprised besides the taxes included in the Sewai Juma a variety of other imposts, the most considerable of which was a tax of 17 p.c. on the sale of a house.[13]

2. Census

Sometimes, when the normal means of the government proved inadequate for meeting the financial pressure, the government levied a *Jasti Patti* or *Karja Patti* on all land-holders, Inamdars included, and the tax generally amounted to a year's income. Some of the above-mentioned levies were farmed and some of them were paid in kind. But as we have seen in relation to the assessment and collection of land revenue, the Peshwa's government relied much on inspection and what may be regarded as statistical reports. Thus we find that an officer was sent to take a census of the houses, and she-buffaloes, in Pargana Ghosala in the year 1741-42, and papers of the preceding year's census were given to him.[14]

"Ganesh Dattaji has been sent to ascertain the taxable houses and she-buffaloes (belonging to cow-herds) in the Pargana of Ghosala; give him the papers of the preceding year". The next year (1742-43) Karkuns were deputed for the same purpose to Tarfs Pal, Ashtami, Nagothane, Ghosala, Birwadi and Mamla Tale.[15] It, therefore, seems that such statistical information was annually gathered (as Tarf Ghosala is mentioned also in the previous document).

3. Exemption of Government Officers and Prabhus

But government officers were generally exempted from Ghar Patti (house-tax) and the Prabhus in the Konkan enjoyed similar exemption with the Brahmans.[16]

"Sanads to Kamvisdars: The Huzur has been informed that in the Konkan, house-tax is demanded from the Prabhus whilte it is not levied on the Brahmans. Don't levy that tax on the houses of the Prabhus in the Konkan Prant and you should return what you have already realised from them on that account". Consideration as usual was made for the poverty of the taxpayer in levying these extra taxes also. Thus we find that Moro ganesh Behare of Satara was exempted from house-tax because the gentleman with his brother had been robbed twice and was, therefore, not in a position to pay (1776-77).

"A letter to Krishna Rao Anant, Mukkam Satara: Moro Ganesh Behare is a resident of Satara. The Huzur is informed that you have dunned his family for house-tax due to the government. The year before last the aforesaid gentleman was robbed by dacoits beneath Morgiri and lost his property. After that, his brother at Vadutha was also robbed last year of all his goods and killed. Therefore he is under great difficulties. So we have taken pity on him and exempted him from this tax. Do not, therefore, dun his family."[17]

The principle was that the levy should be *Jivan maphak* or in proportion to the resources of the tax-payer and these various taxes, although they look tremendous on paper, could not be very oppressive except in the hands of bad rulers like Baji Rao II. It is significant that although most of these taxes fell on lands, Mirasi lands always fetched as high a price as ten years' purchase. Some of these taxes however were not levied on the Rayats at all. Vancharai for instance was levied really to safeguard the interests of the peasants. The tax was imposed on the professional shepherds or *khilaris,* whose flocks were often let loose to graze freely in the fields and villages (mountainous regions where cultivation was difficult). To put a check on them these khilaris were required to take a licence for their sheep and if the number ever exceeded that sanctioned in the licence they had to pay a tax of Rs. 6 per hundred sheep. But the Rayats, whether Dhangar or Kunb, was not to be taxed for the sheep that they might keep. This principle of levying Vancharai is clearly set forth in a letter written to Bapu Rao Yeshwant in 1767-68.

"A letter to Bapurao Yeshwant: You had been deputed to make an enquiry about the sheep of the khilaris, but complaint has reached us that you have levied Vancharai even upon the sheep of the Rayats. Though there was no custom of levying that tax upon the Rayats, in the past you extorted Vancharai from them, and so they felt oppressed. It has, on this account, been settled that you should not exact it from the Rayats. Therefore make an enquiry about the sheep not belonging to the Rayats. Those who have got a licence should be let alone, but those who graze their sheep along with the licence-holders give trouble to the Rayats. Therefore carefully find out the number of unlicensed sheep and levy Vancharai at the rate of Rs. 6 per hundred. Deposit in the Sarkar what you can on account of Vancharai and take a receipt for it. But the Rayats, whether Dhangar or Kumbi, are not to be on any account troubled for the sheep that they may keep."[18] In fact these khilaris with their flocks had become such a nuisance to the farm lands as well as to the wood lands that in 1770-71, the government was compelled to take the drastic measure of confiscating the licensed as well as the unlicensed flocks grazing in Prant Shirval. The licensed flocks, of course, were restored to their owners shortly afterwards.[19]

4. Forests

Now to pass on to the preservation of government forests for they were a source of income to the Peshwas. Forests do not seem to have yielded much in cash. We find that a man paid Rs. 154-10 for a farm of the bherali palms in Pargana Ghosala for one year (1743-44)[20] and of course the Peshwas got something by selling their permission for cutting wood both for building purposes and for fuel; the usual fee for fuel was As. 4 per bullock load. The honey from the beehives, whatever it might have yielded, formed another item of the forest revenue. But it seems that the *kurans* were, also included in the forest department. The Peshwas preserved the forests and kurans more for their direct produce than for any revenue as will be seen in the document below:

"Balaji Krishna was appointed to the Mamlat of the Kurans and the following instructions were issued to him:

1. He should deliver to Government in Poona fifteen lakhs of bundles of grass, and should keep a similar quantity ready for Government use in Kurans within a radius of five or six Kos from the city. (This last quantity should be given to the stables and camel stables, on presenting a letter from the Peshwa's officers).

2. He should take in his charge all the Kurans existing within a radius of fifteen to twenty Kos of Poona, whether belonging to Government or to private individuals, and there establish Government Kurans.

3. He should deliver to Government in Poona 1,600 khandis of fuel and 150 khandis of coal.

4. Out of the timber, fuel, grass, bamboos, leaves and other produce realised in a private Kuran, a quantity sufficient to meet his annual wants should be given to the owner. The rest should belong to the Government and should be sold, excepting such portion as may be required for Government

purposes, and the proceeds credited to the Government.

5. A duty of As. 4 per bullock load, or if possible more, should be levied from all traders carrying wood on bullocks, and Vancharai should be levied on all cow-herds grazing their flock in the Kuran and the proceeds should be credited to the Government".[21]

The Peshwas sometimes allowed government officers to take timber free for constructing their houses. Sometimes building materials were given to villagers in distress and in need of public help.

"The houses of the Kunbis of Mauja Talawade belonging to Moro Babu Rao having been burnt, Keso Krishna is ordered to give them 750 bamboos from the Kuran of Manja Chas in Tarf Chakan".[22] For works of public utility building materials could be freely obtained from government forests with the sanction of the Peshwa, very easily obtainable on such occasions.

5. Mints

A third source of revenue was the mint. The mints during the Peshwa period were, unlike those of our own days, in private hands. "The Hindu financer", says Mr. Ranade, "whose opinions were so prominently referred to in one of the articles on Indian affairs published in a recent issue of the *London Times,* reflected the views of his countrymen faithfully enough when he observed that "No Government has the right to close its mints, or to say that the currency of the country was either deficient or redundant. That was a question solely for the bankers, traders and merchants to consider. If they do not require money they will not purchase bullion to be coined. The duty of Government is merely to assay all bullion brought to the mints for coinage and to return the value of the Bullion in money."[23] Shivaji also advocated the same policy in his reply to the prayer of the

English that their "money should go current in his dominions".

Its natural consequence was that no less than twenty-six different sorts of gold coins of different value were current in Shivaji's times, and "in an official table published for the guidance of the Civil Courts in the Bombay Presidency, the names of no less than thirty-eight gold coins and over one hundred and twenty-seven silver coins are mentioned as still so far current in different parts of this Presidency as to make it worth-while to give the relative intrinsic values of these local currencies in exchange for the Queen's coin".[24]

The inevitable corollary of this system was private minting; not free but licensed. For this licence, the Sonar (the owner of private mints was usually a Sonar or Goldsmith) had to pay some royalty to the government which varied indifferent cases. But the licence-holder had to stipulate for keeping up the standard proportion in the alloy and the purity of the metal used for coining purposes. A branch of this contract meant fine or forfeiture of the licence. Even a random quotation of a document bearing on mints will illustrate the principle well.

"Balaji Bapuji is permitted to establish a mint at Kasba Nagothane and coin piece ten Masas in weight. If pice of the prescribed weight is coined it will be all right; but if the pice is made of a less weight, he will be fined". The permission was given for three years and for the licence Balaji Bapu had to pay Rs. 50 for the first year (in four instalments of Rs. 12-8 each), Rs. 75 for the second year (four instalments), and Rs. 100 for the third year (four instalments).[25] Mr. Ranade points out that the document quoted above furnishes the first notice of such licensed private mints in the Peshwas' Daftar, and both Shahu and the Raja of Kolhapr had their own mints.

Though the Peshwas granted licence for private mints they were by no means ready to tolerate unlicensed mints or debased coins. But in some provinces the Zamindars established their own mints and issued counterfeit coins. The most notorious in this respect was Subha Dharwar, and it was not very easy to put a stop to this corrupt practice, so profitable to the offenders. The first notice of counterfeit coins we find in a document of Balaji Baji Rao dated 1760-61.[26] It states:

"In Subha Dharwar the mints for coining Hons, Mohars, and Rupees issue false coins. In the old mints good coins were struck. Recently the Zamindars have established mints almost at every house and are issuing bad coins". The remedy proposed was to abolish these spurious mints and to establish one central mint for which a licence was granted to Pandurang Murar.

"It causes loss to the government. You represented that all these mints should be abolished and in their place one central mint should be established at Dharwar. Bad coins should be discontinued and good coins issued. Such a measure will be profitable to the government. Therefore agreeing with your view that the continuation of the issue of bad coins is not desirable and should be discontinued, the management has been entrusted to you. You should pull down the mints established in different places and establish a central mint at Dharwar. You should also destroy the bad coins and issue good ones." The mint charges were fixed at seven per thousand (six coins for the government and one for the manager). "The customary charge from former time is one Mohar for each thousand Mohars and one Rupee per thousand. The work of the mint should be profitable, therefore the Sawkars have been exempted from this charge for one year from Rabilakhar, San Ihide, to Rabilakhar, San Issanne Sitain. After this you should take the customary due of six per thousand coins and remit the same to the government. In addition to this, take one coin more with the free consent of the Sawdars in your own name, and remit that also to the government. Your dues will be afterwards fixed according to your service." But this reform could not be carried out till 1765-66 when the first Madhava Rao had to issue a circular letter to the Kamavisdar, Zamindars and

Sawkars telling them that no payment should henceforth be accepted by the government except in new coins. We have many other instances of suppression of spurious mints and counterfeit coins.[27] But the government confined itself to supervision only, and the actual control of the currency was never undertaken. The currency was further strengthened by an extensive use of *hundis* or credit instruments. The Peshwas always instructed their revenue officers to make use of hundis in the transmission of money to the central treasury. How popular the use of hundi had become is seen in letter written by one Ganesh Bhat, where he says that he has remitted Rs. 13-8 by hundi.[28]

6. Customs Duties

We may now turn to the Peshwas' income from customs duties and other taxes levied on traders. These duties fell under two classes, Mohatarfa or duties on traders, and Zakat which included duties on sales and purchases as well as octroi duties. A chart of the rates of Mohatarfa during the administration of Balaji Baji Rao Peshwa can be framed from four documents, a letter to the Kamavisdar of Mamla Revdanda written in 1742-43,[29] a letter to Nathuram Chaudhari dated the same year,[30] a Sanad to the officer in charge of Janjira Revdanda (1750-51)[31] and a Sanad to Shridhar Jivaji issued in 1752-53.[32] The Kamavisdar of Mamla Revdanda was asked to levy Mohatarfa at the following rate.

7. Mohatarfa

1. The Kolis should be taxed at the rate of Rs. 8, 5 and 2 per palanquin (per year) according to its size and nature.
2. Shop-keepers should be taxed at the rate of Rs. 5, 6 and 7 per shop per year.
3. The blacksmiths should be taxed at the rate of Rs. 4 per shop per year.
4. The shoe-makers should be taxed at the rate of Rs. 4, 5 and 6 per shop per year.

5. The rate of tax on oilmen should be Rs. 5, 6 and 7 per oil mill per annum.
6. The rate of tax on goldsmiths should be Rs. 3 per shop per annum.
7. The rate of tax on potters should be Rs. 3 per wheel per annum.
8. The rate of tax on basket-makers should be Rs. 3 per house per annum.
9. The Gondhlis (worshippers of Devi or goddess of small-pox) to pay for their profession Rs. 3 per year.
10. The tax on boats passing the channel should be four annas for each small boat (fit to carry a load of five khandis) and eight annas for each big vessel.

Nathuram Chaudhari was informed that he should collect Mohatarfa from beldars (stone-quarry-men) at the rate of 5 per cent of the their income. Similarly Moroji Shinde, officer in charge of Revdanda, was told to levy Mohatarfa from masons, stone-cutters, and stone-diggers, at the rate of one day's income per month, and Shridhar Jivaji was informed that the current rate of Mohatarfa to be paid by the carriers was Rs. 1-4 for every bullock carrying cloth and grocery. The Zakat included the Thalbharit (tax to be paid at the place of loading), the Thalmod (tax to be paid at the place of sale) also Chhapa, a stamping-duty and Hashil which again in one document at least is described to be consisting of three items—Tafavat Dhakhala, Dasturi and Tallab Dhakhala. In another document a tax called Shingshingoti (levied on cattle) is also included in the Zakat.

8. Zakat

The Mohatarfa, as the above list will show, varied with the means of each individual shop-keeper, and can, therefore, be regarded as an income-tax. The Zakat was levied separately in every district, and this naturally led goods to be stopped frequently in their transit. This, however, was not peculiar to Maharashtra or to India. Tradesmen and merchants were similarly troubled in pre-revolutionary France, and, in Germany before the Zollverein. The Maratha merchants could evade the difficulty. "To remedy this inconvenience, there was a class called Hoondeckurrees in towns, who undertook for a single payment to pass articles through the whole country. These men arranged with the farmers of the customs, and where answerable to them for the sums due."[33] The Peshwa was not unaware of the inconvenience of frequent stoppage of merchandise in course of transit. In 1745-46, Peshwa Balaji Baji Rao ordered that goods passing between Sironj and Burhanpur should pay octroi (Zakat) at one place only.[34]

"A letter to Sankaraji Nikam: Zakat on elephants, and horses carrying goods of different descriptions from Sironj to Burhanp should be collected at Sironj. Nothing should be charged at Burhanpur. If there is any custom of taking something as `pansupari' gift, that alone should be taken. This practice has been observed from early times. When things of various descriptions are sent from Burhanpur, Zakat should be levied there and not at Sironj. This being the practice, we have been informed that you have demanded Hashil at Burhanpur although it was duly paid at sironj. This letter is written on this information. You should collect only according to the customary practice, and should not introduce any innovation".

9. Zamindars and Darakhadars

It may be noted here that Zakat was generally farmed to a person for a fixed sum, but these men were strictly warned not to oppress the people or to levy any unauthorised tax. As in the administration of land revenue the Peshwas followed the policy of encouraging the merchants and securing their prosperity and as the farming system was bound to be more or less inefficient from that point of view, we find that government officers were appointed during the administration of the second Madhava Rao for assessment and collection of Zakat. These officers often replaced the farmers all together, but sometimes they simply supervised their work. The collection of Zakat, when under a government department, was conducted according to the Kamavis system and to it also the same checks of Zamindars will Darakhdars were applied. Two documents will be quoted here to illustrate the working of the principle. The first of these recounts the duties of the Zakat-Fadnis, of Bandar Pen, as follows:

1. The settlement of the fixed sum to be levied from any trader on account of octroi, should not be made without the consent of the Fadnis.
2. The account of octroi on exported goods should remain with the Fadnis.
3. All correspondence regarding octroi should be conducted and all orders regarding credit and debit should be issued by the Fadnis.
4. The octroi farms being abolished and the revenue being departmently managed, writing work should be done by the Fadnis.
5. The Fadnis should be prompt in his work and should issue notes or passes without delay.[35]

The second document illustrates how the Zakat officers were also checked by Zamindars and hereditary officers or Darakhdars. Krishnaji Viththal, Jamenis of octroi, in Prant Kalyan, had some difference with the Zamindars about official duties. The following instructions were therefore issued to Uddho Dadaji and Apaji Vishwanath, Joint Kamavisdars of Zakat in the Prant:

1. "The Jamenis shall ascertain the amount of octroi to be levied, under orders of the Mamlatdar and in the presence of the Zamindars and shall prepare rough memorandum thereof on the spot, another memorandum being prepared by the Zamindar.
2. The Jamenis shall write the draft agreement setting forth the conditions on which a sub-contract of the

octroi farm is given. The Majumdar shall enter the totals and when the agreement is approved by the Mamlatdar, the Fadnis shall write the *sanad*.

3. Passports to traders carrying bullock-loads from forts shall be written either by the Zamindars or by the Darakhdars. as may be customary at the particular post. In the former case the Fadnis shall date the passports, the Majumdar shall make his mark thereon, and the Mamlatdar shall see them. In the latter case the passports shall be sent through the Zamindars.

4. At the end of the year the Jamenis shall compare his rough memoranda of receipts with those kept by the Zamindars and submit a detailed account to the Mamlatdar.

5. The Zamindars represent that the amount to be levied from the traders is fixed by them according to custom or according to Kauls granted to them, and that in their absence, the work is performed by the Mamlatdars. As the Zamindars keep separate accounts of the tax, the rates should be fixed with their cognizance. The memorandum fixing the amount leviable, either for particular Mahal, or for the whole tract, from the post to the province, above the ghaut should be written by the Jamenis and marked by the Mazumdar, and it should bear the approving endorsement of the Mamlatdar. It should then be given to the Fadnis for being registered and finally recorded by the Mamlatdar. The copy to be sent to the *Thana* should be made by the Jamenis. The Zamindar should take a copy for reference.

6. Kauls to traders shall be written by the Jamenis; the Fadnis shall date them, and they shall bear the Zamindar's mark and the Mamlatdar's seal."[36]

10. Remission of Zakat and Mohatarfa

In the above document mention has been made of kauls to traders. This will naturally remind us of the Kauls granted to cultivators for improvement of cultivation and other measures adopted for the same purpose. As land revenue was remitted from time to time in consideration of poverty of the Rayats, failure of rain, and above all, for the general and all-embracing reason of the improvement of agriculture, so these Zakat and Mohatarfa taxes were also, from time to time remitted. The Peshwa's government never meant to make their assessment and collection rigid; flexibility was preferred as it suited the circumstances well. In the year 1763-64, a greater supply of ghi, oil, jaggery and turmeric being considered necessary the Kamavisdars in charge of Zakat, in Prants Poona and Junnar, were ordered to levy Zakat at half the usual rate.[37]

"A Sanad to Mahadaji Narayan and Sadashiva Raghunath Kamavisdars, Zakat, Prants Poona and Junnar: levy Zakat at half the usual rate upon the traders from Desh who would bring ghi, oil, jaggery and turmeric, etc., till the festival of Dasra and excuse the other half, as it is necessary to import a greater quantity of these articles." Similarly the levy of *Tag* (a tax on balance—it came under the Mohatarfa) newly imposed on traders at Poona was abolished in 1769-70 on their representation as it pressed heavily on them.[38] The Peshwa's attention was not confined to the sellers alone, the consumers as the party most affected by trade regulations also shared is consideration. Thus in a letter addressed to the Kamavisdars of Zakat, Prants Poona and Junnar 1763-64, we find that (1) "rice and salt and groceries brought from the Konkan were to pass free of Zakat. (2) Bhusara grains (pulses) were always exempted from Zakat. (3) Cultivators carrying grain and salt from Poona were to be exempted from Zakat as their property had been recently lost owing to war. (4) No fee was to be levied on cultivators purchasing bullocks and buffaloes in Prant Poona as they had been deprived of their cattle during the disturbance this year: traders, however, should pay the usual duty."[39]

11. Communication

In times of famine and searcity, the favourite remedy of English statesmen during the first four decades of the 19th century had been a sliding scale of tariff, intended to secure agricultural interest, and at the same time to procure relief to the distressed. The Maratha government on such occasions boldly met the difficulty by the total suspension of Zakat and temporary introduction of free import of foodstuff and agricultural necessities. But the means of communication in those days were not so advanced and in spite of these wise measures famine had often terrible consequences. Means of communications, such as ferry-boats and roads, were to be neglected by the Peshwa's government. The government sometimes granted money for the construction of ferry-boats, and the roads were in general good, particularly in the neighbourhood of big cities. The Duke of Wellington, then Sir Arthur Wellesley, remarks in his despatches "The roads are excellent except when the rain is heavy". Among the papers of the second Madhava Rao, we find a letter to Balaji Mahadev, Mamlatdar of Taluka Shivner (1783-84), ordering him to repair the road through the pass of Malje in Tarf Shivner, one-fourth of the total expense was to be paid from the land revenue of the district and the remaining three-fourths were to be raised by the Kamavisdars of Zakat. The same road was for a second time repaired nine years later. The contribution to the major portion of the expenses by the Kamavisdars of Zakat shows that these roads mainly meant for trade purposes.[40]

12. Foundation of New Market-Towns

We have casually noticed the kauls granted to traders. The cultivators, we have seen, got a kaul for bringing waste land into cultivation and for the improvement of agriculture in general, and kauls were granted to merchants for repopulation of old and deserted market-towns, for foundation of new market places and for the improvement of trade and commerce in general. A kaul was granted to the Shete Mahajan, shopkeepers and traders, and persons following other occupations of Kasba Mukhde in Pargna Patode, of Sarkar Sangammer in the Subha of Khujiste Buniad in 1750-51, because business in the old market of the aforesaid village was not thriving well owing to some disturbance. The kaul was granted not only for the improvement of the trade and for the benefit of the tradesmen, but also because it was to the profit of the government as well. By this kaul old residents of the place were to be exempted from export and import duties for three years, and to be subjected only to the payment of house-tax (levied according to the profession of the house-owner); and new-comers were to be exempted from export and import duties for five years, and from house tax for three years.[41]

Similarly, when a new *peth* or suburb was established at Kasba Barshi in 1777-78, a kaul was granted to traders exempting them from all taxes for seven years.[42] In the year 1776-77 Chabidas Gulabdas of Burhanpur was exempted from half the usual Hashil for opening a new shop of cloth and embroidery.[43] and in the year 1789-90 two merchants, Pomaji Naik and Govind Naik Bhake, got a refund of money illegally exacted from them by a Mamledar of Zakat on bhusara grains, especially because their supply proved a great source of relief in time of a famine at Poona.[44]

It is to be noted here that special inducements were offered to new traders to come and settle in the Peshwa's territories. Vithoji Krishna Kamat, a Shenvi merchant, having offered to come with five ships and settle at Bassein as a trader, Peshwa Balaji Baji Rao ordered a palanquin and clothes of honour to be given to him in addition to partial exemption from Zakat.[45] Sometimes when tradesmen were pressed hard for money by their creditors, the government interfered in their favour and induced the money-lenders to accept easy terms of payments.

13. Shete Mahajan

Generally the task of establishing a new suburb or market town was entrusted to an enterprising man, who was rewarded on the successful conclusion of his labours with a watan of *Shetepan*. The perquisites of his watan were quite analogous to those of the village officers, and in this case too the Peshwa got important services without any payment whatever from the government treasury. The shopkeepers and traders, who actually paid the Shete's remuneration, had no reason for grumbling, as he was, like the Patil, the natural guardian of his clients' interests. The perquisites of the Shete watan were as follows:

1. One betel-nut on every weekly market day from each Bania's shop.
2. Five betel leaves every day from each shop of the leaves sellers.
3. Nine *taks* (½ seer) of oil every week from every oilman's shop.
4. Hill a seer of gram for each bag of grain sold in the market.
5. Quarter seer of groceries for every bag of grocery sold.
6. A handful of vegetables from every vegetable shop.
7. One *pasodi* (a kind of rough cloth) a year from the weaver community in the suburb.
8. Two pairs of shoes from the shoe-maker community in the suburb.
9. Quarter seer of wheat or rice from every shop on such festivals as Dasra, Diwali, Shimga and Varsha Pratipada.
10. A handful of grain for every bag of corn measured by the measure of the Shetes.
11. Flesh and dried fish to be taken when offered for sale in the market by butchers and fish-sellers.

12. A piece of cocoanut at every marriage celebrated in the suburb.
13. The houses of the Shetes to be exempted from house-tax.[46]

14. Government Intervention

The Peshwa's government interfered actively in commerce and manufacturing industries. Merchantmen required a dastak or passport for coming to or leaving a port in the Peshwa's territories.[47]

The Peshwas were perfectly justified in regulating the weights and measures, a otherwise retail dealers could cheat their customers with impunity. But the same thing cannot be said of Chhapa, or stamping of cloth for which also a fee was charged. The stamping duty on cloth was 5 p.c. *ad valorem* on imported cloth, and 2½ p.c. on cloth locally manufactured, and sellers of unstamped cloth were ordered to be fined.[48]

Government interference did not stop here; the manufacturers of turbans were, actually told, what metal they should melt for the manufacture of the brocade and what should be the length of the turbans.[49]

"Instructions about the manufacture of brocade for *sangas* at Kasba Jalnapur in the Pargana of the same name:

1. At present brocades are made by melting Chandvad Rupees. Their quality is therefore bad. Formerly Malharshai, English, surati or Patani coins were melted for making brocades. The same practice should be renewed.
2. `*Khar*' made by burning plantain trees is now used in preparing silk; brocades therefore become blackish. Manufacturers should be warned and made to use *datyakhar* (Kharsalt).
3. *Pagotas* are now made of a length of twelve to fifteen cubits; this is not proper. Their length should

not be less than thirty cubits. Manufacturers should be warned, and asked to make pagotas of a length of thirty cubits."

15. Monopoly

Monopoly was also given for purchase and sale of cocoanut, ghi, and even for brokerage in some cases. Sometimes the government went to the extent of fixing a price for certain articles. We should however judge the Peshwas by their motives. The principle of Laissez Faire had not gained any recognition in Europe in those days, and even in England, the future birthplace of free trade, protective duties and bounties were in fashion; and what was the sliding scale of duties on corn but an attempt to fix a minimum price for agricultural produce of the land? The Peshwas also did the same thing, and, on the whole, their subjects were not badly off.

16. Ship-building Encouraged

We have seen how owners of new shops and importers of cheap grains were partially exempted from Hashil. An over-seas trade had grown up. The Peshwa encouraged building of ships or gallibats.

"Chimnaji Ganesh Sathe of Kaliye in Tarf Majgaum in Taluka Ratnagiri having built a new ship was exempted from Octroi and other taxes on goods brought in the ship from other ports to his village for household use. His ship was also exempted from liability to forced service." (Marathe's Translation).[50] And we find Maratha merchants settling in coast towns of Arabia, and Maratha merchantmen visiting Chinese waters. (One Narottam Joshi is described as a resident of Muscat, in a letter to Admiral Ananda Rao Dhulap).[51]

In a document published by Mr. V. K. Rajwade in the 10th volume of his "Sources of Maratha History", one Asaram Vinayak is spoken of in the following terms: "He is a merchant of high position. His ships go to China. He has considerable trade with the English."[52]

We may note here that the Maratha naval officers could not claim salvage money from a subject of the Maratha empire for recovering ships from pirates.

"A merchantman with a cargo on board on its way to Bassein was taken by pirates. From them it was recovered by men serving in the navy under you and you also came to know that the ship belonged to the merchants. Therefore enquire whether the ship belongs to the merchants and Krishnaji Raghunath. If it belongs to them, restore to them the cargo that you may have found and the gallibat, and get from them an acknowledgement of receipt." It is to be noted that no salvage money is mentioned in any part of the document; such an item was not likely to be omitted by a Maratha officer, because even *antast* or bribers mentioned in state papers.[53]

17. Excise

Excise duties, as a source of income, may be ignored altogether. For in controlling the manufacture and sale of liquor, the Peshwa acted not only as the secular head but also as the ecclesiastica head of the state. Here, his revenue policy was influenced by religious ideas. Drinking was forbidden by the *Shastras* and the Peshwa, as the head of a great Hindu empire, tried to enforce this injunction. In the year 1775-76, during the administration of the second Madhava Rao, Balaji Ganesh, the officer in charge of Taluka Devgad, was ordered to stop the manufacture of liquor from cocoanut trees from the beginning of the next year.[54] A similar order was sent to the officer at Vijaydurg on the same date.[55]

But a government cannot expect to enforce religious injunctions strictly without causing hardship to the people, and these orders were from time to time modified in order to mitigate such inconvenience. Some of the Rayats earned their living by the manufacture of liquor mainly for the Portguese and Christian soldiers in the Peshwa's employ. Some provision had to be made for these people. Accordingly Peshwa Balaji Baji Rao allowed the Bhandaris and Kolis of

Prant Figure to manufacture wine (1754-55), but they were strictly ordered not to sell or to give wine to Brahmans, Prabhus, Shenvis and government servants.[56]

For the convenience of the European soldiers in the Peshwa's service, the second Madhava Rao allowed them to distil liquor for their own use.

"Some Portuguese and Christians are employed under Syed Ahmad Gardi, who is serving under Ragho Vishwanath. They always require liquor. Let them therefore establish a distillery and manufacture wine for their own consumption. Do not present any obstruction to it."[57]

18. Government Servants Exempted from Zakat

We may take here a passing notice of the exemption from Zakat enjoyed by government servants. "The Konkanstha Brahmin Karkoons." says Ranade, "who had monopoly of all the Secretariat or Daftar offices, and received respectable salaries, obtained the privilege of having their goods exempted from Custom duties and ferry charges when they imported grain and other goods from outside ports and places."[58] In justice to the Peshwa, it ought to be pointed out that the Brahman Karkuns enjoyed these privileges, not as Brahmans, but as government officers. Government officers, other than Brahmans, also shared these advantages. In 1744-45, Babaji Chapaji Shenvi, the farmer of Zakat in Prant sasti (Salsette) was informed that:

1. "Fish purchased by government servants for their own consumption should be exempt from duty.
2. That the following articles when purchased by government officers to the amount mentioned below, should also be exempt—twenty-five plantains, five cocoanuts, gur, dates, dried dates and sugar, to the amount of five seers.
3. That government servants and Brahmans should be exempt from ferry charges."[59]

On the whole the revenue administration of the Peshwa was conducted on sound principles, well calculated to secure the wealth and welfare of the Rayats. But the weak point of the system was not the dishonesty of Maratha officers which could be checked, but the absolutism of the Peshwa which found its worst exponent in Baji Rao Raghunath. The system worked so well under Balaji Baji Rao and his son that it could be favourably compared with the revenue system then prevalent in European countries. Its great advantage was that assessment and collection were flexible and could be regulated according to the actual condition of each individual district.

19. Total Revenue

We do not know what was the total revenue of the Peshwa's government. Lord Valentia estimates it at Rs. 7,164,724.[60] But we do not know how far this figure is reliable, and upon what data it is based. Mr. J. Grant estimated the total revenue of the Maratha Empire at six crores towards the close of the 18th century. According to him the Peshwa's revenue "reckoning chout from the Nizam, Tippoo, and Bundelcund Rajputs, will be found to amount to at least three crores of rupees.[61] Mr. Elphinstone's estimate is more moderate. According to him the total revenue of the Peshwa' dominions, excluding, Ahmedabad and the lands resumed from Bastin, amounted in December, 1815, to Rs. 9,671,735. They arrived at this figure after a detailed examination of the Peshwa's revenue[62] and he has supplied figures for every province and every district. These figures were compiled by him for the information of the Governor-General and his Council. And as he suggested in his covering letter these would be useful should occasion for territorial exchange ever arise. As Elphinstone was at Poona at the time and in close touch with the Peshwa's government we may accept his estimate as fairly accurate. He had no reason to give his superiors an exaggerated figure and in his estimate the Chauth naturally found no place. According to Lt.-Colonel

Blacker, the Peshwa's "clear Revenue was two crores and ten lacs of rupees annually."[63]

REFERENCES

1. Jarrett, Aini-Akbari, Vol. II, pp. 43, 44.
2. *Ibid*, p. 45.
3. Pp. 168-196.
4. *Studies in Mughal India*, p. 191.
5. *Ibid*, p. 192.
6. *Ibid*, p. 194.
7. *Ibid*, p. 196.
8. P. D., Vol. III, pp. 289-295.
9. Aghnides, *Mohammedan Theories of Finance*, p. 379.
10. Elliot and Dowson, Vol. VII, p. 43.
11. Irvine, *Army of the Indian Moghuls*, pp. 192-193.
12. Manucci writes about the oppression of the Mughal army: "Besides all these inflications they have other losses, for when the soldiery passes through they plunder every thing they can lay hands on, cattle, food-supplies, grass straw; they destroy houses to get fire wood and on the villagers' heads they load their baggage, and by dint of blows force them to carry it." Manucci, ed. Irvine, Vol. II, p. 452.
13. Elphinstone's spelling is retained here. The list is not exhaustive. Many local taxes are not mentioned.
14. P. D., Vol. III, p. 328.
15. P. D., Vol. III, p. 329.
16. P. D., Vol. VI, p. 298.
17. P. D., Vol. VI, p. 298-299.
18. P. D., Vol. VII, p. 103.
19. P. D., Vol. VII, p. 105.
20. P. D., Vol. III, p. 250.
21. K. B., Marathe's Summary, P.D., Vol. VI, p. 256.
22. P. D., Vol. VI, p. 255.
23. The Miscellaneous Writings, p. 330.
24. Ranade, The Miscellaneous Writings, p. 331.

25. P. D., Vol. II, p. 157.
26. P. D., Vol. II, p. 164.
27. P. D., Vol. VII, p. 291-297.
28. Rajwade, M. I. S., Vol. X, p. 21.
29. P. D., Vol. II, pp. 299-301.
30. P. D., Vol. III, pp. 301-302.
31. P. D., Vol. III, p. 303.
32. P. D., Vol. III, p. 304.
33. Elphinstone's Report on the Territories conquered from the Peshwa, p. 30.
34. P. D., Vol. III, p. 312.
35. P. D., Vol. VI, pp. 293-94. K. B. Marathe's summary.
36. P. D., Vol. VI, pp. 294.296. K. B. Marathe's translation.
37. P. D., Vol. VII, p. 69.
38. P. D., Vol. VI, p. 281.
39. P. D., Vol. VII, p. 68.
40. P. D., Vol. VIII, p. 215.
41. P. D., Vol. II, pp. 134-135.
42. P. D., Vol. VIII, p. 223.
43. P. D., Vol. VIII, p. 225.
44. P. D., Vol. VIII, p. 225.
45. P. D., Vol. II, p. 139.
46. For another paper recounting similar perquisites see P. D., Vol. VII, pp. 284-285.
47. See letter to Ananda Rao Dhulap. Peshwa's Diary. Sawai Madhava Rao, Vol. III, pp. 226-227.
48. P. D., Vol. III, pp. 320-321.
49. P. D., Vol. VIII, pp. 236-237.
50. P. D. Vol. VIII, p. 226.
51. Rajwade, M. I. S., Vol. VIII, p. 226.
52. Rajwade, M. I. S., Vol. X, p. 263.
53. P. D. Vol. II, pp. 141-142.
54. P. D. Vol. VI, p. 300.

55. P. D. Vol. VI, p. 300.
56. P. D. Vol. III, p. 332.
57. P. D. Vol. VI, p. 300.
58. The Miscellaneous Writings, p. 351.
59. P. D. Vol. III, pp. 308-310.
60. Scott Warning, Hist. of the Marathas.
61. J. Grant, An Historical and Political View of the Deccan, London, 1798, pp. 23-24 and 26.
62. Unpublished papers in the Imperial Records Office, Calcutta, Secret papers, Nos. 42-43, 1816.
63. Blacker, *Memoir of the Onerations of the British Army in India,* p. 27.

APPENDIX E

Elphinstone's Estimate to the Peshawa's Revenue.

Poona, December, 1815.

Sir,

I, have the honour to enclose the Details of the Paishwas Revenue, of which transmitted an Abstract, in my Despatch to His Excellency the Governor-General. I did not forward these Papers at that Time as they are of no General Interest, I send them now because occasions may arise (such as exchanges &c.) when it would be convenient to refer to them and it is therefore desirable to have them on Record. In the same view I enclose a statement of the land assigned to Holcar. The date is old and the amount of the Revenue must have altered since then. Holcar may also have much acquisitions in the Interval that has past but this Document contains the possessions of his Family seventeen years ago and the changes in that Period may be ascertained by a Reference to recent Transactions.

I have the honour to be

Sir,

Your most obedient humble servant,

M. Elphinstone.

To

J. Adam, Esq.,

&c. &c. &c.

Abstract of the Paishwah's Revenue.

Praunt Kokun	25,68,594
Praunt Carnatic including Beejapoor	19,52,183
Praunt Candeish including Bauglana and Berar	10,05,344

Praunt Poona, Joonair, Nuggur & Painair	7,28,118
Praunt Gungterree	5,65,769
Praunt Wye Sattara	2,99,142
Praunt Swadeish, Ballaghaut	4,66,023
Praunt Gazerat	9,76,362
Praunt Serole	0,03,866
Country North of the Nurbudda	0,17,843
Mawul	1,63,927
Praunt Kurhar	7,34,322
Batta of 8 P. Ct. upon the Khasgee	1,90,240
Total	96,71,735

To the above is to be added the revenues of Ahmedabad and of the Lands resumed from Bastin.

4

District and Provincial Governments

1. The Deshmukh and the Deshpande

Before the time of Shivaji the Deshmukhs and the Deshpandes were in charge of the Parganas. They were also called Zamindars. Their control over the villages led to oppression of the rayat, and Shivaji decided to do away with their agency. At the same time, the great Maratha ruler did not forget that if the Zamindars were turned out of their office without any provision whatever, an economic revolution would follow creating a number of beggars who had once seen opulence; and the remedy would be worse than the disease. He, therefore, took away their authority, but left them in the enjoyment of their customary dues, and appointed government officers in their place. The Peshwas simply continued this practice of Shivaji, and the change was not produced "by the policy and avarice of the Brahmins" as Elphinstone seems to suggest, but it was really "attended with beneficial effects," as he himself further adds—"as delivering the people from the oppression and exactions of the Zemindars."[1] In fact during the Peshwa period the Deshmukh and the Deshpande became the sincere friends of the rayat, and never failed to bring to the notice of the Peshwa their grievances. We find the Zamindars accompanying the Khots and Patils of Prant Rajpri to Poona to inform their master how insecure the rayats felt and how the lands were left uncultivated owing to the disturbance of the Shamal (siddi) (1760-61).

"The rayats of Prant Rajpri have been much oppressed by the disturbance of the Shamal, and their lands have not been cultivated. Disturbance takes place everyday. The Zamindars, the Khots, and the Patils came to Poona and prayed that the Swami should therefore take pity on them and make collection according to a new inspection of the aforesaid Prant in the present year."[2]

Again in 1763-64, The Deshmukh and the Deshpande represented to the authorities that the villages of Prant Junnar had been burnt and plundered by the Mughals, and suggested that some concessions to the cultivators should be made.[3]

But although the Deshpandes and the Deshmukhs were relieved of their original duties, their watan was not altogether a sinecure. "Long after the Zamindars ceased to be the principal Agents," says Elphinstone, "they were still made use of as check on the Mamlutdar; and no accounts were passed, unless corroborated by corresponding accounts from them." In fact the hereditary officers were preserved as a check on their non-hereditary superiors in almost every department of the Peshwa's government. In addition to this, the Deshmukh served as a depository of old records and the past and the present history of all watans, grants, and inams. So, whenever there was any dispute about land, the Deshmukh was asked to produce his old records and he had also "to keep a register of all new grants of transfer of property either by the Government or by individuals." It seems that the Deshmukh had an official seal for stamping these deeds, and it was usual for the senior owner of the watan to be the custodian of this seal, while the junior owners simply enjoyed the inam lands. Two documents are quoted here in support of this statement.

"Trimbak Rao, son of Gamaji Mhaske, Deshmukh Pargana Sangamner, came to the Huzur at the Mukkam at fort Purandhar and informed that half the Deshmukhi of the aforesaid Pargana belonged to his family and the other half to the family of Shelke. That in his family he was the senior and that the accepted custom was that the senior man in the family should have the entire right of using the official seal, putting his signature and doing the other duties of half the share of the aforesaid Pargana; while his co-shares should enjoy their customary share of the inam, and that the senior should grant them such pecuniary assistance as he deemed fit for their needs. That he had been exercising his right of seniority in the above style. Coming to the above conclusion we give you this letter of authority. Continue in the enjoyment of your right of seniority, generation after generation, use the seal of the family of Mhaske as before, do the Deshmukhi work of 150 villages and exercise your right of seniority by putting your signature, giving your co-shares their due share of the inam, and granting them pecuniary helps is customary and as their needs demand" (1776-77).[4]

"Dadaji Dev Rao Deshmukh, Tarf Haveli, Tarf Ale, Tarf Votur and Tarf Minher, Prant Junnar, came to the Huzur and represented that of the above-mentioned four Tarfs half the Deshmukhi belonged to Tuljali Sakhoji Hande Deshmukh and the other half to him. That the old custom prevailing in the Mughal regime required the senior member of the family to reside at court, and accordingly on the death of his father Dev Rao, he, as the senior owner of their half, remained with the Mughals at Killa Shivner and asked his uncle Ananda Rao, the younger brother of Dev Rao, to carry on the work of the Deshmukh. Ananda Rao conducted the work for twenty years and upon his death his son Shivaji continued it for ten years more. But he did not submit any account to Dadaji nor did he give the latter the produce of the watan. Dadaji therefore urged that, as the senior owner, he should have the management of the watan to which Ananda Rao had no legal claim, and Shivaji Ananda Rao should be warned that he should have the rights of a simple junior sharer only. Upon that Shivaji Ananda Rao was brought to the Huzur and on enquiry it was found that he had no claim to the management. All past account should be submitted and explained to you (Dadaji), you should manage the above-mentioned half Deshmukhi. You are accordingly ordered to do the customary work of the management of half the Deshmukhi, put your signature and use the seal and enjoy the rights and perquisites of the watan (*Hakdadk, Manpan, Inamat, Isafat*)." [5]

2. The Deshmukh's Rights and Perquisites

The Deshmukh's office, like that of the Patil, was very lucrative. The following remarks of Ephinstone are interesting: "The daishmook's profits are very great; generally, I am told, about five per cent. not only on the Revenue, but on the land; five acres in each hundred for example, will belong to the Daishmook, and a twentieth of the collections besides; and various claims in kind, as a pair of shoes, every year from each shoe-maker, a portion of ghee from those who make that preparation, etc., etc."[6] "It seems to be thought, that they ((Deshmukh and Desphande) cannot sell their Offices (though Patils and Coolcurnees can) and it is even doubtful, if they can sell their fees, though they may pawn them. Their land they can certainly sell." Whether they could sell their fees or not we do not know but that at least on one occasion the Deshmukh's fees were transferred by a *bakshishnama* is certain. The deed[7] in question has been published by Mr. V. K. Rajwade. According to this document, the Deshmukh got only two per cent of the revenue and not five per cent as Elphionstone says. As it recounts all the rights and perquisites of Deshmuh and Deshpande watans, a part of it at least is worth quoting.

1. The custom is to pay Rs. 3 from each village; out of that the Desphande will take Re. 1 and you should take the remaining Rs. 2.

2. The Shirpav from government should be taken by you first and by the Deshpande afterwards.

3. On the documents relating to watan, etc., you should put your signature, and by the side of your signature the Deshpande will put his.

4. Presents should be placed before the government officer by you first, and the Deshpande should make his presents after you.

5. Betel leaves from government as well as from others should first be taken by you and by the Desphande afterwards.

6. As for other Manpan, etc., pertaining to the watan you should accept them first and the Deshpande afterwards.

7. In the aforesaid Kasba, there is a plot for the Deshmukhi watan. You should erect a building there and live therein.

8. Take the customary dues of green vegetables from markets in the different villages and in the aforesaid Kasba, etc.

9. You should enjoy old inam land both *jirayat* and *bagayat*.

10. Take the customary bundle of fuel from the Mahars from each village at the time of the festivals.

11. Take from each village till at the time of Sankranti and *ghi* at each Shradh ceremony performed.

12. Two bhets (presents) should be taken by you and your representative employed for the work of the aforesaid Pargana.

13. Take one blanket annually from every village where Dhangars work their looms.

14. Take shoes from the shoemakers at the rate of a pair per year per village.

15. Take the customary *sayvan* dues from the said Kasba.

16. The sweepers of the mosque of Shah Daval Pidar pays Rs. 3 per year as *tabruk*; out of that Re. 1

belongs to the Deshpande; you should take the remaining two.

17. The bread money from each village should be divided equally between you and the Deshpande.
18. The musician should be rewarded by you first and then by the Deshpande.
19. Of the miscellaneous dues for miscellaneous work, you should give one-third share to the Deshpande and keep for yourself the remaining two-thirds.
20. Of the dues to the government in connection with the Pargana, the Deshpande should pay one-third and you two-thirds.

It is therefore clear that the remuneration of the Deshmukh and the Deshpande was in every way analogous to that of the Patil and the Kulkarni, and was paid by the people of their Pargana and not by the government. Their interest was therefore, closely bound up with that of the people, and for the sake of public interest, it seems that women were sometimes considered unfit to hold these offices, although the affairs of great military fiefs were often under the charge of ladies. Umabai Dabhade was often addressed by the Peshawa on matters of great political weight and we all know how skilfully the famous Ahalya Bai managed the helm of the state bark voiced by the Panch of Sarkar Junnar had decided in 1772-73 that "No Deshpande watan should in future be continued in the name of a female."[8]

3. The Kamavisdar and the Mamlatdar

During the regime of the Adilshahi and the Nizamshahi dynasties the Maharashtra country was, for revenue and administrative purposes, divided into Parganas, Sarkars and Subhas. Shivaji, however, true to his nationalising principles, divided his dominions into Mauja, Tarf and Subha. In his days the officer in charge of a Tarf was called a Havaldar, and the officer in charge of a Subha was styled as a Subhedar or Mukhya Deshadhikari. During the Peshwa period, however, we find all these terms Tarf, Pargana, Sarkar and Subha, in indiscriminate use. But the Subha was also called a Prant and Tarf and Parganas also came to be styled as Mahals. Over the small divisions were placed the Kamavisdars, and the Mamlatdars held the charge of the bigger divisions. The Mamlatdars held their office directly under the central government except in the three provinces of Khandesh, Gujrat and the Karnatak, where they were placed under officers known as Sarsubhedars. "In the Carnatic he (Sarsubhedar) was answerable for the Revenue, and appointed his own Mamlutdars; but in Candeissh he had only a general superintendence; every Mamlutdar giving in his own accounts, and making his payments direct to Government." We may, however, enter into an enquiry about the remuneration of these high officials before discussing their powers and privileges, rights and responsibilities.

4. Their Pay

A comparison of the documents will show that all the Kamavisdars did not enjoy they same remuneration, their allowance varied with the importance of the districts under their charge. Thus Trimbak Hari was appointed Kamvisdar of Sarkar Hande in the year 1740-41 on a salary of Rs. 1,000 per annum[9] while Ramchandra Ballal, Kamavisdar of Pargana Bhupal, enjoyed in the year 1743-44 a salary seven times as large.[10] The general principle seems to have been to give the Kamavisdar 4 per cent of the money advanced by him (thus in the case of the Kamvisdar of Pargana Bhupal—your salary is Rs. 7,000 at the rate of 4 per cent on the revenue of one lac and seventy-five thousand).[11] But this rule does not appear to have been uniformly followed. In the case of the Kamavisdar of Kasba Puntamba[12] quoted in the footnote it was clearly stipulated in his appointment letter that he should pay at least Rs. 20,000 in advance every year. His salary according to the former rule should have been Rs. 800 but as it was, the officer did not get more than Rs. 200 ("of the sum contracted Rs. 20,000 are to be paid in advance every year. Pay therefore Rs. 20,000 annually and get receipt."..."The salary of the Shibandi and the officers of the aforesaid Mahal as before—Rs. 200 Kamavisdar").

Generally a lump sum was granted for the Kamavisdar's office and officers minutely specifying the salary of each and every Karkun, even the ordinary foot-men not being omitted. One document will sufficiently illustrate the whole arrangement and we shall quote here that addressed to Trimbak Hari, Kamavisdar, Sarkar Hande.

"The following sum, on account of the establishment to be kept by Trimbak Hari, Kamavisdar of Sarkar Hande ,was sanctioned—

Rs. 1,000	The Kamavisdar.
Rs. 660	Palanquin for 11 months at Rs. 60 per month, service to be taken for 12 months.
Rs. 7,500	Troopers 50.

Two hundred peons to be entertained at Rs. 2-8, Rs, 2-12, or Rs. 3 per month; the salary to be paid for 12 months.

Twelve Karkuns to be employed when necessary at the chaukis (out-posts) at Rs. 3-8 per mensem.

Karkuns at the following monthly salaries payable for 10 months, service being taken for 12 months:

Rs. 25—Mazumdar.

Rs. 25—Naroram Fadnis.

Rs. 25—Shivaji Dadaji Chitnis.

Rs. 25—Shirmaji Avji (a Karkun).

Rs. 20—Janardan Bhashkar (a Karkun).

Rs. 60—Four Karkuns-Visaji Yadava, Bhikaji Tandev, Moro Shamraj, and Girmaji, on Rs. 15 each.

Rs. 48—Four Karkuns on Rs. 12 each, viz., Babuji Trimall, Govind Shivdev, Shivaji Ram and Venkaji Anant."

It shows how much attention was paid even to minute details. Two points in this document demand our special notice. We find here the peculiar custom of paying for ten or eleven months, while a full year's service was demanded from the officer in question. The practice was, however, not peculiar to the civil departments only, but was followed with equal persistency in the army, navy and the forts. The second point is the allowance granted for the Kamavisdar's palanquin. It should not be compared with the travelling allowance of modern days, or with the allowance granted for the Governor's household. In those days, paanquin and sunshaders were granted to officers of special merit in recognition of their public service, as the British Indian government confers titles like Rai Bahadur or Khan Bhadur on distinguished public servants. All such honours were accompanied by suitable grants for their proper upkeep, because the Peshwa was anxious that his officers should not find their hard-won honours burdensome.

5. Their Duties

The Mamlatdars and the Kamavisdars were the Peshwa's representative in their districts. So their duties and responsibilities were of a most comprehensive character and embraced all possible aspects of affairs. They had to look after the welfare of the cultivator, they had to devise means for improving agriculture, they had to encourage new industries, they had to enquire into disputes of both civil and criminal nature, and appoint a Panchayat for decision. This however does not exhaust the list of their innumerable duties. The Shibandi of the district was under their control and so was the police force. Religious and social questions were often referred to the enquiry, and even the devil with all his evil powers was not beyond their jurisdiction, they could compel the devotees of his black majesty to recall the evil influence of their dread master. It is needless to say that these ample powers gave their owners ample opportunities for corruption and the Maratha officers sometimes did succumb to the charms of gold. Fryer and Broughton, writing at different times and of different courts, alluded to the Maratha officer's inordinate love of presents. Fryer says how an officer of Shivaji's court actually told the English ambassador that if he would have his Work speedily effected, and without any impediment, it was necessary to be at some more charge to present Officers with *Pamerins*, who were not in their List of Presents." Broughton similary describe how Daulat Rao Scindhia did not hesitate to demand a *khelat* for a nephew that was no more, on the plea of soothing the feelings of the disconsolate mother. This love of presents, in vulgar language called bribe, was no monopoly of the Maratha officer alone. His Muhammadan, or even his English, brother was no better. Hawkins and Roe's account of the Mughal officer's curiosity about the contents of the merchants' bales is not complimentary to those grand dignitaries;and Shakespeare's picture of "the justice in fair round belly with good capon lined" found man imitators. It was a common failing all over the world which people in those days were ready to wink at.

6. The Darakhdars

Fryer and Broughton's censures were meant for the officers of the court. Our friends in the districts—the Kamavisdars and the Mamlatdars were not above the common temptation; and as a check upon them were utilised the hereditary officers. Of these we have already come across one set—the district officers, known as Deshmukhs and Deshpandes, and we know they were used as a check on the Mamlatdars, and no accounts were passed, unless corroborated by corresponding accounts from them (Elphinstone). The other set may be conveniently described as the provincial hereditary officers generally known as Darakhdars or feemen. These Darakhdars were always used as a check on the chief officers of every department, the army and the navy included. None of these hereditary officers could be dismissed by the Mamlatdar, nor could he compel them to perform any duties except those specifically assigned to them by long practice and custom. Not that the

Mamlatdars never tried to do away as with their independent subordinates; but in such cases the Darakhdar could confidently look to wards the Peshwa's authority to back him and reinstate him in his ancestral office, and the peremptory order always ended with the usual phrase "that the work of the office should be taken from his hands." On the provincial staff besides twelve Karkuns there were (1) Dewan or Minister, (2) Auditor or Mazumdar, (3) the Registrar or Fadnavis, (4) Secretary or Daftardar, (5) Treasurer or Potnis, (6) Assay clerk or Potdar, (7) Petty Registrar or Sabhasad and (8) Under-Secretary or Chitnis. As these officers had not to depend on the Mamlatdar for their pay, they were in every respect independent of him. It was therefore, quite natural that they were expected to be efficient checks on any intended malpractice on the part of the Mamlatdar and to report to the central government all lapses on his part if any ever happened. Moreover their duties were divided and assigned in such a manner that the Mamlatdar could not act independently of them. "The *divan* as the chief factor under the *mamlatdar* countersigned all letters and orders. The Auditor or *majumdar* approved deeds or accounts before they went to the registrar or *fadnavis*. The *fadnavis* dated all deeds and orders, prepared a daily waste book, fastened notes to the money-bags, dated the yearly village rent settlements, and brought the books to the head-quarters. The *daftardar*, from the registrar's waste book, made up the ledger and sent a monthly abstract to the head-quarters. The *potnis* kept a record of collections and the balance of cash, and helped in writing the waste book and the ledger. The *potdar*, of whom there were always two, examined the coins. The *sabhasad* kept a register of petty suits and reported them to the *mamlatdar*. The *chitnis* wrote and answered despatches."[13] A ninth officer the Jamenis is mentioned in a document of the time of the first Madhava Rao and his duties are enumerated as follows:

"(1) The records of the inspection of Jirayet and Bagayet lands by the inspecting officers, should be laid by them before the Jamenis, whose duty it will then be to fix the revenue demand after such enquiry as he may think necessary and to report the fact to the Karbhari.

(2) The Jamenis should receive all revenue accounts and watch the closing of the accounts and see that the collections and arrears are correctly noted.

(3) The Jamenis has authority to increase the revenue of a village or to grant remissions, or to reduce the revenue for a term of years.

(4) Orders for the recovery of arrears from villages should be issued by the Jamenis.

(5) Kowls for the abatement of revenue should be issued by the Jamenis.

(6) A ledger showing the amount received and the amount due from each village, should be prepared by the Jamenis from the day-book of the Fadnis." (Joshi's translation).[14]

These Darakhdars, severally and jointly, served as a check not only upon the Mamlatdar but upon each other as well.

A glance at the following two lists enumerating the duties of the Mazumdar and the Daftardar will show how the Mazumdar supervised the work of the Jamenis, Fadnis and Chitnis, and how the Daftardar while auditing the accounts submitted by the Kamavisdar had to explain every matter to the Fadnis. In the year 1764-65 a letter was written to Vyankat Narayan, Mamlatdar of Dharwar, recounting the duties of his Mazumdar, Ragho Ganagadhar, as follows:

(1) He should see that the day-book is balanced every-day.

(2) He should authenticate every letter and account prepared by the Fadnis or Chitnis.

(3) He should see that the salary registers of sowars and soldiers newly employed are correctly totalled. He should muster every month the sowars and soldiers already in service.

(4) He should prepare estimates of receipts and expenditure in regard to the portion of the taluka proposed to be entrusted to a Sub-Mamlatdar, and the detailed account to be taken from the Mamlatdar should be received through the Mazumdar.

(5) Change of Mamlatdars should not be made without his knowledge (B. P. Joshi's Translation).[15]

Another letter in the same year and to the same officer lays down the duties of the Daftardar as follows:

(1) The day-book should be written by the Fadnis and the ledger should be prepared from it by the Daftardar.

(2) The annual estimates of receipts and expenditure should be prepared by the Daftardar; the detailed accounts submitted by the Kamavisdars at the end of the year should be examined by him with reference to the records.

(3) He should enquire into loans advanced, and their recoveries.

(4) He should examine the accounts relating to the sowars entertained from the Mahal.

(5) He should explain every matter to the Fadnis, and they both to the officer Vyankatrao Narayan (Mamlatdar). Orders to subordinates should not be issued by the Fadnis direct, but through the Daftardar. During the Fadnis's absence his work should be done by the Daftardar, (Joshi's Translation).[16]

7. Beheda and Rasad

We may now turn to two measures generally adopted to restrain the Mamlatdaar from misgovernment. The first was the payment of a big advance paid at the time of his appointment to be realised later on from the revenue of the district under his charge. This advance served as a security against misconduct and at the same time relieved the Peshwa of his financial difficulties to a certain extent. Interest was however paid on this *rasad* at a rate varying from 1 to 1½ per cent per month. The second was the *beheda*. It was an estimate of possible income and expenditure most carefully drawn up by experienced officers in the Peshwa's daftar, and with a knowledge of minute details and yet unsurpassed and unequalled. In his revenue collection the Mamlatdar had to be guided by this annual estimate or beheda and in the case of the Sub-Mamlatdar or Kamavisdar under him—the beheda was drawn up by the Mamlatdar's Mazumdar as we have already seen. But all these cautions could not entirely prevent evil practices in the Peshwa's government; and *antast* or bribe became a regular and quite and ordinary item in their accounts. Elphinstone remarks that "The sources of their profit were concealment of receipts (especially fees, fines, and other undefined collections), false charges for remissions, false musters, non-payment of pensions, and other frauds in expenditure. The grand source of their profit was an extra assessment above the revenue, which was called Sauder Warrid Puttee. It was levied to pay the expenses of the district not provided for by Government, and naturally afforded a great field for speculation: one of the chief of these expenses was called the Durbar Khurch of Untust. This was originally applied secretly to bribe the ministers and auditors. By degrees, their bribes became established fees, and the account was audited like the rest; but as bribes were still required, another increase of collection took place for this purpose; and as the auditors or accountants did not search minutely into these delicate transactions, the Mamlatdar generally collected much more for himself, than he did for his patrons." The Mamlatdar, however, took good care that the imposts might not fall heavy on the rayats, for it was to his interest that they should be well off and, as Elphinstone himself points out, the only party that suffered was the government.

The Mamlatdar and the Kamavisdar were generally appointed for short terms, and in Shivaji's time transfer from one district to another was frequent. During the Peshwa period, however, they generally succeeded in getting their term of office repeatedly renewed, unless they were guilty of any serious abuse of their authority; and frequently the Mamlatdar was left in charge of the same district for thirty or forty years. After his death his son might succeed him in his office, not as a matter of right but as one of favour. Consequently the Mamlatdars thought they had permanent interest in the prosperity of their districts, and whatever they did they always remembered that the goose that lays the golden egg must not be roughly handled. If a bad Mamlatdar intent on present gain at the cost of permanent interest forgot this axiom of good government, he was promptly removed from his office by the Peshwa. (This remark however does not apply to Baji Rao II).

The small division called Mahals or Tarfs were also governed on the same principle. A non-hereditary officer, the Havaldar, was checked and assisted by two hereditary officers, Mazumdar and Fadnis in revenue matters. The duties of the Mahal Mazumdar and Mahal Fadnis corresponded to those of the provincial officers of the same names. In addition to these revenue officers there were in every Mahal four militia officers who demand our notice here. The Hashamnavis kept a roll showing each man's name, family name, his native village, arms, and pay. The Asham Fadnis had to keep the accounts of the militia and had also to keep records of the musters if there was no separate officer for that purpose. The Hazirinavis, as the name of his office implies, kept the muster roll, and the Asham Daftardar made the militia ledger book.

It is needles to say that these officers did not generally interfere in the internal administration of the village. The Mamlatdar of the Kamavisdar assessed the rent for each village in consultation with the Patil, sent a Shibandi force for revenue collection if the Patil asked for any, appointed Panchayats in course entertained complaints against the village officers. In short, they served as a link between the local authorities at the base and the Secretariat at the top.

7. Classification of Lands

The Muhammadan theories of revenue had been enunciated by the Arab theologians long before the conquest of India, and the Hindu principles had been laid down by old lawgivers like Manu centuries before the birth of the Prophet of Mecca. The growth of these two sets of Revenue theories without and within India had therefore been altogether independent of each other. Yet they sometimes happened to be so similar that their interaction on each other had the same effect as the union of two similar Mendelian gamets. This happened with regard to the principles governing the classification of land in particular. We have already seen how Kautilya and the author of the Shukranitisara recognised the distinction between dry and irrigated land and the method of irrigation as a determining factor in assessment. The Marathas variously classified their land according to fertility, the nature of the crops, and the method of irrigation. This principle of classification was recognised by Musulman theologians also. "Al-Mawardi discusses as follows the factors which determine the tax-bearing capacity of land. The person who assesses the *kharaj* on a piece of land should consider the capacity of land, which varies according to the three factors, each factor affecting the amount of *kharaj* more or less. One of the factors pertaining to the land itself is the quality of the land by virtue of which the crop grown on it is rich, or the defect which causes the produce to be small. The second factor released to the kind of crop, since grains and fruits vary in price, some fetching a higher price than the others, and the *kharaj* must therefore be assessed accordingly. The third factor pertains to the method of irrigation, for the crop that has been irrigated with water carried on the back of beasts or raised by a water-wheel, cannot stand the same rate of *kharaj* which could be charged on land watered by running water of rain."[17]

The Muhammadan rulers in India did not always strictly follow the financial theories of Muhammadan theologians. Thus in Akbar's classification of land we find that more attention was paid to the state of cultivation than to the factors enumerated by Al-Mawardi[18] although the *polaj* and *porauti* lands were divided into three classes,—good, middle and bad. But Akbar permitted special rates for some special crops as Abul Fazl informs us: "The revenue from indigo, poppy, pan, turmeric, pignut (*Trapa biopinosa*), hemp, kachalu (*Arum colocasia*), pumpkin, pinna (*Lawsonia mermis*), cucumbers, badrang (a species of cucumber), the egg plant (*Solanum melongena*), radishes, carrots, karela (*Momordica charantia*), kakura, tendas and muskmelons, not counted as produce, was ordered to be paid in ready money at the rates hereafter mentioned."[19] Murshid Quli Khan, during his Dewanshi of the Deccan, not only "distinguished arable land from rocky soils and water-courses," but also recognised "the method of irrigation as a determining factor in assessment." "Where the crop depended on rainfall, the State took one half of it. Where agriculture depended on well irrigation the share of the State was one-third in the case of grain, and from one-ninth to one-fourth in the case of grape, sugarcane, anise, plantain, pea-wort, and other special and high priced crops requiring laborious watering and length of culture. Where the field was irrigated from canals (pat) the proportion of the revenue to the crop varied, being sometimes higher and sometimes lower than in lands irrigated from wells."[20]

In Murshid Quli's system we come across almost all the characteristics of the Maratha practice. The arable land is distinguished from rocky soils and the different methods of irrigation are taken into consideration. The Muhammadan system, however, did not in these respects make any new contirbution to the evolution of the Maratha system. But a special rate for "special and high priced crops requiring laborious watering and length of culture" was the new feature introduced by the Muhammadans. In fact the Marathas went a step further; they did more for the cultivation of palms, jack trees, and Undani trees than what Murshid did for grapes, sugar-cane, anise, plantain and pea-wort, and they continued the Musulman practice with regard to sugar-cane plantations.

8. Principle of Assessment

Let us turn to the principles of assessment, and in this connection our attention is naturally attracted by the istawa system which prevailed under the early Hindu rulers. This system was not revived by the Marathas, as it was a living practice, a principle familiar both to the rulers and the ruled, when Shivaji founded an independent kingdom. We must therefore look to the Muhammadan historians, and not to the old Sanskrit works on law and polity, for the history of its transmission. It is not possible to supply every link and give a connected story, but it is certain that the principle was well-known in Akbar's days and probably in the age of Sher Shah also, for Akbar was indebted for many of his revenue regulations to the great Pathan Emperor. The istawa principle was applied by Akbar in the assessment of *chachar* and *banjar* lands. Abul Fazl writes, with regard to the assessment of *chachar* land, "When either from excessive rain or through an inundation, the land falls out of cultivation the husbandmen are, at first, in considerable distress. In the first year, therefore, but two-fifths of the produce is taken; in the second three-fifths; in the third, four-fifths and in the fifth, the ordinary revenue."[21] The same writer observes about *banjar* lands, "In *banjar* land for the first year, one or two *sers* are taken from each bigha in the second year, five *sers;* in the third year, a sixth of the produce; in the fourth year, a fourth share together with one *dam;* in other years a third suffices. This varies somewhat during inundations. In all cases the husbandman may pay in money or kind as most convenient."[22] Here also the process of evolution is perceptible. While Akbar applied the istawa principle in the assessment of chachar (land that has lain fallow for three or four years) and banjar (land uncultivated for five years and more) land alone, the Marathas applied this principle in the assessment of all classes of lands, good, bad or middling, whether under cultivation or fallow. It should also be noted that the husbandman, under the Peshwa's Government, did pay in cash or kind whatever was convenient to him.

9. Payment by Instalment

Payment by instalment was also allowed by Muhammadan rulers. In a farman addressed to his officers, Akbar advises them thus, "Let them collect rent from the subjects in an easy manner, in order that all lands may be cultivated and blessed with population. In collecting rent from the cultivators, do so piecemeal, and deviate in no degree from the agreement which has been made."[23] The Muhammadan theologians also advocated collection of the Jizyah by instalments. "Abu Yusuf maintains that it should be collected by instalments every two months and Muhammad Ibn al-Hasan, every month, in order that the tax may become more onerous for the tax-payers and more beneficial to the Moslems."[24] Akbar's intention on the contrary was to make the payment more easy. We do not know for certain whether he followed the guidance of Abu Yusuf or Muhammad Ibn al-Hasan in recommending collection by instalment, but it is certain that he acted on far different principles.

10. The Agency of Collection

The agency of collection was practically the same under the Muhammadans and the Marathas. The village communities flourished undisturbed and the village headmen were responsible for revenue collection and the village accountant kept the accounts. The account books were sent to the government officials almost in the same manner under both the Governments. "The *Patwari,*" says Abul Fazl, "of each village was to apportion (the village) name by name, among the various subordinate agents, and the collectors were to send the cash under the seal of the Patwari to the treasurer."[25] The Maquaddams were considered to indispensable that Murshid Quli Khan, during his Dewanship in the Deccan, found it necessary to appoint new village headmen where the old family had either died out or migrated to some other place.

11. Remission of Rent

Like the *paymalli* compensation remission of rent in times of famine were also made by Mughal Emperors. They thus set a strong precedent for the Marathas to follow, even though the principle was not new. One case of such remission of rent will suffice here. In 1629 Gujrat and the Deccan were visited by a terrible famine, and Abdul Hamid Lahori tells us that, "Under the directions of the wise and generous Emperor taxes amounting to nearly seventy lacs of rupees were remitted by the revenue officers—a sum amounting to nearly eighty *krors* from *dams,* and amounting to one eleventh part of the whole revenue. When such remissions were made from the exchequer it may be conceived how great were the reductions made by the nobles who held *jagirs* and *mansabs.*"[26] Akbar was contented, when a similar calamity overtook Hindustan, with the distribution of alms as Shaikh Nurul Hakk informs us, "During the year 1004 H. there was a scarcity of rain throughout the whole of Hindustan, and a fearful famine raged continuously for three or four years. The king ordered that alms should be distributed in all the cities, and Nawab Shaikh Farid Bokhari, being ordered to superintend and control their distribution, did all in his power to relieve the general distress of the people. Public tables were spread, and the army was increased in order to afford maintenance to the poor people."[27]

Another commendable example that the Mughal Emperors set before the Marathas was that of granting rent-free land to deserving physicians for rendering their professional service free of charge to the suffering humanity. Muhammadans and Hindus believed alike in astrology and long association and spirit of inborn tolerance had generated in the Hindus that reverence for the mosque and the saints of their Musulman neighbours which devotees of one faith seldom entertain for another. The Sultans of Bijapur and Ahmadnagar therefore granted rent-free lands in *inam* to successful and learned Hindu astrologers while rent-free lands were granted by Shivaji and his successors for the maintenance of mosques and shrines of Muhammadan saints. The Maratha rulers also granted such *inam* to physicians of all faith and nationality for free distribution of medicine. Here, however, they had the example of the Muhammadan rulers before their eyes. In the year 989 of the Hijira a farman was granted to a Parsi physician which runs as follows—"Order,

Let the revenue collectors and officials and *Desais* and *Qanungos* of the township of Navasari be informed that whereas the Parsi Mahr Tabib (physician) is a deserving person and does not possess any other means of subsistence, and whereas he has offered himself as a sacrifice, for the blessed life of His Exalted Majesty (May God perpetuate his dominion), the extent of four *Auls* of cultivated land and culturable waste, one *Aul* of cultivated and three *Auls* of culturable (waste), within the environs of the aforesaid township, has been settled upon him as his *wazifah.* As soon as they receive intimation of this Parwanah, they should hand over to him the said land after fixing its boundaries and setting it apart, so that having tilled it according to his ability, he may spend the proceeds thereof in (providing) the means of subsistence and devote himself with a tranquil bind to praying for the permanence of His Majesty's powerful Kingdom. Let them know their duty and regard obedience in this matter as a positive obligation and do nothing contrary to the same. Written on the 21st of the sacred month of Muharram 989."[28]

It is certain that the Parsi Tabib did not get the *inam* in question for merely "Praying for the permanence of His Majesty's powerful Kingdom," but for his professional services to the suffering subjects of His Majesty. Any doubt on this point is removed by another document quoted by Professor Hodivala in his *Studies in Parsi History.* "The children of Qiam Tabib beg and request the evidence of all those, who have any knowledge of the matter, to state whether the person aforesaid cures the ailments of the needy poor and distressed of the township of Navasari and whether his means of subsistence depend on fifty Bighas extent of land with trees thereon, in the said township. If any one is cognizant of the fact of the aforesaid Tabib having cured the diseases of the needy and the indigent, let him affix, for God's sake, his testimony below (for which), he will receive his reward from the Lord and deserve thanks from men."[29] The request was answered by several Muhammadan gentlemen who attested to the truth of the statement and attached their seal and signature to the paper quoted above. It should be noted that the children of Qiam Tabib were the descendants of Mahr Tabib of the first document and it is clear that they enjoyed the *inam* in lieu of the service their anncestor and father rendered to the needy and the indigent of their native town. The Peshwas did not open hospitals and charitable dispensaries, they considered their duties performed when they granted some rent-free land in *inam* to some physician, whether he was a Hindu or a Muhammadan or even a Portuguese did not matter much, who had the public spirit and generosity of treating the poor and the indigent sick free of charge.

12. Kauls

Kauls have been referred to in the farmans addressed to Muhammad Hashim and Rasikdas and we have seen in Book II how common this pratice was in the Peshwa days. There is reason to believe that the Marathas were indebted to the Mughals for this excellent practice although the theory under lying it was older than the Muhammadan conquest. While engaged in a war against the Portuguese the Mughal officers often tried to induce the frightened peasants to come back to their villages and carry on the cultivation of their deserted fields by granting them kauls. Manucci, who had first-hand knowledge of the Deccan affairs, writes as follows: "As soon as the governor approached the Portuguese villages, the frightened peasants took to flight. Upon noticing this the governor sent for the village headmen and treating them courteously reasured them, and told them that they ought to remain in their villages and go on cultivating their fields as usual. For, so he assured them, no one would interfere with them. He sent them away contented, giving presents to each according to his merits."[30]

13. Taxes and Cesses

If the Mughals had been instrumental in the survival of many good Hindu practices, they were no less responsible for many of the vexatious cesses and dues. This was but natural, human nature begin what it is. The Muhammadan rulers, on their assumption of the Government of India, found that many taxes and cesses were levied by its former rulers and they were in no hurry to abolish them. Sometimes the conscience of such orthodox Musulman Emperors as Firuz Shah Tughlak, and Aurangzib was pricked because some of these taxes did not quite conform to the injunctions of the Qurran and they abolished them. Benevolent despots like Akbar and Jahangir abolished many extra cesses and abwabs because they were irksome to the trader and cultivator. But these prohibitions had little effect in the distant provinces where the local officers and jagirdars paid but scant respect to the Emperor's wishes. Only in the big cities and the metropolis could these prohibitions be enforced, but even there it had only a temporary effect. After a few years the vexatious cesses and abwabs were all revived; and the Marathas continued to levy these dues when they became the masters of the land.

1. Lagnapatti or marriage cess was certainly one of these old dues, levied by Hindu rulers of Vijayanagar and abolished by them in the sixteenth century. We find Lagnapatti and Patdam frequently mentioned in Marathi documents, and the cess survived till the British conquest. The Marathas did not rise to power immediately after the abolition of the marriage cess by the Vijaynagar rulers in the 16th century, but in the meantime the great Akbar continued to levy it in his empire. Abul Fazl informs us, "His Majesty also takes a tax from both parties,

to enable them to show their gratitude. The payment of this tax is looked upon as auspicious. *Mancabdars* commanding from five to one thousand, pay 10 Muhars, Mancabdars commanding from one thousand to five hundred 4 Muhars, Mancabdars to commanders of forty 1 Muhur, do to commanding commanders of ten 4 R. The latter fee is also paid by rich people. The middle classes pay 1 R. and common people one *dam*. In demanding this tax, the officers have to pay regard to the circumstances of the father of the bride."[31] During the Peshwas regime the marriage cess was levied at the rate of 8 annas in case of a marriage and 1 Re. when it was a re-marriage.

2. Among the taxes remitted by Akbar is mentioned *Sardarakhti*[32] a tax on each tree. Jahangir also says, "Thanks to the Almighty God, that no revenue on fruit trees has been taken during my reign; and I gave orders that if any one were to plant a garden in cultivated land he was not to pay any revenue."[33] So it is evident that sardarakhti was levied before Jahangir and Akbar, but though abolished by them it was revived later on. In Maratha days the tax was known as jhadjhadora.

3. Ashva Zakati is a cess we have mentioned in a previous Book. It is interesting to note that a similar tax is mentioned by Abul Fazl. "From foresight and on account of the large profits of the horse-dealers, His Majesty enforced a tax of three Rupees for every Iraqi Mujammas and Arab, imported from Kabul and Persia; two and a half Rupees for every Turkish and Arabian horse imported from Quandahar, and two for Kabul horses and Indian Arab breed."[34] Manucci also mentions a similar tax.[35] "Most of the horses used by the duty Mogul come from the regions of Balkh, Bukhara and Kabul. Thence come every year more than one hundred thousand, and

on them the King makes a great profit by the duty he imposes. At the crossing of the Indus alone a payment twenty-five per cent on their value is made."

4. There cannot be any doubt that *gau shumari* or a tax on each head of oxen[36] abolished by Akbar, was the Mughal prototype of the Maratha Shingshingoti, but it is needless to multiply instances. "Rahdari which was collected on every highway frontier and ferry, and brought in a large sum to the revenue," and Pandari (or (Pandharpatti) a ground or house cess, which was paid throughout the Imperial dominions by every tradesman and dealer, from the butcher, the potter and the green-groccer to the draper, jeweller and banker" had both been prohibited by Emperor Aurangzib.[37] This prohibition however was not quite effective. Khafi Khan tells us, "Although his gracious and beneficent Majesty remitted these taxes, and issued strict orders prohibiting their collection, the avaricious propensities of men prevailed, so that, with the exception of pandari, which, being mostly obtained from the capital and the chief cities, felt the force of the abolition, the royal prohibition had no effect and faujdars and jagirdars in remote places did not withhold their hands from these exactions." And again, "The rahdari in particular is condemned by righteous and just men as a most vexatious impost, and oppressive to travellers but a large sum is raised by it. In most parts of the Imperial territories the faujdars and jagirdars by force and tyranny, now exact more than ever from the traders and poor necessitous travellers."[38] So it is no wonder that the Marathas should continue to exact rahdari and taxes analogous to pandari as the Mughals did before them. They had accepted the bad as well as the good points of th administrative system which they found in operation when they wrested the land from their Islamic masters.

It is needless to go into details about every tax and cess. It will suffice here if some of the taxes and cesses levied by Muhammadans and afterwards continued by the Marathas are mentioned.

1. Beth Begari[39]
2. Belekati
3. Telpati
4. Tup
5. Hejib
6. Mohtarfa
8. Churpatti
9. Bat Chapai
10. Kotowali
14. Wancharai.[40]

Khafi Khan has mentioned, among other taxes, cesses and abwabs, prohibited by Aurangzib, "the fourth part of debts recovered by the help of Magistrates from creditors." We have seen in Book II, how creditors had to pay a fee amounting to twenty-five per cent of the money recovered from debtors with state help under the Peshwa regime. Customs, specially when favourable to the powerful, die hard indeed!

Customs and transit duties were levied in India by her Hindu rulers from very early times. The Muhammadan kings who succeeded them continued the old duties as usual and sometimes added to their incidence. In the early years of the Mughal rule, when Babar laid the foundation of his power at Delhi, "there was a duty levied on the frontier on goods" and "there were transit duties on merchandise transported from one part of the country to another."[41] Jahangir prohibited transit duties[42] but there cannot be any doubt that they continued to be levied. "Mundy, Thevenot, and Tavenier, who took an interest in such topics, show us a regular system of transit dues in force throughout large portions of the country, and Father Sebastian Manrique tells how the passport granted to him as an ecclesiastic to travel from Lahore to the mouth of the Indus was used by a merchant of his party to evade many demands during the journey."[43] Thevenot counted, on the road from Aurangabad to Golkonda, sixteen taxing posts in twenty-three leagues.[44] Customs, tolls and transit duties were collected throughout the territories of the Sultan of Golkonda even at the time of the Mughal conquest.[45] The Marathas did not cease to impose these time-honoured duties, but in their time the hardship of the merchants and tradesmen were considerably ameliorated as a class of men known as Hundikaris undertook to transport all commodities from one place to another for a single payment.

Customs duties were during the Peshwa regime farmed out to tax-contractors for a specified sum. Here also the Marathas seem to have followed in the footsteps of the Mughals. Manucci not only mentions tax-contractors, but gives a graphic account of their shameless conduct.[46]

Thus we find that many of the cesses and taxes had been inherited by the Marathas from their ancient Hindu ancestors through the Muhammadans, while for others they were indebted to the Muhammadans alone. The term Zakat they must have borrowed from their Islamic rulers; but their Zakat could hardly be identified with the Poor tax which every follower of the Prophet of Mecca deemed it his bounden duty to pay for the benefit of the poorer and more indigent members of their community. The payment of Zakat formed part of the Islamic faith, technically therefore it could not be levied for the benefit of the State nor was an unbeliever entitled to pay it.[47] But it has to be remembered that Zakat was collected from tradesmen too for complete *nisabs* of articles of trade they possessed by the ashirs. "The ashirs were collectors stationed by the *imam* on the public road in order to collect the Zakat of Moslem traders, as well as the tolls imposed on the *dhimmi* and *harbi* traders who pass him." It is not difficult to guess how the Zakat which originally formed an obligation on the part of all Muhammadan householders who possessed the taxable amount of property, became a source of income of the Non-Muslim Maratha rulers. The Muhammadans of course brought their theories of finance with them and tried to enforce them as far as possible, and as the payment of Zakat was an obligation on the part of all true believers, they continued to pay them. Gradually the more unscrupulous of the Muslim rulers began to appropriate the Zakat collected by public officers for their own use instead of properly disbursing it according to the injunctions of the Quran. The Hindus also became familiar with its collection by officers on the roadside and whether they were familiar or not with its origin, they began to regard it as source of revenue like other taxes and cesses. When therefore the Marathas replaced the Muhammadans the term lost its original Quaranic sense and acquired a far wider meaning. It was collected from all traders irrespective of their faith, caste and creed, and like some other taxes were farmed out to a contractor. But sometimes as we have seen a Kamavisdar of Zakat was appointed to check the oppression and corrupt practices of the tax-contractors.

14. Standardisation of Price

Before concluding this chapter on the revenue principles we may take a passing notice of a Hindu practice transmitted to the Marathas by the Muslims. All Maratha rulers from Shivaji to Baji Rao II actively interfered in the manufacturing industries of their land and tried to control the prices of the necessaries of life. This practice is as old as the Artha Shastra of Kautilya. But it must be conceded that the Muslim rulers of India did much to keep it alive. Allauddin Khiliji tried to keep down his military expenses by keeping down the price of all necessaries of life. He did not try to achieve its purpose by a skilful balancing of demand and supply. These principles were perhaps undreamt-of in his time in Europe and Asia. But like a true autocrat he arbitrarily fixed the price of all necessary articles of food. Anybody who was detected in demanding a higher rate was severally punished.[48] But

Allauddin was not the only prince to aim at a standardisation of prices. In Mughal days it was one of the duties of the Kotwal to supervise the purchase and sale of goods in the market place. Akbar fixed the price of building materials after a careful enquiry to the satisfaction of all as Abul Fazl informs us.[49] And the principle of state-controlled price survived till the English introduced the idea of free trade and economic non-interference in India.

REFERENCES

1. Elphinstone, *Report*, p. 21.
2. P. D., Vol. III, p. 220.
3. P. D., Vol. VII, p. 19.
4. P. D., Vol. VI, pp. 322-323.
5. P. D., Vol. VI, pp. 323-324.
6. Elphinstone, *Report*, 2nd edition, pp. 21-22.
7. Rajwade, *Sources of Maratha History*, Vol. X, p. 114.
8. The circumstances of the case are as follows:

   In the year 1768-69. Girmabai, widow of Krishnaji Hari Deshpande, represented that there had been no lineal descendant in her family for 4 or 5 generations, and that it was therefore usual in the family for the widow to adopt a son and have the watan continued in her adopted son's name: that the adopted son had agreed to enter her name along with his, but after sometime he had omitted to do so. Her adopted son Bhagvant Rao died leaving a boy of five or seven years, and his officers refused to recognise the authority of the lady. The lady, therefore, urged that her joint authority with the boy should be recognised, and the prayer was granted. The unreasonable interference of the lady, however, led to mismanagement, and three years later we find Amrit Rao petitioning the government that some measures for good management should be taken. He also pointed out that if the claim of Girmabai was recognised by the government as a principle, the same claim would be made after her death by Amrit Rao's step-mother. The government appointed a Panchayat for decision, and they gave their verdict entirely in favour of Amrit Rao. They decided that not even a moiety of power should be surrendered to Girmabai, her name however should be continued in documents so long as she lived, but in future no watan should be continued in the name of a female, P. D., Vol. VII, pp. 112-113.

9. P. D. Vol. III, p. 254.
10. P. D. Vol. III, p. 255.
11. P. D. Vol. III, p. 255.

I beg to differ from Rao Bahadur D. B. Parasnis who seems to think that in the above two cases the officers got as their salary 4 per cent of the revenue of their districts. In his English summary of documents Nos. 407 and 409, Vol. I, `Balaji Baji Rao Peshwa', he says—"the remuneration of the Kamavisdar of Bhopal was fixed at Rs. 4 per cent of the revenue received." And again "The Mamlat of Bundelkhand was entrusted to one person, and Rs. 3,20,000 were received from him in advance on account of land revenue. His remuneration was fixed at Rs. 12,800 at Rs. 4 p.c. of the revenue." It is doubtful whether the word *rasad* in these two documents means—revenue, it stands rather for the money that these officers had to advance at the time of their appointment, and a simple calculation shows that the salary amounted to just 4 p.c. of what they had paid in advance. Ramchandra Balla Kamavisdar of Bhopal had paid Rs. 1,75,000 and his salary was Rs. 7,000. Lakshman Shankar Mamlatdar of Bundelkhand paid Rs. 3,20,000 and got Rs. 12,800 for his salary. Trimbak Babu Rao was appointed Kamavisdar of Kasba Puntamba (in the year 1759-60) for 5 years. The revenue of the village was to rise at the following rate:

1759-60	45,000
1760-61	46,000
1761-62	47,000
1762-63	48,000
1763-64	49,000

So his salary at the rate of 4 p.c. of the revenue would have been at least Rs. 1,800 but actually it was Rs. 200 only (see p. 269, Balaji Baji Rao, Vol. 1). Nor can the Rao Bahadur urge that the *rasad* demanded always amounted to one year's revenue. We have a series of documents in the same volume contradicting such a supposition.

12. P. D., Vol. III, p. 277.
13. *Bombay Gazetteer*, Poona Volume (XVIII), p. 332.
14. P. D., Vol. VII, pp. 123-124.

15. P. D., Vol. VII, pp. 125-126.
16. P. D., Vol. VII, pp. 126-127.
17. Aghnides, p. 381.
18. Jarrett, *Ain-i-Akbari*, Vol. II, p. 63.
19. Jarrett, *Ain-i-Akbari*, Vol. II, p. 65.
20. Jadunath Sarkar, *Aurangzib*, Vol. I, pp. 192-193.
21. Jarrett, *Ain-i-Akbari*, Vol. II, p. 67.
22. *Ibid*, p. 68.
23. Bird, *Statistical History of Gujrat*, p. 394.
24. Aghnides, p. 405.
25. Elliot and Dowson, Vol. VI, p. 64.
26. Elliot and Dowson, Vol. VII, p. 25.
27. Elliot and Dowson, Vol. VI, 193.
28. Hodivala, *Studies in Parsi History*, pp. 172-173.
29. Hodivala, *Studies in Parsi History*, pp. 186-187.
30. Manucci, ed. Irvine, Vol. II. p. 229.
31. Blochmann, *Ain-i-Akbari*, Vol. II, p. 66. Also Thomas, *Revenue Resources of the Moghul Empire*, p. 170.
32. Jarrett, *Ain-i-Akbari*, Vol, II, p. 66. Also Thomas, *Revenue Resources of the Moghul Empire*, p. 17.
33. Elliot and Dowson, Vol. VI, p. 365.
34. Blochmann, *Ain-i-Akbari*, Vol. I, p. 215.
35. Manucci, ed. Irvine, Vol. II, p. 371.
36. Jarrett, *Ain-i-Akbari*, Vol. II, p. 66.
37. Elliot & Dowson, Vol. VII, p. 247.
38. *Ibid*, p. 248.
39. Forced labour existed under the Portuguese in a very rigorous form. Even the Brahmans were not exempted from it. See da Cunlm. Origin of Bombay, pp. 116-118.
40. For these see Thomas, *Revenue Sources of the Moghul Empire*, pp. 5, 16-19. Manucci, ed. Irvine, Vol. II, pp. 386-387. Elliot and Dowson, Vol. VII, pp. 247-248. Bird, Gujarat, pp. 113-114. Jarrett, *Ain-i-Akbari*, Vol. II. pp. 66-67. The Portuguese generally took care to preserve the old revenue customs and usages as far as possible. A Commission with Antonio Francisco Benjamin Pinto as

President and Xavier da Cunha, V. A. Ceaser de Mello, Francisco João Jacob Coutinho as members were appointed (2nd, May 1867) to report on the practices, usages and customs regarding payment of rents. etc., in the villages of Daman. They submitted their report on the 24th August, 1871. The report has been published in *Noticias E Documentos Para A Historia de Damao Antiga Provincia Do Norte* by Antonio Francisco Moniz Junior (1900 Bastora). It recounts all the rights, taxes cesses and privileges enjoyed by the State and the landlords, and we find (p. 168) that *jirayet* land was recognised for revenue purposes as in Maharashtra (terra alta Chamado Jerat) that cocoanut trees were taxed (p. 169) (pagaao por cem cajuris...dez rupias) and that rent varied according to the nature of the crop cultivated. Mention is made of a due called Dan (p. 172), most probably analogous to Dani of our list. Poruma Viga de terra de Undo do produççã de Dangue, ou cara com jerat pagosse vinte e dois parās e sem jerat Vinte a titulo de Dan.

41. Erskine, *A History of India under the First two Sovereigns of the House of Taimur*, Vol. I, p. 530.
42. Elliot and Dowson, Vol. VII. pp. 290-291.
43. Moreland, *India at the Death of Akbar*, p. 49.
44. *Ibid*, p. 50.
45. Irvine, *Manucci*, Vol. II, pp. 387-388.
46. Manucci, ed. Irvine, Vol. II, p. 175.
47. For Zakat see Aghnides, *Muhammadan Theories of Finance*.
48. Briggs' *Ferishta*, Vol. I, pp. 355-360.
49. Blochmann, *Ain-i-Akbari*, Vol. I, pp. 221-223.

    From papers mentioned in *Catalogo does Manuscriptos da Bibliotheca publica Eborense,* it appears that the Portuguese Government also deemed it their duty to regulate the price of rice, etc. See p. 360.

5
Administration of Justice

1. Primitive Simplicity of the Maratha System

The system of administration of justice was simple and suited to the temper of the time. Codified law there was none and procedure was uncertain and informal. For one, the judiciary depended upon the old Sanskrit treatises on law like Mitakshara and Manu's Code, for the other, they had to depend upon old customs. And as those old customs prescribed, among other forms, trial by ordeal, the Maratha judges allowed ordeal by fire and water as well as appeal to divine intervention in the form of an oath taken in a sacred temple. But the Chhatrapati Maharajas and the Peshwa after them acted more like the patriarchs of old than modern judges. What law there was, was not strictly enforced in civil suits. Legal exactitude was not their ideal. Amicable settlement was encouraged, and an attempt was always made to give a suitor every facility for proving his case. Sometimes consideration was made for a defeated party, to ensure good feeling between the parties in future. Thus in the suit of Maloji bin Shahaji Bhanga *vs.* Hiroji bin Narsoji Bhanga about the proprietary right of a Patilki the *Panch* directed Maloji to give Hiroji a site to build a house on and 30 bighas of land.

"A piece of land about 30 cubits in length and about 15 cubits in breadth in the inhabited portion of the aforesaid village and the Patilki right of 30 bighas of the superior, ordinary and inferior classes out of the cultivable land of the village have been given to Hiroji, son Narsoji Bhanga by the assembled *got*."[1] (*Got*—castemen)

2. Pratap Sinha's Yadi

The old customs about procedure were compiled and arranged in a *yadi* by Pratap Sinha Maharaj, Chhatrapati of Satara. Pratap Sinha reigned from 1808-1839 A.D. and the fall of the Peshwas took place in the year 1818. His reign, therefore, coincided with the early period of English administration in the Bombay Presidency. But the rules and regulations drawn up by him in his yadi were based upon the old customs of the land, and give us a clear idea of the policy by which the old Maratha rulers were guided in the administration of justice. Says Chhatrapati Pratap Sinha in the *Nyayadhish Prakaran* of his yadi—"The good old rule of this realm has been to make amicable settlement of all disputes through the proper exertion of the neighbours and to call a *Panchayat* only when there is no other remedy"[2]. He goes on to say that this excellent custom should be encouraged and the Patils, Mamledars and Shete Mahajans (in towns and market places) should try to induce the parties, if they came to them, to settle their dispute by arbitration. Even serious quarrels, beyond the jurisdiction of Patils and Shete Mahajans and Panchayats appointed by them, says the Raja, it would be well if settled through the arbitration of neighbour.[3] Intent on the welfare of his subjects, and perhaps impelled by the good old custom, the Raja says that in case of settlement by arbitration the parties would be exempted from the payment of *Harki*, which they would have to pay, if the case was referred to Royal Courts or Royal officers. In case the parties failed to settle their disputes amicably, they should go to an arbitrator and the Raja assures us that such an arbitrator need not fear Royal displeasure for his laudable efforts.[4]

3. The Separation of the Executive and the Judiciary Unknown

When such efforts for amicable settlement or settlement by arbitration failed, the parties had recourse to the regular instruments of justice. The judicial officer in the village was the Patil as usual, above him the Mamlatdar and the Sarsubhedar and above all the Peshwa or his minister as the representative of the theoretical head of the state, the Raja of Satara, who was like the King of England, the fountain of justice and honour. In towns, learned judges, well-versed in the Shastras, were appointed for judicial duties and were called Nyayadhish. Thus we see the Maratha statesmen were not acquainted with the theory of the separation of the Executive, the Legislative, and the Judiciary. The Peshwa and his minister, the Sarsubhedar, the Mamlatdar and the Patil in the village exercised all these widely different functions. The Nyayadhish was a judiciary pure and simple.

4. Panchayat

The great instrument of administration of civil justice was the Panchayat. Pratap Sinha Maharaja says that for cases of minor importance the Patil in the village and the Shete Mahajan in the towns and market-places could appoint Panchayats. The parties on such occasions had to sign a *Rajinama* or agreement to abide by the decision, and the Panchayat was then to proceed with its enquiry, draw up a *saransh* or summary of the case and pass its judgement. The judgement had to be confirmed by the Mamlatdar. But if it was discovered that the Panchayat was corrupt or prejudiced against a party, the case was to be reported to the Mamlatdar, and if the Mamlatdar after proper enquiry found the Patil's report correct, the case was to be sent to the Sarkar. If the Patil refused to appoint a Panchayat or to dispose of the case in a legal manner, or if the parties rejected a Panchayat of their own village, the case was to be referred to the Mamlatdar; it would then be the Mamlatdar's duty to appoint a Panchayat with the Patil's cognizance to assemble a Panchayat at a place other than the village of the disputants. In serious cases beyond the jurisdiction of the Patil or officers of his rank, the Mamlatdar was to appoint in the first instance an arbitrator with the consent of the parties. Failing this measure a Panchayat in the usual manner had to be appointed and the usual Rajinama had to be signed. The decision of the Panchayat was generally confirmed and upheld by the Government unless there was a charge of corruption against the members of the Panch.

5. Panchayat and Jury

The trial by Panchayat was in many respects like the trial by jury. The members of the Panch, it may be noted, were not paid out of the government treasury like the amateur judges of ancient Athens, and it is not certain whether they got any allowance for their trouble. Elphinstone says that they sometimes got some reward from the parties if the case was a protracted one. But Pratap Sinha strictly forbids and such gratification, and in theory at least it seems such private presents were not permitted. The Chhatrapati threatens to punish both the giver and the taker of bribe even if the former happened to be the party in the right.[5]

But the Panchayat was not exactly like the modern jury. The modern jury is presided over by a judge, but the Panchayat was not always presided over by a government officer, and when a Panchayet from the disputants' village was chosen (as was generally done), the members were bound to be more or less acquainted with the facts of the case and came to take their judicial seat with more or less bias. Moreover the parties were sometimes allowed to nominate the members of the Panchayat, each party naturally nominating its own advocates. In modern times, although the parties cannot nominate the jury, they can considerably influence the empanelment by exercising the right of challenging a juryman. As the attendances of the members of a Panch depended simply upon their sense of duty and dread of public opinion, it was bound to be more or less irregular. And when they were nominated by the parties perhaps they sometimes acted more like pleaders than judges. They were also hampered by the absence of any authority on their part to enforce their decision. Their order unless vetoed by the government was enforced by the Mamlatdar who also placed at their disposal a peon for summoning the defendant and witnesses to their presence.

6. Decision, in the Absence of a Party, not Binding

It is noteworthy that a decision arrived at in the absence of either of the parties was not deemed legally valid and the absent party could afterwards appeal against it and have it quashed. But very severe pressure was sometimes put upon the relatives of the absentee to make him appear in the court.

"After that, hard times ensued and to earn my living I left my daughter and mother in the village and went in search of some service. Then Valimbe went to Ramchandra Pandit and had my mother arrested. My mother was there but put to great trouble for four months and was then made to sign an agreement that she would produce her son in court within three months" (Statement of Shamji Ganghadhar Adkule in Shamji Ganghadhar and Gopal Tukdev Adkule *vs.* Bakdev and Gopal Ganghadhar Valimbe).[6] A man of rank could send his Karkum to represent him.

The defeated party had always to sign a document called *Yejitkhat* by which he renounced all claims to the property in question in favour of his opponent, and the winner had to pay a *Sherni* or *Harki* generally amounting to twenty-five per cent of the value of the disputed property or watan. But, as in assessment of revenue, consideration was made for his pecuniary condition and sometimes he was exempted from payment altogether and often a reduction adequate to his means was made. The Harki of twenty-five per cent even should not be regarded as excessive, as the suitors in the Maratha courts were not required to pay any court-fee, and the services of professional lawyers were both unknown and unnecessary.

7. Appeals

An appeal against the decision of the Panchayat could be made only on the plea of corruption, but if the appellant failed to substantiate his charge he had to pay a fine or

Gunhagari, and as his co-villagers generally sat on the Panchayat the appellant ran the risk of suffering in the public opinion. The gunhagari was usually fixed according to the means of the appellant and it may also be noted here that both in appeals as well as in original suits parties had to give security for abiding by the decision of the court.

For hearing appeal cases a fresh Panchayat could be appointed or the Peshwa's minister or the Mamlatdar (as the case might be) might decide the case without a Panchayat. Original cases might also be disposed of in a similar method. But as Elphinstone points out 'though it rested with him (the Government officer) to decide whether or not the case required a Panchayat, yet it was reckoned gross injustice to refuse one on a question at all doubtful, and it was always reckoned a sufficient ground for ordering a new investigation when there had been no Panchayat".[7] This popularity of Panchayats clearly proves that they were not generally open to corruption; although Elphinstone thinks that "the Panchayats themselves were open to corruption and to partiality". The Panchayats were popularly called *"Panch-Parmeshwar"*, and the members of the Panch in many documents are addressed by the parties as their parents (माय बाप). The people of Maharashtra would not have regarded the voice of the Panch as the voice of God, unless it fully deserved their confidence.

8. Members of the Panch

Before we proceed further we may take note of the status of the men who were called upon to serve on the Panch. The Panchayat called to decide the suit of Bhanga *vs.* Bhanga already referred to, consisted of the Deshmukh, Deshpande and the gots (*got* literally means a caste as considered collectively, or relations, and kindreds considered collectively). Hence it was a trial by peers. Elphinstone says that in deciding boundary questions the Panchayat was constituted of Patils, Deshmukh and Deshpande, assisted by the Mahar. We know from the reports of other cases that in suits about watans, the Zamindars of neighbouring Parganas as well as the Patils of the adjoining villages were called upon to serve on the Panchayat. In fact these justice judges were expected to be well acquainted with the unwritten customary law of the country. In a document published in *Sanads and Letters* of Rao Bahadur Ganesh Chimuaji Wad (edited by P.V. Mawjee and D. B. Parasnis) we find mention of a Majalasi (a council) consisting of Rajsabha and Brahmansabha appointed to hear an appeal case. The members of the Majalasi are described as people who have property (veritti) and who are directly or indirectly acquainted with the customary law of property. Consonant with this principle a dispute relating to the right of priesthood (Appana Bhat *vs.* Shripat Bhat) was referred to the Brahman community of Karhad for settlement[8] and the witnesses summoned were Joshis or fellow priests.

9. Government Sanction Necessary for a Panch

A Panchayat however qualified, could not legally proceed to perform judicial duties unless properly authorised by the government, but such irregularities were sometimes overlooked by the Peshwas in consideration of the motive of the Panchayat. A case in illustration may be quoted here:

"A dispute between Pilaji bin Atmaji Ambare, and Sambhaji bin Krishnaji Ambare, in regard to the Khoti of Chirani in Rarf Khed of Taluka Suvarnadurga was without authority decided with the aid of a Panch by Ragho Vishwanath Canpule, a Karkun attached to the temple of Shri Bhargavaram, and a document bearing the seal of the deity was issued by him. His brother was therefore taken to the Subha and was called upon to account for Ragho's conduct. The matter having reached the Peshwa, a pardon was given to Ragho, and his brother was ordered to be released".[9] The decision by this informal Panchayat was also ordered to be revised.

10 Evidence

In civil disputes the parties were required to produce documentary as well as oral evidence, according to the nature of the case. They could however demand a decision by ordeal, of which various forms were in practice.

Let us see who the witnesses generally called upon to give oral evidence were, and before whom an ordeal, if resorted to, was undergone. These were generally the village officers, the *Pandhar* or the villagers and the gots or caste people, men well-versed in the history and traditions of the village or supposed to be so. From the evidence of old people handed down to us through the carefully recorded summaries of civil suits, we learn that the past history of the village and its old traditions were orally transmitted from generation to generation. Of the Pandhars the most important witnesses were the balutas who, it seems, were fairly well acquainted with the traditional history of the village and its watan-holders. That their evidence had very great weight and was considered essentially necessary will be found at a glance at the list of witnesses still preserved for us in the old records. Here we shall give three lists only. In a dispute (1749-50)[10] regarding the Joshi and Kulkarni watans of Jalgaon in Pargana Supa and Jalgaon in Tarf Karhepathar in Prant Poona. Bado Shivdev, the defendant, signed a Rajinama, or agreement to abide by the decision (literally evidence of the Pandhar of the villages in question.

The names of the witnesses summoned are as follows:

1. Sultanji bin Duryaji Patil.
2. Limbaji bin Mankoji Patil.
3. Subhanji bin Bapoji Patil.
4. Shetyaji bin Rayaji Patil.
5. Piraji bin Santaji Jadhava Chaugula.

Balutas

1. Babu bin Monjoji Sutar (Carpenter).
2. Suryaji bin Udaji Lohar (Blacksmith).
3. Subhanji bin Navji Kumbhar (Potter).
4. Udaji bin Mankoji Chambhar (Shoe-maker).

5. Subhanji bin Jivaji Gurab (attendant of village temple).
6. Vaghoji bin Limbaji Koli (fisherman and carrier of water).
7. Malharji bin Raju Nhavi (Barber).
8. Maniknak bin Rajnak (Mahar).
9. Yesnak bin Nimbnak (Mahar).
10. Sambnak bin Ajnak Mang (Drummer).

In a dispute about the patilki watan of Wadgaon Budruk[11] (1741-42) separate statements were made by different groups of Pandhars, and their names are quoted below in groups as in the document:

GROUP 1

1. Bud Mali (Gardener).
2. Shivaji bin Kondji Nhavi (barber).
3. Bajaji bin Badjoji Parit (Washerman).
4. Raynak bin Saynak (Mahar).
5. Hasa bin Chandnak (Mahar).

GROUP 2

1. Nimbaji bin Janoji Sutar (Carpenter).
2. Badja bin Bahira Chambhar (Shoe-maker).

GROUP 3

Sukha Mali bin Sant Mali aged 75 formed a group by himself and seems to have been better informed than the preceding witnesses.

GROUP 4

Patils of neighbouring villages:

1. Kavji bin Kalji Patil (Ambegaon Budruk).
2. Rakmaji bin Malji Mate Patil (Khadakbasle).

3. Hemaji Patil Pola (Dhayti).
4. Yesji bin Gopji Patil Borate (Barje).
5. Yesji bin Yelboji Patil (Narhe).
6. Amai Borati Patlin (Hingne Budruk).

GROUP 5

1. Hasa Mahar.
2. Lingnak bin Padamnak (Mahar as the name shows).
3. Raya Mahar.
4. Taba Mahar.

GROUP 6

1. Moro Narhar Kulkarni.
2. Har Mali bin Mant Mali.
3. Sant Mali bin Raj Mali.
4. Shivmabla bin Raumabla.
5. Daj Varta.
6. Raya bin Ramnak.
7. Tahanak bin Santnak.

The difference in their statements is explained by the fact that they were not equally well informed about the past history of the village watans.

We get our third list from a case, Shivaji son of Tanhaji and others *vs.* Satwaji about the Loharki and Sutarki watans of Khodad in Tarf Narayangaon.[12] In this case also the parties signed a Rajinama to abide by the evidence of the Pandhar, and security as usual was taken from them. The Pandhars summoned were then taken singly and questioned about the past history of the watan after *bel bhandar* (analogous to copper and *tulsi,* तामा तुलसी of Bengal) had been given to them. Here also we find the witnesses divided into two groups according to the fullness or scantiness of their information;

and a glance was in these disputes about watans, and here we find the age of the witnesses given against their names.

GROUP 1

		Age
1.	Khandoji valad Subhanji Gaikwad	45
2.	Bahirji valad Ranoji Kuchila	34
3.	Ramji valad Padaji Kharmala	60
4.	Kachu valad Khandoji Gaikwad	35
5.	Mahadaji valad Harji Yeranda	50
6.	Condji valad Ranoji Raut	55
7.	Nimbaji valad Yesaji Kumbhar	60
8.	Malharji valad Umaji Koli	35
9.	Hari valad Gangaji Dabra	60
10	Lokha valad Amaji Chambhar	50
11.	Yesaji valad Tanhaji Mahar	60
12.	Uma valad Pangnak Mahar	35
13.	Pemnak valad Yesnak Mahar	60
14.	Jabiya valad Satba Mahar	25
15.	Luma valad Hema Mahar	60

GROUP 2

1.	Javji valad Gangaji Patil Thorat	34
2.	Sakhoji valad Satbaji Mule	34
3.	Khandoji valad Shetyaji Mule	60
4.	Gundaji valad Pilaji Patil Dhete	35
5.	Hangoji valad Malji Dhangale	70
6.	Chahu valad Mahadji Parit	35
7.	Aman valad Lakshman Mali	55
8.	Nagoji valad Muktaji Mule	35
9.	Jarya valad Nama Mang	25
10.	Nimbaji Panman and his mother Rakhmai	65

The winner in this case paid a Harki of Rs. 200.

11. Trial by Ordeal

Although the parties signed a Rajinama to abide by the evidence of the Pandhar, and furnished security for their obedience, the defeated party might claim a fresh decision by ordeal and if one ordeal failed he could ask for a trial by an ordeal of a different sort. Sometimes he changed his mind about the selection of ordeal before the first proposed by him had been tried. How much indulgence was given to a Maratha suitor, in order that he might be satisfied that no injustice had been done to him, and how often he changed his mind can be shown by a document quoted by Mr. Bhaskar Vaman Bhat in the Tritiya Sammelan Vritta of Bharat Itihas Sanshodhak Mandal.[13] "Upon that, on the second day Somaji refusing the decision of the *gots* demanded an ordeal by water. He said that the man drawn by hand out of the water by the Pandhri should be regarded as in the right. When you were asked whether you were willing to undergo that ordeal you answered in the affirmative. The next day he changed his mind, refused the ordeal by water and suggested that the case should be decided by an oath in the mosque at Kasba Ranjangaon; on the third day he rejected the idea of an oath in the mosque and again demanded an ordeal by water. Then it was ordered that the plaintiff and the defendant should pour water over each other's hands. He who would pass this ordeal should enjoy the watan. Somaji rejected this proposal also and prayed for an ordeal by fire".

Of the ordeals enumerated in the above document the first deserves our special notice, because it was to all intents a trial by the Pandhar or by the *got*. The parties and the Pandhars were sent to a sacred river like the Krishna, or better, to a *sangam* of special sanctity like the Krishna-Vena sangam. There, at an auspicious moment the Pandhars stood on the bank after their bath in the sacred stream. The defendant and the plaintiff still remained standing in the river. Either the patil or some other trustworthy man there present was then ordered to draw the rightful party from the water and pass a conscientious verdict. An ordinary man would not deliberately give a wrong verdict at such a place, at such a moment and in the presence of all his co-villagers. He would not only ensure for his soul eternal prediction after death, but also public execution while alive. This ordeal was therefore not unreasonable, specially in those times of strong faith in religion and of stronger superstition. In a dispute regarding the Patilki watan of Fursangi, in Tarf Haweli, of Pargana Poona, between the Kamthes and the Gaikwad Harpales, such an ordeal was resorted to. While the assembled Pandhars stood on the sandy banks of the Krishna, Yeknak, a Mahar was ordered by the gots and the balutas to draw the rightful owner of the watan from the river bed and he loudly declared his verdict."[14]

12. Ordeal by Fire and Heated Metal

There were so many forms of ordeal that it will not be possible to describe them all. We will here take notice of the more important ones only. One of the most common ordeals was to draw a piece of metal out of a pot full of boiling oil. This had to be performed in a temple of special sanctity and at an auspicious moment previously fixed by the government. The ordeal had to be witnessed by the co-villagers of the parties as well as by a government officer deputed for that purpose. An ordeal with a piece of metal in heated oil is thus described in the summary of a dispute regarding a Patilki watan between Devji and Shankarji Dangat: "You were then sent with Rajshri Apaji Hanmant Subhedhar and Balaji Dadaji and Baghoji Raut, officers from the Huzur and the District to Pali for the performance of an *Agnidivya*. The *got* of that place assembled in the temple and they lighted a fire and heated *ghi* and oil mixed in customary proportion. You bathed and after a declaration of your right, took two pieces of meal from the heated liquid in the presence of all. Then your hand was bandaged and sealed. The next day the aforesaid parties were brought to the Huzur by the Karkun of the District officer. On the third day, in the presence of the Majalasi the bandage was taken off and the seals broken. On your hand were found only the marks that formerly existed there. Nothing more, nothing less; you passed the ordeal successfully"[16].

Another ordeal is described in a document quoted by Mr. Bhat in the journals of the Bharat Itihas Sanshodhak Mandal.[16] There, the palm of the man is first bandaged with leaves of peepul tree and new thread. Then a heated ball is placed on his hand. He is then made to walk over seven concentric circles. After completing the seventh circle he drops the metal ball on a little heap of grain which is burnt and it is thus shown that no fraud has been practised. These ordeals were undoubtedly the relics of a bygone age. But the fallacy of such trials was not altogether undetected; in one case at least we find the Sabha Naik objecting to the demand of a *rava* (drawing out a piece of metal from heated oil) on the ground that when reliable evidence was available, an ordeal should not be permitted. Fire ordeal was in fact very seldom resorted to in ordinary cases.

Ordeals with boiling water and with burning lamps are also mentioned. In the latter case truth was supposed to be indicated by the period of burning. When an oath in a temple or mosque was taken, a period was fixed within which divine intervention was expected to take place. If the man lied, some illness or other mishap was expected to befall him or his family; but if he was left undisturbed, it was believed that his assertion had been corroborated by the god of the temple. On one occasion a man took an oath on the feet of Shahu Chhatrapati, and as fate would have it, died of cholera within a month.[17] "Then Bhikaji Harpala said that the Maharaja's feet were the Krishna to him and he would take an oath on his (Raja's) feet. Accordingly he swore that the watan in the aforesaid Mauja belonged to him and that Kamthe was a Thalvaik (Mirasi) peasant. Within a day or two of this oath Bhikaji Gaikwad got cholera, he had to be carried back to the village on the back of a bullock and there he died after a month in consequence of that false oath taken on his behalf".

Boundary disputes between two villages were often settled by ordeal. One of the Patils walked on the right boundary with a cow's hide on the head; here also a fixed period was allowed to elapse for the manifestation of divine confirmation. But the Patil had afterwards to undergo a Prayaschchitta for defiling his body".

13. Nivad Patra and Watan Patra

At the conclusion of the case a *nivad patra* or a *watan patra* was given to the winners in the Peshwa's name—for all judicial measures were taken in his name. The winner was allowed to take away the original, but a true copy was always kept in the Peshwa's Daftar. There copies were sometimes useful in testing the genuineness of the old records. In a dispute regarding a Deshmukhi watan in 1792-93 an old document of doubtful character was produced. The seals affixed on it had become indistinct and unreadable. It was then compared with old documents of similar dates and with similar seals and its authenticity was proved beyond doubt.[19]

Elphinstone says that generally great favour was shown to men of rank. In all countries, in all ages, men of wealth and influence have for all practical purposes defied law with more or less impunity.[20] It does not seem that in Maratha countries they enjoyed any unusual advantage. In the 11th volume of his *Sources of Maratha History,* Mr. V.K. Rajwade has published a long but incomplete account of a suit about the inheritance to the property of the Chaskar family. The Chaskars were near relations of the Peshwa (1779 A.D.) and the case was brought before the celebrated Nyayadhish Ram Shastri.

The procedure was, of course, informal, but that was not because the parties concerned were near relatives of the Peshwa. Even the procedure of village Panchayets were extremely informal. Sometimes Ram Shastri was interviewed in his own house in private. Sometimes he consulted a common friend of the disputants; but on the whole he conducted the business with firmness and with an attitude of strict justice. In fact Ram Shastri was not the person to deviate from the path of justice for the sake of any man in the world. And Ram Shastri was not the only Nyayadhish famous for uprightness in Maratha history. European observers cared more for form and procedure and hard and fast rules. The absence of these led them to pass sweeping remarks on the judicial system of the Marathas. Even an acute observer like Elphinstone could not rise above this ordinary prejudice. Not that the rich and powerful could not buy justice sometimes, but that was by no means the general rule; we find high officials punished for misdemeanours, and their watans and inams attached for liquidation of debts. Powerful Sardars, however, could not be brought under law. This was the bane of feudalism, till then prevailing in European countries too. So far as the European critics of the Maratha system are concerned, it was a difference of ideals more than anything else that shocked them so much.

13. Fees in Civil Suits

Let us now enquire what fees the Peshwa's government usually demanded from suitors in civil cases. In suits relating to money bonds, the usual fee was twenty-five per cent of the money realised, sometimes a lower fee, that of twenty per cent was charged. The creditors however had very seldom to go to the law courts of the land for realisation of the money lent. The custom of the country allowed them to practise dunning, the most extreme form of which was *dharna,* which debarred the debtor from taking any food or drink before satisfying his creditor. Dharna could be practised against men of the highest rank in the country, the Peshwa not excepted. Daulat Rao Scindhia was subjected to it by some Muhammadan soldiers, as Broughton tells us.[21] Government interference for realisation of loan could therefore be necessary only in exceptional cases, and a fee of twenty-five or twenty per cent cannot be regarded as too high. These cases were sometimes referred to a Panchayat. "Fair bankrupts," says Elphinstone, "seem to have been left off pretty nearly as with us. Fraudulent ones were made to pay when discovered, notwithstanding previous release."[22] In partition suits however, property up to the value of Rs. 300

was exempt from any charge, property above that value was charged at the rate of ten per cent. Some estimates may also be formed of the customary laws from the summaries of the civil suits preserved in the Peshwa's Daftar. In inheritance cases we find the eldest son could not be altogether disinherited. So far as watans were concerned, the right of seniority belonged to a son of a *lagna* marriage, although younger than a son of *pat* (widow remarriage). A mother could claim maintenance from her son and also money for religious performances as well as for going on a pilgrimage. Although the property of a man without any issue belonged by law to the government, still consideration was made for his widows. Brothers were sometimes allowed to inherit the property of a childless brother on the payment of an inheritance tax, and adoption of a child always required a formal sanction of the government, which ordinarily could be secured without any difficulty. The property of a foreigner dying within the Peshwa's territory was carefully preserved, and investigation was made about the legal heirs of the dead. When they could not be found, the property of the dead man was spent in charity for the welfare of his soul in the other world. In disputes about watans, the disputed property was placed under attachment to force quick settlement.

14. Elphinstone's Structures

Elphinstone says, "The judicial system seems to have been very imperfect. There was no regular administration of justice: no certain means of filing a suit: and no fixed rule of proceeding after it had been filed. It rested with the officer of Government applied to, to receive a complaint or to neglect it altogether. The reception of your appeal from his injustice, equally depended on the arbitrary will of his superior. The other occupations of these officers rendered it difficult for them to attend to judicial affairs, even if well disposed, and these occupations increasing with the rank of the officer, the *Paishwa* (or the minister) who was the mainspring of the whole machine, must have been nearly inaccessible to all men and entirely so to the poor."[23] Perfection of course cannot be claimed for the Maratha institutions or for any human institution in the world—there would have been no room for evolution had everything been perfect. But the observations of the great historian, to say the least, do not touch the heart of things. No doubt the Kamavisdars and Mamlatdars had other works to do. But their judicial duties mainly consisted in appointing a Panchayat and confirming its decision. Their work was more of supervision than of direct participation in the administration of justice. Moreover, there were provincial courts under the District Nyayadhish in important towns. If every one of these officers refused to receive a complaint, the plaintiff could still approach the Nyayadhish or Chief Justice at Poona, and the Peshwa himself. The chief court at Poona had always been put under a brilliant set of scholars and independent judges like Ram Shastri and his successors from 1760 downwards to the time of Baji Rao Raghunath, when Balkrishna Shastri Tokekar held that important office. The Peshwa was not at all inaccessible to his subjects, rich or poor. The students of old documents known well how many of these watan patras and nivad patras begin with the customary clause,—"You came to the Swami at such and such a place and complained to him, etc."

The Peshwas went out on tour every year and received complaints and punished offenders. In the month of Rabilaval of San Ihide Arbain Maya wa Alf only (1740-41) Peshwa Balaji Baji Rao visited no less than eleven places (Pali, and some neighbouring forts and villages Parli, Vadvathar, Poona, Garade, Pargaon, Bhuinj and Satara).[24] Nor was this journey of exceptional length. Similar tours were made almost every year if not every month. Even the worthless Baji Rao Raghunath used to go out on these tours and on one occasion he punished some miscreants.[25] The Maratha princes were always accessible even to the poorest of their subjects—and Broughton, by no means an admirer of things Maratha, was struck with the case and informality with which Daulat Rao Scindhia could be approached even while on an expedition by the seekers of justice.[26]

15. Maratha and English Judicial Institutions Compared

The fact is judicial institutions were still going through a process of evolution in India as elsewhere, and evolution proceeded on different lines in different countries. In England for instance more stress was laid on procedure. English jurists had given a scientific turn to their legal studies and the Legislature of the land had by a series of Acts made a systematic effort to remove any ambiguity where it previously existed as to the purpose and intents of the existing laws. Even the unwritten customary laws had been given a definite shape through the decision of the courts. There was a well organised machinery for enforcing the laws of the land and there was a body of professional men well versed in laws to help the judges in interpreting them. The English suitor knew quite well where to file his case in the first instance and to whom to appeal and he was ordinarily sure of a fair decision provided he could afford to pay the costs of a lengthy suit, for good lawyer always charged a high fee and a chancery suit caused proverbial delay.

The Maratha system on the other hand excelled in simplicity. There was no codified law, no fixed procedure, and even a lengthy suit hardly cost the parties anything but the unavoidable worries and anxieties. But these advantages were marred by the disadvantage caused by the lack of settled procedure. The suit could be prolonged indefinitely by the obstructive tactics of an unscrupulous party. He could claim a trial by ordeal after the Panchayat had already delivered a judgement. And if he found one ordeal inconvenient he might demand a second trial by an ordeal of a different description. If the Mamlatdar was a dishonest man, and he was seldom proof to present, the losing party might still get the decision arrived after so much delay and so many ordeals cancelled, and one who had an influential and highly placed friend at the court had always some advantage over his less fortunate adversary. To add to these difficulties there was no professional lawyer and the provisions of the law, written and unwritten, were not always clear and definite. The old Hindu law-givers did not always agree and differences were sometimes accentuated by their commentators. Customs varied in different districts and offered no valuable aid to the bewildered judge. The result was that the honest poor might often find it difficult to defend his rights against the dishonest rich. But the English laws and English lawyers and English courts would hardly help him better. For in the first instance the poor man could not expect to engage as able a lawyer to defend him as his wealthy adversary and the heavy expenses of a lengthy suit would ultimately prove his ruin, even if he was so fortunate as to get a favourable verdict. It is unnecessary to labour this point any further. It is clear that both the systems had their merits and demerits. Elphinstone passed very severe strictures upon the weak points of the Maratha judicial system, because in his own country he had not been familiar with them. But he was by no means blind to the merits of the Panchayat as he had recommended its continuation even after the British conquest of the Peshwa's territories.

16. Dr. Hope's Views

It should be noted in this connection that British courts of law were at first unpopular in India. Their settled code of procedure, which ought to have commanded itself to the Indian suitors was at the beginning regarded as an unnecessary innovation. The punishment inflicted by these courts, the rapidity with which their judgements in some cases were enforced, also bewildered the illiterate Maratha peasant, and it is no wonder that they sighed for the Panchayat with which they were familiar.

In fact the simplicity of the old judicial system readily caught the imagination of European writers and Dr. Hope, who had first-hand knowledge of India, definitely expressed himself in favour of the original Maratha judicial system. He says, "We have found much to admire and very little to detest in the administration of public officers at Gwalior. Such is our conviction knowing well that if the people of India—the 180 millions—could go to the poll on a choice of governments an almost countless majority would prefer a native one to one which was ever supervising and controlling every act of their public life and haunting them with a vision of an English court of Law."[27]

17. Serious Crimes Very Rare

In the administration of criminal laws also the authorities were the same as in civil cases; —the Patil in the village, the Kamavisdar or Mamlatdar in the District, the Sarsubhedar in the province and the Peshwa and the Chief Justice at Poona above all.

If we judge by the effect, the administration of criminal justice in Maharashtra was as efficient as that of civil justice under the Peshwas. Although he does not miss any opportunity of denouncing the system as a whole, Elphinstone himself admits, "The country was peculiarly free from crimes. Gang robberies have never, since I have been in the country, reached to such a pitch, as to bear a moment's comparison with Bengal, described in the paper laid before the Parliament".

18. Panchayat in Criminal Cases

It does not seem that a Panchayat was so frequently resorted to as in civil cases; but that it was sometimes called to make enquiry into the facts of a criminal case as well as to pass judgement thereon, admits of no doubt. In the year 1760-61, Yeshvant Rao Kshirsagar of Kameri in Tarf Valve, of Prant Karhad, and two others were killed in consequence of a dispute about land revenue, and Kshirsagar's son complained against the murderers. We find that the Patil, Kulkarni and Rayats of the village were summoned to the Huzur for an enquiry into the case, and afterwards the compensation to be paid to the murdered man's son was settled by a Panchayat.[28]

"Upon that Shidoji bin Firangoji Kadam surnamed Ludge, half Patil of the village, Anaji Tukdev and Janardan Baburao Kulkarni and other Rayats were summoned to the

Huzur. After proper enquiry and by the evidence of the Patil, Kulkarni, and the Rayats of the village, the charge of the three murders was proved against the aforesaid Sultanji and Baji. This dispute had to be disposed of, and according to the suggestion of the Panchayat it was ordered that out of the Inam lands of Sultanji and Baji Patil and the Mirasland of the Kunbi two houses and sixty-five bighas of lands with boundary duly described should be granted to the complainant as a hereditary Inam." This document not only shows that a Panchayat was appointed for trying homicides, but also that the relatives of the murdered person had to be compensated by the murderer.

19. Fine According to the Resources of the Offender

Capital punishment in the days of Shahu Chhatrapati and Balaji Baji Rao seems to have been unknown. Murder and treason were punished with fine, confiscation of property, and imprisonment. The Maratha rulers seem to have realised that punishment was to be used as a corrective only and not to drive the offender to the extreme of despair and convert him into a sworn enemy of human society. That explains the queer but common prayer on the part of convicted offenders that the fine inflicted should not exceed their means; and why Government agreed not only to take the offenders' income into consideration while fixing the amount of fine, but also allowed them to pay the sum so fixed, by instalments.

"Morshet Bani, a resident of Peth Somvar accused of murdering his wife. He was brought to the Huzur and examined. He was found guilty and he confessed that he had committed the crime. He also represented that a fine should be levied upon him, taking into consideration what his debtors owed to him and he should be absolved of his sin."[29]

Although the guilty had to pay a fine according to his means, the innocent, if accused, could not escape without any payment. Perhaps that people should suspect him was thought a sufficient offence. In 1752-53 Rupaji bin Rambhaji Mudtadak was accused of pelting Setya, the younger son of Jakhoji bin Setyaji Bhadag Vanjare, to death, and although his innocence was proved, he had to pay a Harki of Rs. 1,500.[30] Elphinstone rightly remarks, "the innocent might sometimes suffer, but the guilty could scarcely ever escape".

When the government levied Harki upon the innocent, a false accuser could not expect mercy when detected. Fine was the usual punishment for such an offence. Three cases of false complaints are found in the Selections from Balaji Baji Rao's Diaries. In the first, Vithoji Jingar was fined Rs. 75 for bringing a false charge of theft against covindaji Jagannath Deshmukh.[31] In the second we find how Rama, a barber of Kashba Saswad, had brought a false charge of witchcraft against Subhanji Jingar and was fined Rs. 40. The Gunhagari as usual was "*Jivan Mafik*".[32] In the third instance Soyraji of Fort Narayangad was fined Rs. 50 for accusing Maini, daughter of Rakhamaji Repal of adultery with Shivaji a washerman.[33] It is noteworthy that Maini proved her innocence by an ordeal by metal (that or drawing out a piece of metal from a potful of boiling oil). So in these three cases of false complaints, the fine varied from Rs. 40 to 75. Evidently the offenders were men of small means, for during the administration of the same Peshwa and only ten years later, we find that Hanmant Bhat, brother of the Pratinidhi, was fined Rs. 1,000 for giving false evidence.[34] This explains the policy of levying fine in proportion to the means of the offender. What would be a preventive in case of Rama, a barber, could not be a preventive in case of the Pratinidhi's brother. Therefore the latter had to pay a fine twenty-five times more than what was levied upon the former, although the offence committed by the barber might have been more serious.

20. Witchcraft

The offence of the barber mentioned above brings to our notice a crime that would certainly appear novel to us, witchcraft. Yet the European states had taken serious steps for its suppression. Witchcraft was made criminal in England by a statute of Elizabeth which had not been repealed till 1736. In the meantime no less than 30,000 men and women had lost their lives on the charge of selling their souls to the Devil. The most inhuman of these murders were those of Mrs. Hicks and her daughter a girl of nine in 1716. In Austria the law against witchcraft was suffered to disfigure the statute book as late as 1766. The Peshwas, however, thought fine and imprisonment sufficient penalty for intercourse with evil spirits. Only one case is recorded of capital punishment. But special measures were taken against prisoners convicted of witchcraft and sorcery. In 1775-76, Martand Joshi Rairikar was imprisoned in Killa Ghangad for practising sorcery, the warders in charge were instructed not to allow him to apply sacred ashes or sandal mark on his forehead or to perform the daily religious rites and to recite sacred hymns.[35] He was not to be allowed to take more than one meal per day, and he was required to prepare his own food. Sometimes the peshwas went further, and took direct measures to deprive the supposed offender of his infernal power. In 1775-76 Moraji, a resident of Poona, was accused of killing a man through the instrumentality of evil spirits. His offence was proved beyond any doubt by the evidence of fifty of his caste people! They further prayed that in order to render his witchcraft ineffectual, two of his upper teeth should be extracted, and he should be made to drink water from a Chambhar's reservoir, and lastly he should be excommunicated. This pious prayer was, for public safety, granted; and further, as the persecuted wizard had threatened to practise witchery against his caste people through Berads and Mangs, if he was excommunicated, the Peshwa ordered him to be imprisoned in the fort of Kohaj and there kept under strict guard.[36]

When a man was charged with causing harm to others by sorcery and witchcraft, he was generally fined and ordered to recall the evil spirits under his commands. Public opinion and common suspicion were regarded as sufficient profits[37] of his offence. Only in one case was a man banished on the charge of witchcraft. So anxious was the Peshwa to save the person and property of his subjects from the infernal influence of the evil spirits in the service of the sorcerers and wizards that two officers were appointed to make a thorough enquiry about the sorcerers in the Talukas-Anjanvel, Suvarndurg, Ratnagiri, Vijayadrug, Devgad and Saudal in the year 1774-75. The first officer was asked to visit the villages of Talukas Anjanvel and Suvarndurg, and he got two Karkuns and six peons to assist him, and he was also authorised to employ five more peons if necessary. The second officer was appointed on an annual salary of Rs. 350 and an additional allowance of Rs. 261 for Karkuns and peons and stationery. He was to levy fine on the wizards when detected, but here also the principle laid down was that the amount of fine should not be exorbitant. The document clearly states that in the instructions about enquiry framed by the Sarsubha the amount of fine prescribed was from Rs. 25 to Rs. 50. But the Rayats of the Konkan were poor and the Sarsubha wrote a letter in the year San Salas that taxes and fine should not be insisted on. Therefore you should fix Gunhagari (fine) according to their means".[38] Even highly placed people often suffered for suspected intercourse with the evil spirits. A Kashmiri general in the Sindhia's employ was disgraced on this account in the early years of the 19th century.

21. Adultery

Here we shall take notice of another offence, adultery; the punishment being so far as the female offenders were concerned, slavery and penal servitude. They were, however, let off if any of their relations offered to stand surety for their future god conduct. In 1741-42 one such female slave was released on the application of her husband who offered to replace her by another slave.[39] In 1754-55 a Koli woman arrested on a charge of adultery was saved from the ignominy of a slave's life on the application of her caste people, but she had to pay a fine of Rs. 50.[40]

In 1785-86 Janki Lagdin, an adulteress, then undergoing penal servitude at fort Visapur, was released on her father standing surety for her good conduct.[41] In one case we find that mutilation was substituted for slavery. In 1781-82 Ahili, wife of Janoji Davra of Dholwad in Prant Junnar committed adultery with Devji Khandoji Chinchvada. Devji was fined and Ahili got her liberty at the loss of her nose.[42]

Girls thus condemned to slavery had to work hard in fortresses. Generally they had to do building work. But sometimes they were sold off like ordinary articles of sale. A Brahman Gangadhar Bhat Karve bought a female convict for Rs. 30 only in 1755-56.[43] The male offenders on the other hand were generally let off with a fine, and sometimes after a term of imprisonment.

22. Slaves Well Treated

The institution of slavery in Maharashtra had not the horrors of slavery of Europe and America. The slaves were treated well. They were sometimes freed on the occasion of great festivals, or simply because they were old. Moreover the slaves in the Maratha country were allowed to possess property, and sometimes actually secured their release by purchasing a suitable substitute for their owners. In the year 1773-74 two female slaves were bought by Fuli and Tulshi, female slaves belonging to the government.[44] Salves on the government establishment were specially well treated. We find that in 1762-63, Rs. 1,303-4 was granted for clothes to be given to female slaves of government on the Dasra festival.[45] In the same year Badi a slave was released and allowed to go wherever she pleased.[46] In 1774-75 the daughter of a Muhammadan female slave attached to the cavalry under Sakhoji Mule was decently married to a Muhammadan boy.[47] It may be noted here that legal marriage of a slave girl meant her manumission.

"A letter to Eshi, a woman, when you were at Purandhar, Rajashri Ranoji Bhonsle represented that you were his female slave's daughter. There upon you had been summoned to the Huzur, but it was found that the gentleman had formerly given you in marriage. Therefore he cannot force you to slavery. Nobody has any right to interfere with your liberty."[48]

The condition of the slaves in other parts of the Maratha empire was equally good. Broughton tells us in his *Letters from a Mahratta Camp* how well treated the slaves were in Sindhia's country. His knowledge was first-hand. Two female slaves belonging to Mamma (relative of Daulat Rao Scindhia) came to his camp one day. "They told me," says Broughton, "that they were brought up on a family of Mamma, where they led a very easy life; their only employments, during the day, being to attend upon his wives, of whom he had three in camp, and rub the old gentleman's legs when he lay down to repose; and at night they were at liberty to dispose of themselves as they pleased. The Muha Raj's favourite wife has a number of these girls about her, from every part of India, who receive their daily food and two suits of clothes annually, and are allowed to earn as much more as they can and in any way they think proper. The *Butkees* (female slaves) remain attached to the family during their lives."[49]

Jenkins writes of the treatment accorded to slaves at Nagpur: "These are brought up on the families of their purchasers, generally as domestic servants, and are frequently placed almost on an equality with their master's children in regard to food and clothing; and it is not uncommon for persons who have no children of their own, to adopt their slaves as their sons, and leave their property to them at their death. Task-labour, or any work beyond what would be expected of a hired servant, is never exacted from slaves; and in general, they are treated with kindness and consideration, and become more than attached servants, and it may be said friends of the families in which they have been nurtured, than the degraded slaves, from whom no labour can be obtained except what is extorted by fear of punishment."[50]

23. Bigamy and Forcible Marriage

Conjugal infidelity reminds us of two other offences connected with marriage, bigamy and forcible marriage. Polygamy in India was of course, no crime for a man, but bigamy on the part of a girl, specially when she was a Hindu, was unthinkable. Yet a few instances of this rare offence are recorded. The guardians of the girls were really to be blamed, the innocent victims were still in their minority. The usual punishment for forcible marriage was confiscation of property or ex-communication or both. Sometimes the offender was fined. In one case in irregular marriage of a girl of three years, with a Brahman bridegroom forty-five years old, performed by force while the parents of the victim lay unconscious, was declared null and void and a second and more formal marriage with a suitable bridegroom was ordered. The offenders in this case were fined.[51]

Of bigamy we have two cases only. In 1752-53, Nimbaji vallad Yesu Jhagda of Sinnar married the wife of Dhondji Mali of the same village according to the past system. The aforesaid Dhondji had been away from home, and Bapuji Mali, his father-in-law, got his daughter married for a second time. But Nimbaji did not enquire whether Dhondji was living or dead before he married the girl. He was therefore fined Rs. 80.[52] In the second case the punishment inflicted was imprisonment. In 1770-71, Bhiu Bai Vyas, a Brahman lady got her daughter married twice and the whole family consisting of mother, daughter and a son was imprisoned at Shivner.[53] The boy in this case was clearly free from any guilt and here comes one of the drawbacks of the Maratha system. In order to overawe would-be offenders, the Peshwa's government committed to prison innocent children and helpless wives of convicted prisoners and absconding offenders. Repeated instances of such measures are found in the papers of the Peshwa's Daftar. We will here choose three only from those of the first Madhava Rao's administration. In 1765-66 we come across a paper which pitily states that Khandya Berad of Chakan having committed theft, his mother, wife and three children (two belonging to him and one to Somya Berad) were sent to fort Kohaji.[54] "In 1766-67, certain Bhats having been caught thieving, 11 women and 12 children of their families were condemned to rigorous imprisonment. Their daily ration was fixed at one seer for each adult and half a seer for each child."[55]

In the same year Baji Sonar was imprisoned at Killa Visapur for committing theft, and his wife was sent to prison at fort Sinhagad.[56]

24. Mutilation—A Punishment

We have seen that capital punishment was not inflicted even for murder during the administration of Shahu Chhatrapati and Balaji Baji Rao. But the two Madhava Raos not only condemned offenders convicted to treason, murder, causing grievous hurt, dacoity and theft, to death, but sometimes caused them to be mutilated. Robbers and thieves were mercilessly deprived of their hands and feet. Here, of course, we find the revival of the old principle of removing the offending limb recommended to the Hindu kings by the compiler of Manu's code, in bygone days of antiquity. Among the papers of the second Madhava Rao have been preserved long lists of convicts condemned to lose their hands and feet. One of these lists enumerates the following sentences for theft:

Capital punishment	20 men
Right hand and left leg to be cut off	13 men
Right hand only to be cut off	18 men
Right hand and one ear to be cut off	4 men
Right hand and right leg to be cut off	1 man
One ear to be cut off	1 man

and one man was to be first paraded ludicrously dressed and then nailed to death.[57]

These punishments were undoubtedly cruel, but it should not be forgotten that humanitarian principles had very little influence on the criminal laws in India as well as in England in the first decade of the 19th century. These inhuman penalties therefore were perhaps less shocking to the people of the time than to us. Even in the native country of Peel and Mackintosh the criminal law was hardly humane. For, while the thief in the Maratha country escaped with the loss of a hand or a foot, his English cousin forfeited his life for the same offence. Capital punishment was prescribed by English law for offences which the Maratha judge would punish with imprisonment only. To the natural severity of English criminal laws was added the influence of the rich. Sir Spencer Walpole says,—"The least influential member of parliament had sufficient power to have any offence made a capital felony, without benefit of clergy. In 1815 it was capital offence to steal goods to the value of 5*s*. in a shop. It was capital offence to steal 40*s*. from a dwelling house. It was capital offence to break frames. It was made a capital offence in 1816 to destroy machines. It was a capital offence to steal a horse or sheep. Up to 1808 it had been a capital offence to pick a man's pocket. Up to 1812 it had been a capital offence for soldiers and mariners to beg. It was seriously proposed in 1813 to punish the fraudulent debtors with death." "There are no less than two hundred felonies," said Mackintosh in 1819, punishable with death." The result was that although "more people were hanged in England than in all Europe besides", crime went on increasing. When this was the state of things in England, it is no wonder that in India mutilation should be inflicted on convicted criminals by Indian and English rulers alike. According to Busted, mutilation was executed on criminals in Bengal under the orders of the British Government.[58] Elphinstone found the Maratha country peculiarly free from crimes. The reason was that the rulers were not naturally cruel. They would make every consideration for a deserving offender. Even treason was sometimes pardoned or slightly punished. Some of Sumer Singh's (murderer of Narayan Rao Peshwa) accomplices were let off with a small fine. This want of vindictiveness on the part of the Peshwa's government, and absence of hard and fast criminal laws, enabled the judicial officers to be lenient, and so when an exemplary sentence was passed to overawe would-be offenders, it never failed to strike terror.

REFERENCES

1. P.D., Vol. I, pp. 179-181.
2. B. I. S. M., *Tritiya Sammelan Vritta*, pp. 51-52.
3. *Ibid.*
4. The original document has been published in the Tritiya Sammelan Vritta of the Bharat Itihas Shanshodhak Mandal by Mr. Bhaskar Vaman Bhat.
5. B. I. S. M., *Tritiya Sammelan Vritta*, p. 53.
6. Watan Patren Nivada Patren, p. 3.
7. Elphinstone's *Report*, p. 538.
8. P. D., Vol. VII, p. 143.
9. P.D., Vol. VII, p. 145. Mr. Bapu Purushottam Joshi's summary.
10. P. D., Vol. I, pp. 172-177.
11. P. D., Vol. I pp. 159-166.
12. P. D., Vol. VII, pp. 133-139. The first six of group I were Patils.
13. P. 42.
14. P. D., Vol. I, p. 168.
15. P. D., Vol. I, pp. 165-166.
16. *Tritiya Sammelan Vritta*, p. 44.
17. P. D., VII. I, p. 168.
18. P. D., Vol. I, p. 131-133. For another ordeal to settle such disputes see P. D., Vol. VIII, p. 69.
20. That things were not much better in this respect at Bombay during the Governorship of Elphinstone can be proved by the interesting revelation made in the Journal of Lady West. I quote here only one extract: "Aug. 24 (1823), Mr. G. has the natives flogged without any examination, trial or usual formality. A friend sends a note to him and says pray flog the bearer and it is done". For other instances of high-handedness see *Bombay in the days of George IV*, ed. Drewitt, Longman, 1907.
21. Broughton, pp. 31-32.

22. Elphinstone's *Report*, p. 65.
23. Elphinstone's *Report*, p. 65.
24. P. D., Vol. II, p. 238.
25. See letters of Parashram Bhat and Malhar Ramchandra Kulkarni to Rajashri Nanaji. Rajwade, *Sources of Maratha History*, Vol. X, p. 398.
26. Broughton, Letters from a Maratha Camp.
27. The House of Scindia, p. 5.
28. P. D., Vol. II, pp. 54-56.
29. P. D., Vol. II, p. 50.
30. P. D., Vol. II, pp. 47-48.
31. P. D., Vol. II, p. 61.
32. *Ibid*, pp. 61-62.
33. *Ibid*, p. 63.
34. *Ibid*, p. 61.
35 P. D., Vol. VIII, pp. 114-115.
36. P. D., Vol. VIII, p. 115.
37. The published documents do not tell us how wizards were detected in the Peshwa's dominions. A curious mode of trying witches in Behar has been described, in the Annual Asiatic Register (1801), Tracts, pp. 91-92. Jenkins says that the method of detecting witches by the Nagpur Government was as follows: "The usual test by which witches are discovered, is that of plunging them, tied up in a bag, into the water; if they sink, they are innocent, if they swim, guilty: and they are punished sometimes with death, at others their teeth are drawn: they are made to drink the water in which the skins of dead animals have been immersed, are beaten with twigs of a particular bush, supposed to have peculiar properties and are turned out of their caste, and sometimes out of the village." Jenkin's Report, p. 60.
38. P. D., Vol. VIII, pp. 112-114.
39. P. D., Vol. I, p. 214.
40. P. D., Vol. II, p. 67.
41. P. D., Vol. VIII, p. 108.
42. P. D., Vol. VIII, p. 108.
43. P. D., Vol. II, p. 68.

44. P. D., Vol. VIII, p. 249.
45. P. D., Vol. VII, p. 249.
46. *Ibid*, p. 318.
47. P. D., Vol. VII, p. 250.
48 P. D., Vol. I, p. 213.
49. Broughton, p. 75. Compare with this the harsh treatment by the Portuguese of their slaves—'She imprisoned in her house one other slaves for having stolen something. By reason of severe punishment and deprivation of food he died, and was buried in the dunghill ... This murder of slaves and slave girls is common among the Portuguese, and few are the houses in which the skeletons of their bodies would not to be found". Manucci, ed. Irvine, Vol. III, p. 113.
50. Report on the Territories of the Rajah of Nagpore (Calcutta, 1827), p. 63.
51. P. D., Vol. VIII, pp. 107-108.
52. P. D., Vol. II, p. 69.
53 P. D., Vol. VI, p. 211.
54. P. D., Vol. VI, pp. 203-204.
55. P. D., Vol. VI, p. 204.
56. P. D., Vol. VII, p. 204. It should be noted that uncommon severity was practised in those days for effectively suppressing robbery. Warren Hastings found it necessary "to order that every convicted Dacoit should be executed in his own village in all the forms and terrors of the law and that his whole family should be made slaves and that every inhabitant of the village should be fined". Hunter, *The Annals of Rural Bengal*, p. 73.
57. P. D., Vol. VIII, pp. 96-99.
58. *Echoes from Old Calcutta*, pp. 116-120.

6
Social Affairs

We have at another place remarked that the Peshwas and the Chhatrapatis before them were not only the secular but also the ecclesiastical head of the state. They united to a certain extent the rights and prerogatives of the Pope and the Emperor. This peculiar position left its mark on the criminal laws of the time. Murder was to them not only a crime but a sin also. And as the crime had its legal punishment, the sin had its religious penance as prescribed by the Shastras. So a murderer even when pardoned had to perform the necessary Shastric penance. During the region of Shahu Chhatrapati one Shidoji Raut murdered his concubine and cousin. At the intercession of his brother Shetyaji, Shidoji obtained a free pardon, but he was ordered to perform the prayashchitta for cousin-murder.[1] An Abhayapatra granted to Shetyaji Raut: "Your brother Shidoji had a concubine and his cousin Bakaji induced her to commit adultery. They did not pay any attention to warning given once or twice. Thereupon Shidoji caught his concubine and cousin at the same place in his house and killed them. A written information was sent to the Huzur with a prayer for pardon. A free pardon is given, but he should get himself absolved of the sin of cousin-murder by performing Prayashchitta".

1. Social Affairs

This combination of the secular with the religious authority naturally led the Peshwa to regulate social affairs, and he could not logically avoid this duty even if he would. We have seen how Sambhaji Maharaj had sanctioned the decisions of the Chhandogyamatya as the ecclesiastical head of the state. Similar orders were often issued in the name of Shahu Chhatrapati. Feudal chiefs like the Angrias had undertaken similar duties within their fiefs. On the *shuklatritiya* of Ashwin, Shaka 1656 (the third day of the lighter half of Ashwin or October 6, 1734) Sambhaji Angre Sarkhel with due salutations referred the case of a Brahman woman Savitri to the Dharmadhikaris and other Brahmans well-versed in the Vedas and the Shastras of Kasba Karhad.[2] It is to be noted here that on these social questions the decision of the *got* or caste people was often confirmed and the Panchayat was appointed for enquiry about old customs as well as decision thereupon. An unreasonable judgement of the got was seldom if ever upheld.

The Peshwas did not exercise this authority of regulating the social affairs because they were Brahmans. It formed part of their duties as the chief magistrates of the state. In one of the documents we find that cases of social customs and rights were sometimes decided by Muhammadan rulers like Aurangzib.[3] As the Joshis assert, "On a previous occasion, the servants of the fort and from two to four thousand Mahars of the province applied to Aurangzib Padsha that the Jyotishis should be ordered to officiate in their marriages. After an enquiry about the old customs, he decided that the Jyotishis were not to officiate in Mahars' marriages and up to this time we have worked according to that decision".

2. Jurisdiction Over Non-Hindus

As the non-Hindu ruler of the country was required to enquire about the social customs of the Hindus and decide disputed social and religious questions, so the Peshwas were also called upon to decide about the religious rights and customs of their non-Hindu subjects. Thus in the year 1754-55, a dispute (Bhikaji and Rustumji Andharu *vs*. others) about the priesthood of the Parsis was decided by an officer of the Peshwa.[4]

In the year 1769-70 a Portuguese clergyman asked for a government patent for his claim to officiate as Priest in the church of Ramedi in Salsette.[5] "Padre Farelpadra Majardesh, a resident of Revdanda came to the Huzur at the Kukkam of Kasba Poona and informed that the Padreship of the church of Ramedi in Salsette belonged to him. Accordingly Ramaji Mahadev had granted the Padreship to him and the Sarsubhedar also had given him a letter (of confirmation). A patent from the Huzur should be given him. The padreship was therefore granted to him and he was ordered to enjoy its customary dues. A letter to Ramaji Mahadev:— As the abovementioned clergyman is in government service and cannot attend his duties at the church, he should be allowed to send an agent to perform the duties of the church".

3. Spirit of Toleration

It appears that this extensive jurisdiction effectively exercised by the Peshwas over the social and religious affairs of their non-Hindu subjects did not cause any discontent, for these Brahman rulers were uncommonly tolerant and generous to people who professed a faith other than their own. The grants and farmans issued by the Muhammadan rulers were not only continued but from time to time new Inams were given for the maintenance of mosques and shrines. They liberally contributed to the preserved forests was frequently supplied for such purposes. Cannons were fired thrice at the request of a Portuguese clergyman to celebrate a Roman Catholic festival at Revdanda. Baji Rao II permitted the Portuguese clergymen at Bassein to exercise all their old rights with the single exception of cow slaughter, an act so repugnant to Hindu sentiments.[6] And the other Maratha rulers did not lag behind in this respect. Daulat Rao Scindhia and his officers always joined the Muharam procession dressed in green as Muhammadans should do, and even today Muharam remains the most popular festival at Sindhia's capital.

4. Superstition

Their solicitude for the suppression of witchcraft shows that the Peshwas were by no means free from superstition. Further instances of their superstitious beliefs are met with-in their religious and social regulations. In 1721-22, one Rupee was given as a present to an Agnihotri to counteract the evil effects of the fall of a lizard in the hall of audience.[6a] When on the Dasra-day 1740, the flagstaff of the fort at Mahuli was struck by lightning, one hundred Brahmans were feasted and *Shantijap* was repeated a hundred-thousand times.[7] In the year 1751-52, there was an earthquake in the province of Kalyan Bhivandi and good Brahmans were ordered to assemble for a *Shanti* ceremony (to appease the supposed wrath of the gods).[8] In 1753-54 performance of a similar ceremony was ordered at fort Visapur,[9] because of unusual prevalence of sickness in the fort. We come across a set of similar orders during the administration of the second Madhva Rao. In 1773-74 the idol in the famous Pandharpur temple was touched by a lizard, and *Shanti* and *Maharudra* ceremonies were performed; over and above this one thousand Brahmans were fed.[10] In 1775-76 the Brahmans of Kasba Trimbak represented that they were seriously troubled since the discontinuation of the customary sacrifice of a buffalo to the local goddess on the Dasra-day, and the practice was ordered to be reintroduced.[11]

5. Influence of Orthodox Views

Sometimes the Peshwas were influenced by orthodox ideas. In 1744-45, the Peshwa was informed by a person from Bassein that during the Portuguese regime some Brahmans of the Yajurvedi class introduced the new unorthodox practice of giving their daughters in marriage to nephews (by sisters). But now as a righteous government was established and as the new practice was quite contrary to the *Dharmashastras,* a fine of Rs. 50 together with the punishment of excommiunication should be inflicted on those who adhered to this practice. The suggestion was accepted and instructions were accordingly issued to the officers in charge of Bassein.[12]

The first Madhava Rao excommunicated Sakho Moreshwar Belsare Joshi Kulkarni of Jejuri and confiscated his Kulkarni and Joshi watan because he did not observe mourning for a death in another branch of his family. Copies of the order were sent to government officers and the Brahman community to Jejuri.[13] In 1789-90 during the administration of Madhava Rao II the Prabhus were ordered to desist from pronouncing Vedic *mantras* and other practices peculiar to Brahmans. They were strictly ordered not to obstruct the remarriage of a willing widow in their community.[14] But it appears from an order of Baji Rao Raghunath dated 1796-97 that the Prabhus had the right of wearing sacred thread like the Brahmans.[15] Baji Rao II tried to enforce the old Shastric regulations about marriage specially in the Brahman community. He ordered that no Brahman should sell his daughter or keep her unmarried after she was nine years old.[16]

To Mamledar and other officers in Talukas and Mahals. "The Huzur has been informed that Brahmans sell their daughters to their castemen and keep them unmarried after the age of nine years. Thereupon this letter is addressed to you. You should strictly warn all Brahmans in every village under your jurisdiction against sale of girls and keeping them unmarried after nine years. Failure to observe this will not be excused. Make careful enquiry from the day of the receipt of this letter and excommunicate every one who may have sold daughters after the receipt of this letter. About their re-admission into the caste necessary orders will be passed by Huzur."

6. Widow Remarriage

Liable to be guided by superstition and orthodox views as the Peshwas were, a modern student will be struck more by the liberal spirit that pervades their social regulations than their occasional tinge of narrowness. We in Bengal are more concerned with the question of widow remarriage and readmission to society of students returning from foreign lands. We have often come across the tax known as *Patdam* (tax upon widow remarriage) in documents previously quoted and among the regulations about religious conduct of the Prabhus we have seen them stipulating that they would not oppose the remarriage of any willing widow of their caste. Widow remarriage was a common practice among the non-Brahmans of Maharasthra. There were two forms of remarriage—Pat and Muhurta; the Pat seems to have been more informal. Justice Telang says that the celebrated General Parshram Bhau Patwardhan had contemplated the remarriage of his young widow daughter although the custom did not prevail among the Brahmans and it is said he got the sanction of no less an authority than the celebrated Nyayadhish Ram Shastri.[17] Why Parashram gave up this bold idea is not known, and Brahman widows in Maharashtra like their unfortunate sisters in Northern India have been condemned to life-long misery and austerity.

Among the non-Brahmans, however, not only widow remarriage but marriage of a woman to second husband in case of prolonged and continued absence of the first, depriving her of anv means of livelihood, was also permitted. An instance of such a marriage is found among the papers in the Daftar of Shahu Chhatrapati. The facts of the case are as follows: One Godji Gaikwas, Patil of Mauja Bahuli, Farf Mutherkhore, represented to the Huzur that Jani, daughter of Manaji Ghorepada Patil of Sayagaon was given in marriage to Jotyaji Savant of Kasba Dahigaon. Jotyaji however left her and went away. She waited for her husband for ten or twelve years but he did not return. In the meantime her parents died and there was nobody in her husband's family to maintain her. Then she went to the King and represented that as she had none to support her, she should be advised what she should do. The King, thereupon, ordered her to marry a second husband according to the Pat rites. Then she came back to Muthekhore and informed the Deshmukh, Deshpande, and the *got* of the purport of the Raja's order, and they married her to Godji Gaikwad according to the Pat rites. But the latter was arrested by Pant Sachiv and asked by whose authority he had performed the Pat ceremony. Godji answered that he had the authority of the Raja and as he was afraid that in future he might be similarly troubled by others, he requested the King to give him a written authority. An Abhaya Patra was accordingly granted to him.[18]

7. Victims of Violence

The Hindus of Maharashtra in those days were more considerate towards the gentler sex than they are now, and the government always extended its support to the women in difficulties whenever necessary. The following case will perhaps make the orthodox leaders of the Hindu society gape in wonder. The original document was discovered in the house of the Dharmadhikari of Karhad by Mr. V.K. Rajwade, and has been published by Mr. Datto Vaman Potdar in the reports of the Bharat Itihas Sanshodhak Mandal: "Sambhaji Angre Sarkhel informed with due salutations, all the good Brahmans well-versed in the Vedas and the Shastras and the Dharmadhikaris of Kasba Karhad that Savitri, wife of Purushottam Palsura, a resident of Dhopsehwar in Tarf Rajapur, was going to her mother's house in the village of Rayepatan. On the way she was violated by a Muhammadan, Malik Abdala. The woman returned to her house and related the incident to her people, and a written report of the case was thereupon sent to the headquarters at Vijayadurg. The Muhammadan was brought to the Huzur and decapitated. The woman however prayed that as she was violated by force and against her will and as the Saheb was the upholder of religion, some Prayashchitta should be prescribed for her so that she might conduct herself in the proper way. Thereupon it has been settled that she should perform Prayaschitta in the holy place of Karhad in the presence of the Brahmans and she should be then admitted to the right of dining with her caste people, and to other ordinary rights. Therefore this letter is addressed to you so that you may prescribe a Prayashchitta in accordance with the *Shastras* for the lady in order to admit her as before to the caste and the rights of the Brahmans and give her a letter for her caste people in Prant Rajapur"[19]

Another document[20] discovered by Mr. Rajwade and published by Mr. Potdar gives an account of a low caste woman who was simply attacked by an intending violator, but was rescued by a wayfarer. The woman although quite innocent and chaste was outcasted. On her taking a solemn oath about her innocence after the usual bath at one of the Sangams she was not only given a *shuddhapatra* or acknowledgment of her innocence but was also publicly honoured by government.

It is a pity that after a century and a half of western education we are still unprepared to show that sympathy for such unfortunate victims that the Peshwas readily extended to them under similar circumstances. The Peshwas compelled a reluctant husband to take back his deserted wife, through a sense of social duty, for restitution of conjugal rights could not be claimed by a Hindu wife.

8. Informal Marriage

But neither the Peshwas nor the people of those times were unreasonable. Sometimes they would tolerate the omission of from if the motive was good, as the case quoted below amply illustrates. Sambhaji, son of Harji Gauli of Mauja Abte of Tarf Nid in Prant Kalyan came to the Huzur and represented that alter the death of Singrup Gauli, his wife, after wandering here and there, came to Sambhaji's father Harji and lived with him. Harji had by her a son named Chimaji before the *Muhurta* marriage could be performed.

After that both Harji and the woman died. At the time of his death Harji requested his son Sambhaji to get Chimaji legitimatised with the consent of the *got*. Thereupon Sambhaji and his uncle brought the whole fact of the case of the notice of the *got*, and they consented to get Chimaji married in a Poona family. He requested that the Saheb should issue orders to the *got* of Poona. A letter was issued and the Gaulis of Poona also admitted Chimaji into their caste.[21]

An informal marriage, though not complete for legal purposes, was declared valid of children were born to the pair. In 1755-56 the carpenter community of Sarkars Junnar, Sangamner, Baglan, and Daulatabad were ordered to acknowledge a *Shastra Vivaha* between Khandoji Banrao, a carpenter of Mauja Redgaon, and a woman after she had borne him a son. Khandoji had to pay a Nazar of Rs. 1,001 to the government on this occasion. "A letter to the Sutar community of Sarkars Junnar, Sangamner, Baglan and Daulatabad: Khandoji Banrao, a Sutar of Mauja Redgaon and Sirbande, of Pargana Chandvad, came to the Huzur, and represented that his first and second wives legally married to him (wives of Lagna marriage) were without any issue. His third wife, a woman of the carpenter caste, was married to him according to the *Shastra Vivaha* rites. Her name as Haibati, and she had borne him a son. He therefore prayed that his caste men should be ordered to admit her into the caste after the usual assembly of the community. The *got* is ordered to assemble and admit Haibati to their caste."[22]

It seems this laxity in marriage laws was allowed only among the lower castes. But in one case at least, we find that a parent's fault was not allowed to add a lasting stigma to the social position of the son even among higher castes. A letter from Shrinivas Parashram Pratinidhi to the Brahman community of Karhad relates that, the mother of Apaji Ram of Masur, was accused of adultery, and went to her parent's house, but Apaji should have the right of dining with his caste people and he has been purified by a Prayashchitta ceremony. All Brahmans should therefore procure that right for him.[23]

9. Involuntary Social Offence

We may now turn to those unfortunate outcasts who could not avoid dining with their captors, while prisoners in a Muslim camp. In those days of constant warfare, when everybody ran the risk of being taken a prisoner by their Muhammadan enemies, and as the Muhammadans of Janjira in particular treated their Hindu captives with scant consideration, their friends and relatives had to treat them leniently on their return home. The caste people of the unfortunate man were generally sympathetic and all that the Peshwa had to do was to sanction the decision of the *got*, receive a Nazar from the grateful outcast, and to prescribe the necessary Prayaschchitta for his readmission to the caste. Sometimes when the Peshwa was directly approached, a Rajsabha (or assembly of the nobles) and a Brahman-Sabha were called for considering the case, and a letter was then issued to the Brahmans or to the *got*. One case here, casually selected, will illustrate the system of readmission as it prevailed during the regime of Shahu Chhatrapati. "Putajibin Mudhoji Wadghar, Chaugula of Kasba Jiti in Tarf Chambargonde, while employed under Davalji Somvanshi, went with the army to Surat. He fell into the hands of the Mughals and was polluted by them. He remained in the Mughal camp for a year. When Balaji Pandit Pradhan was returning from Delhi, Putaji joined his army and came to his village. He related the facts to his castemen who decided upon admitting him into the caste. The Patils of Chambhargonde, Rasni and other villages communicated the decision of the caste to the Raja and asked his permission to carry it into effect. The Raja directed that Putaji should be first purified according to the Shastras and then admitted into the caste" (Parasnis's summary).[24]

Although the caste people could, subject to the government sanction, readmit a polluted member into their rank, they could not without such order exclude anybody from his caste. In 1742-43 Malharji Jadava, a Kunbi, was excluded from society; his caste people and the Shete Mahajan of Ahmadnagar were ordered by Shahu to readmit him into the caste.[25]

Not only could an innocent man be protected from the unreasonable oppression of his caste-men, but a man who had willingly or unwillingly committed a social offence could, if repentant, and willing to perform the necessary penance, be forced into his caste. Very recently a Brahman Barrister had petitioned the Bombay High Court to order his caste people to invite him to their ceremonial dinners on the strength of the old practice that prevailed during the Peshwa regime; but their Lordships did not think they could exercise all the prerogatives that the Peshwas enjoyed.[26]

10. Exaction of Dowry Prohibited

As the clergy in mediaeval Europe had tried to bring under their jurisdiction everything directly or indirectly bearing a religious character, so the Peshwa also, as the head of the society, exercised a control over everything social and religious. The question of adoption and marriage came as a matter of course under these headings. The marriage peshwas evinced a liberal spirit that may be profitably imitated by their modern descendants. Baji Rao II strictly forbade any exaction by the bride's father from the bridegroom, and threatened to punish all parties concerned in such transactions.[27]

"The officers of Talukas of Bassein, Vijayadurg, Anjanwel and Revadanda are directed to issue orders preventing the relatives of the bride from taking any sum either as a present or as a loan from the relatives of the bridegroom. The relatives of the bridegroom or other persons settling a marriage were directed to give immediately after the marriage, information to Government of any amount paid by them to the relatives of the brides in contravention to the above order. The following penalties were prescribed:

1. The relatives of the bride receiving any such sum to return it to the relatives of the bridegroom and to pay an equal amount as fine to the government.
2. If the relatives of the bridegroom or any person settling the marriage failed to give information to government of the amount paid to the relatives of the bride, the relatives of the bridegroom should forfeit to government double the amount paid by them to the relatives of the bride, and the person settling the marriage double the amount received by him" (Summary by B. P. Joshi.)

11. Forcible Marriage

These regulations are based on the strict injunctions of the Shastras, but the Peshwas did not hesitate to take advantage of technical flaws to declare a forcible marriage null and void. A marriage was nullified in 1778-79, although *Kanyadan* and other ceremonies were over and the *Hom* alone remained to be performed.[28] Such a marriage is still legally incomplete, but a Hindu will regard such an excuse as flimsy on a Hindu monarch's part. But what seems particularly strange is that they should sometimes go out of their way to order the wedding of marriageable girls without being approached by their parents.[29] In fact his double function made the Peshwa's position unique in the world. The Pope could excommunicate a man, but he could not force the execution of his order by a threat of confiscation of property outside his own kingdom. The King can condemn a man to penal servitude, but he cannot further embitter his position by excommunication. The Peshwas could do both yet the combination of these double authority did more good to the Hindu society than harm. In fact it is a matter of wonder that the spirit of reform gradually but surely growing under the auspices of the native rulers, should have been checked and retarded in the Bombay Presidency for more than a generation after its contact with the West.

A peculiar method of demanding justice may here be noticed, because it had its origin in the religious aspect of murder as a sin. Aggrieved parties sometimes drew the attention of the authorities to their grievances by committing suicide.[30] The aggressor, or the party giving cause of offence, was held responsible for such deeds, and not only justice was done but the aggressor; was sometimes required to perform a penance.

12. Prisons

We may now enquire how prisons were managed and how the great department of police, so necessary for prevention as well as detection of crimes, was worked.

There being no regular prisons some rooms in forts were generally used for that purpose. Elphinstone remarks that "imprisonment in hill forts and dungeons was common and the prisoners unless they were people of consideration, were always neglected, and sometimes allowed to starve. Hard labour in building fortifications was not unknown". Elphinstone's remarks were undoubtedly based on his experience of the worst days of the Maratha administration under that bad prince Baji Rao Raghunath. Hard labour, it has been found, is better for the health, both physical and mental, of the prisoners. And as for the rest, it seems they were treated according to the standard of the time. In Maratha prisons allowance of food was regulated by weight and not by price, and in apportioning prison rations the rank of the prisoner was taken into consideration. But such distinction is not unreasonable; because the standard of living differs in different stations of life. Even in British India, we find some difference in rations allowed for European and Indian prisoners.

13. Leave for Religious Duties

The Maratha prisoners sometimes got leave for going home to perform some religious ceremonies like the Shradh of dead parents, marriage of grown-up daughters, and the sacred thread ceremony of grown-up sons, which the Peshwa as the ecclesiastical head could not permit to be neglected.

In 1760-61 Govind Rao Apaji, was released from his prison at fort Chandvad, as his two daughters were ten and eleven years old and could not be kept unmarried any longer, and for the marriage expenses, an order was issued to give him in cash or in ornaments Rs. 1,000 out of his family estate which was probably confiscated by the government.[31] In 1776-77, the wife and son of Trimbak Ganesh Bhat, then imprisoned at Ratnagiri, were released for the performance of the sacred thread ceremony of the boy.[32] They were however to come back to their prison after the ceremony was over. In the same year Dhondo Gopal Kelkar, an adherent of the pretender, died in his prison at fort Ghangad. His wife was imprisoned at Ratnagiri. Order was issued to release her for the performance of the Shradh ceremony of her dead husband.[33]

14. Consideration for the Prisoner's Health

At times some consideration was made for the health of the prisoners. In 1753-54 Tulaji Bhosle was transferred from Vyaghragad to Wandangad because the climate of the former place was very cold and unsuitable to the prisoner's health. Among the papers of the elder Madhava Rao's Daftar (1766-67), we find a list of nine persons imprisoned in different places for complicity in a plot with Tulaji Angre.[34] The eight male prisoners were all put in irons, while the single convict of the other sex was differently treated. The fact is worth noticing as the names of the male prisoners show that some of them were Brahmans, while the female was an ordinary Kunbin or slave girl. In 1776-77, the shackles of Dhondo Gopal Kelkar were ordered to be removed because his feet were swolien, and he was in consequence unable to stand or sit.[35] In 1773-74, Hari Sakhoji and his wife imprisoned in the fort of Sinhagad were released, [36] because they were seriously ill. The next year saw the release of nine persons belonging to the family of one Ramchandra Viththal,[37] for the climate of the fort Sinhagad did not suit their health. The cause of imprisonment in this case was evidently political, for the brother of Ramchandra, then at large, was ordered to be imprisoned in their stead. In 1781-82 four female prisoners in the fort of Ghangad got *saris,* bodices and blankets as the place was cold.[38] That one of these women was not a Brahman can be easily guessed from her name Darki Kayasthin. Keso Moreshwar Phadke and his wife Rakhmabai were imprisoned at Revdanda. The lady became pregnant in 1806-07. The fort was an unsuitable place for her delicate condition and Baji Rao Raghunath ordered her to be released and to be sent to her relatives.[39]

The wives and relations of prisoners were sometimes permitted to live with them in their prison rooms to look after them whenever their health demanded it. The servants and the relatives in such cases were fed by the government during their residence in the prison. In 1777-78, during the administration of the second Madhava Rao, it was ordered that the wife of Mahadji Ganesh Phadke, a prisoner in the fort of Chandangad, and a female attendant should be permitted to reside with him, for the prisoner felt indisposed and the usual ration should be given to them.[40] Similar permissions were given to the family of Madhava Rao Krishna Bhingarkar in 1785-86.[41]

15. Treatment of Political Prisoners

But it should be remembered that no prisoner could demand any privilege as a matter of right. They had to depend entirely on the favour of those in authority and not infrequently had to pay for it. Sakharam Hari Gupte, a faithful friend and adherent of Raghoba, was very inhumanly treated in the prison. He was loaded with heavy irons, he was kept in unhealthy places, and ultimately ill health, bad food and unusual rigours of the prison life brought about his death. His wife had left no stone unturned in order to secure the government permission for nursing her husband in the prison. She spent her all and paid heavily for the favour which was granted to others. But when the favour was finally purchased her husband needed no nurse. He was out of all troubles.

But the political prisoners were ordinarily well-treated. Good arrangements were made for their boarding and lodging, as well as for other comforts, although they were strictly watched, and their communication with the outside world, and sometimes with their own warders, was strictly prohibited. Mr. Ranade has made mention of the rigour with which the supporters of Raghoba Dada and the pretender were treated. But we have to remember what trouble these men gave to the state. The Maratha statesmen were not naturally cruel. The pretender was not thrown under the feet of an elephant until he had fled from his prison and endangered the security of the government. The ordinary soldiers of his party were leniently treated, as were some of the adherents of Sumer Singh, the murderer of Narayan Rao.

It is a pity that we know very little about the internal management of prisons under the Peshwas. In Europe philanthropists and reformers like John Howard and Elizabeth Fry visited the prisons and exposed their horrible condition. Unfortunately, however, no such graphic accounts of the Maratha prisons have come down to us. In England we are told, "the people were made worse in prison. They left it better instructed in crime than when they entered". We do not know what the effect of a term of imprisonment was upon the morals of a Maratha offender. But whilst the denizens of English perisons in the 18th century were mostly small debtors, it appears that the prisoners in Maratha hill forts were mostly criminals, and some attempts were made to secure their moral welfare. Kashi, wife of Trimbakji Chawan, left her home and began to practise adultery. She was sent to the imprisoned in the fort of Sarasgad with instructions that strict watch should be kept over her to prevent her immoral practices.[42]

The offenders convicted for adultery were always imprisoned at different places, so that the man could never in future meet the woman.

Some extra precaution, it seems, was taken in the case of Brahman prisoners. The death or suicide of a Brahman was commonly believed to bring calamity upon the country. Brahman prisoners tried to secure their release by threats of suicide, and were therefore put under a very strict watch.

The greatest defect in the Maratha system was that the prisoner had hardly any right. He might be very leniently treated and he might suffer from all sorts of hardships. Everything depended on the nature of his offence, his rank and wealth; but ordinary offenders escaped uncommon hardship on account of their obscurity.

16. The Police

From the prison we shall now turn to the police. Here, as in the judicial administration, it will be convenient to begin from the village. The village police was under the Patil, and the chief police officer in the rural republics was the Mahar. The district police was under the Mamlatdar.

In detection of crime the *Jaglas* or village watchmen, consisting generally of Mahars and Mangs, were helped by criminal tribes as the Ramoshis, Bhils, and Kolis. Unless the stolen property could be recovered or the offence could be traced to some other village, the Police and the criminal classes had to compensate the party robbed. All responsibility however ended with the detection of the offenders or tracing the offence to another village. In the latter case the inhabitants of the place to which the offence had been traced were liable to make compensation. But sufficient proof had to be put forward for such suspicion before the police and the criminal tribes could shake off their responsibility. Mr. V.K. Rajwade had published an incomplete report of such a tracing of offence in the 10th Volume of his Sources of Maratha History. The case is so interesting that we wish that the rest of the report could have been recovered. Abaji Khando, an officer, was going home with a report from Dada Saheb. He was robbed by thieves near Khandyala. The people of Khandyala traced the offence as far as Bhuinj. Thence it ought to have been traced towards Chingholi, but the Ramoshis, by a common compact, asserted that the Ramoshis of Khadki had committed the offence and also induced Abaji Khando to support their assertion. The Ramoshis of Khadki were thereupon thrown into prison, but there was no proof whatever against them. Abaji Khnado's loss was valued at Rs. 30, and it was settled that the Ramoshis of seven villages should subscribe the amount.

17. Criminal Tribes

The peace of the country was generally disturbed by Bhils and Kolis living a semi-independent and altogether uncivilised life in the hills and jungles. Complete subjugation of these hill tribes was impossible. Hence their chiefs were held responsible for any theft and disturbance committed by them. For the Police duties performed by the Bhil Naiks, they were permitted by the government to levy certain customary dues or *Haks*. So successful was this Police arrangement that in spite of its evident theoretical defects, Elphinstone recommended its continuance in the early days of the British administration in the Bombay Presidency.

When there was any unusual outbreak of theft and robbery, an additional force from the local Shibandi or the neighbouring forts was sent to help the local police. A force of 101 Rohila *Gardis* was sent in 1782-83 to help the Kamavisdar of Naski, because thefts and dacoities had increased there.[43] The expenses of these additional police force were met by a house-tax payable by everybody including Brahmans, but the poor were generally exempted. In the year 1777-78 Krishna Rao Anant had to employ 33 Berads and Mangs at an annual expenditure of Rs. 2,104. He was instructed to raise this amount by taxing the well-to-do alone.[44]

Such additional Police force was also sent on temporary duty for maintaining peace and order in holy places of pilgrimage like Pandharpur and Nasik at the time of great religious festivals when people of all descriptions flocked there. In 1753-54, one hundred and fifty men from the forts of Satara, Chandan and Wandan and twenty-five horsemen were deputed to Pali for one month to maintain order at the annual fair.[45] In 1788-89 one hundred *Gardis* were sent to Naski to keep order among the pilgrims visiting the place during the *Sinhastha*.[46]

18. The Kotwal

In big cities the police was placed under an officer called Kotwal. His duties included regulation of prices and taking of census. The duties of the officer are enumerated as follows in a document issued in 1767-68, for the guidance of Janardan hari, when he was appointed to the Kotwalship of Poona:

1. Minor disputes in the Peths in the Kasba should be disposed of by the Kamavisdars of the several Peths: disputes of importance should be disposed of by the Kotwal.
2. The Kotwal should fix the prices of goods and list of the prices fixed should be daily submitted to the Government.
3. The Kotwal should arrange to supply labourers as required by Government from among the artizans and the members of the several castes in the city; sales and purchases of land sites should be made with the permission of the Kotwal who should prepare the necessary documents and receive the fees due to Government.
4. The Kotwal should take the census; he should keep a record of all persons coming into and leaving the city. The Kamavisdars of the Peths should supply him with information on the point.
5. Should the Kotwal consider any regulation followed by the last Kotwal or any new regulation to be fit for adoption, he should report it to the Huzur and act in accordance with such orders as might then be issued.
6. All disputes relating to roads, lanes and houses should be disposed of by the Kotwal.

7. The Kotwal should furnish monthly accounts to Government.
8. The Kotwal should issue orders for any proclamation being made by the beat of drum.
9. Professional gamblers should not gamble without the permission of the Kotwal who should levy from them the usual fees. Other persons are not allowed to gamble.[47]

It is needless to say that his ample authority gave the Kotwal ample opportunities for abusing it. The abuse of power reached its climax in the notorious Ghasiram, a Kanojia Brahman, who occupied the post of Kotwal at Poona during the administration Nana Fadnavis. Much capital has been made out of his case by European writers. Grant Duff remarks, 'No instance of greater neglect on the part of an administration, or of more extraordinary criminality in a subordinate officer, is recorded in the annals of any state than the case of Ghasiram, Kotwal, or Police Superintendent, of the City of Poona. This man, a Brahman native of Hindoostan, employed the power with which he was vested in perpetrating the most dreadful murders. People disappeared and no trace of them could be found. Ghasiram was suspected, but Nana Fadnavis refused to listen to complaints, apparently absurd from their unexampled atrocity." I do not think that Ghasiram's case reflects any discredit on the administration in general.

19. Forbes on Ghasiram's Case

It appears from a contemporary English account that there was not a tithe of evidence against Ghasiram, and he was an unfortunate victim of undeserved suspicion. According to Forbes, who derived his information from no less a personage than Sir Charles Malet, the mob was encouraged "by many persons desirous of mortifying the ruling minister through the ignominy of the cutwal his dependant". The Peshwa weakly surrendered the 'foreigner' into the hands of an infuriated mob that subjected the Kotwal to all sorts of humiliation and finally stoned him to death.[48]

The officers of Indian Police in those days were not without their faults, and we cannot say that supervision by English officers has absolutely purged that department of corruption even now. About thirty years ago, a Brahman officer of Bengal Police was accused and convicted of an offence, which would make Ghasiram blush and cry shame. That does not prove any neglect of supervision on the part of the higher authorities. Abuse there was, but it seldom assumed such a serious character as to be accounted as a great public danger. Elphinstone remarks, "The Police however was good on the whole, murder or robberies attended with violence and alarm were very rare; and I have never heard any complaints of the insecurity of property."

Baji Rao II, weak and wicked as he was, did much for the improvement of the police. A special officer called *Tapasnavis* was appointed by him for general supervision and inspection of the police force. They were quite independent of the Mamlatdars and their jurisdiction did not always coincide with revenue districts.

20. The Metropolitan Police

The Metropolitan Police at Poona became a model body during the administration of the last of the Peshwas. The efficiency and honesty of this body had extorted the applause of cities like Elphinstone and Tone. William Henry Tone served in the army of Baji Rao II, and he had first-hand knowledge of the Peshwa's Government. His remarks therefore claim our best regards. Tone says, "It is little remarkable for anything but its excellent Police which alone employs thousand men. After the firing of the gun, which takes place at ten at night, no person can appear in the streets without being taken up by the Patrols, and detained prisoner until dismissed in the morning by the Kotwal. So strict is the discipline observed that the Peshwa himself had been kept prisoner a whole night for being out at improper house." No less than Rs. 9,000, Elphinstone tells us, were spent for the upkeep of this splendid body consisting of a large number of peons, horse patrols and Ramoshis. Lt. Edward Moor and his brother officers visited Poona in 1792 and they heard that the police of Poona was "uncommonly well regulated."[49]

We cannot say that the London police of the time was as efficient as the Poona police, before its reorganisation by Peel. Sir Spencer Walpole says, "There was no efficient police force in London. A small horse patrol nominally guarded the suburbs; a small foot patrol nominally guarded the metropolis. The horse patrol consisted of only fifty-four, the foot patrol of only one hundred men. The peace of London, otherwise, depended on the parish constables in the day time, on the old watch at night. The ingenuity of man could have hardly devised a feebler protection."

The Maratha institutions, compared branch by branch with those of contemporary Europe, cannot fail to extort our admiration by superiority and excellence in many cases.

REFERENCES

1. P. D., Vo. I, p. 183.
2. B. I. S. M., *Tritiya Sammelan*, p. 93.
3. P. D., Vol. VIII, pp. 279-281.
4. P. D., Vol. II, pp. 24-25.
5. P. D., Vol. VII, p. 342.
6. Bikar, Vol. X, p. 276; Sen, *Historical Records at Goa*.

6a. P. D., Vol. II, p. 195.

7. P. D., Vol. II, p. 195.
8. P. D., Vol. II, p. 204.
9. P. D., Vol. II, p. 205.
10. P. D., Vol. VIII, p. 255.
11. P. D., Vol. VIII, p. 257.
12. P. D., Vol. II, p. 198. This custom prevails among the Gauda Sarswat Brahmans commonly known as Shenvis.
13. P. D., Vol. VII, pp. 360-361.

14. The order runs as follows: The Brahmans of Kasba Pen in Pargana Sakse came to the Huzur and complained that the Prabhus did not behave according to the regulations formerly made during the administration of the late Peshwa Narayan Rao about their religious conduct and secretly celebrate the Brahman rites. An enquiry should therefore secretly celebrate the Brahman rites. An enquiry should therefore be made and order passed. It has been found that during the regime of the late Peshwa Narayan Rao the following regulations were made and the Prabhus had signed an agreement to behave in accordance to these:

    (1) That they would perform no religious rite accompanied by a recital of Vedic Mantras.

    (2) That they would not pronounce Vedic Mantras, if any occurs (in course of their religious rites).

    (3) That they would not use cooked rice in offering oblations to the dead.

    (4) That in performing daily oblations, etc., they would pronounce Pauranic Mantras only and they would not feed Brahmans at their house.

    (5) That they would not worship the Shaligram deity.

    (6) That they would visit only the temples frequented by Shudras.

    (7) That they would salute Brahmans by calling out the word *Dandavat* and use the same word in saluting men of their own caste.

    (8) That they would not oppose the remarriage of any willing widow of their caste. The Peshwa orders strict observance of these regulations, made in his father's regime, and threatens any failure to do so with severe punishment. The Government officers in different Mahals are entrusted with the execution of the above order (for original document see Peshwa's Diaries, Sawai Madhava Rao, Vol. III, pp. 287-292). This document does not prove the illegality or otherwise of the Prabhu claims, and is cited simply as an instance of state interference in social affairs. I have not the least intention of participating in a controversy which has already become acrimonious, and nothing will hurt me more if the quotation of this document here is given an interpretation likely to offend my many esteemed Prabhu friends.

15. P. D., Vol. V, pp. 251-252.

16. P. D., Vol. V, pp. 259-260.
17. Vasudev Shastri Khare has proved conclusively that there is no evidence for this assertion; see his Adhikar Yoga.
18. P. D., Vol. I, p. 218.
19. Tritiya Sammelan Vritta, pp. 93-94.
20. *Ibid*, p. 97.
21. P. D., Vol. VII, pp. 325-326.
22. P. D., Vol. II, p. 208.
23. B. I. S. M., Tritiya Sammelan Vritta, p. 96.
24. P. D., Vol. I, p. 215.
25. P. D., Vol. I, p. 219.
26. I am indebted for this information to Sir Devaprasad Sarvadhikari.
27. P. D., Vol. V, pp. 266-268.
28. P. D., Vol. VI, pp. 260-261.
29. P. D., Vol. V, p. 259.
30. This was by no means peculiar to Maharashtra. Drury noticed the custom in Travancore also. See Drury, Life and Sport in Southern India.
31. P. D., Vol. II, p. 76.
32. P. D., Vol. VIII, p. 141.
33. P. D., Vol. VIII, p. 142.
34. P. D., Vol. VII, p. 239.
35. P. D., Vol. VIII, p. 142.
36. P. D., Vol. VIII, pp. 136-137.
37. P. D., Vol. VIII, pp. 139-140.
38. P. D., Vol. VIII, pp. 151-152.
39. P. D., Vol. V, p. 225.
40. P. D., Vol. VIII, p. 143.
41. P. D., Vol. VIII, pp. 152-153.
42. P. D., Vol. VIII, p. 190.
43. P. D., Vol. VIII, pp. 133-134.
44. P. D., Vol. VIII, pp. 132-133.

45. P. D., Vol. II, p. 72.
46. P. D., Vol. VIII, p. 136.
47. P. D., Vol. VII, pp. 233-236. Summary by B.P. Joshi.
48. Forbes, *Oriental Memories*, Vol. II, p. 135. The full account of the affair will be found in a letter published in the 9th volume of Aitihasik Lekha Sangraha by Vasudev Shastri Khare.
49. Moor, *A Narrative of the Operations of Captain Little's Detachment* (London, 1794), p. 364.

7
The Police

1. The Kotwal

The Maratha Government like the Mughals had nothing to do with the rural police. The village headman kept rural peace as best as the could with the help of his Mahar watchmen. But the urban police was maintained by the state, and here in also we find another instance of the Marathas adopting the Muslim practice. The head of the city police was the *Kotwal,* and the origin of his office, as the name indicates was certainly Muhammadan. His principal duties as enumerated in a document dated 1767-68 were (for full particulars see Book II) (1) to dispose of important disputes within his jurisdiction, (2) to fix the prices of goods, (3) to supply labourers for Government work and to supervise sales and purchases of land, (4) to take a census and keep a record of all persons coming to and leaving the city. And over and above these he had to maintain peace and order in the city.

According to Abul Fazl also, "He (the *Kotwal*) should keep a register of houses, and frequented roads, and engage the citizens in a pledge of reciprocal assistance and bind them to a common participation of weal and woe." "Of every guild of artificers, he should name one as guild master and another as broker, by whose intelligence the business of purchase and sale should be conducted." "He shall discover thieves and goods they have stolen or be responsible for the loss." "He should use his discretion in the reduction of prices and not allow purchases to be made outside the city." And "he shall examine the weights."[1] According to a Farman addressed by Akbar to all his officers, the *Kotwal* was required to supervise the purchase and sale of goods.[2] The *Kotwal* should according to Sastur-ul-Aml, "summoning the watchmen and sweepers, take bonds from them that they should daily report to him the occurrences of every *mahalla* (ward of the city) without suppression of exaggeration." "Do justice," the *Kotwal* is advised, "that people may liken you to a quazi in the power of arriving at the truth of a case. On the public streets of the cities post careful men to act as watchmen from sunset to 9 P.M. to dawn, to scrutinise the wayfarers and arrest those whom they consider to be thieves and evil-doers, and bring them to you."[3] Manncci says that it was the *Kotwal's* business to stop the distillation of arrack (spirits) the *cau-de-vie* used in the Indies. He obtains information about all that goes on so as to be able to send in his report. He also has the duty of arresting thieves and criminals. It is also his business to collect the income from the town."[4]

A comparison of the above two lists, the Maratha and the Mughal, of the Kotwal's duties leaves but little doubt that the Maratha Kotwal had to perform almost the same duties as those entrusted to his Muslim brother in a Mughal town. We have noticed elsewhere that the Maratha Kotwal's duties were to a great extent similar to those of the Nagaraka, the Mauryan Town Prefect. But it is doubtful whether the Marathas went so far from their own times in search of their ideal for a Police officer when it was easily available in the neighbouring Mughal cities.

2. Compensation for Stolen Property

We may also take note of a police rule of undoubted antiquity which was adopted by the Mughal rulers of India. Whenever anything was stolen it was the duty of the Police officers of the place to recover the property or compensate the owner for his loss. This compensation was on rare occasions paid out of the state funds but more generally by the Policemen concerned. The Ain-i-Akbari lays down, "He (the Kotwal) shall discover thieves and the goods they have stolen or be responsible for the loss." Manucci tells us that loss from robbery was compensated by the state during Shah Jahan's reign.[5] The same writer, whose statement is based on actual observation, says to the Kotwal, "If any one is robbed within the bounds of his jurisdiction, he is forced to make good what has been taken."[6] The Faujdars who supervised roads had similar responsibilities. Manucci informs us, "These *faujdars* have to supervise the roads, and should any merchant or traveller be robbed in day light, they are obliged to pay compensation. If robbed at night, it is the traveller's fault for not having halted earlier, and if he loses all, without his complaints being heard."[7] This practice survived in the Central Indian principalities till the middle of the 19th century. The Maratha policy towards such criminal tribes as the Kolis and the Bhils who infested their frontier was also an inheritance from the Muhammadan rulers they had replaced.[8]

3. Mutilation

From the Police let us turn to the punishment inflicted on thieves detected or arrested by them. Thieves often suffered capital punishment towards the close of the Peshwa period. Capital punishment for the same offence was by no means an exception under the Mughal days. Manucci tells us that Aurangzib decapitated no less than 500 thieves in order to "terrorise the perverse."[9] And again "Once when I was living in Lahore, fifteen thieves of this tribe were caught. They had robbed a house at midnight; they were seized and sentenced to death. When the officers of justice were taking them to be executed in front of that very house, they passed in front of my door."[10]

Mutilation of criminals also was as common a practice under the Mughals as under the Marathas. Jahangir ordered his *amirs* "Not to punish any person by ordering him to be blinded or to have his nose or ears cut off."[11] But the Wakiat-i-Jahangiri gives at least one instance of the Emperor's inflicting a terribly cruel punishment on an unfortunate Hindu offender. 'After conviction," says the Emperor, "I ordered that his tongue should be cut off, that he should be kept in prison for life, and that he should be fed at the same mess as the dog keepers and sweepers."[12] Nor was mutilation uncommon when Manucci wrote. The Emperor Aurangzib prohibited the sale of wine and other intoxicants and "he directed the kotwal to search out Muhammedans and Hindus who sold spirits, every one of whom was to lose one hand and one foot."[13] Convicted offenders lost their limbs during the Pathan period also as we are informed by the benevolent and humane Firuz Shah Tughlak, who put a temporary stop to this practice. "In the reigns of former kings, the blood of many Musulmans had been shed, and many varieties of torture employed. Amputation of hands and feet, ears and noses; tearing out the eyes, pouring molten lead into the throat, crushing the bones of the hands and feet with mallets, burning the body with fire, driving iron nails into the hands, feet and bosom, cutting the sinews; sawing man as under; these and many similar tortures were practised. The great and merciful God made me, His servant, hope and seek for His mercy by devoting myself to prevent the unlawful killing of Musulmans, and the infliction of any kind of torture upon them or upon any men."[14] Mutilation was a common punishment in the Kingdom of Golkonda and Manucci says that a Persian lost his offending hand for giving a slap to a Hindu who had given him offence.[15]

4. Trial by Ordeal

In the administration of justice, "Akbar encouraged the use of trial by ordeal in the Hindu fashion."[16] Ordeal by heated metal was commonly resorted to by the ignorant people of Sind even after the Muhammadan conquest of the province. Ali Sher Kani, the author of *Tuhfalu-l Kiram* writes, "An ordeal, still practised among the most ignorant, is that of taking a red-hot spade. Green leaves of a tree are tied on to the hand of the suspected person with raw thread, and an iron spade, heated to redness, being then placed on his palm, he must carry it for several spaces quickly and it has often been seen that neither the thread nor the leaves have been in the slightest degree affected by the heat of the red-hot iron, although when cast to the ground it scorched it like the sand in the oven of a parcher of grain."[17] James Forbes, an intelligent observer of Indian customs and manners, says that trial by ordeal was allowed under Muhammadan Governments.[18] And the Maratha documents show that trial by ordeal was very common under Southern Muhammadan potentates. Trial by ordeal is distinctly opposed to the principles of Islam though one may come across a rare instance of taking an oath after circumambulating the Kaba in vindication of one's innocence. Jalal-uddin Khilji wanted Siddy Mowla and his accomplices to undergo a fire ordeal. Ferishta gives the following account of that affair: "The king caused both Siddy Mowla and Kazy Julalood-Deen Kashany to be apprehended, and brought before him for examination. They persisted in their innocence, and as no other witness appeared against them, the accusation was rendered doubtful. The king, therefore, caused a fire to be prepared in the plain of Bahadurpoor, in order that they might be submitted to the fiery ordeal to purge themselves of their guilt; and having left the city to see the ceremony, he ordered a circle to be railed off round the pile. Siddy Mowla and the other accused were then brought, in order that they might walk through the flames to prove their innocence. Having said their prayers, they were just about to plunge into the fire, when the king stopped them, and turning to his ministers, asked, if it was lawful to try Mussulmans by the fiery ordeal?

They unanimously declared, that it was the nature of fire to consume, paying no respect to the righteous more than to the wicked; and they also pronounced the practice to be heathenish, and contrary to the Mahomedan law, as well as to reason."[19] Probably this heathenish practice was confined among the Hindus and was not resorted to, as in the above case, if the parties concerned were Muhammadans. The only logical conclusion possible under the circumstances is that the Southern Muhammadan rulers had simply helped the survival of trials by ordeal in the Deccan and were in no way responsible for its introduction.

REFERENCES

1. Jarrett, *Ain-i-Akbari*, Vol. II, pp. 41-42.
2. Bird, *Gujrat*, p. 402.
3. Sarkar, *Mughal Administration*, First Edition, pp. 94-95.
4. Manucci, ed. Irvine, Vol. II, pp. 420-421. Mr. Ramsbotham tells me that Eau-de-vie is more generally used for brandy, arrack was a rough kind of rum.
5. Manucci, ed. Irvine, Vol. I, p. 204.
6. Manucci, ed. Irvine, Vol. II, p. 4.
7. Manucci, ed. Irvine, Vol. II, p. 451.
8. Bird, *Statistical Hist. of Gujrat*, pp. 409 ff.
9. Manucci, ed. Irvine, Vol. II, p. 421.
10. Manucci, ed. Irvine, Vol. II, p. 458.
11. Elliot and Dowson, Vol. VI. p. 325.
12. Elliot and Dowson, Vol. VI, p. 314.
13. Manucci, ed. Irvine, Vol. II,. p. 6.
14. Elliot and Dowson, Vol. III, p. 375.
15. Manucci, ed. Irvine, Vol. III,. p. 131.
16. V.A. Smith, Akbar the Great Moghul, p. 345.
17. Elliot and Dowson, Vol. I, pp. 329-330.
18. Oriental Memoirs, Vol. II, pp. 389-330.
19. Briggs, Ferishta, Vol. I, p. 299.

8
Military Organisation

I

1. Mansab and Saranjam

For their military organisation the Marathas were more directly indebted to the Muhammadans than for their Revenue system. The Revenue principles were mostly Hindu in origin, but the Maratha military regulations were directly inspired by the practice in the Muhammadan armies. After the foundation of the Bahmani kingdom, the Marathas enlisted in large numbers in the Pathan army and during the Nizam and Adil Shahi regime they rose to very great prominence. High ranks and rich jagirs were willingly conferred on competent Maratha generals by their Muslim masters, and it is no wonder that they completely assimilated the military tactics of the Muslim rulers of South India. Having once formed a component part of the Ahmadnagar and Bijapur forces, Shivaji's early followers were naturally familiar with the Muhammadan military organisation. In fact Shivaji often enlisted deserters from his enemy's army. But it should be remembered that the genius of Shivaji warned him against a slavish imitation. While therefore the organisaton of Shivaji's forces had been largely influenced by the uncommon genius of their great leader, the Peshwa army in its organisation differed but little from that of their Mughal foes. While Shivaji's generals held their office at the

King's goodwill and got no jagir for maintaining their forces, the Peshwas had, to the detriment of the solidarity of their empire, introduced the military jagir system and granted *Saranjams* to their Generals in imitation of the Mughals. Like the Mughals again they exaggerated the value of cavalry and suffered their infantry to deteriorate. Foreign critics like Tone oberves that the Marathas had no infantry worth the name. And by giving preference to foreigners, the Peshwas and their officers deprived their army of that national spirit which formed the strongest characteristic of Shivaji's followers. But while differing in the fundamental principle underlying his military organisation, Shivaji had yet to retain many Muhammadan practices in his army administration. He recognised the distinction between Shiledars and Bargirs as the Peshwas did after him. In his methodof enlistment and payment he followed his Muhammadan predecesors. He honoured his men and officers for distiguished services in the battlefield almost in the same manner as the Muslim Sultans and Emperors. Even his tactics, which made the Maratha horseman famous in the military annals of India, were not unknown to the Muslim Generals. Malik Ambar had employed the same tactics against the Mughal invaders of Ahmadnagar, and the Bijapur officers on more than one occasion had found the same tactics equally useful against their heavily armed and armoured enemies.

2. Method of Enlistment

Let us now consider in more detail the extent of Shivaji's indebtedness to his Muslim teachers for some of the practices prevailing in his army, for instance, his method of enlistment. Sabhasad says, "Of the forces, the musketeers, the spearsmen, the archers and light armed men should be appointed after the Raja himself had carefully inspected each man individually (and selected) the brave and shrewd. The garrison in the fort, the Havaldar and the Sarnobat should be Marathas of good family. They should be appointed after some one of the royal personal staff had agreed to stand surety (for them)."[1] So the spearsmen, the archers and the light armed men were appointed after a personal inspection by the King himself and a surety was also demanded from them. The Emperor Akbar also apointed ahdis after personal inspection and taking a security. Abul Fazl informs us, "Without partiality or accepting bribes he takes daily several before His Majesty, who examines them, when they have been approved of the pass through the *Yaddasht*, the *Taliquah*, the descriptive roll and accounts. The paymaster then takes a security and introduces the candidate a second time to His Majesty who increases his pay form an eighth to three-fourths, or even to more than six-sevenths."[2] The practice of taking surety from soldiers of all rank was very common when Manucci lived in India. He writes, "All soldiers high and low, Generals and Captains, are forced to give surety and with out it they cannot obtain employment. This practice is so common and so general that even the princes find it necessary to conform to the custom."[3] And again, "All the said soldiers, Captains and Generals, whatever their birth or position, are obliged to furnish sureties. Without this they will not be taken into the service. This thing is universal and no one can complain. Nor is there any ground for complaint, the same rule being observed in the case of prices of the blood royal."[4] No wonder, that in those days of treachery and disloyalty a surety should be the inevitable condition of employment and the practice that was universal in the Mughal army, as the Italian writer says, should commend itself to the good sense of the shrewd Maratha leader.

3. Payment

In Shivaji's time and in the Peshwa days too, soldiers were paid partly in money and partly in clothes.[5] In Book II we have taken notice of a queer practice that deprived the Maratha official of a month's or two months' salary although he had to serve the State for full twelve months. Every Maratha soldier was familiar with *"baramahi chakri* and *dahamahi* or *akra mahi pay."* Here also the Maratha government simply imitated a common practice of the Mughal army. Akbar deducted one month's pay every year on account of the horse.[6] Abul Fazl informs us that, "The commander of every contingent is allowed to keep for himself the twentieth part of the pay of his men, which reimburses him for various expenses."[7] We read in Harivansanchi Bakhar, that Purushottam *alias* Daji Patwardhan used to deduct one month's pay for the same reason. In Manucci's time the Mughal soldier did not get even ten month's pay. Writes the Italian adventurer, who had personal knowledge of the Mughal practice, "For in respect of one year's service they receive six or eight months' pay. Even that is not all in coin; they are always foisted off in respects of two months pay with clothes and old raiment from the house-hold."[8] The Marathas found it specially convenient to pay partly in clothes because this enabled them to dispose of a portion of the spoils that they got in their Mulukhgiri expeditions.

4. Mulukhgiri

The term Mulukhgiri is of Muhammadan origin, derived from Persian *Mulk*, country and *giriftan* to take. The Sultans of Gujrat also regarded Mulukhgiri as a legitmate source of income.[9] Professor Jadunath Sarkar observes in this connection. "The coincidence between Shivaji's foreign policy and that of a Quranic sovereign is so complete that both the history of Shivaji by his courtier Krishani Anant and the Persian official history of Bijapur use exactly the same word, Mulk-giri, to describe such raids into neighbouring countries as a regular political ideal. The only difference was that in theory at least, an orthodox Muslim King was bound to spare the other Muslim states in his path, and not to spoil or shed the blood of true believers, while Shivaji (as well as the Peshwas after him) carried on his Mulkgiri into all neighbouring states, Hindu no less than Islamic, and squeezed rich Hindus as mercilessly as he did Muhammadans."[10] In practice, however, the Muhammadan invader had very litle mercy for his brother in faith and while some of the Maratha expeditions were but a prelude to the conquest and annexation of the country invaded, all the Mulukgiri expeditions led by Muhammadan Generals, whatever might have been their aim, were not rewarded with similar success.

5. Rewara for Military Services

In rewarding distinguished services in war, the Maratha rulers followed the Muhammadan precedent. Titles were conferred on successful Generals, they sometimes obtained the honour of using Sunshades or *Aftagirs, Palquis* and *Nalquis* and another distinction which brave officers could expect was the use of *Chaughada*. And Sabhasad tells us that Shivaji rewarded his soldiers with gold bracelets, earrings, necklaces, crests and medallions,[11] after his success against Afzal Khan, while officers of rank got horses and higher ranks. According to Irvine jewelled ornaments, weapons with jewelled hilts, palkis, with fringes of gold lace and pearls, horses with gold mounted and jewelled trappings and elephants were presented by Mughal Emperors to their military officers in acknowledgement of their services to the State.[12] Aftabgir is mentioned in the Ain-i-Akbari and Irvine says that in the Mughal army only royal princes were entitled to this high distinction. He writes, "*Aftabgir*--This sun screen shaped like an open palm leaf fan was also called Suraj mukhi. By the Moghul rulers it could only be granted to royal princes. In the eighteenth century, however, the Marathas adopted it as one of their commonest ensigns, and even the smallest group of their cavalry was in the habit of carrying one."[13] Aftagir was conferred by Shivaji on his Generals and officers of lesser rank as early as the seventeenth century. Similarly the honour of carrying *Jari Patka*, the golden standard, conferred on distinguished Maratha Generals, was also quite in accord with the Mughal custom. Irvine remarks that in the Mughal army "apart from titles or money rewards, or ordinary gifts, a man might be awarded," among other distinctions *(i)* "the right to carry a flag or simple standard and *(ii)* the right to use kettle drums and beat the naubat."[14] The Chaughadas granted by Maratha rulers were nothing but kettle drums[15] and the principal Maratha Sardars had their naubats as well.

Shivaji had conferred upon two of his generals, Kadtaji Gujar and Hansaji Mohite, the titles of Pratap Rao and Hambir Rao respectively. Rajaram also honoured his officers with high-sounding titles, but a mere glance at the list of the titles the conferred will at once convince one that the Chhatrapati was simply following the practice of the Badshah of Delhi. Hukmatpanha, Shamsher Bahadur, Shahjang, Rustamrao, Amir-ul-Umara, Sharfanmulk, Madarulmaham, Saphejang Bahadur, Shahajatmulk and Fattejang Bahadur[16] were undoubtedly of Muslim origin and not Hindu titles.

6. Pension

Irvine does not say whether the Mughals paid any pension to the minor children and widows of soldiers killed in action as the Marathas did, although Balban had granted to his old veterans a full-pay pension. The principle of helping the children and wives of such men was not unknown to the Muhammadan monarchs. "A rule was established by the Sultan (Mahmud Bigarah) that if an *amir* or any soldier was killed in battle or died a natural death, his *jagir* was confirmed to his son; if there was no son, half of the *jagir* was given to the daughter; and if there was no daughter, a suitable provision was settled upon the dependents, so that there might be no ground of complaint."[17] The Emperor Humayun also provided for the widows and orphans of his soldiers, as his step-sister Princess Gulbadan informs us, "To widows and orphans, land kins folk of men who had been wounded and killed at Chausa and Kanauj or Bhakkar, or who were in the royal service during those intermissions, he gave pensions, and rations, and water, and land, and servants. In days of His Majesty's good fortune, great tranquillity and happiness befell soldiers and peasants. They lived without care, and put up many an ardent prayer for his long life."[18]

7. Branding of Horses

Sabhasad tells us that Shivaji captured about four thousand horses at Surat and "a cavalry force was organised with them. As the distinctive mark of this force, a quardangular sign was branded on the right buttock of the horses."[19] For this practice of branding horses the Marathas were certainly indebted to the Muslims. Branding was first introduced by Allauddin Khiliji, but the practice was discontinued by his immediate successors. It was however revived by Sher Shah and finally introduced into the Mughal army by Akbar, to continue till the downfall of his dynasty.[20] Abul Fazl has given detailed information about the branding of horses in Akbar's time. Manucci, who was quite familiar with the military regulations of the great Mughal, is not silent about it. "All the horsemen," writes he, "who are *mansabdars* under the kind must have impressed on the right flank of their horses a mark made like this, which is the royal brand. From the day that they get this mark made their pay begins. The Generals also cause a brand to be placed on the horses of their troopers, but it is made on the left flank. Their brand is usually the first letter of their name, and their men's pay begins also on the day that the brand is imprinted."[21] It seems that Shivaji first branded his horses after the second sack of Surat. By that time he must have become well acquainted with the military regulations of his Mughal enemies. But we do not know certain whether this practice of branding horses survived Shivaji in the Maratha army.

8. The Shieldars

From the horses let us turn to their owners, the Shieldars. The Shieldar had to purchase his own horse and was not compensated for its loss, whether in war or otherwise, by the State. From a paper published in the Itihas Sangraha, it appears that this rule was suspended by Chimnaji Appa during his campaign against Bassein and the horseman who lost his horse in the siege operations got its price. But this was an exceptional case, the general practice was the same as that prevailing in the Mughal army. The Shieldar's horse was his own property and he seldom risked its loss. Irvine writes of the Mughal army, "The constitution of the army was radically unsound. Each man was, there can be no doubt, individually brave, even to recklessness. Why then do we find them so ready to retreat from a battle-field, so anxious to make off after the slightest reverse? Simply because they had so much to lose and so very little to gain. A trooper rode his own horse, and if it was killed he was ruined irretrievably." Irvine further remarks, "Moor noticed among the Maratha cavalry that the same cause produced the same effect. A reluctance to charge will be frequently observed; which does not proceed from any deficiency in personal courage, but from this cause: a great part of the horses in the Mahratta service are, we have understood, the property of the riders, who receive a certain monthly pay, according to the goodness of the horse, for their own and their beast's services. If a man has his horse killed or wounded, no equivalent is made of him by the Sirkar, but he loses his animal and his allowance; he will, therfore, of course, be as careful as possible to preserve both."[22] Moor wrote in the last decade of the 18th century, and we do not know whether his remarks hold good of Shivaji's army. It is however certain that many of his military regulations were suffered to disapear during the Peshwa period, and the Peshwas not only tried to imitate the pomp and splendour of the Mughal court, but also organised their army on the Mughal model. The organisation of the Peshwa army therefore was equally unsound.

9. Pendharis

Before we take leave of the Maratha army let us take a passing notice of the Pendharis who accompanied it. Authorised thieves were known in ancient India, and they accompanied the Mughal force also, to harass the enemy's country. Manucci says, "Along with the armies there march privileged and recognised thieves called Bederia (Bidari); these are the first to invade the enemy's territory, where they plunder every thing they find. The handsomest items are reserved for the General; the rest they sell on their own account. Prince Shah Alam, when he was within the territories of Shivaji, near Goa, had in his army seven thousand such, whose orders were to ravage the lands of Bardes because of my non-return, as I have stated in my Second Part."[23] Irvine remarks in a note that these Bidaris are sometimes confounded with the Pendharis. Such confusion or identification is not however absolutely unwarranted.[24] The Pendharis and the authorised theives mentioned by Mannucci shared several common characteristics. They accompanied a regular army to ravage and plunder the enemy's territories. The Pendharis paid a tax which amounted to 25 per cent of their booty, while the Bidari reserved the choicest items for the General. It may be noted that the authorised theives and robbers who accompanied the Maratha army were variously called the Pendharis and Lamans and in extreme south Bedars. It may not therefore be altogether unreasonable, though the objections of so great an authority as Irvine cannot be lightly rejected, to suppose that the Pendharis of the Peshwa army had their prototypes in the Bidari who followed the Mughal forces. It should be noted that it is not known whether Shivaji had, like the Peshwas, and auxiliary force of authorised robbers. Naturally the Peshwa army organised on the Mughal model shows more points in common with the Mughal army than does the earlier Maratha army that earned eternal fame under Shivaji's leadership.

REFERENCES

1. Sen, *Siva Chhatrapati*, p. 29.
2. Blochmann, *Ain-i-Akbari*, Vol. I, pp. 249-250.
3. *Manucci*, ed. Irvine, Vol. II, p. 377.
4. *Manucci*, ed. Irvine, Vol. IV, p. 407.
5. Ranade.
6. Blochmann, *Ain-i-Akbari*, Vol. I, p. 264.
7. *Ibid*, p. 265.
8. Manucci, ed. Irvine, Vol II, p. 379.
9. Mirat-i-Ahmadi.
10. Sarkar, *Shivaji*, First Ed., p. 480.
11. Sen, *Siva Chhatrapati*, p. 25.
12. Irvine, *Army of the Indian Moghuls*, pp. 29-30.

13. *Ibid*, p. 34.
14. Irvine, *Army of the Indian Moghuls*, p. 35.
15. For an instance of Chaughada see Peshwanchi Bakhar, p. 74.
16. Chitnis's *Sambhaji and Rajaram*, ed. Sane, p. 52.
17. Bayley, *Gujarat*, p. 167.
18. Beveridge, A. S., *The Humayun Nama of Gulbadan Begam*, pp. 178-79.
19. Sen, *Siva Chhatrapati*, p. 88.
20. Irvine, *Army of the Indian Moghuls*, p. 46.
21. *Manucci*, ed. Irvine, Vol. II, pp. 376-377.
22. Irvine, *Army of the Indian Moghuls*, pp. 298-299.
23. *Manucci*, ed. Irvine, Vol. II, p. 459.
24. It is worth noticing that Sabhasad thinks that Dilel Khan was accompanied by a body of Pendharis when he laid siege to Kondana. It is therefore clear that these Bidaris were known to their Maratha contemporaries as Pendharis. See Sen, Extracts and Documents, Vol. I, p. 52.

9

The Karkhanas

1. The Council

We have seen how in their revenue system, military and police organisation the Marathas had been influenced by Muhammadan ideas and Indian Muslim practices. Other departments had not been unaffected. Most of the members of the Astha Pradhan Council had Muhammadan designations before these were replaced by new Sanskrit designations at the time of Shivaji's coronation. But even then later heads of the Maratha Empire were known to the world outside, by their Muslim designation of the Peshwa while the Sanskrit Mukhya Pradhan seems to have been used in state papers alone. Even during the Peshwa period such Persian designations as Dabir and Surnis had not altogether fallen into disuse while, provincial governors were known, like their Mughal brothers as Subhedars. Karkuns, Kamavisars and Mamlatdars are words of Persian origin and must have been borrowed from the Muslims. Though the Astha Pradhan Council owed its origin to Hindu ideas and Hindu works on polity, its polity, its original members, the Peshwa, the Dabir, the Surnis, the Waknis, the Mazumdar and the Sar-i-Naubat had at first been appointed in imitation of the Muhammadan courts of the South. Thus in spite of its later re-organisation Shivaji's council never lost its original Muslim impress.

2. State Documents

We have seen in a preceding Book how every royal grant, sanad, and other paper had to be signed and sealed by the several Pradhans or ministers of state and how the accounts of the Provincial government had to be passed by the several *Darakhdars.* This practice was in all probability derived from the Muhammadans. under Akbar every parwanah and barat had to be signed and sealed by several officers and it will not be altogether unreasonable to infer that the later Maratha practice originated from the previous Muhammadan one. Let us now see what exactly the Muhammadan officers did or were expected to do with regard to the above-mentioned documents Abul Fazl writes, "The *Sarkats* are entered in the daftars of all *Sub-Bakshis* and are distinguished by particular marks. The *Diwan* then keeps the *Sarkhat* with himself, prepares an account of the annual and months salary due on it and reports the matter to His Majesty. If His Majesty gives the order to confer a jagir on the person specified in the Sarkhat, the following words are entered on the top of the report; *Ta' liqah i-tanqalmi numayand.* This order suffices for the clerks; they keep the order, and make out a draft to that effect. The draft is then inspected by the Diwan who verifies it by writing on it the words *sabt numaynad.* The mark of the Daftar and the seal of the Diwan, the Bakshi and the Accountant of the Diwan are put on the draft in order, when the Imperial grant is written on the outside. The draft thus completed is sent for signature to the Diwan."[1] Other instances of this practice will be found in the same Ain.[2] About the order of the seals Abul Fazl writes, "Farmans, Parwanchas, and Barats, are made into several folds beginning from the bottom. On the first fold which is less broad, at a place towards the edge where the paper is cut off, the vakil puts his seal; opposite to it but a little lower, the Mushrif of the Diwan puts his seal in such a manner that half of it goes to the second fold. Then in like manner, but a little lower, comes the seal of the Cadre. The Mir Mal, the Khan Samman, the Parwanchi, etc. seal on the second fold, but in such a manner that a smaller part of their seal goes to the first fold. The seals of the Diwan, and the Bakshi do not go beyond the edge of the second fold, whilst the Diwan-i-Juz, the Bakshi-i-Juz and the Diwan-i-Buyutal put their seals on the third fold. The Mustaufi puts his seals on the fourth, and the Cahib-i-Tauji on the fifth fold. The seal of His Majesty is put above the Tughra lines on the top of the Farman where the princes also put their seals in Taliqahs."[3] The Marathas, so far as we know, did not go to such niceties in affixing their seals, but in their case too every paper passed through several hands and several officers sealed it before it became legally valid. In spite of this slight difference even a cursory comparison will convince every one that the Muhammadan rule was the progenitor of the Maratha practice.

3. Karkhanas

Let us now turn to the Karkhanas. There were eighteen of them and twelve mahals, as we have seen in Book I, and both of these terms are of Persian extraction. First organised in Shivaji's time they continued down to the close of the Peshwa period. They had been, in all probability, most of them copied from Muslim originals. Mr. Beveridge tells me that all of them had Persian synonyms. Firuz Shah Tughalak had thirty-six Karkhanas or royal establishments. The treasury (Khajina of Sabhasad), the treasury for precious stones (jawahir khana, Sabhasad), the mint (Tanksal, Sabhasad), the harem (Daruni, Sabhasad), the Farash Khanah, the Abdar Khanah, the Imperial kitchen (Mulbak khana, Sabhasad), the Arsenal, the elephant stables (pilkhana), the horse stables, the camel stables, the gaukhana or cowsheds, are mentioned in the Ain-i-Akbari as forming different departments. A Mir Shikar[4] is mentioned and the mention of hunting leopards and falcons under the same Ain leaves but little doubt that here we find the origin of Shivaji's Shikarkhana. Sabhasad, unlike Abul Fazl, gives no detailed account of these departments. But so far as the Shikarkhana is concerned the necessary information can be fortunately called from a much later work, the Peshwas' Bakhar. In the Shikarkhana of the second Madhava Rao, wee seven or eight talking Mynahs and talking green parrots. There were several Chandols, (the pyramid-crested wood lark), several ducks, cormorants, several pairs of peacocks, one hundred or two hundred deer, hunting leopard, tigers and rabbits.[5] An adequate number of keepers were appointed to look after these animals. This bakhar also tells us that these leopards were used for hunting. Although this small menagerie offers but a poor comparison to the grand hunting department of Akbar consisting of hundreds of animals and birds. Yet there is little doubt that the Peshwa's Shikarkhana was an imitation of that of the Mughal Emperor.

In fact the Mughal influence had so strongly pervaded the different strata of the Hindu society that it could be perceived in their dress, in their manners and even in their religion and festivities. Thus a discerning observer might notice it even in the coronation darbar of Shivaji, the founder of the Hindu Padshahi and the recognised leader of the Hindu revivalists. While describing Shivaji's coronation Prof. Jadunath Sarkar remarks, "The coverings of the royal seat were a grotesque combination of Hindu asceticism and modern Mughal luxury: tiger skin below and velvet on the top!" But this was not all. "On the two sides of the throne, various emblems of royalty and government were hung from gilded lance-heads. On the right hand stood two large fish heads of gold with very big teeth, on the left several horses' tails (the insignia of royalty among the Turks) and a pair of gold scales on a very costly lance-head (the emblem of justice). All these had been copied from the Mughal court. At the palace gate were placed on either hand pitchers full of water covered with bunches of leaves, and also two young elephants and two beautiful horses, with gold bridles and rich trappings. These latter were auspicious tokens according to Hindu ideas."[6]

This was typical of the whole Maratha administrative system. It was a happy combination of Hindu and Muhammadan institutions. The Muslim conquerors came to India with readymade principles of government and finance but they were confronted in their new home with another set of principles and ideas, much older and in a sense more systematic than their own. To their credit they did not reject these old ideas that prevailed in their newly conquered kingdom nor did they set themselves to enforce their own principles at the point of the sword. When two civilisations meet under such circumstances they naturally interact on each other. The result was that while the Muhammadans borrowed something from their Hindu subjects, the Hindus in their turn got much in return from their Muslim rulers. Hindu influence was evident in the Muhammadan government and many Muhammadan sects and subsects in India.[7] And Muslim influence was equally evident in the Hindu literature of the time, in the Vaishnavism of Chaitanya and the Sikhism of Nanak. The Marathas founded their kingdom when this process of mutual influence and interaction had had free play for several centuries. And so in their literature in their language, in their dress and customs. Muslim influence was clearly visible, and in their government we naturally find a combination of two different sets of principles, indigenous and foreign, old and new, Hindu and Muhammadan. The basis was Hindu but the superstructure had many Muhammadan characteristics.

REFERENCES

1. Blochmann, Ain-i-Akbari, Vol. I, p. 261.
2. *Ibid,* pp. 262-263.
3. Blochmann, Ain-i-Akbari, Vol. I, pp. 263-264.
4. Blochmann, Ain-i-Akbari, Vol. I, p. 282.
5. Peshwanchi Bakhar, ed. Sane, pp. 111-112.
6. Sarkar, Shivaji, First ed., p. 277.
7. The Timuride princes of Delhi had imbibed during their long sojourn in India many of the superstitious beliefs of the original Hindu inhabitants of the country. Their belief in astrology was probably characteristic of that age, but Sir Thomas Roe, the English ambassador at the Court of the Emperor Jahangir, speaks of one superstitious rite that is still current among the native Hindus and was undoubtedly of Hindu origin. Writes Sir Thomas

Roe—"Then the king descended the stairs with such an acclamation of Health to the king, as would have out-cryed cannons. At the staires foote, where I met him, and shuffled to be next, one brought a mighty carpe, another a dish of white stuffle like starch, into which he put his finger, and touched the fish, and so rubbed it on his fore-head; a ceremony used presaging good fortune." In that "might carpe" and "a dish of white stuffle like starch" it is not difficult to identify a *Rohit* fish and a pot of *`Dadhi,'* things of good omen that every orthodox Hindu likes to touch and look upon when he sets forth from his home for a new place, even to-day. The Hindu and Muhammadan had lived side by side for so many centuries that they had naturally learnt to tolerate and unconsciously imbibe each other's social customs, common beliefs and even superstitious rites, and the process must have begun long before the conquest of India by Babar and his immediate successors. Towards the close of Tughlak period, the Muhammadans of India had earned such a notoriety for their heathenish practice among their co-religionists outside India that Timur regarded his invasion of India as a real Jehad; according to him most of the Indian Muhammadans were no better than heathens. In the *Malfuzat-i-Timuri* we read that the expedition was directed mainly against "the infidels and polytheists of India." The Muhammadans were neither in country "there were those who called themselves Mussalmans but had strayed from the Muhammadan fold." From a description of some heretics left by Firuz Shah Tughlak it appears that some of the Muhammadan heretics were influenced by the *Tantras* while others followed the Vedantic system of thought and yet others had taken to idolatry. See Hinduism and Muhammadan heretics, Surendranath Sen, Calcutta Reviews, January 1924.

GLOSSARY[1]

Abhayapatra—a paper promising security or impunity.

Abhiṣeka—literally ceremonial ablution, coronation.

Apṭā—a tree, *Bauhinia tomentosa,* for the origin of apṭā worship, see Valentia, Vol. II

Bāgāyat or bāgāīt—ground planted with fruit tree or vegetables.

Bakhsīnāmā—a deed of gift.

Bhárgava Rám—an incarnation of Visnu who exterminated the fighting race for no less than twenty one times.

Bāzār— a market.

Belbhanḍhār—a solemn oath on leaves of Beltree and turmeric. On one occasion even such an oath was dismissed as of little consequence by a Maratha Chief with the sarcastic remark that *bel* was but the leaf of a common tree and banḍhār he ate every day.

Beraḍ—a class of professional robbers, otherwise called Rāmosī.

Bhanḍārā—a feast given to the Gosāvīs or the Bairāgīs.

Bhusār—a generic term for the cereals, the grasses and the esculent culms.

Chāmbhār—a shoe-maker or skin-dresser.

Dānpatra—a deed of gift.

Darakhdār—a holder of a hereditary public office especially Diwān, Mazumdār, Faḍnīs, Sabnīs, Karkhānnīs, Chiṭnīs, Jāmdār and Potnīs.

Dasrā—the tenth of the lighter half of Áṣvin; for a description of the festivities celebrated on this day, see Valentia, Vol. II, Parasnís, Poona in Bygone Days and Gupte, Hindu Holidays and Ceremonials.

Dewāli, more correctly Diwāli or Dīpāvali—a festival with

nocturnal illuminations. For a scholarly discussion of its origin, see Gupte, Hindu Holidays.

Dhangar—they are shepherds and herdsmen and weavers in wool.

Dharṇa—"The person who adopts this expedient for the purpose mentioned, proceeds to the door or house of the person against whom it is directed, or wherever he may most conveniently intercept him; he there sits down in *dherna,* with poison, or a poignard, or some other instrument of suicide, in his hand; and threatening to use it if his adversary should attempt to molest or pass him, he thus completely arrests him. In this situation the brahmin fasts; and by the rigour of the etiquette, which is rarely infringed, the unfortunate object of his arrest ought also to fast; and thus they both remain until the institutor of the *dherna* obtains satisfaction." Lord Teign mouth, quoted by Forbes, Oriental Memoirs, Vol II, p. 391. Lord Teign mouth laboured under the idea that only Brahmans could institute a dharṇā. This is a mistake, even a Muhammadan creditor could sit in dharná at the gate of his Brahman debtor.

Farmān—a royal mandate, commission, or patent

Gālichā—a small variegated carpet of wool upon a cotton ground.

Gāneś and Gaur—Gaṇeś is the elephant headed son of Śiva and Gauri. He is the god of wisdom and remover of all difficulties. For the ceremonies connected with Gāneś and Gaurī, see Gupte, Hindu Holidays.

Gardi—an infantry soldier trained in European methods of war fare.

Ghānā—an oil mill.

Ghāsdānā—a contribution like the Chauth levied by Maratha chiefs.

Gondhli—a caste or an individual of it. They are musicians and singers and makers or Goṇdhal.

Gunhegāri—a fine.

Gurav—a caste among Śudras. They are employed in the service of the temple and are worshippers of Śiva.

Hakkadār—Any one having a claim or a right.

Harijāgaraṇ—vigil kept in the lunar days named *ekādaśī* in honour of Hari or Viṣṇu.

Harkī—money paid to the court, in token of gratification by the successful suitor or litigant.

Hāsīl—a tax or duty.

Hom—offerings made to gods particularly in form of libation thrown into fire.

Hoṇ—a gold coin, also called Pagoda. See Prinsep, Useful Tables, price commonly between three and five Rupees.

Huzur—the roval court or presence-chamber: also the royal person or the regal office and excellency as personified or as viewed concretely answering to *His Majesty, The Government, etc.*

Inām—a grant in perpetuity.

Jābtā—a regulation, law, statute, also a schedule; a describing statement.

Jāsud—a scout.

Jāwār—a plant and its grain, *Holcus sorghun.*

Jirāyat also Jirāīt—a land fit for agriculture as distinguished from bāgāyat land.

Kanyādān—giving away of a daughter.

Kārkun—a clerk, scribe.

Kārkhānā—a royal establishment as Prof Dowson translates it. Prof. Sarkar translates kārkhānā as a factory in his *Mughal Administration,* but the Marathas classed even the zenana as a kārkhānā (see Ramchandra Pant Amatya's Rājniti) and therefore Prof. Dowson's translation is quite appropriate.

Kasbā—the chief town of a Parganá.

Kaṭyār—a dagger.

Kaul—a writing of assurance, agreement or engagement as granted by Government, but in the Deccan this word was sometimes used in a still wider sense, see Ananda Ranga Pillai's Diary.

Khār—salt, mineral or vegetable.

Khārīp—the autumnal harvest.

Khelāt—a robe of honour.

Khijmatgār—a servant.

Khot—a farmer of land revenue, for particulars see Bombay Gazetteer.

Killedār—office in charge of a fort.

Kolī—either a hillman of that tribe or a caste or individual thereof who supply water.

Kumbhār—a potter.

Kuṇbī—a peasant.

Lohār—a blacksmith.

Mahāl—a small subdivision, or a Government department as in the twelve Mahals.

Majālasī—a royal court or an assembly; also an assembly in general of great, learned or respectable persons.

Mālī—a florist, a gardener.

Maṇtra—an incantation or a mystical verse, a spell.

Mártanḍa—the sun god.

Maujā—a village.

Māwalī—an inhabitant of Máwal.

Mokāsi—the holder of a mokāsā (rent free land) or the farmer of the revenue of it on the part of the person holding or of the state.

Mokdam properly Mukaddam, a title of the Pātīl or the managing authority of a village.

Muhūrta—the second marriage of a Sudra widow.

Mujāvar—a sweeper of a mosque.

Mukkām—a residence or encampment.

Musāhirā—a salary or a stipend.

Naivedya—an offering of some eatable to an idol.

Nala (Nālā)—A deep ditch.

Nāṅgar—a plough.

Nazar—a present to a superior.

Nhāvī—a barber.

Oḍhā—a pit.

Pāgoṭā—a turban.

Pānsupāri—a term for betel leave and all the ingredients composing the roll, a small bribe.

Pārasnīs—a Persian Secretary

Parīṭ—a washerman.

Prwārī—a village watchman, gate-keeper or porter.

Pāṭ—a second and inferior sort of marriage among widows of the lower classes.

Paṭṭī—a tax or cess.

Polā—an agricultural festival, bullocks are on that day exempted from labour, variously decorated and paraded.

Prāyaśchitta—a penance.

Rabī—the vernal crop.

Rājināmā—agreement.

Rāmosī—see under Beraḍ.

Rupees—Chāndvaḍ seems to be the Chandory Rupee of Prinsep's list; its weight was 172 grains and its intrinsic value 95,939. Malhāršaī derived its name from Malhar Rao Holkar; its weight also was 172 grains but its intrinsic value was 93.646. The old Surat Rupee weighed 144.50 grains and its purity was 99.367. See Prinsep's Useful Tables.

Sanad—a commission or a warrant.

Sangā—a cloth.

Saṇgām—the confluence of rivers.

Saraṇjām—villages granted for maintaining an army.

Sarkārkun—a minister.

Sāyvān—an awning, canopy.

Seer (Ser)—a Bombay seer = 11 oz. 3-1/5 dr. 40 seers make a maund, a Poona seer = 1 lb. 15 oz. 8-1/9 dr.

Shanti (Sānti)—an appeasing ceremony.

Sherni (Serṇī)—same as Harkī.

Shelā (Selā)—a sor of scarf.

Shiralshet (Sirālseṭ)—a corndealer who became king for about an hour, an earthen image of him is worshipped and then thrown into a well or tank.

Shirpav (Sirpāv)—a turban bestowed by a Raja or grandee as a mark of favour.

Shradh (Srādha)—a funeral ceremony consisting of offerings of water and food to the manes.

Sinhastha—the position of the planet Jupiter in the sign of Leo.

Sonār—a goldsmith.

Sūtār—a carpenter.

Swāmi—Maste equivalent to your Majesty or your Highness.

Tabrūk—presents from a Pīr's shrine by way of a blessing.

Tagri (Tāgdī)—a balance or pair of scales.

Ṭāk—a weight equal to about a grain.

Tāṅḍel—boatswain.

Tape—a small subdivision or district.

Thānā—the head station of a tālukā: also a post, station or lodge under the civil authority.

Til—*Sesamum orientale,* the plant and the seed pot have been nicely shown in a plate in Forbes, Ornetal Memoirs.

Ṭilak—a mark made with coloured earth or unguents upon the forehead.

Toran—a lintel.

Tulśī—A shrub veneraed by the Hindus. *Ocymum sanctum.*

Upādhye—A priest.

Varāt—An assignment or order upon the revenues or a treasury.

Varṣhāsan—An annual allowance or stipend granted to Brahmans.

Vavri (vāvḍā)—a paper kite or ornamental paper work.

Waf—(Vapha) a literally the pit which receives the boiled juice of the sugarcane, hence an indefinite measure.

Wakil—an hereditary estate, office, right, due; any hereditary right whether in land or in office.

Watandar—one whole has a watan.

Yadī—a memorandum, a list, roll.

REFERENCE

1. Compiled mainly from Molesworth's *Marathi-English Dictionary*.

10

Organisation of the Navy

Soon after his conquest of the Konkan, Shivaji found it necessary to organise a navy strong enough to check the raids of the Siddi's fleet on his coast. His fleet consisted mainly of Gallivats and Ghurabs as well as many river crafts of various description. Sabhasad tells[1] us that no less than four hundred Ghurabs, Tarandes, Tarus, Gallivats, Shibads and Pagars were built and organised into two squadrons of 200 vessels. Each squadron was placed under the supreme command of an Admiral, Dariya Sarang, ad Muhammadan officer, and Mai Naik, a Bhandari. Dariya Sarang was not the only Muhammadan officer in Shivaji's fleet. Another prominent Muhammadan Admiral, Daulat Khan by name, entered Shivaji's service a few years later. The fleet was in all probability manned mainly by the Kolis and other sea-faring tribes of the Malabar coast. What was their uniform, or whether they had any, we do not know. At Malwan, the principal port of Shivaji, there is a statue of the Maratha hero with the peculiar Koli hat on his head.[2] It will not, therefore, be unfair to suppose that the sailors of Shivaji's fleet generally wore a similar headgear.

Subhasad tells us that Shivaji's fleet not only harassed the indigenous sea powers of the suth, but also plundered the ships and possessions of such European powers as the Portuguese, the Dutch and the English. That Shivaji's navy was a menace to these traders is quite true, but he was not so fortunate in his navy as in his military organisation. He could hardly hold his own against the Siddis in the sea and the numerical strength of his fleet was perhaps highly exaggerated by his son's court historian. Robert Orme informs us that "The fleet of Sevagi had by this time (1675) been increased to fifty-seven sail, of which fifteen were grabs, the rest gallivats, all crowded with men."[3] Fryer saw on his way to "*Serapatan* (Kharepatan), to the *South* of *Dan de Rajpore* a Strong Castle of *Seva Gi's* defended a deep Bay, where rode his Navy, consisting of 30 Small Ships and Vessels, the Admiral wearing a White Flag aloft",[4] Prof. Jadunath Sarkar[5] points out "that the English reports never put their number above 160, and usually as 60 only". In all probability Shivaji's men-of-war did not exceed 200 in number, but he had a large mercantile navy. On land Shivaji depended more on the equality than on the number of his men, on the sea, however, his fleet was decidedly inferior to that of the English in efficiency, though not in number. The President of the Surat Factory was of opinion that "one good English ship would destroy a hundred of them without running herself into great danger".[6] This weakness was mainly due to the lack of good artillery as well as the want of a naval tradition.

The main strength of the Maratha fleet consisted in the gallivats and the ghurabs, vessels peculiar to the Malabar coast. The ghurabs and the gallivats of the Angria's fleet have been thus described by Robert Orme:[7] " The grabs have rarely more than two masts, although some have three; those of three are about 300 tons burthen; but the others are not more than 150; they are built to draw very little water, being very broad in proportion to their length, narrowing however from the middle to the end, where instead of bows they have a prow, projecting like that of a Mediterranean galley, and covered with a strong deck level with the main deck of the vessel, from which, however, it is separated by a bulkhead which terminates the forecastle: as this construction subjects the grab to pitch violently when sailing against a head sea, the deck of the prow is not enclosed with sides as the rest of the vessel is, but remains bare, that the water which dashes upon it may pass off without interruption: on the main deck under the fore-castle are mounted two pieces of cannon of nine or twelve pounders, which point forwards through the port holes cut in the bulkhead, and fire over the prow; the cannon of the broadside are from six to nine pounders. The gallivats are large row-boats built like the grab, but of smaller dimensions, the largest rarely exceeding 70 tons: they have two masts of which the mizen is very slight; the main mast bears only one sail, which is triangular and very large, the peak of it when hoisted being much higher than the mast itself. In general the gallivats are covered with a spar deck, made for lightness of bamboos split, and these only carry petteraroes fixed on swivels in the gunnel of the vessel; but those of the largest size have a fixed deck on which they mount six or eight pieces of cannon, from two to four pounders: they have forty or fifty stout oars and may be rowed four miles an hour". It is not difficult to understand why such clumsy vessels manned by inexperienced sailors should not be able to contend with the English on their peculiar element on equal terms. But we should note that Shivaji's sailors had on more than one occasion attacked Portuguese men-of-war with success.

Of the other vessels mentioned by Sabhasad the *tarande* was a sailing vessel of large dimension; the *shibad* was a flat-bottomed two-masted craft without any deck, and the *pagar* was only a well smoothed canoe. Most probably some of the crafts belonged to the mercantile navy. It may not be out of place to note here that Shivaji had a strong mercantile fleet that plied between its ports and the coast towns of Arabia. Unlike man of his contemporaries the great Maratha had realised that a strong naval power without a strong mercantile navy was an impossibility.

Besides doing police work against the Siddi's pirate fleet Shivaji's navy was also employed in taking possession of foreign vessels wrecked on his coast and collecting duties from trading ships. In Shivaji's time it was considered the duty of the state to regulate prices of articles.[8] This was done mainly by regulating export and import duties.

The naval spirit roused by Shivaji did not die with him. The Angrias maintained the naval reputation of Maharashtra till the destruction of their fleet by the combined efforts of the Peshwa and the English. The Peshwas also had a strong fleet for defending the western coast. The mercantile spirit of the Maratha traders also found a greater scope with the expansion of the Maratha empire. In Shivaji's time merchantmen plied between Arabia and the Malabar coast; during the Peshwa period the Maratha traders actually settled in Arabian coast towns like Muscat[9] and their trading vessels visited China. The naval policy of Shivaji therefore bore ample fruit, though long after the Maratha Alfred had passed away.

REFERENCES

1. Sabhasad, p. 68. Sen, *Siva Chatrapati*, pp. 93-94.
2. See *Itihas Sangraha*, Sphuta Lekha, p. 1.
3. Orme, *Historical Fragments*, p. 53.
4. Fryer, p. 145.
5. Sarkar, *Shivaji*, p. 336.
6. (F. R. Surat, 86, 26 No.) quoted in Sarkar's Shivaji, p. 339.
7. *Military Transactions* (2nd Ed.), Vol. I, pp. 408-409.
8. Rajwade, *M.I.S.*, Vol. VIII, pp. 21-23.
9. See Book, II.

11

Rajputs and Marathas

Rajput States Over Maratha Domination (1761-76)

During this period several attempts were made by the Rajputs to dislodge the Marathas from Rajputana. Sawai Madho Singh initiated it but was defeated in the battle of Mangrol. Guman Singh of Kota and Jawahar Singh of Bharatpur unsuccessfully tried to form coalitions against the Marathas. After the death of Sawai Madho Singh, the relations between the Marathas and the Rajputs were cordial for some time. The Maratha Generals by their plundering activities spoiled them.

The news of the arrival of Ahmad Singh Abdali in the Punjab alarmed the Marathas. The impending battle made the Peshwa to recall his Generals from Rajputana. Hectic preparations were seen in the Maratha camp. The Peshwa ordered Sadashiv Rao Bhau[1] to command the Maratha forces against the invader. He sent deputations to the Rajput courts to win them over to his side. But the predatory incursions and forced impositions of the Marathas had completely alienated the sympathies of the Rajputs.[2] So they decided to watch the outcome of the battle in a detached manner.[3] Sadashiv Rao Bhau's invitation to Madho Singh and others to send a contingent to repel the menace of Abdali was not heeded by them.[4] The Kachwaha Raja instead deputed Sadhu Singh, Dhaju Singh and Mool Chand to the court of Ahmad Shah to ask what his intentions were.[5] He even actively conspired to help Abdali as asked by him.[6] Because of his hatred of the Marathas Madho Singh made the other seventeen Kachwaha sardars in a deed under threat of being excommunicated, if they broke their neutrality in the conflict between Mohammedans and Marathas.[7] Abdali also intimated to Madho Singh of his intention to crush the Maratha power. He requested him to keep engaged those Maratha soldiers who were quartered in his dominions so that they might not reach the battle-field.[8] The Maharaja therefore attacked the Marathas in his dominions. He captured their `thanas'[9] of Udairana, Khetri[10] and Paharikhori.[11]

The defeat of the Marathas at the hands of Ahmed Shah Abdali in the third battle of Panipat on January 14, 1761 swept away every chance of Maratha predominance for the time being. The fog of their invincibility was dispersed.[12] Under Malhar Rao Holkar and Madhav Rao Scindhia, commonly known as Mahadji Scindhia,[13] the Maratha recovered from this defeat in less than a decade.

The Marathas had completely overtaken Rajputana by their ravaging activities. Therefore, the Rajputs did not hesitate even to side with foreigners against them. This attitude of the Rajputs was not liked by the Marathas. The return of Ahmad Shah Abdali[14] was a signal for the Marathas to commence their predatory incursions in Rajputana once again.

Soon after the debacle of Panipat, the Rajput princes stopped the payment of tribute to the Marathas.[15] Madho Singh made a systematic attempt to dislodge the Marathas from Rajputana. He began to look for allies and sent envoys to Najib Khan, Yakub Ali, and the Emperor,[16] Shah Alam II. He also deputed Barhet karnidan to Jodhpur[17] to seek help against the Marathas. The rulers of Mewar,[18] Kota,[19] Bundi and Karauli[20] were also invited. There was no effective response from either the Rohilas or the emperor. The past jealousies of the Rajputs came in the way of their union against the Marathas. Mewar was weak and had an inexperienced youth[21] at the head of affairs. Jodhpur, the only powerful state next to Jaipur, persisted in the hostile attitude encouraged by the support that Ram Singh[22] was getting from Madho Singh, which might cost Bijay Singh his throne. At the same time Bijay Singh disliked the idea of antagonising Mahadji Scindhia with whom he had formed a treaty in Posh, 1817 V.S. (December 1760) against Ram Singh.[23] The Hadas of Kota refused to be a party to the alliance as they suspected that Madho Singh's real intentions were to establish his supremacy over that part of Rajputana. This was corroborated by the hostile attitude that Madho Singh adopted towards his semi-independent nobles and his undue haste in recapturing the fort of Ranthambore. Madho Singh contended that Kota and Bundi should accept his sovereignty by virtue of his being the master of Ranthambore. This claim was unpalatable to Kota. Kota also could not afford to quarrel with the Marathas because of its geographical proximity to the Marathas. Finally, as Malhar Rao Holkar was lying near Kota so the latter refused to join the league.[24] Bundi and Karauli were negligible powers in comparison. So the Rajputs could not form a united front.

The failure did not, however, deter Madho Singh from taking upon himself the responsibility of ejecting the Marathas from Rajputana.[25] He had also decided to fight the Hadas as early as Chaitra, 1818[26] V.S. (March-April 1761). He had a dual purpose at the moment—that of driving out the Marathas and of establishing his hegemony over Kota. He was displeased at the attitude adopted by Mahararo Chatrusal in not accepting his invitation to form a united front against the Marathas. Raja Balbhadra Singh informed him that refractory nobles, namely, Soohag Singh Roop Singh of Sagod, Roop Singh of Palighat and Megh Singh of Rahelwan, were willing to join him against Kota.[27] The sole reason for such an estrangement lay in the fact that Madho Singh wanted the Kotries or *fiefs*[28] to pay him `Peshkush'.[29] These principalities of Hadas were under the protection of the sarkar of Ranthambore, administered by an imperial Faujdar, who used to collect the taxes and pay them to the imperial treasury. Sawai Jai Singh, in course of time, took it on lease from Emperor Mohammad Shah, and collected the revenue. When the fort of Ranthambore was transferred to Madho Singh by Ahmad Shah Abdali in 1753 A.D., the Kotries refused to transfer their allegiance to Jaipur. They, instead, sought protection of the Maharao of Kota because of his sympathetic attitude.[30] The Maharao took upon himself the responsibility of defending them against Madho Singh.[31]

The Kachwahas could not permit the annexation of territory by the Hadas and Marathas. So Madho Singh with his troops marched towards Rantambore. He set up his camp at Chatsu and called Raja balbhadra Singh to his help.[32] He led his troops as far as Uniara, a Jagir touching the boundaries of the Kotries, and levied a tribute to thirteen lakhs of rupees.[33] Flushed with this initial success, Madho Singh returned to Ranthambore. His troops marching forward clashed with the Maratha General at Lakheri, and made him leave the fort.[34] Never was next besieged. Another force attacked Keshori Paten. Both surrendered to the Kachwahas. Malhar Rao was in the know of the move initiated by Madho Singh for dislodging the Marathas.[35] The attack on his territory made him aware of the impending danger. He sought the permission of the Peshwa to invade Jaipur.[36] He marched from Indore and entered the Mukandara pass. Here he was detained due to rains. He encamped at Madhkargarh.[37]

The Maharao of Kota initiated to join hands with him against Madho Singh. He deputed Akhay Ram for this purpose and also sent friendly letters for Holkar.[38] Even before this, Kota had cordial relations with Malhar Rao and made presents to him whenever he passed *en route* to Kota. At the time of his visit in 1817 V.S. (1760-61) provisions worth one lakh were supplied to his forces.[39] Again, on hi return from Delhi, he was met by Akhay Ram at Namana and was given a *'Nazar'* of Rs. 51,000.[40] Next, when he came from Ujjain, he was offered Rs. 13,672.[41] Malhar could not let slip the opportunity easily when the Maharao was inclined to bear expenses. So he agreed to join Kota forces.[42] The papers of the postwar period show that the least conditions must have been the paying of allowances ranging from the minimum of one anna and a half to a maximum of four annas per day during the actual days of fighting for each soldier[43] and treatment of the wounded at the cost of Kota.[44]

The strength of the Jaipur army was nearly twenty-five thousand.[45] Hamir Singh of Ramgarh and Ajit Singh of Isarda accompanied Jaipur forces. Roop Singh of Palaitha, Nath Singh of Rajgarh. Chand singh of Sarthal and Guman Singh of Nagoda[46] assisted Kota. Malhar Rao personally led his own foreces. From the eight Kotries Sanman Singh of Pipalda, Amir Singh, Khuman Singh of Karwad and Khusal Singh of Gainta brought their own levies. The total strength of their levies was about 500.[47]

Jaipur troops crossed the Kota territory at Palighat.[48] The responsibility for defending this ford was that of the Jagirdar of Sultanpur. He resisted but was killed. The troops reached Bhatwara,[49] four miles from the tehsil headquarters of Mangrol. Here they came face to face with the combined forces of Zalim Singh[50] and Malhar Rao Holkar. The Kota forces numbering 15,000[51] were commanded by Zalim singh and assisted by Akhay Ram Pancholi and Dhai Bhai Jaskaran.[52] In early November, the combined forces had all the advantages of an easy retreat if necessary, but the retreat of the Kachwahas was difficult on account of the two rivers that they had to cross, the Banganga and Kali Sindh.

The action began on Magsar Sudi 3, 1818 V.S.[53] (29.11.1761) with the firing of Jaipur Artillery. It resulted in the instantaneous death of 700 men of Kota.[54] At this critical juncture Ballu Hada and Zalim Singh made a devastating assault,[55] on the Kachwahas. Malhar Rao also attacked, but the battle remained indecisive. On the third day, both sides fought desperately. the battle lasted till the afternoon of Magsar sudi 5, 1818 V.S.[56] (1.12 1971). Some 3,000 fighters of both sides perished and an equal number lay wounded on the battlefield.[57] Nine important jagirdars were killed from the Kota contingent.[58] The camp and property of Madho Singh were plundered by Malhar Rao Holkar and the Handas.[59] Malhar's skin was grazed by a bullet.[60]

The defeat of the Kachwaha forces sent a wave of consternation throughout Jaipur. Madho Singh, who had been watching the battle from Ranthambore, now hastened back to the capital. The garrison at Amber[61] was strengthened. The Maharaja asked Rawat Prithvi Singh[62] and Rawat Salim Singh,[63] the commanders of outlying detachments, to reach Jaipur immediately. Madho Singh himself stayed at Jaipur with light equipment and sent his family to Amber which was a safe place.

Malhar Rao Holkar chased the fugitives up to Khapra.[64] He halted at Mansharpur[65] to enforce his demand of tribute. The Marathas began plundering the territory of Jaipur. Kani Ram, the Dewan, opened negotiations with the Marathas for a settlement. While the peace negotiations were going on, Providence came to the rescue of Madho Singh. Malhar Rao was compelled to leave Rajputana due to the invasion of Bundelkhand by Shah Alam II and his Wazir, Shuja-ud-daulah. His retreat, naturally, disheartened all Maratha officers[66] who, on proverbially flimsy pledges of Madho Singh sent arrears, retired from Jaipur during February, 1762.

The Battle of Bhatwara established the supremacy of the Marathas over Jaipur, which had been temporarily eclipsed due to the disaster of Panipat. The centre of their activities was once again transferred to the sandy desert of Rajputana. They made themselves a formidable force against the Rajputs and were not easily to be appeased. The Rajputs woke up to the folly of their ways but it was too late for them to manage their affairs independently. Every state of Rajputana invited the Marathas by making lucrative promises—never to be fulfilled—to settle their mutual disputes till the British power intervened.

The defeat of Madho Singh made the Rajputs conscious of their weakness. For some time all attempts at uniting the

Rajputs against the Marathas were given up.[67] The Rajput Rajas, to avoid spoilation of their land, began to mix up with these marauders. They attempted to adjust the disputes amicably and deputed their Vakils to the court of the Marathas for this. When these representations could not make a headway, the Rajputs once again turned to forge coalitions against the Marathas but their traditional rivalries and the recovery of Mahadji Scindhia after the defeat of Panipat came in their way.

The mutual jealousies of the Rajputs made the Marathas the arbiter of the fate of Rajputana. Mewar, because of her ignoble strife, fell a prey to such acts of the Marathas. She was virtually bereft of everything she possessed till she was rescued temporarily by Zalim Singh who came into prominence by this battle.[68]

The victorious force returned to Kota on the 7th day of the later half of Magsar[69] (December 1761). Maharao Chatrusal received them at a distance of four miles from the capital. Malhar Rao Holkar and his officers, namely, Bithal Mahadev, Krishnaji Tantiya, Pandit Rao Karkun received gifts and honours.[70] Malhar Rao was presented a "Saropao" and Rs. 500/- besides Rs. 101/- for the treatment of his wounded elephant.[71] The total expenses of the battle of Bhatwara came to Rs. 35,598-7-9,[72] including 2,561-5[73] which was spent on garrison of Malhar Rao Holkar before he accompanied the Kota forces to Bhatwara.[74]

Both the Rajput and Maratha sources claim the battle as a victory for their forces. For Kota, it was a trial of strength between the Hadas and Kachwahas, while, for the Marathas, it was a question of their very existence in Rajputana.

Madho Singh, jealous of the dominance of the Marathas, wanted to get rid of them. By 1761, the dues amounted to twenty lakhs of rupees. He was unable to pay them. The defeat of the Marathas at Panipat made him atttack an already shattered house divided against itself. So he marched against Holkar after the monsoon of 1761. But singleness of purpose had never been his characteristic and, therefore, he thought of claiming the possession of the Kotries also. This led to his ruin at the hands of the combined forces of the Hadas and Marathas.

Holkar started for Jaipur, waiting for a favourable opportunity attack. He was invited by the Maharao to make a combined cause against the Kachwahas as the Maratha sources claim. The Rajput historians depict that Malhar Rao, who was encamping nearby, was hired by the Hadas to plunder the retreating Jaipur army.

Both the sources suffer from exaggeration so common in their annals. According to the Rajput sources, the Kota forces present at the battle-field numbered 15,000 only.[75] Chatrusal knew the preparations of the Kachwahas long before. With his meagre forces he could not have dared oppose a 25,000 strong force equipped with artillery.[76] He was also not confident regarding the Bundi contingent which actually came to Kota but did not participate in the battle. Therefore, he won over Malhar Rao by sharing the responsibility of financing the project and furnishing forces that Kota could afford. This was why Kota paid the troops of Malhar Rao and got the wounded treated at her expense. Malhar Rao stood in sore need of money. This was fulfilled by Kota, and he prepared himself to avenge the wrongs done by the Kachwahas. Had Malhar Rao Holkar been hired for the plunder alone, Kota would not have undergone such heavy expenses. Had it been an action between the Hadas and Kachwahas, the latter would not have sued for peace with Malhar Rao Holkar. But the opening of the negotiations between Malhar Rao and Madho Singh prove that Malhar was the dominant and not a secondary party. It appears that Malhar Rao had reached some understanding on the Kotries as after this battle the cause of the Kotries was never espoused by any Kachwaha King.

The Rajput sources claim that Madho Singh was at the time too weak to face Malhar Rao Holkar whose contingent had returned intact[77] from the battle-field of Panipat. But, on the other hand, Madho Singh tried to exploit the so-called predicament of Malhar Rao Holkar—his exhausted treasure, rivalry with Scindhia and the disillusionment of his forces. Malhar's aggressive movements indicated an invasion on his dominions and so Madho Singh prepared to meet him before he entered his state. The only misfortune for him was that he had a duality of purpose, which prompted the Handas and Marathas to pool their resources. Thus it is clear that the action was a joint venture of the Marathas and Hadas against Madho Singh.[78]

Between 1762 and 1764, the Marathas could not pay any attention to Jaipur on account of internal dissensions at Poona. During this time the Marathas reminded Madho Singh for payment. Kedarji Scindhia asked for the arrears of tribute amounting to twelve lakh of rupees.[79] Madho Singh, it appears, paid half of it as the subsequent demand amounted to 6 lakhs only.[80] Again at the persuasion of the Peshwa, Madho Singh agreed to pay[81] four and a half lakhs of rupees. Out of this Rs. 2,50,000 were to be paid immediately in banker's bills and 2 lakhs later on by instalments. But Madho Singh could not fulfil his promise and so constant reminders poured in throughout the year 1820 V.S.[82] (1762-63). The Rajputs evaded payment so long as it was not backed up by force of arms. This was the only course left open to the Rajputs, for between their rapidly falling revenues and constantly increasing demands of the Marathas, they could not effect a way out.

The immediate reason for the renewal of the action was that Madho Singh first delayed[83] and then denied to despatch two thousand of his forces for the help of the Peshwa to settle the Deccan affairs. When peace was restored at Poona, Malhar Rao proceeded towards Rajputana to put pressure on Madho singh for payment. He encamped at Chatsoo[84] and demanded the tribute. Madho Singh summoned his nobles for giving battle to Malhar Rao Holkar. They advised him to save the country from devastation by agreeing to pay the Maratha chief.[85] Bijay Singh did not favour the cause of Madho Singh against Holkar.[86]

When the payment was not forth-coming Malhar Rao proceeded to Jobner[87] and began to plunder.[88] Madho Singh then deputed Vidya Guru Bhatt, Raja Sada Shiv, Raj Singh and Shiam Singh to settle the dues.[89]

The meeting of rival representatives was fruitful. Malhar Rao made the Kachwahas acquiesce in his demand for Rs. 35,00,001 in stipulation of the clearance of all is arrears.[90] Out of this Rs. 10,00,001 were to be paid in four instalments—the first of Rs. 4,00,001 to be paid immediately and the rest each of Rs. 2,00,000 to be paid on Magh Sudi 1, 1821 V.S. (22.1.1765), Phalgun sudi 15, 1821 V.S. (7.3.1765) and Asadh Budi 1, 1822 V.S. (4.6.1765) respectively. The rest of the amount of Rs. 25,00,000 was to be paid during the next 6 years in annual instalments of which Rs. 4,25,000 each in the year 1822 to 1825 V.S. and Rs. 4,00,000 each in 1826 to 1827 V.S. In addition to this the Parganas of Tonk and Rampura were ceded to the Marathas. A jagir worth Rs. 1 lakh was bestowed upon Mala Rao, son of Malhar Rao Holkar, of Maharaja's own accord. Having reached the agreement Malhar Rao left Jaipur.

The understanding was no more than a mere scrap of paper. It was dire necessity for Madho Singh to reach an understanding to save his kingdom from being ravaged. Sawai Madho Singh gained his objective by paying Rs. 4,00,001 immediately and making vague promises for the rest. But the severance of Tonk and Rampura from the Kachwaha state was a permanent loss to him not only in terms of money alone, but it gave the Marathas a stronghold in the heart of Rajputana whence they could carry on their operations conveniently. The Maharaja paid the instalments punctually during 1822 V.S. (1765-66), after which he again stopped payment.[91]

For Malhar Rao Holkar the treaty not only riveted the chains of his supremacy on Jaipur but also provided an immediate payment of a handsome sum by which he could set his affairs in order. It also served to mark his superiority on the Peshwa against his rival Mahadji Scindhia as he had subdued the powerful Kachwaha Raja all alone for the time being.

The battle of Bhatwara brought to the fore-front another chain of events which deserve our consideration. Maharao Chatrusal was pained at the attitude which Rao Raja Ummed Singh had adopted at the battle of Bhatwara.[92] The feeling of revenge was desperate and soon he got an opportunity. Budh Singh helped Maharaja Abhay Singh of Jodhpur when Mahadji Scindhia and Kedarji Scindhia invaded Marwar to punish the ruler for the untoward behaviour meted out to Jayaji Rao Scindhia. Mahadji Scindhia himself was pressing Bundi for payment of the tribute three years in arrears. Maharao Chatrusal deputed Akhay Ram Kayastha and his son Keshav Ram to meet Mahadji Scindhia,[93] at Majok. Akhay Ram promised that the Kota forces would help him in his venture against Bundi.[94] Bundi foresaw such a move and so sounded Madho Singh for help.[95] Soon a treaty was concluded by which they promised mutual help to each other.[96]

On the other hand, Mahadji Scindhia, for playing off one Rajput against the other, accepted it and the combined forces of Kota and Mahadji encamped at Nanwak near Bundi. They ravaged the country.[97] Abhay singh Rathor[98] and Dewan Kani Ram[99] were deputed to appeal to the Marathas to restore peace, but the outbreak of hostilities seemed inevitable.[100] The Marathas through Pancholi Hira Nand and Purohit Jai Krishna demanded 7 lakhs of rupees as "Fauj Kharch". They also claimed the tribute for the last 3 years.[101] When the peace negotiations failed, Ummed Singh got ready for the battle. He asked Madho Singh to send his contingent[102] under Raj Singh Harshav.[103] Shahpura contingent under Malim Singh also joined him.[104] A small skirmish took place between the rival forces but Ummed Singh, feeling himself weak, sued for peace.[105] Neither the Kota records nor Marathi sources throw any light on the terms of the treaty, but Kaviraj Devi Dan mentions that Mahadji Scindhia was sent off by paying his dues.[106] Kota incurred an expenditure of Rs. 1,84,000 on the expedition.[107] Mahadji got a foothold in this part of Rajputana.

When the Marathas were busy with these affairs, Jawahar Singh, the Jat Raja of Bharatpur, took advantage of this opportunity. The Jaipur Raja had, of late, espoused the cause of Najib-ud-Dollah, the sworn enemy of Jawahar Singh. Therefore, he hired an army 25,000 strong of Sikh mercenaries under Jassa Singh and Tara Singh[108] and entered Jaipur. He began plundering it.

Madho Singh realising that he alone could not face the danger, sought the help of the Marathas. He requested Malhar Rao Holkar and Mahadji Scindhia to help him.[109] Malhar Rao sent his forces under Santaji Bable and Govind Rao, promising to come later in person.[110] Scindhia ordered Achyut Rao Ganesh, who was plundering near Kishangarh, to hasten to Jaipur.[111] He was promised a subsidy of Rs. 5,000 daily. This intervention of the Marathas on behalf of Jaipur made Jawahar Singh nervous, for he could not fight single-handed with them. He patched up a truce with Madho Singh through Nawal Singh. Jaipur was saved from the atrocities of the Jats due to the timely help of the Marathas. The Jat menace compelled Jaipur to adopt a pro-Maratha policy.

Jawahar Singh's plans were frustrated due to the undue interference of the Marathas and so he was jealous of the power which the Marathas wielded over Rajputana. He, therefore, decided to expel them. He marched to Pushkar, near Ajmer, where Bijay Singh met him by invitation on Kartik Sudi 15, 1824 V.S.[112] (6.11.1767), and exchanged turban as a token of brotherhood.[113] They vowed to wage a war jointly against the Marathas and drive them across the Narbada. Bijay Singh invited Madho Singh to join the league but the latter spurned the offer in abusive terms.[114] It offended Jawahar Singh. Madho Singh wisely plotted to attack Jawahar Singh's kingdom in his absence with the help of the Marathas. He got the help of Bikaner[115] through Krishna Kant and Vyas Bhawani Das.[116] Bikaner provided some troops for his help. Raja Ragho Dev Rawat Singh and

Arjun Singh brought some forces from Udaipur.[117] Raja Ragho Dev was also sent to Kota and secured a force 3,000 strong.[118] Friendly letters were also addressed to Tukoji Holkar[119] who acceded to his request.[120] A respectable number under Shiv Gangadhar joined Madho Singh.[121]

Madho Singh's preparations were not a secret. At his instance, Yashwant Rao Bable and Raj Singh attacked Deeg and Kumbher.[122] Bijay Singh, hearing of such developments, requested Madho Singh not to harass the Jat Raja on his return journey and he promised it. Bijay Singh then returned to Maroth.[123] Contrary to the promise, the Kachwahas and the Marathas attacked the Jat army on Posh Budi 9, 1824 V.S.[124] (14-12-1767). The Jats and Rathors were completely routed.[125] The Jaipur forces lost a number of their heroic Sardars.[126] When Bijay Singh came to know of this, he reprimanded Madho Singh for such a treacherous act.[127]

The emergence of the Jat power under Jawahar Singh commplicated the political atmosphere of Rajputana. His rivalry with Madho Singh and the Marathas confused the situation. Upto this time the rivalry was restricted to the Rajputs alone but now the Jats became the sworn enemy of both the Rajputs and Marathas alike. Had this state of affairs continued, it would have proved ruinous to Rajputana, but the death of Jawahar Singh and Madho Singh[128] lessened the tension. By Jawahar Singh's death, the Marathas were relieved of a perpetual enemy who was opposed to their penetration into Rajputana.

This conflict with the Jats proved costly to Jaipur as it encouraged the chief of Macheri to make a bid for his independence from Jaipur. He took refuge with the Jat Raja and ultimately succeeded in it.

The same feeling of vengeance was felt by the other Rajput chiefs. At heart they disliked the predatory habits of the Marathas and were always on the look out for an opportunity to expel them. Though the Hadas were traditional friends of Holkar, yet they initiated a move to forge a united front of Jaipur. Jodhpur and Mewar against the Marathas.[129] Bijay Singh sent Padam Singh to the Maharana of Udaipur.[130] Vyas Raghu Nath and Purohit Hathi Ram were sent to Jaipur and Jodhpur respectively.[131] Kota contemplated an early action and asked Pancholi Ram Krishna to bring with him a respectable army.[132] They decided to assemble at Nathdwara[133] under the guise of making a pilgrimage. Guman Singh, the new ruler of Kota, asked Sowan Singh Sisodia to come fully prepared at a meeting of Rana Ari Singh, Bijay Singh had been fixed up with him at Nathdwara.[134] Maharao Guman Singh reached Nathdwara. He was followed by Maharaja Bijay Singh. Maharana Ari Singh was the last to arrive and was received at a distance of three miles.[135] The meeting took place as scheduled on Kartik Sudi 10, 1823[136] V.S. (11-11-1766), but as the Kachwahas did not participate and Mewar showed disinterestedness, nothing could be achieved. All the participants started on their journey back home. Guman Singh reached Kota on Magsar Sudi 4, 1823, V.S.[137] (5-12-1766). Realising the consequences of the failure of his move, Maharao Guman Singh asked Pandit Abhaji to impress upon Malhar Rao Holkar his fidelity to the Marathas.[138]

Though this move failed to achieve any tangible results, yet it signified resentment against the destructive character of Maratha influence in Rajputana. It clearly demonstrated that it was the weakness and disunity among Rajput states which strengthened the Marathas. The attitude of the Rajputs toward the Marathas was ambivalent. On the one hand, they sought the help of the Marathas to settle their scores with their Rajput rivals, while, on the other hand, they were tired of their demands. These divergencies came in their way of a united front against the Marathas. thus a period of active conspiring against the Marathas came to an end.

After the death of Sawai Madho Singh in March 1768, his son, Prithvi singh, ascended the throne. The Peshwa, Madhav Rao, sent a `Pagri' recognising him as the lawful heir. He desired to maintain good relations between the two `durbars.'[139] Sawai Prithvi Singh also reciprocated the friendly sentiments of Madhav Rao.[140] But these profuse professions could only be maintained as long as Maratha interests were intact.

By the end of march 1769, the Peshwa had şubdued his enemies in the south. He ordered Ramchandra Ganesh and Visaji Krishna to proceed towards the North with 15,000 state cavalry.[141] The object was to re-establish the hold of the Marathas in the North. It implied the realisation of a war indemnity from the Jat Raja according to the treaty of May 26, 1754, and to possess the lands granted by the Delhi Government to the Marathas for the help up to 1754.[142] They marched towards the Khechi country of Raghogarh and encamped at Aroni.[143] While proceeding towards Narsingarh,[144] Tukoji[145] and Ramchandra Ganesh[146] caused a huge devastation. These depredations made Raja Balbhadra Singh appeal for help to Sawai Prithvi Singh.[147] He also requested him to instruct his Vakils with Tukoji for prevailing upon him to stop this devastation.[148]

Sawai prithvi Singh's letter to the Maratha chiefs had no effect.[149] Tukoji also did not care for the offer of mediation.[150] The Raja at last offered Rs. 4,65,000 as the Maratha dues.[151] Out of this two lakhs were immediately paid, the paraganas of Aroni and Madusudangarh were handed over to the Marathas[152] for Rs. 1,65,000 and for the balance the Raja himself accompanied the Maratha forces.[153] Once again in the year 1830 V.S. (1773-74), Sawai Prithvi Singh addressed a letter to Tukoji Holkar and Nanaji Pandit reminding them of the happy relations between the two darbars and requested them to be lenient towards Raja Balbhadra Singh in realising the dues.[154]

While in Khichiwara, the Marathas demanded Rs. two lakhs and seventy thousand as the dues from Kota.[155] The Maharao was uncertain as to the policy to be followed towards them. He instructed Pancholi Shiv Nath to handle the problem tactfully so that neither side might feel offended.[156] The Maharao's inability to meet the demand brought the Marathas into Kota territory.[157]

Tukoji Holkar entered the southern part of Kota territory and looted the villages of Bharant, Ganeshpura, Nimana, Borkheri and Alpo.[158] Ramchandra Ganesh also came to help him.[159] They plundered Mangrol, Itawa, Barod and Kishanganj.[160] The raids continued throughout October-November, 1769. As the Kota forces were no match for the Maratha sardars the Maharao deputed Naroji, a Deccani Pandit, to placate the invaders by offering costly presents. Ramchandra was urgently required in the North, and, therefore, he accepted them and retired. Tukoji was left in charge of the operations.

He attacked Bakani, a small fort in the south of Kota. He besieged the four hundred Hadas in it and demanded their surrender. The siege continued for two weeks and, at last, the fort was handed over to him. Then he directed his energies towards Suket, again a small fort nar Bakani. The Hadas left the fort under cover of darkness. The fort fell into the hands of Tukoji.

In Magsar, 1826 V.S. (December, 1769) Holkar again entered Kota territory from the south and ravaged the parganas of Atru, Atoni, Kundi, Modpur, Baran, Mangrol, Basthuni and Barod.[161] He demanded a huge sum for his withdrawal. He even prepared himself to raid Kota and crossed the river Chambal at Jhampayat, a few miles north of Kota city. The Maharao, apprehending danger, appeased him by making a substantial payment and made him leave Kota.[162]

Zalim singh had, by this time, returned to Kota from Mewar. He met Holkar at Suket[163] and complained to him against his raids on Kota, as Kota had been a tributary. Zalim Singh made Holkar agree to deduct Rs. 2,50,000 as compensation from the amount payable in 1827 V.S. (1770-71).

Kota enjoyed a respite from the invasions of the Marathas till 1833 V.S. (1776) when Mahadji Scindhia's Generals Ambaji, Manuji, Mahipat Rao and Ikhuji raided the Parganas of Kota.[164] They crossed the river Parvati near Atru. Zalim Singh was very offended at this move of Scindhia. He despatched his troops under Pandit Tantiya and Bakshi Akhay Ram. The rival forces faced each other from January to April 1776.[165] Scindhia was alarmed at the preparations of Zalim Singh and so withdrew his forces on Jaisath Sudi 9, 1833 V.S. (26.5.1776).

Even though the Maratha were busy at Kota, yet they did not spare Jaipur whenever there was an opportunity for it. At Raghoghar the Vakils of Jaipur met Ramchandra and Visaji. They promised to send the dues regularly. As they failed in it[166] so the Marathas entered Jaipur territory.[167] The Maharaja satisfied them by paying the dues. He utilised the opportunity in provoking them against the Jats for their invasion of his territory during the time of Jawahar Singh.[168] The Maharaja even promised to assist the Maratha Generals with a contingent.[169] But it appears that the Kachwahas were playing a double game as Ramchandra Ganesh and Visaji reminded Prithvi Singh, "We waited for your forces yet they have not joined us till now. Raja Sahaj Singh was always assuring us that the forces will arrive soon but this did not materialise. You have deputed Har Lal to the court of Jat Raja Nawal Singh with a view to effecting a compromise."[170] At last, a Kachwaha force 7,000 strong joined the Marathas.

A battle ensued between the forces of Nawal Singh and the Marathas on Chaitra Sudi 11, 1827 V.S.[171] (6.4.1770). Nawal Singh was defeated. He took shelter in Deeg. The Jats suffered heavily. The suppression of the Jat Raja with the help of the Kachwaha forces facilitated the northern enterprise of the Marathas.

But the victory over the Jats brought about an open rupture between Scindhia and Holkar. While Scindhia sensing the hostile designs of the Rohilas advocated a mild policy towards the Jat Raja, Holkar opposed it vehemently.[172] This open conflict between the Maratha chiefs stultified the activities of the Marathas. After overcoming the Rohila menace, Scindhia took to escorting Shah Alam II to Delhi in 1772. He requested Sawai Prithvi Singh to send a contingent to be in attendance to the Emperor.[173] It was complied with.[174] The temporary reconciliation between the two established the hold of Mahadji on the Mughal Emperor.

The timely help of Prithvi Singh could not appease the Marathas with regard to their `mamlat' dues. Jaipur had settled rupees one lakh and nine thousand in quarterly instalments, through Sahej Singh.[175] The Peshwa, Madho Rao Ballal, reminded Prithvi Singh that the instalment has fallen in arrears and that it should be paid forthwith to Bapooji Vaman.[176] He again asked Prithvi Singh that the instalment be paid to Apaji Narain.[177]

The constant stream of reminders made the Maharaja depute Manorath Ram and Shah Khub Allah Khan to settle the long standing arrears.[178] They brought over Ghodoji Govind, the Peshwa's vakil, for waving off the dues. The Peshwa, again, complained that the arrears had not been received by him and that his Vakil who has been detained there should be sent back with the money.[179] Prithvi Singh showed his willingness to pay and informed him that Ghodoji would be sent back after his return from Delhi.[180]

Even though Jaipur paid the `mamlat' dues, yet the various Maratha Generals laid waste the country. Ramchandra Ganesh devastated the country[181] and was paid 5 lakhs of rupees. Next came Mahadji and he was given one lakh and demanded the same amount more.[182] Visaji Krishna was also given a hundi of one and a half lakhs and kind worth Rs. 50,000.[183] Prithvi Singh asked Narain Rao, the new Peshwa, to check the Maratha Generals[184] who were creating disturbances in his country. These invasions made Jaipur unable to pay the `mamlat' dues for the year 1830 V.S.[185] (8.7.1773 to 25.2.1774).

Thus, the ascendancy of Sawai Prithvi Singh created a semblance of cordiality between the Rajputs and the Marathas. The former were ineffective for obvious reasons, and the latter were preoccupied with their affairs in the Deccan.

REFERENCES

1. Sada Shiv Rao Bhau was the cousin of Peshwa Balaji. He had successfully conducted wars in the south.

2. (a) D.O.A.B.: From Inder Singh to Maharaja Sawai Madho Singh, dated Phalgun Budi 14, 1816 V.S. (15.2.1760), Kharita Section, Bundle No. 10.

   (b) D.O.A.B.: From Maharaja Sawai Madho Singh to Peshwa Madhav Rao, dated Chaitra Sudi 9, 1817 V. S. (25.3.1760), Kharita Section.

   (c) D.O.A.B.: from Bapuji to Sawai Madho Singh dated Shrawan Budi 6, 1819 V.S. (12.7.1762), Arziat Section Bundle No. 15.

3. Tikakar, R. Sharipat, (Sardesai Commemoration Volume, Bombay: Keshav Bhikaji Dhwale (1938), p. 144.

   Duff, J. Grant: *History of the Marathas* (Vol. I, 3rd edition, Times of India Office, 1873), pp. 313-15.

   Bijay Singh had signed an agreement, through the good offices of Karnidan, with Jankoji in January 1761, to help the Marathas against Abdali. Jankoji promised that he would not help his rival. Ram Singh. In spite of this, Bijay Singh remained neutral during the fateful contest as he was afraid of the Abdali menace and at the same moment he did not favour to renew hostilities with the Marathas. S.P.D. XXI, 187.

4. *Ibid.*

5. D.O.A.B.: Dastari records, Basta No. 9, File No. 4, letter No. 1, dated Magh Sudi 7, 1817 V. S. (11.2.1761). From Maharaja Sawai Madho Singh to Maharaja Bijay Singh.

6. D.O.A.B.: From Maharaja Sawai Madho Singh to Maharaja Sawant Singh dated Phalgun Sudi 8, 1817 (14.3.1761). Draft Kharita, Bundle No. 9.

7. D.O.A.B.: Agreement between Madho Singh and seventeen Kachwaha sardars, dated Jaisath Budi 9, 1816 V.S. (20. 5.1759) No. 776, Kapat-dwara. The Seventeen Kachwahas were as follows: Jaswant Singh, Gulab Singh of Bagru, Jodh Singh, Jagat Singh, Nand Singh, Rao Bikramaditya, Dalel Singh Rajavat, Rao Sardar Singh, Zalim Singh Nathawat, Ratan Singh Nathawat, Sultan Singh Naruka, Salim Singh, Chhaju Ram Naruka, Chand Singh, Fateh Singh, Ajit Singh and Dalel Singh.

8. D.O.A.B.: From Ahmad Shah Abdali to Maharaja Sawai Madho Singh, No. 197, Kapat-dwara.

9. D.O.A.B.: From Maharaja Sawai Madho Singh to Maharaja Sawant Singh dated Bhadra Budi 5, 1817 V.S. (31.8.1760), Draft Kharita, Bundle No. 9.

10. D.O.A.B.: From Maharaja Sawai Madho Singh to Bhoop Singh, Nawal Singh, Anoop Ram, Sampat Rai, Arjun Rai, Pawae Singh, Mubarik Rai, Kishan Singh, Ummed Singh, and Naruka Rao Anoop Karan Singh of Pipal Khedi, dated Chaitra Sudi 2, 1817 V.S. (19.3.1760), Draft Kharita, Bundle No. 9.

11. (a) D.O.A.B.: From Maharaja Sawai Madho Singh to Raja Hari Singh, dated Baisakh Budi 7, 1817 V.S. (7.4.1760), Draft Kharita, Bundle No. 9.

    (b) D.O.A.B.: From Maharja Sawai Madho Singh to Raja Hari Singh, dated Asadh Budi, 5, 1817 18 V.S. (7.4.1760), Draft Kharita, Bundle No. 9.

12. Gupta, H. R.: *Marathas and Panipat* (Vol. I, Ist edition; Chandigarh, Panjab-University, 1961), p. 261. Sethi, R.R.: *Consequences of the Battle.*

13. Mahadji Scindhia was an illegitimate son of the Patel of Kamar Khera, 16 miles from Satara, the slipper bearer Ranoji Scindhia. Ranoji left five sons. Mahadji was the younger but one. All his brothers, namely, Jayappa, Dattaji, Takuji, and Jotiba, died before the third battle of Panipat.

14. Abdali gained the victory at so great a cost that he returned to his highlands early in March, 1761. His ambitions were baulked by the mutiny of his soldiers.

15. S.P.D.: Vol. XXIX, letter No. 21, dated 27.10.1761.

16. (a) S.P.D.: Vol. XXIX, letter No. 21, dated 27.10.1761.

    (b) Sharma, *op. cit.,* II, p. 437.

17. D.O.A.B.: Dastari records, Basta No. 9, File No. 4, letter No. 1, dated Phalgun Sudi 9, 1817 V.S. (15.3.1761). From Maharaja Sawai Madho Singh to Maharja Baijay Singh.

18. Sharma, *op. cit.,* II, p. 437.

19. S.P.D.: Vol. II, letter No. 18, dated October 1761.

20. D.O.A.B.: From Brij Nath Pondrik to Maharaja Sawai Madho Singh, dated Baisakh Sudi 4, 1818 V.S. (8.5.1761), Arziat Section, Bundle No. 15.

21. Maharana Raj Singh II.

22. Ram Singh was the son of late Maharaja Abhay Singh. Bakht Singh succeeded in 1751 A.D. but could rule only for a year. The succession was disputed by Ram Singh against Bijay Singh.

23. D.O.A.B.: Dastari records, Basta No. 4, File No. 6, letter No. 2, dated Posh Sudi 9, 1817 V.S. (15.1.1761). From Madho Rao Scindhia to Maharaja Bijay Singh.
24. D.O.A.B.: From Rai Badri Bhan to Maharana Raj Singh II, dated Chaitra Budi 7, 1817 V.S. (27.3.1761). Holkar was lying at Mukandgarh in the Aravali hills after returning from Panipat.
25. D.O.A.B.: From Maya Ram to Maharaja Sawai Madho Singh, dated Chaitra Budi 2, 1818 V. S. (22.3.1761), Arziat Section, Bundle No. 15.
26. D.O.A.B.: From Maharaja Sawai Madho Singh to Ram Singh dated Chaitra Sudi 14, 1818 V.S. (18.4.1761), Draft Kharita, Bundle No. 9, Draft No. 62.
27. D.O.A.B.: From Raja Balbhadra Singh of Raghogarh to Maharaja Sawai Madho Singh, Kharita Section. No Date.
28. They were eight in number: Pipala, Gainta, Karwad, Pusod, Indergarh, Khatoli, Balban and Antarda.
29. The tribute.
30 Shyamal Das, *op, cit.*, pp. 1418-19.
31 A.O.K.: Bhandar No. 5, Basta No. 15.
32. D.O.A.B.: From Maharaja Sawai Madho Singh to Raja Balbhadra Singh, dated Jaisath Budi 4, 1818 V.S. (23.5.1761), Draft Kharita, Bundle No. 9, Draft No. 389.
33. S.P.D.: Vol II, letter No. 18, dated October 1761.
34. S.P.D.: Vol. XXIX, letter No. 93, dated December 1, 1761.
35. S.P.D.: Vol. XXIX, letter No. 81.
36. S.P.D.: Vol. XXVII, letter No. 269, dated June 19, 1761. Holkar marched from Indore in early November.
37. The place to-day is known as Mandargarh.
38. A.O.K.: Bhandar No. 5, Basta No. 15.
39. A.O.K.: Bhandar No. 1, Basta No. 58. Do Varkhi Parchazat.
40. A.O.K.: Bhandar No. 1, Basta No. 58, File No. 10. Do Varkhi Parchazat.
41. A.O.K.: Bhandar No. 1, Basta No. 59. Nal KaBhandar; Bhandar No. 1, Bundle No. 58, File N. 10.
42. A.O.K.: Bhandar No. 5, Basta No. 15.
43. A.O.K.: Bhandar No. 1, Basta No. 58, Samvat 1818-20 (1762-64). Do Varkhi Parchazat.

44. Das, Thakur Lakshman: History of Kota (MISS.) Kotri Ka Daftar, Kota.
45. A.O.K.: Bhandar No. 5, Basta No. 15.
46. A.O.K.: Bhandar No. 1, Basta No. 58, Samvat 1818-20 (1762-64); Do Varkhi Parchazat.
47. *Ibid*.
48. Six miles north of Dhipari in the territory of Indegarh.
49. A.O.K.: Bhandar No. 5, Basta No. 15. Manuscript History of Kota State.
50. Jhala Zalim Singh was born on the 5th day of the light fortnight of Masgar 1796 V.S. (24.11.1739). He was a posthumous son of Prithvi Singh Jhala, son of Gopal Singh Jhala, who died early after his marriage. The young boy was adoped by his uncle, Jhala Himmat Singh whose Jagir of Nainta, he inherited and also succeeded him to the post of the Faujdar of Kota. When Zalim Singh became the Jagirdar, the Marathas were at the height of their power. Their power extended in the north as far as Peshawar and by the majority of people they were looked upon as the masters of the country.
51. A.O.K.: Bhandar No. 5, Basta No. 15. Manuscript History of Kota State.
52. A.O.K.: Bhandar No. 1, Basta No. 58, Samvat 1818. (11.3.1762 to 27.2.1763).
53. D.O.A.B.: Vakay Papers, Samvat 1818-20 (1762-64).
54. A.O.K.: Bhandar No. 5, Basta No. 15.
55. A.O.K.: Bhandar No. 5, Basta No. 15. Manuscript History of Kota State.
56. A.O.K.: Bhandar No. 1, Basta No. 58, Samvat 1818-20 (1762-64). Do Arkhi Parchazat.

    Sir J. N. Sarka in "Fall of the Mughal Empire," Vol. II, mentions that the battle started on November 28, 1761 and concluded the next day i.e. on November 29, 1761. But the daily accounts of the battle preserved in the Kota Archives clearly reveal that the battle started on Magsar Sudi 3, 1818 (29.11.1761) and continued up to Magsar Sudi 5, 1818 (1.12.1761). Even some very minor skirmishes were witnessed on 2.12.1761. In view of these original and authentic evidences the view of Sarkar is hardly acceptable.
57. A.O.K.: Bhandar No. 5, Basta No. 15.

58. A.O.K.: Bhandar No. 1, Basta No. 58, Samvat 1818-20 (1762-64). Do Varkhi Parchazat. The Jagirdars were of Rajgarh, Nanta, Railawan, Malikhera, Gainta and Pipalda.
59. Das, *op. cit.*

    The Kachwahas lost their five-coloured flag, some eighteen guns, seventy-three pieces of cannon and 1,800 horses. (Kota Archives, Kagzat Samvat, 1818).
60. Sarkar, *op. cit.*, p. 372.
61. The Old capital of Jaipur.
62. D.O.A.B.: From Maharaja Sawai Madho Singh to Rawat Prithvi Sing dated Posh Sudi 14, 1818 V.S. (9.1.1762), Draft Kharita, Bundle No. 9, Draft No. 447 (d).
63. D.O.A.B.: From Maharaja Sawai Madho Singh to Salim Singh, dated Chaitra Sudi 4, 1819 V.S. (29.3.1762), Draft Kharita, Bundle No. 10, Draft No. 9.
64. S.P.D.: Vol. XXIX, letter No. 27, dated 30.12.1761.
65. Forty mile north of Jaipur.
66. S.P.D.: Vol. XXIX, letter No. 33.
67. S.P.D.: Vol. XXIX, letter No. 18.
68. A.O.K.: Bhandar No. 1, Basta No. 56. Samvat 1813-18 (1757-62). Zalim Singh worked under Akhay Ram Pancholi for many years. After his heroic deeds at Bhatwara he acquired prominence and eclipsed his importance. The entire power of administration centred in his hands. He was appointed Musahib-i-Ala on December 28, 1764. Such was his manoeuvring skill that he befriended the Marathas on the one hand and secured the goodwill of the Rajput Rajas on the other.
69. A.O.K.: Bhandar No. 1, Basta No. 58, Samvat 1818-20 (1762-64). Do Varkhi Parchazat.
70. Das, *op. cit.*
71. A.O.K.: Bhandar No. 1, Basta No. 58, Samvat 1818-20 (1762-64).
72. A.O.K.: Bhandar No. 1, Basta No. 58, File No. 10, Samvat 1818-20 (1762-64). Do Varkhi parchazat.
73. *Ibid.*
74. Thakur Laxman Das in his "History of Kota" (MSS) mentions that an amount of Rs. 4 lakhs was offered to Kota as a price of his support but this is nowhere confirmed in the State papers. As such the statement should be taken very cautiously and so long as it is not confirmed by Archieval evidences, should be rejected.

75. A.O.K.: Bhandar No. 1, Basta No. 15.

76. A.O.K.: Bhandar No. 1, Basta No. 58, Samvat 1818-20 (1762-64). Do Varkhi Parchazat.

77. Sidney, J. Owen, The Fall of the Mugul Empire (London: John Murray, Albemarle Street, W. 1912), p. 277.

78. Sarkar in his "Fall of the Mughal Empire", Vol. II, takes this battle as a contest between Madho Singh and Malhar Rao Holkar. His contention rests on three letters written by Maratha officers, which appear in S.P.D. Vol. XXI at numbers 22, 93 and 94. The last two letters written by Kanhoji Jadhav specifically mention that the Jaipur ruler, Madho Singh, had become formidable by this time and defied the payment of the Maratha tribute which had accumulated to a staggering sum of Rs. twenty lakhs. So Madho Singh was not reluctant for a contest with the Marathas and even actually prepared for it instead of paying it. Sarkar could not consult the Rajasthani sources and hence such an erroneous view was the natural corollary.

    The above description rests on the boastful claims of the Marathas who wanted to wash out the haunting memory of the disastrous defeat which they met at the hands of Ahmad Shah Abdali in the third battle of Panipat. If Madho Singh had been strong enough to fight the Marathas single-handed, he would not have negotiated for help with the emperor, the Rohila leader and the Rajput Rajas. This early shows that he was weak and fragile at the moment and could not have even thought of defying the authority of Holkar whose forces had returned intact from Panipat. At the same time his treasury had become, almost, depleted by the huge and unfailings demands of the Marathas, who resorted to plunder and exactions whenever their demands were not met with. To this long chain of difficulties was also to be added the hostile attitude of the Jagirdars who were to be reduced to submission before an encounter with the Marathas could be thought of. As such it is inconceivable that Madho Singh could have taken an initiative to march against Malhar Rao.

79. D.O.A.B.: From Kedarji Scindhia to Maharaja Sawai Madho Singh, dated Jaisath Budi 14, 1819 V.S. (22.5.1762), Kharita Section, G.B.

80. D.O.A.B.: From Peshwa Madhav Rao To Mutsadis of Maharaja Sawai Madho Singh, dated Jaisath Budi 13, 1819 V.S. (15.10.1762), Kharita Section.

81. *Ibid.*

82. (a) D.O.A.B.: From Kedarji Scindhia to Maharaja Sawai Madho Singh, dated Jaisath Sudi 1, 1820 V.S. (28.4.1763), Kharita Section, G.B.

    (b) D.O.A.B.: From Peshwa Madhav Rao to Maharaja Sawai Madho Singh, dated Second Asadh Sudi 10, 1819, V.S. (1.7.1762), Kharita Section.

    (c) D.O.A.B.: From Peshwa Madhav Rao to Maharaja Sawai Madho Singh dated Bhadra Bdi 9, 1819 V.S. (14.8.1762), Kharita Section.

    (d) S.P.D.: Vol. XXIX, letter No. 99 dated 11.11.1762

83. D.O.A.B.: From Maharaj Swai Madho Singh to Peshwa Madhav Rao, dated Shrawan Sudi 11, 1820 V.S. (19.8.1763), Kharita Section.

84. D.O.B.: From Shah Mool Chand to Maharaja Sawai Madho Singh, dated Ashoj Sudi 3, 1821 V.S. (28.9.1764), Arziat Section, Bundle No. 15, Arzi No. 196.

85. D.O.A.B.: From Dhai Bhai Roopji to Rai Ganpati, dated Sharwan sudi 13, 1821 V.S. (9.8.1764), Draft Kharita, Bundle No. 11, Draft No. 87.

86. D.O.A.B.: Arzi Bahi No. 4, p. 244 dated 4th day of dark-half of Shrawan 1821 V.S. (17.7.1764). A letter from Dewan Surat Ram to Dalel Singh of Jaipur.

87. Thirty miles east of Sambhar.

88. D.O.A.B.: From Maharaja Sawai Madho Singh to Subedar Malhar Rao Holkar, dated Shrawan Budi 9, 1821 V.S. (22.7.1764), Draft Kharita, Bundle No. 11, Draft No. 86.

89. D.O.A.B.: Dastoor Komwar, Vol. 9, Samvat 1821 V.S. (1764-65). p. 613.

90. D.O.A.B.: Yad-Dast between Subedar Malhar Rao Holkar and Maharaja Sawai Madho Singh, dated Magh Sudi 9, 1821 V.S. (30.1.1765), Kapat-Dwara No. 784.

91. D.O.A.B.: From Santaji Bable to Maharja Sawai Madho Singh, dated Shrawan Budi 13, 1822 V.S. (15.7.1765). Arziat Section. Bundle No. 11.

92. Sharma, *op. cit.*, p. 449.

93. A.O.K.: Bhandar No. 1, Basta No. 58, File No. 10, Samvat 1818-20 (1762-64). Do Varkhi Parchazat.

94. Mishra, *op. cit.*, IV, p. 3706.

95. D.O.A.B.: From Maharaja Sawai Madho Singh to Rao Raja Ummed Singh, dated Posh Budi 5, 1818 V.S. (16.12.1761), Draft Kharita, Bundle No. 9, Draft No. 446.

96. D.O.A.B.: Yad-Dast between Jaipur and Bundi dated Phalgun Sudi 7, 1818 V.S. (3.3.1762), Bundle No. 9, Draft No. 434.

97. D.O.A.B.: From Bhagat Ram Hada of Indergarh to Maharaja Sawai Madho Singh, dated Posh Sudi 13, 1818 V.S. (8.1.1762), Arziat Section, Bundle No. 15, Arzi No. 138.

98. D.O.A.B.: From Maharaja Sawai Madho Singh to Rao Raja Ummed Singh, dated Bhadra Sudi 10, 1819 V.S. (29.8.1762), Draft Kharita, Bundle No. 9, Draft No. 321.

99. D.O.A.B.: From Maharaja Sawai Madho Singh to Rao Raja Ummed Singh, dated Ashoj Sudi 8, 1819 V.S. (25.9.1762), Draft Kharita, Bundle No. 9, Draft No. 329.

100. (a) D.O.A.B.: From Rao Raja Ummed Singh to Maharaja Sawai Madho Singh, dated Magsar Sudi 3, 1819 V.S. (18.11.1762), Kharita Section, Bundle No. 10.

(b) D.O.A.B.: From Rao Raja Ummed Singh to Maharaja Sawai Madho Singh, dated Magsar Budi 8, 1819 V.S. (9.11.1762), Kharita Section, Bundle No. 10.

101. (a) D.O.A.B.: From Maharaja Sawai Madho Singh to Inder Singh, dated Magsar Sudi 8, 1819 V.S. (24.11.1762), Draft Kharita, Bundle No. 9.

(b) D.O.A.B.: From Maharaja Sawai Madho Singh to Inder Singh, dated Posh Budi 3, 1819 V.S. (2.1.1763), Draft Kharita, Bundle No. 9.

102. D.O.A.B.: From Rao Raja Ummed Singh to Maharaja Sawai Madho Singh, dated Magsar Sudi 9, 1819 V.S. (25.11.1762), Kharita Section Bundle No. 10.

103. D.O.A.B.: From Rao Raja Ummed Singh to Maharaja Sawai Madho Singh, dated Magh Budi 5, 1819 V.S. (4.2.1763), Kharita Section Bundle No. 10.

104. Devi Dan, Vansh Prakash, Vol. II, p. 187.

105. Mishra, *op. cit.*, IV, p. 3710.

106. Devi Dan, *op. cit.*, p. 187.

107. A.O.K.: Bhandar No. 1, Basta No. 58, Samvat 1818-20 (1762-64). Do Varkhi Parchazat.

108. D.O.A.B.: From Maharaja Sawai Madho Singh to Malhar Rao Holkar, dated Ashoj Budi 11, 1822 V.S. (11.9.176), Draft Kharita, Bundle No. 11, Draft No. 53.

109. *Ibid.*
110. D.O.A.B.: From Malhar Rao Holkar to Maharaja Sawai Madho Singh, dated Kartik Sudi 8, 1822 V.S. (21.10.1765), Kharita Section, Indore Bundle.
111. S.P.D.: Vol. XXIX, December 1765.
112. D.O.A.B.: From Maharaja Sawai Madho Singh to Maharaja Hindu Pati dated Magsar Budi 5, 1824 V.S. (26.11.1767), Draft Kharita, Bundle No. 11, Draft No. 344; Shahpura Khayat I, f.149A; Ojha, Jodhpur 2, p. 718.
113. D.O.A.B.: From Dharam Rao Pandit to Maharja Sawai Madho Singh, dated Posh Sudi Purnima 1824 V.S. (4.1.1768), Arziat Section, Bundle No. 15; Asopa, p. 248.
114. Girdas Surat Singhot was sent to Jaipur; Jodhpur Rajya ki Khayat, V. 3, p. 399.
115. (a) D.O.A.B.: From Maharaja Gaj Singh to Maharaja Sawai Madho Singh, dated Posh Sudi 12, 1824 V.S. (2.1.1768), Kharita Section, Bundle No. 9, Kharia No. 342.

     (b) Powlett, Col. P.W. Gazetteer of the Bikaner State, p. 68.

     (c) Dayaldas Ki Khayat, Part II, p. 90.
116. D.O.A.B.: From Maharaja Sawai Madho Singh to Maharaja Gaj Singh, dated Magsar Budi 11, 1824 V.S. (17.11.1767), Kharita Section, Bundle No. 9, Kharita No. 335.
117. D.O.A.B.: From Dhai Bhai Roopa to Maharaja Sawai Pratap Singh, dated Posh Budi 3, 1824, V.S. (8.12.1767), Kharita Section, Bundle No. 12, Kharita No. 342; Jodhpur Khayat 3, p. 399.
118. D.O.A.B.: From Vyas Gopal Rao to Maharaja Sawai Madho Singh, dated Phalgun Sudi 7, 1824 V.S. (2.2.1768), Arziat Section, Bundle No. 15, Arzi No. 115; Ojha, Jodhpur 2, p. 719.
119. Tukoji Holkar was an e-in-e during Ahalaya Bai's time. During that period he was engaged in 1780 in Gujrat with Mahadji Scindhia against the English. He died in 1797 leaving four sons.
120. D.O.A.B.: From Tukoji Holkar to Maharaja Sawai Madho Singh, dated Magsar Sudi 9, 1824 V.S. (30.11.1767), Kharia Section, Indore Bundle.
121. D.O.A.B.: From Tukoji Holkar to Maharaja Sawai Madho Singh, dated Magh Sudi 1, 1824 V.S. (20.1.1768), Kharita Section, Indore Bundle.
122. *Ibid.*

123. D.O.A.B.: From Santaji Bhonsle to Maharaja Sawai Madho Singh, dated Magh Sudi 1, 1824 V.S. 20.1.1768), Arziat Section, Bundle No. 15, Arzi No. 118. Bijay Singh accompanied Jawahar Singh up to Doolia and then via Sambhar returned to Maroth. He left Muhota Manurath Singhvi, Shiv Chand along with some forces; Jodhpur Khayat 3, pp. 400-401.

124. D.O.A.B.: From Maharaja Sawai Madho Singh to Tukoji Holkar, dated Magh Budi 12, 1824 V.S. (16.1.1768), Kharita Section, Indore Bundle.

125. (a) D.O.A.B.: From Subedar Tukoji Holkar to Maharaja Sawai Madho Singh, dated Magh Sudi 1, 1824 V.S. (20.1.1768), Kharita Section, Indore Bundle.

(b) D.O.A.B.: From Santosh Singh to Maharaja Sawai Madho Singh, dated Chaitṛa Sudi 5, 1825 V.S. (23.3.1768), Arziat Section, Bundle No. 15, Arzi No. 178.

(c) Dewan Surat Ram purchased their retreat S.P.D. XXIX, 164.

126. (a) Shyamal Das, *op. cit.*, pp. 1304-05.

(b) The notable among the dead were Dewan Harshav, Bakshi Gur Sahai, Sanwal Das Shekhawat, Guman Singh, Shiv Das Shekhawat, Nahar Singh of Itawa and Dalel Singh. The Jats lost Rathor Surat Singh, Madho Das Mertia and a host of other Sardars. Jodhpur Khayat 3, p. 403.

(c) D.O.A.B.: Letter dated Shrawan Budi 1825 V.S. (July-August 1768), No. 131. The four villages, Katrathal, Doulatipura, Rasidpura and Gangvasar, were granted to Budh Singh Shekhawat's wife to maintain herself.

127. Mishra, *op. cit.*, pp. 3721-27; Jodhpur Rajya ki Khayat 3, p. 404.

128. Madho Singh died in March 1768 and Jawahar Singh was assassinated the same year in July.

129. A.O.K.: Bhandar No. 3, Basta No. 1, dated Ashoj Budi 2, 1823 V.S. (20.9.1766)

130. 2. Ibid. Letter from Nand Gaon to Bhabhi Kachwahayi.

131. A.O.K.: Bhandar No. 3, Basta No. 1, dated Ashoj Budi Amavash 1823 V.S. (3.10.1766). From Nand Gaon to Pancholi Ram Krishna.

132. (a) A.O.K.: Bhandar No. 3, Basta No. 1, dated Kartik Budi 5, 1823 V.S. (23.10.1766). Letter From Nand Gaon to Pancholi Ram Krishna.

(b) A.O.K.: Bhandar No. 3, Basta No. 1, dated Kartik Sudi 2, 1823 V.S. (4.11.1766), Letter From Nand Gaon to Dhai Bhai Roop Chand.

133. On the right bank of the Banas river about 30 miles north by north-east of Udaipur city.

134. A.O.K.: Bhandar No. 3, Basta No. 1, dated Kartik Sudi 8, 1823 V.S. (10.11.1766). Letter From Nand Gaon to Vyas Raghu Nathji.

135. A.O.K.: Bhandar No. 3, Basta No. 1, dated Magsar Budi 11, 1823 V.S. (26.11.1766). Letter From Maji Ranavati.

136. *Ibid.*

137. A.O.K.: Bhandar No. 3, Basta No. 1, dated Magsar Sudi 6, 1823 V.S. (7.12.1766). Letter from Nand Gaon to Pancholi Somnath.

138. A.O.K.: Bhandar No. 3, Basta No. 1, dated Magsar Budi 11, 1823 V.S. (28.11.1766). Letter from Nand Gaon to Pandit Abhaji.

139. (a) D.O.A.B.: From Peshwa Madhav Rao to Bhatt Sada Shivji, dated Posh Sudi 2, 1825 V.S. (10.1.1769).

(b) D.O.A.B.: From Peshwa Madhav Rao to Maharaja Sawai Prithvi Singh, dated Ashoj Budi 8, 1826 V.S. (23.9.1769). Kharita Section.

140. (a) D.O.A.B.: From Maharaja Sawai Prithvi Singh to Peshwa Madhav Rao, dated Chaitra Sudi 2, 1827 V.S. (29.3.1770), Kharita Section.

(b) D.O.A.B.: From Maharaja Sawai Prithvi Singh to Peshwa Madhav Rao, dated Chaitra Sudi 4, 1827, V.S. (30.3.1770), Kharita Section.

141. (a) D.O.A.B.: From Peshwa Madhav Rao to Maharaja Sawai Prithvi Singh, dated Ashoj Budi 8, 1826 V.S. (23.9.1769), Kharita Section.

(b) S.P.D.: Vol. XXXIX. No. 169, dated March 18, 1769.

142. Sarkar, *op. cit.*, III, 5.

143. (a) A.O.K.: Bhandar No. 3, Basta No. 1, Talik Bahi, dated Shrawan Sudi 6, 1826 V.S. (7.8.1769). From Maharao Guman Singh to Sardar Singh and Pancholi Sitaram.

(b) A.O.K.: Bhandar No. 3, Basta No. 1, dated Bhadra Sudi 9, 1826 V.S. (9.9.1769). From Kota to Pancholi Sheo Nath.

144. A.O.K.: Bhandar No. 3, Basta No. 1, dated Ashoj Budi 2, 1826 V.S. (17.9.1769). From Kota to Pancholi Udai Ram and Bhopat Ram.

145. (a) D.O.A.B.: From Subedar Tukoji Holkar to Maharaja Sawai Prithvi Singh, dated Ashoj Sudi 10, 1826 V.S. (10.10.1769), Kharita Section.

(b) A.O.K.: Bhandar No. 3, Basta No. 1, dated Shrawan Sudi 12, 1826 V.S. (14.8.1769). From Kota to Pancholi Shiv Nath.

146. A.O.K.: Bhandar No. 3, Basta No. 1, dated Ashoj Budi 14, 1826 V.S. (28.9.1769). From Kota to Pancholi Shiv Nath.

147. D.O.A.B.: From Raja Balbhandra Singh to Sawai Prithvi Singh, dated Bhandra Budi 2, 1826 V.S. (19.8.1769). Draft Kharita Bundle No. 13, No. 254.

148. D.O.A.B.: From Raja Balbhandra Singh to Sawai Prithvi Singh, dated Ashoj Budi 3, 1826, V.S. (17.9.1769), Draft Kharita, Bundle No. 13, No. 261.

149. D. O. A. B.: From Maharaja Sawai Prithvi Singh, Ramchandra Ganesh and Visaji, dated Bhadra Budi 9, 1826 V.S. (25.8.1769), Draft Kharita, Bundle No. 15, No. 26.

150. D. O. A. B.: From Maharaja Sawai Prithvi Singh to Tukoji Holkar dated Bhadra Budi 9, 1826 V.S. (25.8.1769), Kharita Section, Indore Bundle.

(b) D. O. A. B.: From Raja Balbhadra Singh to Maharaja Sawai Prithvi Singh, dated Bhadra Sudi 6, 1826 V.S. (6.9.1769), Draft Kharita, Bundle No. 13.

151. D. O. A. B.: From Balwant Singh to Maharaja Sawai Prithvi Singh, dated Magh Budi 7, 1826 V.S. (18.1.1770), Draft Kharita, Bundle No. 13. No. 265.

152. *Ibid.*

153. D. O. A. B.: From Raja Balbhadra Singh to MaJi Sahib of Jaipur, dated Magh Budi 7, 1826 V.S. (18.1.1770), Draft Kharita, Bundle No. 13, No. 266.

154. D. O. A. B.: From Maharaja Sawai Prithvi Singh to Subedar Tukoji Holkar and Nanaji Pandit, dated Asadh Budi 12, 1830 V.S. (16.6.1773). Draft Kharita Bundle No. 13.

155. A.O.K.: Bhandar No. 3 Basta No. 1, Samvat 1825-26 (1769-70).

156. A.O.K.: Bhandar No. 3, Basta No. 1, Talik Bahi. From Kota to Pancholi Shiv Nath, dated Shrawan Sudi 9, 1826 V.S. (11.8.1769).

157. A.O.K.: Bhandar No. 3, Basta No. 1, Talik Bahi. From Kota to Thakur Kishan Singh Rawat, dated Shrawan Sudi 10, 1826 V.S. (12.8.1769).

158. A.O.K.: Bhandar No. 1, Basta No. 3, Samvat 1826-32 (1770-76).

159. A.O.K.: Bhandar No. 3 Basta No. 1, Samvat 1825-26 (1769-70).

160. *Ibid.*

161. *Ibid*.

162. A.O.K.: Bhandar No. 3, Basa No. 1, Samvat 1825-26 (1769-70).

163. *Ibid*.

164. A.O.K.: Bhandar No. 1, Basta No. 61, Samvat 1833-35 (1777-79).

165. *Ibid*.

166. A.O.K.: Bhandar No. 1, Basta No. 1, From Kota to Majlis Rai, dated Ashoj Budi Amavas 1826 V.S. (29.9.1769).

167. D.O.A.B.: From Mehta Bala Nand to Maji Sahib, dated Phalgun Sudi 9, 1826 v.s. (6.3.1770), Draft Kharia, Bundle No. 13, Draft No. 276.

168. Sarkar, *op. cit*., III, 6.

169. D.O.A.B.: From Ram Chandra Ganesh and Visai Krishna to Maharaja Sawai Prithvi Singh, dated Chaitra Budi 8, 1827 V.S. (19.3.1770), Draft Kharita, Bundle No. 13.

170. *Ibid*.

171. D.O.A.B.: From Ramchandra ganesh and Visaji to Maharaja Sawai Prithvi Singh, dated Baisakh Sudi 14, 1827 V.S. (8.5.1770), Draft Kharita, Bundle No. 13, Draft No. 249.

172. Sarkar, *op. cit*., III, 10.

173. (a) D.O.A.B.: From Maharaja Sawai Prithvi Singh to Mahadji Scindhia, dated Phalgun Sudi 2, 1828 V.S. (6.3.1772), Draft Kharita, Bundle No. 14, Draft No. 149.

(b) D.O.A.B.: From Mahadji Scindhia to Maharaja Sawai Prithvi Singh to Mahadji Scindhia, dated Phalgun Sudi 13, 1828 V.S. (17.3.1772), Kharita Section, Gwalior Bundle

174. D.O.A.B.: From Maharaja Swai Prithvi Singh to Mahadji Scindhia, dated Chairta Sudi 15, 1829 V.S. (17.4.1772), Draft Kharita, Bundle No. 14. Draft No. 103.

175. D.O.A.B.:From Peshwa Madho Rao Ballal to Sawai Prithvi Singh, dated Jaisath Sudi 4 1827 V.S. (28.5.1770), Kharia Section.

176. *Ibid*.

177. D.O.A.B.: From Peshwa Madho Rao Ballal to Maharaja Sawai Prithvi Singh, dated Kartik Budi 13, 1827 V.S. (1.11.1770), Kharita Section.

178. D.O.A.B.: From Peshwa Madho Rao Ballal to Maharaja Sawai Prithvi Singh, dated Magsar Budi 7, 1828 V.S. (28.11.1771), Kharita Section.

179. D.O.A.B.: From Peshwa Madho Rao Ballal to Maharaja Sawai Prithvi Singh, dated Magsar Budi 7, 1828 V.S. (28.11.1771), Kapatdwara, No. 184.

180. D.O.A.B.: From Maharaja Sawai Prithvi Singh to Peshwa Madho Rao Ballal, dated Magh Sudi 1828 V.S. (1771-72), Draft Kharita, Bundle No. 14, Draft No. 119.

181. D.O.A.B.: From Bohra Khushali Ram to Peshwa Narain Rao, dated Asadh Budi 5, 1830 V.S. (9.6.1773), Draft Kharia, Bundle No. 14, Draft No. 189.

182. D.O.A.B.: From Bohra Khushali Ram to Pandit Visaji, dated Jaisath Sudi 1830 V.S. (June 1773).

183. D.O.A.B.: From Maharaja Sawai Prithvi Singh to Peshwa Narain Rao, dated Asadh Budi 6, 1830 (10.6.1773), Draft Kharita, Bundle No. 14.

184. D.O.A.B.: From Bohra Khushali Ram to Peshwa Narain Rao, dated Baisakh Budi 4, 1830 V.S. (17.4.1773).

185. D.O.A.B.: From Mahadji Scindhia to Maharaja Sawai Prithvi Singh, dated Shrawan Sudi 9, 1832 V.S. (21.7.1775).

12

Jaipur, Jodhpur and the Marathas

Sawai Pratap Singh succeeded his brother Prithvi Singh in 1778. Khushali Ram Bohra managed the administration successfully. In 1779 the Emperor marched to Jaipur. Khushali Ram avoided hostility by agreeing to pay twelve lakhs of rupees. Soon after Khushali Ram was thrown out of power, the Jaipur government stopped payment. An imperial army was sent to realise tribute but it failed. The Emperor then appointed Mahadji Scindhia as Wakil-i-Mutluq. He invaded Jaipur to realise the dues of the Emperor as well as to collect the Maratha tribute. A battle was fought at Tunga in July, 1787. It was indecisive. Mahadji retreated from Jaipur.

He was opposed by the two Muslim chiefs Ismail Beg and Ghulam Quadir. After suppressing them he fought against the forces of Jaipur and Jodhpur at Patan and Merta in 1790. He once again made the Rajputs pay tribute.

The disintegration of the Jaipur Raj commenced with the death of Maharaja Sawai Madho Singh on March 5, 1768.[1] This continued throughout the inconclusive reign of his eldest son Sawai Prithvi Singh, as we have seen. When discord and disunity prevailed in the Kachwahas, the death of the ruler accelerated the chaos. His brother, Sawai Pratap Singh, ascended the throne in 1778 A.D. His neglect of administration resulted in a struggle between the powerful sardars—Khushali Ram Bohra, Daulat Ram and Khushali Ram Haldia, for the position of first servant of the state.

If the Kachwaha state was absorbed in internal strifes the condition of the Marathas was also not better. Mahadji Scindhia retired to Poona by the middle of 1776 where a constant contest was being waged for the Peshwaship. He could not give his attention to Rajputana. His absence was utilised by Mirza Najaf Khan,[2] the powerful new agent of the Mughal Emperor, Shah Alam II, to establish the Mughal hold on the territories which had slipped from its grip.[3]

Najaf Khan ordered his lieutenant Mahbub Ali then to realise the dues of Jaipur tribute, which Himmat Bahadur[4] had failed to collect even after a stay of a year.[5] Khushali Ram Bohra, who was released from the jail, in vain attempted to appease him. War preparations went ahead on both sides. Fortune favoured Jaipur and the Khan's army broke up for want of money. Himmat Bahadur was once again entrusted with the onerous job of collecting it. Khushali Ram reached an agreement with Himmat Bahadur on April 28, 1781. He was given the `Mahals' yielding Rs. 12 lakhs a year, one half of which was to be remitted to Najaf Khan and the rest to be spent on the forces kept for collection.[6] Himmat Bahadur realised Rs. 75,000 and sent it to Najaf Khan. At this time Daulat Ram Haldia returned to Jaipur and was installed as Bakshi.[7] These events were responsible for the subsequent bitterness between the Marathas and Rajputs.

All this time Rao Raja Pratap Singh formed successive plans for being the guardian of the infant Man Singh,[8] Sawai Prithvi Singh, whose claims for the *`gadi'* were set aside by his uncle, Sawai Pratap Singh. Rao Raja aimed at dominating the affairs of both the states.[9] The boy was kept at Kishangarh, his maternal grand-father's house, for purposes of safety.[10] He persuaded Mahadji to support him. Mahadji accepted it as he himself aimed at encircling Jaipur as a base for his operations against the Rajputs. For the moment, Mahadji was engaged in serious problems at Poona and so could not give his whole attention.

During this time, the first Anglo-Maratha was continued. The Governor-General emphasised the need for peace with

Marathas,[11] because of the successive defeats of the Company's troops at their hands and of the danger from Hyder Ali and later on Tipu Sultan of Mysore. The war had severely taxed the resources of Mahadji. He was also not reluctant to accept the offer of peace. Anderson, on behalf of Warren Hastings, the Governor-General, started deliberations with Mahadji and signed the treaty of Salbye on May 17, 1782.

It solved the conflict between Raghunath Rao and the Poona Government and established the ascendancy of the house of Scindhia against his rivals[12]. Not only this but Scindhia came to be regarded as the peace-maker between the Company and Poona Government.[13] Besides this honour, Mahadji also obtained freedom for the management of imperial affairs. It was the greatest advantage that Mahadji scored against the British for it opened up new vistas for him to establish his influence in the North and Rajputana.[14] There were not a few British diplomats who vehemently opposed Governor-General's policy in regard to Mahadji. But Warren Hastings wanted to maintain good relations with him at all cost.[15]

The death of Najaf Khan on April 6, 1782 and the treaty of Salbye left Mahadji attend to the affairs of the Emperor. But before he could do this he had to brush aside his arch enemy, Mohammad Beg Hamdani.[16] In 1783, when Mirza Mohammad Shafi[17] started negotiations with Mahadji, Hamdani got him murdered on September 23, 1783.[18] Similarly, when Afrasiab Khan[19] arranged for a meeting between the Emperor and Scindhia,[20] Hamdani also got him murdered on November 3, 1784. This time the whole Mughal Court was in anger and requested Mahadji to punish him. The Emperor invited him to come and set his house in order. Mahadji attained complete success on November 10, 1784. The Emperor then conferred upon him the office of Wakil-i-Mutluq on December 1, 1784, the highest executive office combining the powers of both Wazir and Mir Bakshi.[21] This again made him much superior against his rival Tukoji. But even more important than this was that Mahadji had achieved it due to his own statesmanship and the Poona Government was relegated to the background.

Mahadji had taken upon himself a great responsibility without funds. By the close of 1784, he had incurred a debt of Rs. 80 lakhs.[22] The arrears of tribute were not forthcoming from Jaipur. In addition to this, he had to realise the dues of the Mughal Emperor too. He felt that his Vakils could not manage affairs at Jaipur and that he had to proceed personally to realise the dues.

Having made preparations, Mahadji made an attack on Mahewa-Ramgarh on the Jaipur frontier.[23] It was captured on December 18, 1784. The Kachwahas, finding themselves unable to bear the brunt of attack, initiated peace offers. Bohra Khushali Ram was deputed for it.[24] It was decided that the Jaipur Darbar would pay two lakhs in cash and two lakhs in Jewels immediately, 10 lakhs by cessation of territory and seven lakhs imposed on the vassal nobles.[25] This being achieved, Scindhia proceeded on his return journey towards Deeg.[26] Throughout the year reminders constantly poured in the Kachwaha capital for immediate payment.[27] To avoid an attack Sawai Pratap Singh sent Raja Sanjay Singh to him[28] and promised to offer hundis worth two lakhs.[29] He kept his promise but induced hostility to Mahadji by asking him to vacate his posts and delaying the payment in kind.[30] Sanjay Singh was closely followed by Bakshi Mitha Lal and Khushali Ram.[31] But all proved futile. Mahadji was now convinced that without a show of arms nothing could be secured from the Kachwaha kingdom.

Mahadji, after the capture of Aligarh in November, 1785, proceeded to Jaipur once again.[32] To give an air of legality to his cause, Scindhia included the Emperor in his camp.[33] The designs of Scindhia made Sawai Pratap Singh depute Bohra Khushali Ram[34] to settle affairs amicably.[35] The negotiations having failed Scindhia resumed his march. He reached Uardain and halted there. He made his army proceed in advance to Sanganer.[36] Maharaja Gaj Singh offered to mediate, assuring Roda Ram of his willing support in case of grave necessity.[37] Though Scindhia reached Jaipur yet the again invited Khushali Ram and Roda Ram for a settlement.[38] The Maharaja wanted to act in close concert with Bijay Singh. He requested him to instruct Naval Rai to accompany the Jaipur envoys.[39] Meanwhile Sawai Pratap Singh began assembling an army.[40]

The negotiations were complicated, on the one hand, by the double-dealing of the Naruka chief, Rao Raja Pratap Singh, who espoused the cause of Man Singh[41] and, on the other hand, by the stiff attitude that the Jaipur envoys adopted towards getting the land vacated by Pratap Singh Naruka and Najaf Quli Khan.[42] As Mahadji was in a peaceful frame of mind, so it was agreed between the two that the Kachwaha Raja would pay Rs. 63 lakhs[43]—60 lakhs as `*Peshkash*' and 3 lakhs as `Darbar charges.' Out of this 11 lakhs were to be paid within a month; 4 lakhs to the be paid on his leaving the state; 4 lakhs after 4 months; another two lakhs were to be set apart for deducting the amount alreadycollected by the imperial forces during their recent occupation. In another 21 lakhs the Parganas of Tomo, Pauto, Ujirpur, Salabad and Shekhawati were handed over.[44] Another 21 lakhs were made good by assignments.[45] All ceded territory was to be jointly administered and evacuated by the Marathas after the payment. Having made this agreement, Bohra Khushali Ram paid 3 lakhs on the spot and took leave for Jaipur to collect another 8 lakhs for clearing the first instalment.

Bohra now became all powerful and extracted money forcibly. He paid the first instalment which made Mahadji begin his return Journey on June 4, 1786 towards Mathura.[46] The Emperor also marched towards Deeg.[47] Mahadji left five thousand horses under Jaiji Patel to enforce the terms of the agreement.[48] Najaf Quli Khan and Rao Raja Pratap Singh were to help him. But the slackness of the former and the treachery of the latter made Sawai Pratap Singh delay the payment. The Kachwaha king as early as May 1786 made an unsuccessful attempt to win over the English to his side against the Marathas.[49] Mahadji's suspicion of Pratap Singh's aggressive attitude was confirmed when pro-Maratha Minister Khushali Ram Bohra was deposed. Daulat Ram Haldia who opposed the Maratha penetration into Jaipur was again invited to form the Ministry. Raja Sanjay Singh constantly reminded the Kachwaha king of the serious consequences in case of non-compliance.[50] In another letter he clearly foresaw the possibility of an armed invasion.[51] He asked the Maharaja to send four lakhs earlier to appease Scindhia as he intended proceeding towards Jaipur very shortly.[52] But neither the threats of Scindhia nor the warnings of Sanjay Singh, made the Maharaja think in conciliatory terms. Scindhia now thought of invading Jaipur.

The Maharaja openly devised measures to resist Scindhia. He successfully persuaded Kishori Das and Amolik Palji, the Rajas of Seopur[53] and Karauli[54] respectively, to despatch their forces. Sawai Pratap Singh also won over Bijay Singh to his side.[55] He advised the Kachwaha Raja to seek the support of the disaffected nobles of Jaipur too. Acting upon his advice he won over the Shekhaot leader of Manoharpur. He swore upon `beal-leaf' to serve the Maharaja on a payment of 7 lakhs of rupees.[56] Shekhaot Devi Singh agreed to throw in his weight on the side of Jaipur[57] if the Raja paid the expenses of his army.[58] Attempts were also made to win over Mohammad Beg Hamdani from the Maratha camp.[59] Raja Bahadur Gopal Das promised to help the Kachwaha Raja.[60] Rawat Him Singh of Udaipur also favoured the Kachwaha cause.[61] Rao Raja Bishan Singh of Bundi also sent his forces under Roda Singh Rathor and Gordhan Dass to help Sawai Pratap Singh.[62] The Kachwaha vassals were asked to cease payment of tribute payable to Scindhia. The Jaipur Raja braced himself to withstand the sieze.[63] Scindhia now became convinced of the necessity of resorting to armed action, to enforce payment. He planned an early invasion.[64]

Scindhia, leaving Brindaban,[65] in November 1786, proceeded towards Mewat to subdue the rebels[66] and then advanced to Deeg with a view of intimidating the Rajputs and making the chiefs subservient to Raiji Patel.[67] Raiji Patel, who had been to Mojavadi to demand payment[68] sustained some reverses.[69] He was further harassed by the attitude of Mughalia troops[70] in his service. They were scandalously ill-paid and so inclined to join the enemy.[71] Therefore, Raiji Patel impressed upon Scindhia to undertake the supervision of Jaipur affairs.[72] So Scindhia marched towards Jaipur.[73] Sawai Pratap Singh was all the time busy assembling his forces.[74] There were ten thousand Rathors ready to join the Kachwahas at Sambhar,[75] whenever the latter should take the field. Scindhia, learning all these designs, proceeded from Deeg on March 16, 1787 and reached Daosa.[76]

Seeing Sindhia's preparations, every Rajput of note advised Sawai Pratap Singh to make an amicable settlement as it was not feasible to unleash a conflict at that time.[77] Negotiations were opened through Shobha Chand.[78] The Jaipur envoys only offered a meagre sum of 12 lakhs of rupees.[79] This was nothing short of defiance. Rana Khan[80] and Raiji Patel[81] advised Scindhia to accept it and retire from Jaipur as the enemy was too strong. On the other hand, Khushali Ram Bohra and Rao Raja Pratap Singh asked him not to do so.[82] Rao Raja thought that Scindhia would compensate the loss by annexing his territories and so advised likewise. Scindhia was in a fix. Sawai Pratap Singh, sensing his ventures culminating in success, became more stiff. He evinced a strong desire to bring the matters to a head.[83] To add insult to injury, the Kachwaha deputies departed from the camp of Scindhia without obtaining the formal leave.[84] Scindhia now had no alternative but to fight.[85] He ordered Mohammad Beg Hamdani to check the collusion of the Kachwahas with the Rathor forces.[86] Ambaji Inglia was also summoned from Karnal.[87] Scindhia himself proceeded towards Bhankri[88] to relieve Raiji Patel and put pressure upon the Kachwaha Raja to accept his terms.[89] Scindhia imagined that by his personal appearance at Jaipur he would be able to impose his terms upon the Raja. But he miscalculated his own strength. The Kachwaha king did not move out of his fort. Mahadji, with diplomatic generosity, made the virtue of necessity and pleaded for a renewal of negotiations.[90] Peace proposals were made through Sewajee Ethul Rao. Sawai Pratap Singh demanded that Rao Raja be forsaken and Scindhia countermanded that the former should defray the expenses of this expedition.[91] The negotiations broke off abruptly. Scindhia decided to fight.

The Kachwahas and Mahadji began to hunt for allies. The Jaipur and Jodhpur Darbars had already decided to their resources.[92] Sawai Pratap Singh informed him that the Marathas were fast approaching and there was a possibility of the outbreak of hostilities.[93] He informed him that he would leave Jaipur on Jaisath Budi 2, 1844 V.S.[94] (4.5.1787) and requested him to send his forces under Bhim Raj.[95] Bijay Singh asked him to make arrangements for such sums as might see them through the conflict[96] and wait for the arrival of Bhim Raj.[97] But Sawai Pratap Singh left his capital under an auspicious star and stayed at Sanganer,[98] awaiting the arrival of Bhim Raj.[99] Bhim Raj, with 10,000 fighting men, joined the Kachwaha camp.[100]

The problem of winning over Mohammad Beg Hamdani had already been undertaken. Hamdani's agents were given assurances of good faith as early as Phalgun Budi Amavash 1843 V.S.[101] (18.2.1787). Hamdani arrived near the Rajput camp on the 23rd of May, 1987,[102] and was received in a very honourable manner by Sawai Pratap Singh. He was formally invested with the command of all the Muhammadan troops.[103] Even before this, small parties had been leaving the Maratha camp and on the 6th May, two Mughal chiefs, namely, Zulfekar Khan and Mansur Khan went over to the Rajputs. The Rathor army was paraded before Mohammad Beg Hamdani and was found most disciplined and well-equipped.[104]

The situation in Mahadji's camp became worse day by day. His starving soldiers demanded their pay. Scindhia made an attempt of making his wife security for the payment but even that offer was not accepted by them.

Scindhia's forces began to flee. A full battalion 7,000 strong abandoned Scindhia and joined the Rajputs.[105] Scindhia suspected the treacherous designs of the Hindustani troops who on the day of battle might turn their guns against him. He also came to know that his convoy of provisions had been immobilised by the Rajputs. Scindhia was completely cut off from his base as Roda Ram Khawas and Daya Bhai blocked the approach roads from the side of Ranthambore and Khushalgarh respectively.

Mahadji was not wanting in gaining support and he sent his men to Kota. Lala Bhola Nath was sent with some forces.[106] Again Pandit Lalji and Joshi Dev Karan were deputed with a small force to join Mahadji.[107] Scindhia deemed it unsafe to remain in the vicinity of the Rajput camp. So he proceeded to Sawlia, 20 miles to the west of Lalsot, where he would be able to engage the Rajputs with greater advantage.[108] Raiji Patel was also asked to join.[109] The withdrawal of the Marathas was followed by the advance of the Rajput forces.[110] Sawai Pratap Singh requested Bijay Singh to join earlier.[111] Scindhia captured Jhalai,[112] and Navai.[113] He collected some provisions and levied a contribution of Rs. 50,000 on the inhabitants.[114] He then moved southwards and encamped at Tonk.[115] But this made the Rajputs cut off his communications with Deeg and Agra. Sawai Pratap Singh followed him at a cautious distance. Scindhia was impatient to engage the Rajputs, so he on the 29th of May marched towards Lalsot.[116] He arrived at Piplai, 15 miles south-east of Lalsot. Scindhia from here could have an easy access to the passes leading into the Agra District. Rajputs followed suit, advanced from Sanganer and reached Madhogarh, 17 miles north-west of Lalsot. From there the Rajputs proceeded to Daosa to attack Scindhia's rear. Scindhia also made a move of about two kos in that direction and encamped near Surajpur.[117] Scindhia now realised the gravity of the situation and the tremendous work of suppressing the Rajputs he had undertaken. Divergent counsels split the Maratha camp. Rao Raja Pratap Singh advocated a bold and surprise attack while others opposed it. Scindhia himself preferred protracting the issue when for want of money his enemies might disperse. He also knew that the Rajput forces, chiefly comprised of peasantry, would retire in August.[118] The interval he utilised in awaiting the arrival of Ambaji Inglia and Apa Khande Hari. They both arrived by the end of July, 1787.[119]

Mahadji now decided for a pitched battle. Sawai Pratap Singh marched towards Lalsot with Daulat Rao Haldia attending him.[120] The Rathors suffered much from Sindhia's artillery and so Daulat Rao was ordered to send Hamdani's forces to the Rathors. Sindhia's ferocity abated for some time. Hamdani was struck by a cannon-ball and died.[121] The troops ignorant of their leader's death pushed forward and repulsed the Maratha right wing. Hamdani's son, Mudjey Ali, was installed in his place.[122] A truce of two days was agreed upon to perform the funeral sites of Hamdani. Again the two forces faced each other. Sawai Pratap Singh marched from his camp and was joined by the Rathors,[123] on first Shrawan Sudi 13, 1844 (28.7.1767). A battle ensured near the village of Soonar. The Marathas lost a number of valiant fighters—Shambuji Patel, Malhar Rao Panwar, and Chimanji Khande Rao.[124] The distinguished sardar Ghazi Khan[125] was killed. The casualties on the side of the Marathas and Rajputs numbered some 1,500 and 1,000 men respectively[126] Shobha Ram Bhandari was among the killed from the Rajput camp.[127] The Rathors lost Shive Singh Rathor,[128] Sarup SinghNahar,[129] Devi Singh and Maha Singh.[130] They captured two camps and 113 guns of the Marathas.[131] The battle lasted till eight in the night.[132]

Mahadji Scindhia seeing his losses ordered a retreat[133] towards Deeg on second Shrawan Badi 2, 1844 V.S.[134] (1.8.1787). Thus only he could save his family left at Deeg and help Lodoji.[135] He left Lalsot with 5,000 cavalry, leaving behind Rana Khan to cover his retreat.[136] Mahadji proceeded ten kos towards Karauli and Dholpur but as the Marathas posted there had been ousted by the Rajputs, so Scindhia took a circuitous road towards Deeg. He reached Thun, 14 miles south-west of Deeg on August 8, 1787, and sent his family to Gwalior under Ambaji.

Scindhia on the 23rd of August disbanded his Hindustani troops for he could not trust them. He, at the head of 13,000 men, proceeded towards Delhi for checking the advancing Rajput army and oust the new Mir Bakshi, Ghulam Qadir.[137] But as he had completely dominated the Emperor so Scindhia marched to Alwar to prepare himself for the future. He stayed there for more than two months.[138] The Rao Raja showed him every consideration.

The plight of Scindhia was a source of relief and merry-making in Rajputana.[139] Letters of congratulations in the name of Sawai Pratap Singh poured in from Shahpura,[140] Karauli,[141] Bikaner,[142] Udaipur[143] and many other places.[144] Sawai Pratap Singh, to keep Holkar away from the contest, maintained cordial relations with him all the time.[145]

Sawai Pratap Singh pursued Mahadji for a short distance but then gave it up.[146] He was satisfied that he had ousted the Marathas from his territory and avoided any engagement with them, if they did not harry his country or demand tribute.[147] The Maharaja took the road towards Manpura and imposed a fine of one lakh of rupees. He then reached Ramgarh where he again extracted the same amount.[148] Then he proceeded to punish the Rao Raja who had been responsible for this expedition. Some astray forts were reduced. A siege was laid on Alwar itself but on the advice of Bijay Singh it was given up.[149] Infructuous attempts were made to win over Najaf Quali Khan who still sided with the Marathas.

The Rathors also could not lag behind and Singhvi Dhanraj from Merta proceeded towards Ajmer to repossess it from the Marathas.[150] The Maratha forces took refuge in Taragarh (Ajmer). The Rathors besieged it. Forces from Jalor and Nagor under Zorawar Mal and Mehta Rai Chand joined the Rathors.[151] Maratha's commander, Sher Khan defended it well but asked for re-inforcements.[152] So Ambaji Inglia with 8,000 forces was sent for help, but Rodoji Khawas successfully opposed him and made him retire with heavy losses. The fort was ultimately occupied by Singhvi Dhanraj.[153] Sawai

Pratap Singh expressed happiness at the laurela gained by the Rathors.[154] Scindhia's hold on Rajputana disappeared with it. The last stronghold of Scindhia in this region had passed into the hands of his Rathor adversary. Bijay Singh wrote to Tukoji Holkar that the land of Rajputana belongs to Rajputs alone. The propriety of the Marathas lay only in befriending the Rajputs. This was not the end of Mahadji's humiliations. During this time the city of Agra also fell into the hands of Mirza Ismail Beg.[155]

Mahadji was hard-pressed all this time and was on the look out for some allies. The emperor was also harassed by Ghulam Qadir. He called Mahadji[156] and met him at Rewari, but could not be won over by Mahadji. He now abandoned all field operations, crossed the Chambal,[157] retreated towards Gwalior and encamped on the south bank of the Kumari brook to prepare himself for the contest against the Rajputs.

The retirement of Mahadji emboldened the Rajas of Karauli and Narwar to discard their allegiance to the Marathas. They joined together, unsuccessfully, to efface the last traces of the Marathas, from their soil.[158] Bijay Singh also tried to efface the last traces of Scindhia's influence from Rajputana. He even wrote to the Peshwa through Tukoji of depriving Mahadji from the leadership of Maratha affairs in Rajputana.[159]

Bijay Singh also requested Tukoji to withold his support to Mahadji.[160] He also did not pay heed to the peace overtures of Mahadji[161] and even unsuccessfully sought the help of the Company against Mahadji.[162] Sawai Pratap Singh also planned to win over Shah Alam II to their side to drape their action in the mantle of legality. Bijay Singh was informed of the plan through Tewari Sri Krishana.[163] They agreed to serve the Emperor by stationing a force 10,000 strong, equally constituted by both of them.[164] The Emperor who was very hard-pressed reached Rewari on Posh Budi 12, 1884 V.S. (5.1.1788) to meet Sawai Pratap Singh.[165] Though a meeting took place on Magh Budi 13, 1844 V.S. (5.2.1788), yet nothing could come out of it.[166] The Emperor hoped to realise his dues and the Kachwaha Raja could not meet it.

The retreat of Mahadji from Lalsot was a death blow to his aspirations of dominating Rajputana and the Mughal Empire alike. In his hour of crisis he entreated the Poona government for help. The intrigues at the Peshwa's court shelved the issue for some time. The idea of Scindhia being powerful in Hindustan served as a constant threat to the other Maratha potentates. His repeated requests at last bore some fruits and Ali Bahadur[167] and Tukoji Holkar were ordered to rush to his help on condition of sharing equally the territory north of the Chambal between Peshwa, Scindhia and Holkar.[168] Ali Bahadur started on September 8, 1787, but could join Scindhia only in October 1788. Tukoji met Scindhia on July 31, 1788. But the appearance of Tukoji weakened Scindhia's cause due to the activities of Himmat Bahadur.[169] The breach between the two was further widened as Tukoji demanded an equal share in the spoils which, according to Mahadji, were more nominal than real.[170]

This open rift between the two Maratha chiefs emboldened the Rajputs to form an anti-Maratha coalition. On the other hand, it put serious demands on the power of Scindhia to crush Ghulam Quadir[171] and Mirza Ismail beg Hamdani.[172] Soon their revolting excesses and division of booty prompted Ismail Beg to come to terms with Scindhia against Ghulam Quadir. He joined Rana Khan, who had been deputed by Scindhia to release the Emperor. Delhi was again possessed by Scindhia in October 1788. His forces were busy in crushing Ghulam Quadir till February 1789.

With the suppression of Ghulam Qadir, Mirza Najaf Quli Khan[173] and Ismail Beg remained the two road-blocks in Mahadji's domination over Delhi.[174] Mahadji successfully employed Ismail Beg against Najaf Quli Khan till November 1789. The break with Ismail Beg came early in March 1790 as Mahadji could not provide him help in his attempt to capture Kishangarh. Ismail Beg wanted to convert it into a strong-hold for himself. Ismail Beg then favoured the Jaipur and Jodhpur Rajas in their designs of forming in anti-Maratha league. Had the Rajput Rajas not been in the know of the cut-throat struggle between the Maratha sardars they would never have thought of aligning themselves with Ismail Beg and offer resistance to Mahadji.

The Rajputs had been apprehending an attack much earlier. Rao Shambhu Singh and Daulat Ram were deputed by the Jaipur Darbar to Jodhpur to seek help against the Marathas.[175] Sawai Pratap Singh prevailed upon him to collect 10,000[176] forces and despatch them under Khushali Ram, who was sent by the Jaipur Darbar for the purpose.[177] Even the Deputies were sent to win over Ismail Beg.[178] When signs of rapture between Scindhia and Ismail Beg became apparent, the Jodhpur Darbar sent a hundi of Rs. 50,000 to the latter through Shobha Chand Shitab Rai.[179] Some forces were also sent under Singhvi Biney Chand and Lodha Shah Mal on Magsar Sudi 10, 1846.[180] (27.11.1789) to help the Mirza. At last in February, 1790, the relations between Scindhia and Ismail Beg became very strained. He then formed a confederacy with the Rajputs against Scindhia. The Rajas of Jodhpur and Jaipur agreed to pay him seven and five lakhs of rupees respectively. Payment of two lakhs of rupees was to be made immediately and the balance after the commencement of war with Scindhia.

Bijay Singh tried to secure the aid of the Company too. He deputed Rathor Sangram Singh to appraise the Governor-General, Lord Cornwallis, of the designs of the Marathas towards the Rajputs and the English.[181] But the Governor-General followed a policy of non-intervention.

Seeing the designs of Mahadji, Maharaja Bijay Singh began collecting his forces, while putting up an appearance of adjusting the matter amicably.[182] He sent Nawal Rai to Scindhia. But he was not granted an interview. An unsuccessful second attempt was made through Ghulam Raza Khan.[183] As such the Rajputs determined to face the inevitable. The Jaipur and Jodhpur Darbars collected a force 40,000 strong.[184] Every effort was made to secure allies. Bohra Bhawani Ram with a force of one thousand strong was sent to Shekhawati to raise an army.[185] There was a general feeling of revolt against the ascendancy of the Marathas in Rajputana and so even hostile chiefs willingly offered their services.[186] The Rajas of Bundi and Shahpura sent their contingents against the Marathas.[187]

The preparations in the Maratha camp were also not lacking. De Boigne[188] was given the supreme command of Maratha forces. He assembled his battalion 10,000 strong with another 30,000 of Lakwa Dada.[189] The force left Mathura in May 1790, on their way to Rewari and had a small skirmish with Ismail Beg's forces. Beg was forced to retreat towards Patan[190] to join his Rajput allies. The Marathas chased Ismail Beg and Ecamped eight miles East of the Patan City. The Rajputs lay encamped about two miles to the east of Patan.[191]

There was no fighting till the 19th of June, 1790. On the 20th of June the Marathas seized the transport animals of their enemies and when attempts to rescue the animals were made, the battle began. During the engagement, the battalions belonging to Mirza Matlab Khan, who was inimical to Ismail Beg, joined the Marathas. Mirza Ismail Beg put up a stiff resistance but in the evening he was defeated[192] and so he left the battle-field. The Marathas swept away every trace of resistance by 9 in the evening.[193] Straight from the battle-field Ismail Beg hurried to Jaipur and was busy in collecting the forces to oppose the Marathas again.[194] Sawai Pratap Singh expressed regrets at losing the battle and impressed upon Bijay Singh the necessity of continuing their efforts to drive away the Marathas from Rajputana.[195]

The Marathas, in the meantime, hotly pursued the Rajputs.[196] Marathas under Jivaji, Gopal Bhau and De Boigne occupied Sambhar, Parbastsar and Rupnagar on the way. The Rajputs took refuge in the fort of Patan. It resisted the Marathas for six hours but ultimately capitulated.[197] The casualties on the Rajput side were heavy.[198] Ismail Beg's army ceased to exist. Bijay Singh proposed peace talks through Rana Khan and Pandit Apa Chitnis but Scindhia did not entertain it.[199] Mahadji aimed at complete reduction of

Jodhpur and possess Ajmer. Bijay Singh then took to collecting his forces at Merta and Nagor.[200] He also asked to Ismail Beg to join him, promising to pay his expenses.

The Marathas after their victory laid siege to the fort of Ajmer for it was strategically important in maintaining the hold on Rajputana.[201] Infructuous attempts were made to capture it and at last De Boigne leaving some forces there proceeded towards Jodhpur which still posed a threat to the Marathas.[202] The Marathas possessed the city of Ajmer but failed to capture the fort. It held out the invaders for more than six months and was surrendered to the Marathas after Jodhpur was defeated.

While the siege of Ajmer was continuing, the Rajputs and Marathas prepared for a second bout on the plains of Merta.[203] Bijay Singh tried to win over De Boigne unsuccessfully.[104] The Rajputs commanded a force 30,000 strong in cavalry, one lakh of infantry and 25 guns. The Marathas under De Boigne commanded an equal number of cavalry, and a strong artillery of 80 guns.[205] During the early hours of the morning on the 10th of September, 1790, the Marathas attacked the enemy. Their artillery fire forced the Rajputs to retreat. The Rathors made a vigorous counter-attack. The Marathas had to retreat. De Boigne arranged his forces in a hollow square. The plan succeeded and the forward march of the Rajputs was put to a stop before it was nine in the morning.[206] The Rajputs were ultimately defeated. Bhandari Ganga Ram was caught while attempting to escape. The Rathor chiefs, namely, Kesho Pandit, Gulabji, Bharat Singh and Arjun Singh were wounded.[207]

Ismail Beg retired towards Nagor and hurriedly collected his scattered forces. He came to Jodhpur and tried to persuade Bijay Singh to continue his struggle. He himself made an unsuccessful attempt to raise a fresh battalion. As the Raja was not inclined for a renewal of hostilities so he had to give up his plans.

The defeat of the Rajputs was complete and there was no alternative to a complete surrender. Fortunately for the

Rajputs, Scindhia and Holkar quarrelled over the spoils of war which saved them.[208] De Boigne was also facing difficulty in maintaining his famished forces. Mahadji Scindhia rushed to the rescue of his General and left Mathura for Rajputana. The Rajput Rajas to avoid his vengeance appointed Deputies to offer terms to him.[209] Ultimately the Jodhpur Vakils[210] headed by Budh Singh met Mahadji at Sambhar on the 25th of December, 1790. An agreement was signed on Posh Sudi 1, 1847 V.S.[211] (5.1.1791). The Rathors committed to pay Rs. 60,00,001.[212] Out of this amount, Rs. 15,00,001 in cash and 3 lakhs in kind were to be paid immediately; Rs. 15,00,001 was to be paid in cash in six instalments in the following manner:[213]

(a) Rs. 8,00,001 to be paid on Magh Sudi 1, 1847 V.S. (4.2.1791).

(b) The next four instalments of Rs. 1,50,000 each were to be paid on Phalgun Sudi, 1847 V.S. (5.3.1791); Chaitra Sudi 1, 1848 V.S. (4.4.1791); Baisakh Sudi 1, 1848 V.S. (4.5.1791); and Jaisath Sudi 1, 1848 V.S. (2.6.1791), respectively.

(c) The last instalment of one lakh was to be paid on Asadh Sudi 1, 1848 V.S. (2.7.1791).

The cash instalments were to be supplemented by payment in kind to the amount of Rs. 7 lakhs out of which Rs. 3 lakhs were to be paid with the first instalment and the balance of Rs. 4 lakhs was to be paid in two instalments during the years 1847-48 V.S. (March 1790-March 1792). For the remaining 20 lakhs, the Pargana of Sambhar, Nabho, Maroth, Parbatsar and Merta were mortgaged with Mahadji.[214] This sum was to be paid like this: Rs. 2 lakhs on Jaistha Sudi 15, 1848 V.S. (16.6.1791); and four equal instalments of Rs. 4 lakhs each were to be paid on every Jaisath Sudi 15 from 1849 to 1852 V.S. (4.6.1792 to 2.6.1795). The rest of the balance of Rs. 2 lakhs was to be written off if the Rathors paid the instalments regularly. Besides this, the fort and parganas of Ajmer were to be evacuated in favour of the Marathas.[215] In addition to this the tributes of Jodhpur and Godwar were settled at Rs. 1,50,000 and Rs. 30,000 respectively, in Brindaban and Lashkar currency respectively. Another agreement[216] was executed between Mahadji Scindhia and Maharaja Bijay Singh through Champawat Budh Singh and Bhandari Kalyan Das, by which they agreed not to employ the aggrieved men of either Raj.

Though there is no reference regarding Ismail Beg in the treaty the correspondence that followed shows that Mahadji had forbidden the two Darbars to provide any protection to him. The Jodhpur Darbar followed it faithfully. Mahadji reprimanded Sawai pratap Singh for he despatched some forces to help Ismail Beg who had left for Kanod[217] where Khande Rao Hari was attempting to drive him out. The Jaipur Darbar informed him that Mirza was no longer in his service.[218] The Jaipur Darbar sent Dewan Rani Chand to join Khande Rao Hari[219] against the Mirza. Rao Raja also sent his forces to help the Maratha general.[220] Ultimately the Marathas defeated Ismail Beg.[221] The defeat turned him into an outcast.

With Jodhpur Darbar under his control Mahadji now turned his attention towards Jaipur which had been the mainspring of his misfortunes during this period. Raiji patel asked Sawai Pratap Singh to depute Thakur Pahar Singh and Khawas Roda Ram to negotiate the terms.[222] The two representatives[223] met Mahadji at Phulia in the Pargana of Shahpura.[224] The arrears of the past tribute and Mughal dues were totalled to the sum of Rs. 63,00,001[225] which was to be paid in cash by Jaipur after deducting the amount already paid to Scindhia.[226] In addition to this, 15 lakhs were settled as war indemnity out of which 3 lakhs in cash and one lakh in kind were to be paid immediately. The balance of Rs. 11 lakhs was to be made good by assignments on the Rajputs in his Raj.[227] A supplementary treaty was also signed by which the Marathas agreed not to interfere in the administration of the Raj and not to take sides against the Darbar. Mahadji agreed to supply forces if and when demanded by the Raj on condition that the latter would bear the expenses of the forces during its stay. The contracting parties swore by their Gods to execute the agreement faithfully. The Maratha forces were to co-operate in the work of collection from Shekhawati out of which 1/3rd would be paid as `Fauj Kharch'.[228] The details of Rs. 15 lakhs were worked out.[229] The Jaipur Raj agreed to pay Rs. 6,48,639 out of which Rs. 5,82,639 in cash including Rs. 50,000 as `Fauj Kharch' and Rs. 66,000 in kind; Rs. 5,36,586 were to be realised from Shekhawati out of which Rs. 3,14,736 were to be realised by Jagoo Bapoo and Lakwa Dada; Rs. 1,17,000 by Scindhia and Rs. 1,04,850 from Sewar and Unaira, 1/3rd of it, i.e., Rs. 1,78,862 was to be paid as `Fauj Kharch'. The balance of Rs. 3,57,724 was to be adjusted against the total amount of Rs. 15 lakhs. The Jaipur Maharaja transferred the Nazar of Rs. 50,000 to be paid directly to Scindhia which had been agreed upon as Nazar from Rao Raja Bakhtawar Singh to him. The total amount thus realised would come to Rs. 10,56,363 (6,48,639 plus 3,57, 724 plus 50,000) leaving the balance of Rs. 4,43,637. Out of this amount Rs. 4,09,637 was to be paid immediately and the balance of Rs. 34,000 in kind afterwards.

The battle of Merta once again flared up the rivalry between Scindhia and Holkar. It proved the undoing of Mahadji and led to utter chaos in the two camps. This paved the way for British penetration into Rajputana.

Having settled the accounts with the Rajputs Mahadji appointed Lakwa Dada to look after the affairs. He retired for Poona.[230] Hardly had he reached Pushkar, when Zalim Singh waited upon him and requested to take Mewar under his protection.[231] Mahadji acceded to the request. He was in a hurry to reach Poona so he left Ambaji Inglia to help the Maharana in crushing the rebels. But Ambaji could not get over them. So Mahadji returned and could finally leave Rajputana in the beginning of 1792.

As the money promised by the Jaipur Darbar was not forthcoming, and De Boigne was hard pressed to pacify his mutinous troops so Mahadji made him the recipient of the dues from Jaipur.[232] He put forth his demand at Rs. 19,43,614/11/6[233] including Rs. 15 lakhs as already agreed upon: Rs. 58,000 as `Fauj Kharch', Rs. 15,000 realised from Borada and Rs. 3,70,614/11/6 as present expenses for collecting the money from the territory of Jaipur. Further details of Rs. 3,70,614/11/6 have been set forth in the agreement as follows:—

Expenditure of Bhao Bhaskar Rs. 2,28,862/-. Out of this Rs. 50,000 to be paid to clerks and Rs. 1,78,862 as `Fauj Kharch' at the rate of 1.3rd of the amount collected from Shekhawati and the rest to be adjusted against tribute. The total to be realised from Shekhwati was taken as Rs. 5,36,586; Rs. 1,88,051/3/6 to be realised from the Chaudharies, Kanungoes of Shekhawati, Torawati, Balhar, Pragpura and Antala. Out of this Rs. 62,683/11/6 was to be paid as `Fauj Kharch' and Rs. 1,25,367/8/- against tribute, Rs. 76,159/- as expenditure of De Boigne through Daulat Ram from Siwar and Unaira and Rs. 2,910 as expenses of Nand Kishor.

The affairs at Jodhpur were also not encouraging. The Jodhpur Darbar had mortgaged the Parganas of Sambhar, Nabha, Maroth, Parbatsar and Merta with Mahadji, yet the villages[234] of Sambhar had not been transferred. He asked the Maharaja to instruct his `*Amildars*' to hand over this territory to his `Kanvishdars.'[235] The Maharaja assured that the matter would be adjusted amicably.[236] The territories were then transferred to Mahadji Scindhia.

The same delay was seen in the cash payment and Scindhia constantly reminded the Darbar for it.[237] In spite of the casual delay, Bijay Singh paid the tribute due to Scindhia up to his death in July, 1793 and remained on friendly and cordial terms with him.[238]

The defeat of the leading Rajput Rajas at Patan and Merta was nothing short of humiliation at the hands of Mahadji Scindhia. Scindhia once again had proved his invincibility to the Rajputs so much so that when the Jaipur ruler again initiated a move against Scindhia in May, 1792, the Jodhpur ruler categorically refused to be a party to it. Mahadji had retrieved his lost prestige in Rajputana which had eclipsed due to the disaster at Lalsot. He was the master of the land in unequivocal terms and had inversely gained what the Rajput Rajas had lost. The defeat of the Rajputs brought in its wake political instability accompanied with financial bankruptcy, giving rise to chaos and turmoil at the Rajput capitals. Not only big chunks of land were transferred by Marwar and Jaipur alike, but under duress, they had to promise a huge sum, much beyond their meagre means, to save themselves from Scindhia.

REFERENCES

1. Sarkar, *op. cit.*, III,. 230.
2. Mirza Najaf Khan was an adventurer from Persia. He held the regency of Delhi from November 1779 to April 1782.
3. Raghbir Singh, *op. cit.*, p. 196.
4. He was Najaf Khan's principal adviser and agent in dealing with the Hindu Princes.
5. Sarkar, *op. cit.*, III, 146.
6. Sitamow: *Muntakhab-i-Akhbar* (Mss.), folio 221 B, dated April 17, 1781.
7. Sarkar, *op. cit.*, III, 237.
8. Parasnis, Delhi Yethil Marathyanche Rajkarna, letter No. 1, dated Dec. 10, 1784.
9. Jaipur & Alwar States.
10. *Ibid.*, letter No. 133, dated Dec. 10, 1784.
11. Dodwell, *Letters of Warren Hastings*, p. 117.
12. Malleson, *op. cit.*, pp. 142-43.
13. Sardesai, *New History ......, op. cit.*, III, 120-24.
14. Malcolm. Sir John, *The Political History of India from 1784 to 1803* (2 Vols,. London: John Murray, 1826), Vol. I. pp. 187-8.
15. Forrest, *Selections from State Papers, 1772-1785*, Vol. III, pp. 1087-89.
16. The most sinister figure among Mirza Najaf's captains.

17. Mir Bakshi and the Supreme Regent. He was also the Subedar of Agra.
18. Sarkar, *op. citl.*, III, 185.
19. Mir Bakshi of the Empire after the murder of Mirza Mohammad Shafi. He was by birth a Hindu grocer's boy. Mirza Najaf had captured him as an orphan, converted to Islam and made him his favourite slave. Najaf Khan had recommended him to the emperor as his successor in office and master of his troops and files.
20. D.O.A.B.: Dastari Records, Bundle No. 9, file No. 4, letter No. 23, dated Kartik Budi 2, 1841 V.S. (30.9.1784). From Maharaja Sawai Pratap Singh to Maharaja Bijay Singh.
21. Parasanis, *op. cit.*, letter No. 106, dated July 1, 1785, and letter No. 139, dated August 1, 1785.
22. Sardesai, *New History*, *op. cit.*, III, 147.
23. (a) D.O.A.B.: From Mehta Swaroop Singh of Bikaner to Roda Ram, dated Magh Budi, 3, 1841 V.S. (29.12.1784).

    (b) D.O.A.B.: From Mehta Rai Sahib Singh to Roda Ram, dated Chaitra Sudi 12, 1842 V.S. (21.4.1785).
24. D.O.A.B. : From Maharaja Sawai Pratap Singyh to Raja Manik Pal, dated Jaisath Budi, 5, 1842 V.S. (18.5.1785). Draft Kharita Section, Bundle No. 18.
25. Sardesai, *Historical Papers ...*, *op. cit.*, No. 358, dated March 1785.
26. (a) D.O.A.B.: From Maharaja Sawai Pratap Singh to Raja Balwant Singh, dated Baisakh Budi 12, 1842 V.S. (5.5.1785), Draft Kharita Bundle. No. 18.

    (b) It is 22 miles West of Mathura.
27. (a) D.O.A.B.: From Subedar Mahadji Scindhia to Bohra Khushali Ram, dated Baisakh Budi 12, 1842 V.S. (22.8.1785), Draft Kharita Nundle No. 18.

    (b) D.O.A.B.: Subedar Mahadji Scindhia to Maharaja Sawai Pratap Singh, dated Bhadra Budi 2, 1842 V.S. (22.8.1785), Draft Kharita Bundle No. 18.

    (c) D.O.A.B.: From Maharaja Sawai Pratap Singh to Amolik Paulji, dated Jaisath Budi 5, 1842 V.S. (22.5.1785), Draft Kharita Bundle No. 18.

    (d) D.O.A.B.: FromMaharaja Sawai Pratap Singh to Saingarji, dated Jaistha Budi 5, 1842 V.S. (28.5.1785), Draft Kharita Bundle No. 18.

(e) D.O.A.B.: From Subedar Mahadji Scindhia to Maharaja Sawai Pratap Singh dated Kartik Budi 10, 1842 V.S. (27.10.1785), Kharita Sectioon, G.B.

28. D.O.A.B. : From Maharaja Sawai Pratap Singh to Raja Balwant Singh, dated Magsar Sudi 3, 1842 V.S. (4.12.1785), Kharita Bundle No. 18.

29. D.O.A.B.: From Subedar Mahadji Scindhia to Maharaja Sawai Pratap Singh, dated Bhadra Sudi 4, 1842 V.S. (7.9.1785), Draft Kharita Bundle No. 18.

30. D.O.A.B. : From Roda Ram to Mehta Rai Sahib Singh, dated Magsar Sudi 5, 1842 V.S. (6.12.1785).

31. D.O.A.B.: From Bakshi Mitha Lal to Khushaliram, dated Jaisath Sudi 10, 1842 V.S. (1.6.1786).

32. D.O.A.B.: Dastari Records Bundle No. 1, File No. 1, letter No. 1, dated Chaitra Sudi 7, 1842 V.S. (5.4.1786). From Ajmer to Maharaja Bijay Singh.

33. (a) D.O.A.B.: From Maharaja Manik Palji to Maharaja Sawai Pratap Singh, dated Magasar Sudi 4, 1842 V.S. (5.12.1785), Draft Kharita, Bundle No. 18.

(b) D.O.A.B.: From Pancholi Gumani Ram to Raja Hamir Singh, dated Magsar Sudi 10, 1842 V.S. (11.12.1785).

34. D.O.A.B.: From Muhonot Gyan Mal to Khawas Roda Ram, dated Posh Sudi 5, 1842 V.S. (5.1.1786). Khatut Ahalkaran, Bundle No. 14, Khat No. 51.

35. (a) D.O.A.B.: From Maharaja Sawai Pratap Singh to Raja Hari Singh, dated Phalgun Budi 13, 1842 V.S. (26.2.1786), Draft Kharita Bundle No. 18.

(b) Banera: From Shah Narain Das to Bhandari-Bhopat Ram, dated Chaitra Budi 13, 1842 V.S. (28.3.1786).

36. D.O.A.B.: From Maharaja Sawai Pratap Singh to Raja Hari Singh, dated Phalgun Budi 13, 1842 V.S. (16.2.1786), Draft Kharita Bundle No. 18.

37. D.O.A.B.: From Bakshi Alam Chand to Roda Ram, dated Chaitra Sudi 12, 1842 V.S. (10.4.1786). Khatut Ahalkaran, Bundle No. 14.

38. D.O.A.B.: From Maharaja Sawai Pratap Singh to Maharaja Bijay Singh, dated Baisakh Budi 12, 1843 V.S. (25.4.1786), Kharita Section, Jodhpur Bundle No. 381.

39. *Ibid.*

40. D.O.A.B.: From Maharaja Sawai Pratap Singh to Maharaja Bijay Singh, dated Magh Budi 14, 1842 V.S. (20.1.1786), Kharita Section, Jodhpur Bundle, Kharita No. 378.

41. Man Singh was the son of Sawai Prithvi Singh. He lived at Bindraban where he enjoyed a Jagir granted by Mahadji Scindhia.

42. N.A.O.I.: F & S, June 23, 1786, cons. No. 32. From G. Harper to GG., dated May 26, 1786.

43. (a) D.O.A.B. : Yad-dast Kalyan Rao Pandit, Baisakh Budi 5, 1843 V.S. (20.1.1786).

    Eleven lakhs were to be made in this manner—cash 7 lakhs; jewels 3 lakhs and elephants, horses, etc., worth one lakh. Sarkar agrees to the total amount of 63 lakhs but differs in the mode of payment, Vol. III, p. 243.

    (b) N.A.O.I. : F&S, April 24, 1786 Cons. No. 21 B. From G. Harper to GG.

44. D.O.A.B.: Yad-dast Kalyan Rao Pandit, Baisakh Budi 5, 1843 V.S. (20.4.1786).

45. *Ibid.*

46. N.A.O.I.: Persian Section, TR. 26, pp. 161-62, No. 71, received June 21, 1786. From Ali Ibrahim Khan to GG.

    As Sawai Pratap Singh's preparations for a showdown with Mahadji were not complete at the moment, so he purchased Mahadji's withdrawal by promising 63 lakhs and paying only 11 lakhs as the first instalment.

47. Sarkar, *op. cit.*, III, 243.

48. Parasnis, Delhi ..., *op. cit.*, Vol. I, letter No. 169, dated August 21, 1786.

49. (a) N.A. O.I.: F& S, June 23, 1786, Cons. No. 30, From G. Harper to GG., dated May 26, 1786.

    (b) Sardesai, *Historical Papers ..., op. cit.*, letter No. 415, dated May 1786.

50. D.O.A.B.: From Raja Sanjay Singh to Pahar Singh, dated Magh Sudi 7, 1843 V.S. (26.1.1787), Draft Kharita, Bundle No. 19, Draft No. 50/4.

51. D.O.A.B.: From Raja Sanjay Singh to Khawas Roda Ram, dated Magh Sudi 9, 1843 V.S. (27.1.1787), Draft Kharita, Bundle No. 19.

52. D.O.A.B.: Dastari records, Bundle No. 1, File No. 1, letter No. 2, dated Magh Sudi 15, 1843 V.S. (2.2.1787). From Ajmer to Maharaja Bijay Singh.

53. D.O.A.B.: From Raja Kishori Das to Vidya Guru Bhattji, dated Phalgun Budi 13, 1843 V.S. (16.2.1787).

54. D.O.A.B.: From Amolik Palji to Vidya Guru Bhattji, dated Phalgun Budi 4, 1843 V.S. (6.2.1787).

55. D.O.A.B.: From Maharaja Sawai Pratap Singh to Maharaja Bijay Singh, dated Posh Sudi 2, 1843 V.S. (22.12.1786); Jodhpur Khyat, 3, p. 425.

 The estranged relations between Bijay Singh and Mahadji made the matters more amicable. The anglo-Maratha rivalry of 1781 and Bijay Singh's overtures with the Company made Mahadji doubt his intentions. Again in 1784, the Rathor Chief supported the Saktawuts while Mahadji was favouring the cause of the Chundawats. Thus a rupture between the two was beyond any doubt. On the other hand, Bijay Singh had entered into cordial relations with the Jaipur Durbar, after the death of Ram Singh in 1772. Bijay Singh had offered his help to Sawai Pratap Singh against Pratap Singh Naruka of Macheri who dreamed to create a territorial sovereignty for himself, independent of the Jaipur Durbar. Bijay Singh had cemented this friendship by giving his grand-daughter in marriage to Sawai Pratap Singh in August, 1785. As such Bijay Singh was easily won over by the Jaipur Durbar.

56. (a) D.O.A.B.: Dastari records, Bundle No. 9, File No. 4, letter No. 28, dated Posh Sudi 12, 1843 V.S. (1.1.1787). From Maharaja Sawai Pratap Singh to Maharaja Bijay Singh.

 (b) Beal-leaf is taken as the symbol of the God Shiva. It is the purest kind of swearing.

57. D.O.A.B.: From Gordhan Dass to Khawas Roda Ram, dated Magh Sudi 14, 1842 V.S. (12.2.1787). No. 27/3.

58. D.O.A.B.: Dastari Records, Bundle No. 9, File No. 4, letter No. 31, dated Phalgun Budi Amavash, 1843 V.S. (18.2.1787). From Maharaja Sawai Pratap Singh to Maharaja Bijay Singh.

59. *Ibid*.

60. D.O.A.B.: From Raja Bahadur Gopal Dass to Maharaja Sawai Pratap Singh dated Posh Sudi 5, 1843 V.S. (25.12.1786). Draft Kharita, Bundle No. 19.

61. D.O.A.B.: From Rawat Bhim Singh to Roda Ram, dated Chaitra Sudi 14, 1843 V.S. (1.4.1787). Draft Kharita, Bundle No. 19.

62. D.O.A.B.: From Rao Raja Bishan Singh to Maharaja Sawai Pratap Singh, dated Magsar Sudi 11, 1844 V.S. (20.12.1787). Draft Kharita, Bundle No. 11.

63. D.O.A.B.: From Maharaja Sawai Pratap Singh to Amolik Palji,

dated Baisakh Budi 7, 1844, V.S. (10.4.1787), Draft Kharita, Bundle No. 19.

64. D.O.A.B.: From Sanjay Singh to Khawas Roda Ram, dated Magh Sudi 9, 1843 V.S. (27.1.1787), Draft Kharita, Bundle No. 19.

65. Sardesai, *Historical Papers ..., op. cit.,* letter No. 489, dated Nov. 24, 1786.

66. D.O.A.B.: From Maharaja Sawai Pratap Singh to Misser Ganga Ram, dated Magh Budi 3, 1843 V.S. (6.1.1787), Draft Kharita, Bundle No. 19.

67. N.A.O.I.: Foreign-Political & Secret, Cons. No. 2, dated March 23, 1787. From W. Kirkpatrick to GG, dated March 3, 1787.

68. D.O.A.B.: From Maharaja Sawai Pratap Singh to Ganga Ram, dated Magh Budi 3, 1843 V.S. (6.1.1787), Draft Kharita, Bundle No. 19.

69. D.O.A.B.: From Amolik Palji to Maharaja Sawai Pratap Singh, dated Chaitra Sudi 5, 1843 V.S. (7.3.1787), Draft Kharita, Bundle No. 19.

70. The Muslim troops under Mohammad Beg Hamdani, Zulfekar Khan, Mansur Khan, etc.

71. P.R.C.: Vol. I, No. 82, pp. 137, dated March 3, 1787.

72. P.R.C.: Vol. I, No. 85, pp. 148-49, dated March 22, 1787.

73. Scindhia reached Dausa on March 6, 1787. P.R.C., Vol. 1, Nos. 71 and 80.

74. N.A.O.I.: Foreign Secert and Political, Cons. No. 1, dated April 20, 1787. From W. Kirkpatrick to GG., dated April 6, 1787.

75. (a) Parasnis, Delhi Yethil ...., *op. cit.,* Vol. I, letter No. 201, dated April 1787; Jodhpur Khayat 3, p. 425.

    (b) 150 kos south of Jaipur.

76. 32 miles East of Jaipur.

    Scindhia was convinced that the reason forwarded by the Jodhpur Vakil Purohit Jivraj, that the forces have been deputed at Sambhar because of the unhappy relations between Kishangarh and Ajmer and that any untoward event may not occur was untrue, made Scindhia proceed from Deeg, Jodhpur Khayat 3, p. 426.

77. D.O.A.B.: From Mitha Lal to Pahar Singh, dated Baisakh Budi 9, 1844 V.S. (12.4.1787).

78. P.R.C.: Vol. I, No. 102, p. 167, dated April, 1787.

79. N.A.O.I.: F & S, Cons. No. 1, dated April 18, 1787. From G. Harper to GG., dated April 10, 1787.

80. He was responsible for saving the life of Mahadji after the rout of Panipat.

81. Jodhpur Khayat 3, p. 427.

82. Parasnis, *op. cit.*, Vol. I, letter No. 201, dated April, 1787.

83. N.A.O.I.: Foreign Sec. & Pol., Cons. No. 5, 1787. From G. Forster to GG, dated April 27, 1787.

84. N.A.O.I.: Foreign Sec. & Pol., Cons. No. 14A, May 23, 1787. From W. Kirkpatrick to GG., dated May 11,1787.

85. N.A.O.I.: Foreign Sec. & Pol., Cons. No. 5, April 20, 1787. From G. Harper to GG, dated April 12, 1787.

86. N.A.O.I.: Foreign Sec. & Pol., Cons. No. 14A, May 23, 1787. From W. Kirkpatrick to GG., dated May 11, 1787.

87. *Ibid.* He was sent to Punjab to encounter an incursion of the Sikhs to the northward of Sindhia's capital.

88. Thirteen miles East of Sanganer Railway station.

89. P.R.C.: Vol. I, No. 104, pp. 168-89, dated April 15, 1787.

90. P.R.C.: Vol. I, No. 105, p. 170, dated April 10, 1787.

91. N.A.O.I.: Foreign Sec. & Pol., Cons. No. 22, Sept. 4, 1787. From W. Kirkpatrick to GG. dated June 30, 1787.

92. (a) D.O.A.B.: Dastari records, Basta No. 9, File No. 4, letter No. 44, dated Asadh Sudi 14, 1844 V.S. (27.6.1787). From Maharaja Sawai Pratap Singh to Maharaja Bijay Singh.

    (b) D.O.A.B.: Dastari records, Basta No. 9, File No. 1, letter No. 4, dated Baisakh Sudi 5, 1844 V.S. (22.4.1787). From Maharaja Sawai Pratap Singh to Maharaja Bijay Singh.

    (c) Conscription was ordered by Bijay Singh in Marwar. P.R.C., Vol. I, 49.

93. D.O.A.B.: Dastari records, Basta No. 9, File No. 4, letter No. 36, dated Chaitra Sudi 12, 1844 V.S. (30.3.1787). From Maharaja Sawai Pratap Singh to Maharaja Bijay Singh.

94. D.O.A.B.: Dastari Records, Basta No. 9, File No. 4, letter No. 38, dated Baisakh Budi 10, 1844 V.S. (13.4.1787). From Maharaja Sawai Pratap Singh to Maharaja Bijay Singh.

95. D.O.A.B.: Dastari Records, Basta No. 9, File No. 4, letter No. 39, dated Jaisath Budi 2, 1844 V.S. (4.5.1787). From Maharaja Sawai Pratap Singh to Maharaja Bijay Singh.

96. D.O.A.B.: Dastari Records, Basta No. 9, File No. 4, letter No. 30, dated Phalgun Budi Amavash 1843 V.S. (18.2.1787). From Maharaja Sawai Pratap Singh to Maharaja Bijay Singh.

97. D.O.A.B.: From Maharaja Bijay Singh to Maharaja Sawai Pratap Singh, dated Jaisath Bud 10, 1844 V.S. (12.5.1787). Khas Rukka No. 278.

98. D.O.A.B.: Dastari Records, Basta No. 9, File No. 4, letter No. 40, dated Jaisath Budi 3, 1844, V.S. (5.5.1787). From Maharaja Sawai Pratap Singh to Maharaja Bijay Singh.

99. D.O.A.B.: Dastari Records, Basta No. 9, File No. 4, letter No. 41, dated Jaisath Budi 9, 1844, V.S. (11.5.1787). From Maharaja Sawai Pratap Singh to Maharaja Bijay Singh.

100. D.O.A.B.: From Maharaja Sawai Pratap Singh to Maharaja Bijay Singh, dated Asadh Budi 5, 1844 V.S. (6.6.1787), Draft Kharita Bundle No. 19, Ojha, Jodhpur 2.

101. D.O.A.B.: From Dastari Records, Basta No. 3, File No. 4, letter No. 31, dated Phalgun Budi Amavash 1843 V.S. (18.2.1787). From Maharaja Sawai Pratap Singh to Maharaja Bijay Singh.

102. N.A.O.I. : F & S, June 11, 1787. Cons. No. 3, Letter from W. Kirkpatrick to GG., dated may 28, 1787: P.R.C. I. 114.

     Hamdani was promised Rs. 3,000 a day to be equally contributed by Jaipur & Jodhpur, Agra & Deeg were to be restored to him if he drives Scindhia beyond the river Narmada, Jodhpur Khayat 3, p. 427.

103. N.A.O.I.: Foreign Pol. & Sc., June 11, 1787, Cons. No. 4. From W. Kirkpatrick to GG., dated May 30, 1787.

104. D.O.A.B.: Dastari Records, Basta No. 1, File No. 1, letter No. 5, dated Asadh Budi 13, 1844 V.S. (13.6.1787). From Maharaja Sawai Pratap Singh to Maharaja Bijay Singh.

105. D.O.A.B.: From Maharaja Sawai Pratap Singh to Manik Palji dated 1st Shrawan Budi 11, 1844 V.S. (11.7.1787), Draft Kharita Bundle No. 19, Draft No. 252.

106. A.O.K.: Bhandar No. 1, Basta No. 66, File No. 22, Do Varkhi Parchazat Samvat 1843 (July 1787 to August 1788).

107. *Ibid.*

108. N.A.O.I.: Foreign Sec. & Pol., May 17, 1787, Cons. No. 3. From W. Kirkpatrick to GG., dated May 3, 1787.

109. D.O.A.B.: From Chaturbhuj to Maharaja Bijay Singh, dated Asadh Sudi 7, 1844 V.S. (22.6.1787).

110. D.O.A.B.: Dastari Records, Basta No. 9, File No. 4, letter No. 43, dated Asadh Budi 5, 1844 V.S. (6.6.1787). From Maharaja Sawai Pratap Singh to Maharaja Bijay Singh.

111. D.O.A.B.: Dastari Records, Basta No. 1, File No. 1, letter No. 5, dated Asadh Budi 13, 1844 V.S. (13.6.1787). From Maharaja Sawai Pratap Singh to Maharaja Bijay Singh.

112. (a) N.A.O.I.: Foreign Pol. & Sec. May 23 1787, Cons. No. 14A. From W. Kirkpatrick to GG., dated May 11, 1787.

(b) Seven miles from Sawlia.

113. N.A.O.I.: Foreign Pol. & Sec. May 30 1787, Cons. No. 8. From G. Forster to GG., dated May 19, 1787.

114. N.A.O.I.: Foreign Pol. & Sec. June 6, 1787, Cons. No. 12. From W. Kirkpatrick to GG., dated May 23, 1787.

115. *Ibid,* 25 Kos from Jaipur.

116. (a) N.A.O.I.: Foreign Pol. & Sec., June 11, 1787, Cons. No. 5. From W. Kirkpatrick to GG., dated June 1, 1787. Jodhpur Khayat 3, p. 429.

(b) Thirty miles South-East of Jaipur.

117. (a) P.R.C.: Vol. I. letter No. 20, dated June 17, 1787, p. 197.

(b) Four Kos from Lalsot.

118. N.A.O.I.: Foreign Pol. & Sec., May 17 1787, Cons. No. 3. From W. Kirkpatrick to GG., dated May 3, 1787.

119. N.A.O.I.: Foreign Po. & Sec., dated Aug. 28, 1787. From W. Kirkpatrick to GG., dated July 28, 1787.

120. Khande Rao arrived on June 26th and Ambaji reached in July 1787, P.R.C. 1, letter Nos. 118, 119.

Scindhia was waiting for his Generals to join him. When they joined Scindhia, he was in high spirits to take the issue to the battle-field. Pratap Singh also waited for more help from Bundi, Bikaner, etc. The arrival of the Maratha Generals in Scindhia's camp prompted him for an early action.

121. D.O.A.B.: From Maharaja Sawai Pratap Singh to Raja Manik Pal, dated Second Shrawan Budi 11, 1844 V.S. (11.8.1787), Draft Kharita, Bundle No. 19, Draft No. 252; Jodhpur Khayat 3, p. 437.

122. N.A.O.I., Foreign Pol. & Sec., Sept. 4, 1787, Cons. No. 16. From G. Harper to GG., dated Aug. 3, 1787.

123. D.O.A.B.: Dastoor Komwar, Vol. IX, pp. 677-82; Gahlot I, p. 54; Jodhpur Khayat 3, p. 430.

124. D.O.A.B.: Dastari Records, Basta No. 9, File No. 4, letter No. 49, dated Magsar Budi 5, 1844 V.S. (19.11.1787). From Maharaja Sawai Pratap Singh to Maharaja Bijay Singh.

125. (a) N.A.O.I.: Foreign Pol. & Sec. Sept. 4, 1787 cons. No. 16. From G. Harper to GG., dated Aug. 3, 1787.

(b) He was the son of Mustafa Khan who was formerly in service of the Subedar of Bengal.

126. D.O.A.B.: From Maharaja Sawai Pratap Singh to Manik Palji, dated Second Shrawan Budi 11, 1844 V.S. (11.8.1787). Draft Kharita Bundle No. 19, Draft No 252; C.P.C. Vol, VII 1551 gives Maratha casualty as 1000.

127. Sarkar, *op. cit.*, III, 266; P.R.C.I, 135, 136, 137.

128. D.O.A.B.: Hakikat Bahi No. 4, folio 425A, dated Ashoj Budi 2, 1844 V.S. (29.9.1787).

129. D.O.A.B.: Hakikat Bhai No. 4, folio 437A, dated Phalgun Budi 14, 1844 V.S. (6.3.1788).

130. D.O.A.B.: Jodhpur Records, Hakikat Bahi No. 4, folio 432B, dated Posh Budi 6, 1844 V.S. (30.12.1787).

131. D.O.A.B.: From Maharaja Sawai Pratap Singh to Manik Palji dated Second Shrawan Budi 5, 1844 V.S. (4.8.1787), Draft Kharita, Bundle No. 19, Draft No. 204.

132. P.R.C. I, 135.

133. (a) D.O.A.B.: From Maharaja Sawai Pratap Singh to Pratap Singh of Bikaner, dated Bhadra Sudi 15, 1844 V.S. (27.9.1787). Draft Kharita, Bundle No. 19, Draft No. 243.

(b) D.O.A.B.: From Tukoji Holkar to Daulat Ram, dated Ashoj Sudi 8, 1844 V.S. (4.10.1787), Kharita Section, Indore Bundle; Jodhpur Khayat 3, p. 439.

134. D.O.A.B.: From Maharaja Sawai Pratap Singh to Raja Manik Palji dated Second Shrawan Budi 11, 1844 V.S. (11.8.1787), Draft Kharita, Bundle No. 19, Draft No. 235, Jodhpur Khayat 3, p. 441; P.R.C. I, 137, 155; C.P.C. Vol. VII, 1572.

135. He was the son-in-law of Mahadji and was acting at Delhi as his deputy.

136. N.A.O.I.: Foreign Pol. & Sec. Cons. No. 17, Sept. 9, 1787. From G. Harper to GG., dated Aug. 6, 1787.

137. Ghulam Qadir had taken possession of the city and the Emperor at the news of Scindhia's defeat at Lalsot. He was appointed Mir Bakshi and Regent plenipotentiary in place of Scindhia.

138. Scindhia reached Alwar on August 24, 1787 and was there up to Nov. 2, 1787.

139. D.O.A.B.: From Bhim Singh to Maharaja Sawai Pratap Singh, dated Phalgun Budi 7, 1844 V.S. (28.2.1788), Draft Kharita, Bundle No. 19, Draft No. 240.

140. D.O.A.B.: From Raja Bhim Singh to Daulat Ram, dated Second Shrawan Budi 5, 1844 V.S. (4.8.1787), Draft Kharita, Bundle No. 19, Draft No. 249.

141. D.O.A.B.: From Madan Mohan to Daulat Ram, dated Posh Budi 2, 1844 V.S. (10.1.1788), Draft Kharita, Bundle No. 19, Draft No. 219.

142. D.O.A.B.: From Maharaja Sawai Pratap Singh to Maharaja Pratap Singh dated Bhadra Sudi 15, 1844 V.S. (27.9.1787), Draft Kharita, Dundle No. 19, Draft No. 243.

143. D.O.A.B.: From Rawat Bhim Singh to Maharaja Sawai Pratap Singh, dated Phalgun Budi 7, 1844 V.S. (28.2.1788).

144. (a) D.O.A.B.: From Maharaja Sawai Pratap Singh to Misser Bal Mukund, dated Bhadra Budi 1, 1844, V.S. (29.8.1787). Draft Kharita, Bundle No. 19, Draft No. 372.

     (b) D.O.A.B.: From Radhika Das to Maharaja Sawai Pratap Singh, dated Phalgun Sudi 9, 1844 V.S. (16.3.1788)

145. D.O.A.B.: From Maharaja Sawai Pratap Singh to Rao Tukoji Holkar, dated Bhadra Sudi 11, 1844 V.S. (23.9.1787). Kharita Section, Indore Bundle.

146. (a) D.O.A.B.: From Maharaja Sawai Pratap Singh to Maharaja Bhim Singh dated Second Sharwan Sudi 4, 1844 V.S. (17.8.1787). Draft Kharita, Bundle No. 19, Draft No. 253.

     (b) D.O.A.B.: From Maharaja Sawai Pratap Singh to Maharaja Bakht Singh, dated Second Sharwan Budi Amavash, 1844 V.S. (13.8.1787). Draft Kharita, Bundle No. 19, Draft No. 226.

     (c) Sawai Pratap Singh was basically interested in punishing the Rao Raja and to regain the territory which he had occupied. He was all the time less interested in ousting the Marathas completely from Rajputana. His lethargic attitude was only in a small degree responsible for giving up the pursuit. Jodhpur Records, Portfolio No. 9, Kharita No. 45, dated bright half of Shrawana 1844 V.S. (16.7.1787).

147. P.R.C. Vol. I, No. 188, pp. 270-71, dated Dec. 9, 1787.

148. D.O.A.B.: From Maharaja Sawai Pratap Singh to Raja Manik Palji,

dated Second Shrawan Sudi 14, 1844 V.S. (27.8.1787). Draft Kharita Bundle No. 19. Jodhpur Khayat 3, p. 441, mentions that a lakh of rupees were levied on Balakheri. It is unsupported by any other primary source.

149. D.O.A.B.: Dastari Records, Bundle No. 9, File No. 4, letter No. 45, dated Second Shrawan Sudi 2, 1844 V.S. (15.8.1787), From Maharaja Pratap Singh to Maharaja Bijay Singh.

150. P.R.C. I, 175.

151. Marwar Khayat, Vol. III, pp. 67-70.

152. P.R.C.I, 175.

153. D.O.A.B.: From Maharaja Sawai Pratap Singh to Maharaja Bijay Singh, dated Magsar Sudi 9, 1844 V.S. (19.12.1787), Draft Kharita, Bundle No. 19, Draft No. 296; Jodhpur Rajya ki Khayat 3, p. 444. Ojha Jodhpur 2, p. 738. P.R.C. I. 192 mentions that Sher Khan took poison to save his honour. After his death only, the Rathors occupied it on December 24, 1787. Marwar Khayat, Vol. III, pp. 69-70 mentions that Sher Khan accepted a bribe of Rs. 20,000 and then surrendered.

154. D.O.A.B.: Dastari Records, Basta No. 9, File No. 4, letter No. 50, dated Magsar Sudi 10, 1844 V.S. (20.12.1787). From Maharaja Sawai Pratap Singh to Maharaja Bijay Singh.

(a) D.O.A.B. : Jodhpur Records, Arzi Bahi No. 3, folio 6 A & B, dated Posh Budi 14, 1844 V.S. (7.1.1788).

155. (a) D.O.A.B.: From Maharaja Sawai Pratap Singh to Maharaja Bijay Singh, dated Kartik Sudi 3, 1844 V.S. (13.11.1787). Draft Kharita, Bundle No. 19, Draft No. 258.

(b) He was the nephew of Mohammad Beg Mamdani and represented the Mughal nobility at the court.

156. D.O.A.B.: From Maharaja Sawai Pratap Singh to Maharaja Amar Singh, dated Magsar Sudi 14, 1844 V.S. (24.12.1787). Draft Kharita, Bundle No. 19, Draft No. 301.

157. D.O.A.B.: From Bhim Singh to Maharaja Sawai Pratap Singh, dated Phalgun Budi 7, 1844 V.S. (28.2.1788). Draft Kharita, Bundle No. 19.

158. D.O.A.B.: From Maharaja Sawai Pratap Singh to Raja Hari Singh of Narwar, dated Magh Sudi 5, 1844 V.S. (12.2.1788). D.K. Bundle No. 19, Draft No. 308.

159. D.O.A.B.: Jodhpur Records, Arzi Bahi No. 4, folio 6 A & B, dated 14th day of the dark half of Posh 1844 V.S. (7.1.1788).

160. D.O.A.B.: Jodhpur Records, Arzi Bahi No. 4, folio 8A, dated Shrawan Budi 5, 1844 V.S. (23.7.1788).

161. P.R.C. I, 312; Hakikat Bahi No. 4, p. 602; C.P.C. Vol. VIII, 617.

162. P.R.C. I, 258; C.P.C. Vol. IX, 161.

163. D.O.A.B.: Dastari Records, Basta No. 9, File No. 4, letter No. 50, dated Magsar Sudi 10, 1844 V.S.. (20.12.1787). From Maharaja Sawai Pratap Singh to Maharaja Bijay Singh.

164. D.O.A.B.: From Maharaja Sawai Pratap Singh to Maharaja Bijay singh dated Posh Budi 6, 1844 V.S. (30.12.1787), Draft Kharita, Bundle No. 19, Draft No. 217.

165. D.O.A.B.: From Raja Radhika Das to Maharaja Sawai Pratap Singh, dated Phalgun Sudi 9, 1844 V.S. (16.3.1788). Kharita Section; Jodhpur Khayat 3, p. 451.

166. D.O.A.B.: From Maharaja Sawai Pratap Singh to Raja Hari Singh dated Magh Sudi 5, 1844 V.S. (12.2.1787), D.K. Bundle No. 19, Draft No. 308.

    The emperor demanded Rs. 5,000 a day and was paid by Mahadji Scindhia. The Rajput Rajas were not in a position to meet it and hence a compromise could not be worked out. The emperor returned to Delhi. Rs. two lakhs were paid to him in fake hundies. Jodhpur Khayat 3, pp. 452-53; Ojha Jodhpur 2, p. 741.

167. Ali Bahadur was the son of the late Peshwa, Baji Rao, by a Mohammadan concubine.

168. Duff, *op. cit.*, p. 475.

169. He had planned against the life of Mahadji Scindhia. He was given shelter by Ali Bahadur. Scindhia demanded his surrender. Tukoji sided with Ali Bahadur.

170. Sarkar, *op. cit.*, IV, 11.

171. *Ibid.*

172 Ghulam Qadir had assumed control over the Emperor after the retreat of Mahadji from Lalsot and in conjunction with Ismail Beg had the audacity of deposing him. They installed Bidar Bakht—the son of the ex-emperor Ahmed Shah—at the entreaty of the Dowager Empress Malika-i-Zamani, who promised to pay them twelve lakhs of rupees. They even had the audacity of extracting both the eyes of the Emperor, for he refused to disclose the hidden treasures. The royal place was robbed of everything.

173. The adopted son of Najaf Khan.

174. Sarkar, *op. cit.*, IV, 2.

175. D.O.A.B.: Dastari Records, Basta No. 9, File No. 4, letter No. 68, dated Magh Budi 3, 1845, V.S. (14.1.1789). From Maharaja Sawai Pratap Singh to Maharaja Bijay Singh.
176. D.O.A.B.: Dastari Records, Basta No. 9. File No. 4, letter No. 72, dated Baisakh Budi 10, 1846 V.S. (20.4.1789). From Maharaja Sawai Pratap Singh to Maharaja Bijay Singh.
177. D.O.A.B.: Dastari Records, Basta No. 9. File No. 4, letter No. 73, dated Baisakh Budi 13, 1846 V.S. (7.5.1789). From Maharaja Sawai Pratap Singh to Maharaja Bijay Singh.
178. D.O.A.B.: Dastari Records, Basta No. 9. File No. 4, letter No. 70, dated Phalgun Sudi 8, 1845 V.S. (5.3.1789). From Maharaja Sawai Pratap Singh to Maharaja Bijay Singh.
179. D.O.A.B.: From Singhvi Khub Chand to Khawas Roda Ram, dated Magsar Budi 2, 1846 V.S. (5.11.1789).
180. D.O.A.B.: Jodhpur Records, Hakikat Bahi No. 5, folio 109 A, dated Magsar Sudi 10, 1846 V.S. (27.11.1789).
181. N.A.O.I.: Persian Section, Translation of Persian Records, Tr. 30, pp. 85-88, No. 94. Received March 1, 1790. From Raja Bijay Singh to GG.
182. (a) N.A.O.I.: Persian Section, Translation of Persian Records. TI. 36, pp. 47-49, No. 102, dated March 15, 1790. From GG. to Raja of Jainagar.

     (b) N.A.O.I.: Persian Section, Translation of Persian Records, TR. 30, pp. 51-52, No. 59, dated Feb. 10, 1790. From Raja of Jainagar to GG.
183. D.O.A.B.: Dastari Records, Basta No.9, File No. 4, letter No. 74, dated Baisakh Sudi 1847 V.S. (14.4.1790 to 28.4.1790). From Maharaja Sawai Pratap Singh to Maharaja Bijay Singh.
184. N.A.O.I.: Persian Section, Translation of Persian Records, TR. No. 30, pp. 51-52, No. 59, dated Feb. 10, 1790. From Raja of Jainagar to GG.
185. D.O.A.B.: Dastari Records, Basta No.9, File No. 4, letter No. 73, dated Baisakh Sudi 10, 1847 V.S. (9.4.1790). From Maharaja Sawai Pratap Singh to Maharaja Bijay Singh.
186. D.O.A.B.: From Khichi Sher Singh to Maharaja Sawai Pratap Singh, dated Asadh Budi 13, 1847 V.S. (10.6.1790), Arziat Section, Bundle No. 17.
187. N.A.O.I.: Persian Section, Translation of Persian Records. TR No. 30, pp. 146-48, NO. 121. Received March 17, 1790. From Raja of Jainagar to GG.

188. Benoit de Boigne was an officer in the regiment of Lord Clare in the King of France's Irish Brigade. He had studied the art of war in that army and afterwards in the army of Catherine of Russia engaged with the Turks in the Levant. Being taken prisoner, he was sold as a slave at Constantinople, but ultimately escaped and came to India. He obtained a commission in the 6th Madras Native Infantry. Soon after he resigned and came to Calcutta. He then entered the service of Scindhia. Firstly he was offered Rs. 4,000 and then subsequently raised to Rs. 6,000 a month. He retired soon after Mahadji's death. He died in June 1830.
189. Lakwa Dada was a Saraswat Brahman. He rose from an humble position to that of a military officer under Mahadji Scindhia and commanded 52 `Risalas'. He displayed great courage and tract against Ismail Beg in the battle of Agra and was honoured by Scindhia who conferred upon him the title of Shamsheer Jung Bahadur. He fought on the side of Scindhia under Ismail Beg at Patan, against Holkar at Lakheri and against the Rathors at Ajmer. Lakwa Dada has been depicted as "the best Maratha General of his time" by Fraser, Military Memoir of Skinner, Vol. I, p. 124.
190. Sixty miles north of Jaipur and eighteen miles south-west of Narnaul.
191. Compton. H., *A particular account of the European Military Adventurers of Hindustan from 1784 to 1808* (London), p. 53.
192. *Ibid.*
193. D.O.A.B.: Sanad Bahi No. 53, folio 145 A.
194. D.O.A.B.: Dastari Records, Bundle No. 9, File No. 4, letter No. 82, dated First Asadh Sudi 10, 1847 V.S. (22.6.1790). From Maharaja Sawai Pratap Singh to Maharaja Bijay Singh.
195. *Ibid.*
196. D.O.A.B.: From Raja Sampat Singh to Bijay Singh, dated Asadh Sudi 13, 1847 V.S. (25.6.1790).
197. P.R.C.: Vol. I, No. 260, pp. 367-68. Intelligence from the Raja of Jainagar dated 7th Shawwal (June 20, 1790).
198. The Kachwahas lost five battalions and the Rathors some 3,000 horsemen. Scindhia lost 52 men from the household cavalry; 301 were wounded. The Marathas collected 105 pieces of artillery, 21 elephants, 8,000 flint locks, 1,300 camels and 300 horses.
199. D.O.A.B.: Jodhpur Records, Arzi Bahi No. 4, foil 166 B, dated Second Asadh Budi 12, 1846 V.S. (9.7.1790).

200. Forces from Jalor, Desuri and Sirohi joined him. Hakikat Bahi No. 5, p. 151.

201. Sarda, Harbilas D.B., Ajmer Historical and Descriptive (1st ed. : Ajmer, 1941), p. 196.

202. D.O.A.B.: From Maharaja Bijay Singh to Thakur Suraj Mal, dated Phalgun Budi 1, 1847 V.S. (19.2.1791).

203. 76 Miles North-East of Ajmer.

204. Keene, *op, cit.*, p. 155. Bijay Singh proposed to make him an independent ruler of Ajmer. Herbert Compton, *op. cit.*, p. 55.

205. Ojha, Jodhpur ......, *op. cit.*, II, 752.

206. D.O.A.B.: Jodhpur Records, Hakikat Bhai No. 5, folio 257 A.

207. D.O.A.B.: Jodhpur Records, Hakikat Bahi No. 5, folio 257 A. The Rathor casualty was 2000 killed and 3,000 wounded. Marwar ki-khayat, Vol. III, pp. 90-91; Mundiyad Khayat, pp. 252-53.

208. Duff, *op. cit.*, p. 497.

209. D.O.A.B.: Jodhpur Records, Arzi Bahi No. 4, dated Posh Sudi 8, 1847 V.S. (12.1.1791), folio 241 B. From Maharaja Sawai Pratap Singh to Maharaja Bijay Singh.

     A deputation was sent under Vyas-Nawal Rai on Sept. 14, 1790. Arzi Bahi No. 4, pp. 161-62, dated Bhadra Sudi 6, 1847 V.S. (14.9.1790). Another deputation under Muhnot Gopal Das, Sukh Ram and Mathura Nath was sent on Sept. 15, 1790. Arzi Bahi No. 4, folio 162 A, dated 7th day of the bright half Bhadra 1847 V.S. (15.9.1970).

210. Budh Singh was accompanied with Bhawani Das Bhandari and Kalyan Das.

211. (a) D.O.A.B.: Dastari Records, Basta No. 6, File No. 6, letter No. 57, dated Posh Sudi 1, 1847 V.S. (5.1.1791). From Mahadji Scindhia to Maharaja Bijay Singh, Jama Kharch File No. 41; Asopa, p. 52.

     (b) Sardesai, Historical Papers ......, *op. cit.*, letter no. 587, dated Jan. 6, 1791. From Apaji Ram to Nana Fadnavis.

     V.V. 2, p. 856; Jodhpur Rajya ki Khayat 3, pp. 98-99.

212. It consisted of 50 lakhs as `Mamlat dues', 5 lakhs as `Darbar charges and 5 lakhs as 'Nazrana' to `Mahadji Scindhia.

213. (a) D.O.A.B.: Dastari records, Basta No. 6, File No. 6, letter No. 57, dated Posh Sudi 1, 1847 V.S. (5.1.1791). From Mahadji Scindhia to Maharaja Bijay Singh; Jodhpur Khayat 3, p. 499.

     (b) Sardesai, Historical papers ..., *op. cit.* letter No. 587, dated

Jan. 6, 1791. From Apaji to Nana Fadnavis. He agrees on the stipulated sum but differs from the Rajput sources in the mode of payment. According to him, Rs. 7 lakhs were to be paid on Magh Sudi 1 and the balance to be paid in 4 equal instalments.

214. (a) Khas Rukka Bahi No. 1, p. 76.

(b) In addition to these five Parganas which were mortgaged, the Maharaja agreed to keep Mahnot Gyan Mal, Singhvi Vyas Manrup and Muhota Banki Das as hostages against good behaviour. Arzi Bahi No. 4, p. 133.

215. (a) Sardesai, Historical Papers ..., *op. cit.*, letter No. 591, dated February 12, 1791. From Apaji to Nana Fadnavis; Jodhpur Khayat 3, p. 500.

(b) D.O.A.B. : From Maharaja Bijay Singh to Thakur Surajmal, dated Phalgun Budi 1, 1847 V.S. (19.2.1791).

(c) Ajmer was occupied by the Marathas in March 1791. Marwar Khayat, Vol. III, p. 99.

216. D.O.A.B.: Dastari Records, Basta No. 6, File No. 6, letter No. 58, No date. From Mahadji Scindhia to Maharaja Bijay Singh.

217. D.O.A.B.: From Mahadji Scindhia to Pahar Singh, dated Bhadra Sudi 14, 1848 V.S. (11.9.1791).

218. D.O.A.B.: From Bohra Khushali Ram to Patel Mahadji Scindhia, dated Ashoj Budi 13, 1848 V.S. (16.9.1791).

219. D.O.A.B.: From Surat Ram to Dewan Shri Rai Chand, dated Magsar Budi 9, 1848 V.S. (20.11.1791), No. 140.

220. D.O.A.B.: From Mahadji Scindhia to Rao Raja Bakhtawar Singh, dated Magh Sudi 5, 1848 V.S. (28.1.1792), Kharita Section.

221. D.O.A.B.: From Gopal Rao and Jivaji Bakshi to Raj Shri Bai Suraj Kanwariji, dated Magsar Sudi 12, 1848 V.S. (7.12.1791).

222. D.O.A.B.: From Raiji Patel to Maharaja Sawami Pratap Singh, dated Posh Sudi 8, 1847 V.S. (12.1.1791), Kapat-dwara letter No. 969.

223. D.O.A.B.: From Duli Chand to Maharaja Sawami Pratap Singh, dated Phalgun Budi 11, V.S. (28.2.1791), Arzadast No. 77.

224. (a) D.O.A.B.: From Mahadji Scindhia to Maharaja Sawai Pratap Singh, dated Magh Budi 6, 1847 V.S. (25.1.1791). Kapat-dwara, No. 1456.

(b) D.O.A.B.: From Mahadji Scindhia to Bohra Khushali Ram and Daulat Ram, dated Posh Sudi 8, 1847 V.S. (12.1.1791).

225. The Mamlat dues amounted to 17 lakhs of rupees.

226. D.O.A.B.: From Mahadji Scindhia to Maharaja Sawai Pratap Singh, dated Magh Sudi 8, 1847 V.S. (11.2.1791).

227. D.O.A.B.: Kapat-dwara, Account sheet of Samvat 1847, No. 153/1318/477.

228. D.O.A.B.: Agreement between Mahadji Scindhia, Khawas Roda Ram and Thakur Pahar Singh, dated Magh Sudi 5, 1847 V.S. (8.2.1791), letter No. 859, Kapat-dwara.

229. D.O.A.B.: Agreement between Mahadji Scindhia, Thakur Phar Singh and Khawas Roda Ram, dated Magh Sudi 14, 1847 V.S. (17.2.191). Letter No. 863, Kapat-dwara.

230. D.O.A.B.: From Maharaja Sawai Pratap Singh to Raja Manik Pal, dated Phalgun Sudi 1847 V.S. (19.2.1791 to 20.3.1791). Kharita Section No. 80.

231. N.A.O.I.: Persian Section, TR. 31, pp. 377-78, No. 256. Received dated Oct. 19, 1791. From Mahadji Scindhia to GG.

232. D.O.A.B.: From Mahadji Scindhia to Sawai Pratap Singh, dated Asadh Sudi 8, 1849 V.S. (27.6.1792).

233. D.O.A.B.: Sikar File, Account sheet of 1849, V.S. (9.3.1792 to 24.2.1793). Grand total demanded by De Boigne and Bhau Bhaskar through Daulat Ram.

234. The villages were Kakarkhi, Sargot and Kuchaman.

235. D.O.A.B.: Dastari Records, Basta No. 6, File No. 6, letter No. 67, dated Ashoj Sudi 14, 1849 V.S. (29.9.1792). From Mahadji Scindhia to Maharaja Bijay Singh.

236. D.O.A.B.: Dastari Records, Arzi Bahi No. 4, folio 48 A, dated Kartik Budi 10, 1848 V.S. (22.10.1792). From Jodhpur to Mahadji Scindhia.

237. (a) D.O.A.B.: Dastari Records, Arzi Bahi No. 4, folio 47 B, dated Bhadra Budi 5, 1849 V.S. (22.10.1792). From Jodhpur to Mahadji Scindhia.

     (b) D.O.A.B.: Dastari Records, Arzi Bahi No. 4, folio 57 A, dated Shrawan Budi 6, 1851 V.S. (18.01.1749). From Jodhpur to Kidar Rao Scindhia.

238. D.O.A.B.: Jodhpur Records, Arzi Bahi No. 4, folio 122 A, dated 5th Jaisath 1848 V.S. (26.5.1792). From Bijay Singh to Pardit Gopal Rao.

13

Marathas and the British Policy

The opening years of the 19th century were important for both the Rajputs and the Marathas. Marquess Wellesley, the Governor-General, who had hooked Hyderabad, Mysore and Lucknow into the subsidiary system, turned his attention towards the Marathas. To stabilise peace, in India, it was necessary that the Company should draw the Maratha power under its protection. The fear of France which served as the mainspring of Wellesley's policy was a smoke-screen designed to silence his critics by playing upon their nervousness regarding French intentions.

Wellesley realised that the success of the campaign against the Marathas would hinge upon the assistance or at least the neutrality of the Rajput chiefs[1] or depriving the enemies of the attachment and resources of the state of Rajputana.[2] For him an alliance with Jaipur and Jodhpur would "be an asset par excellence."

Fortified by the conviction that the State of Jaipur and Jodhpur, chafing at the galling tutelage of Scindhia and General Perron, would be willing to join the system of defensive alliance, he made up his mind to proceed cautiously.[3] The confused state of the Maratha affairs seemed to offer an opportunity for British expansion which Wellesley was loath to leave unused. The French phobia of the times was put forth as a hand excuse to paint his imperialism as purely defensive. The show-down with the Marathas was becoming pressingly inevitable and the desire to win over the Rajput states was necessary.

With this background, Lord Wellesley contacted the two rulers through their Vakils in Calcutta. The immediate despatch of a commission for negotiating the treaty might have failed by the vigilance of Perron and Scindhia.[4] When Maharaja Pratap Singh was informed by his Vakil, Rai Ram Singh, he asked for an "explicit explanation". He desired a public engagement rather than a secret understanding,[5] for he could reject it if unfavourable, and thus cement the wavering faith of his loyalty towards Scindhia and Perron.

Lord Wellesley then conferred upon Lieutenant General Lake an extensive diplomatic authority to conclude treaties with the chiefs of Rajputana. G. Mercer, originally Residency Surgeon at Hyderabad, was appointed to help General Lake.[6] Letters were addressed to Maharaja Pratap Singh[7] and Maharaja Bhim Singh[8] and the proposals of treaties were enclosed with them.

The draft proposed that they would have common friends and foes; that in case of the commencement of hostilities with the Marathas the two Rajas would assist the British forces with their armies and resources on the lines and plans of the Commander-in-Chief of the British forces. In return, the British Government would be responsible to defend them against foreign invaders.

Obviously, the proposals were favourable to the Rajputs, for they guaranteed the independence and territorial integrity of their kigdoms. The proposed defence could act as a check against the Marathas. The two Rajp ut states had hardly been independent since long. They always had to side with some imperial power to save themselves. So they were not reluctant to accept it. But before the draft could reach Jaipur, Maharaja Pratap Singh died on August 1, 1803, and his death was soon followed by the demise of Maharaja Bhim Singh on Kartik Sudi 4, 1860 V.S.[9] (19.10.1803).

Sawai Jagat Singh ascended the throne at Jaipur while Man Singh succeeded his late brother. Though protracted communications continued for long, but the obvious fear of the Marathas and the wavering reliance upon the pledges of the British Government dimmed the prospects. The commencement of hostilities gave it a ceremonial burial.

A short while before, the death of Janardhan Balaji, commonly known as Nana Fadnavis,[10] marked the triangular contest for the helmnship at Poona between Daulat Rao Scindhia, Jaswant Rao Holkar and Baji Rao II, the Peshwa. A truce between the Peshwa and Daulat Rao was effected by which the former promised aid against Jaswant Rao as there were hostile relations between the two. The latter agreed to assist the Peshwa against the friends of the late Nana.[11] While Scindhia was away fighting the forces of Holkar in Malwa, the Peshwa took it into his hands to eliminate all those who had been his and his father's political opponents. He got murdered Vitholi Holkar[12] which made Jaswant Rao to avenge it. He defeated the forces of the Peshwa and Scindhia in October 1802 and entered Poona.[13] The Peshwa fled[14] and found refuge at Bassein where the English were glad to receive him. The Peshwa agreed to enter into the subsidiary system. Wellesley had been trying to bring the Marathas into the subsidiary system but his offers of help and mediation had so long been spurned. Now ill-luck placed the formal head of the Maratha confederacy into his hands and he was determined to make the best use of it. The treaty of Bassein was concluded in December, 1802 between the Peshwa and the Company.[15] It was a general defensive alliance based on reciprocal protection of the territories of the Peshwa and the Company and their allies respectively.

To the Marathas, the treaty meant the annihilation of their independence which they were not ready to acquiese in without a struggle. But even in the face of a common danger they could not sink their mutual rivalries. The English did their best to prevent a coalition and, while Daulat Rao Scindhia and Raghuji Bhonsla, Raja of Nagpur, immediately closed their ranks, nothing could persuade Jaswant Rao Holkar to join the alliance. He retired to Malwa and attached the course of events.

The attempts at peace failed and the British agent Colonel Collins left Scindhia's camp on August 3, 1803, which was the signal for war. The war operations were simultaneously carried on in the Deccan and northern India. General Lake captured Aligarh in August and was the master of Delhi in September, 1803. Agra fell in October and the final battle of northern India was fought at Lasswari in November where Scindhia was defeated. On December 30, 1803, the treaty of Surji-Arjungaon with Scindhia brought the war to an end. Scindhia ceded all his territories between the Ganges and the Jamuna, relinquished his rights over Broach and all land north of Jaipur, Jodhpur and Gohad. Scindhia further agreed to recognise the rights of the Rajput Rajas whom General Lake had won over to his side by signing the treaties with the Jaipur and Jodhpur Darbars in December, 1803, as we will see in the pages to follow. By a separate treaty Scindhia recognised the treaty of Bassein. For some time, the power of Scindhia was reduced in Rajputana.

These incidents, which determined Anglo-Maratha relations, were also events of major importance in the annals of Maratha-Rajput relations. A new factor appeared on the stage and the Company became henceforth a contender for supremacy in Rajputana against the Marathas. The Rajputs sought to apply the healing touch of the British power to the festering sore of the Marataha interference. The Rajputs added to the strength of the Company by adopting a posture of neutrality until one of the owners clearly established its way over the other. This shortened the campaigns of General lake. Henceforth, the Marathas had to pay heavily for the follies they had committed in Rajputana.

While Scindhia was thus busy against the Company, General Perron was demanding tribute from Jaipur.[16] The Maharaja had made persistent calls to Holkar to aid him against Perron. Jaswant Rao consented to it and promised to return to Rajputana[17] immediately after settling the Deccan affairs. Jaswant Rao took a long time and so could not render any help. The Maharaja was forced to pay an yearly tribute of 2 lakhs of rupees regularly to Scindhia.[18] These demands of the Marathas became subsequently the basis for the tribute Jaipur had to pay to the Company.

The laurels gained by General Lake and the proximity to Rajputana made him feel that the Rajput states would willingly agree to an alliance with the Company.[19] But the Rajputs were still unprepared to barter away their freedom for ambiguous assurances.

Jaswant Rao, taking advantage of such a chaos among the Rajputs, tried to exploit it to his advantage. He addressed letters to win over the Kachwaha Raja to his side. He sent Mehta Chabila Ram and Khande Rao to Jaipur.[20] They entreated the Raja to think of the fatal consequences that must flow, should the English become masters. Jaswant Rao addressed a letter to Sawai Jagat Singh telling him that Raghuji Bhonsla and Daulat Rao Scindhia had taken up the task of saving the sacred land and the religion of India against the English, while he had proceeded to maintain intact the dignity of the Rajput Rajas of the North. He requested him to assemble all the Rajputs under his command and save the Hindu religion from being submerged under the ocean of Christianity.[21] He did his best to instigate the Rajput Rajas against the alien domination and frankly maintained that these adventurers were unscrupulous and that there was no point in paying money to them.[22] The past records for the Marathas failed to instil confidence in the mind of the Maharaja.

Jaswant Rao Holkar again reminded him of the over-all calamity that might engulf the whole of northern India.[23] He requested him to let him recruit some forces from Jaipur for the ensuing battle against the English in saving their sacred religion.[24] But the solicitations of Jaswant Rao cut no ice with him. It appears that Jaswant Rao also tried to take Maharaja Man Singh into confidence but he, taking it to be unfavourable at the moment, did not accede to it.[25] The Rajput states relentlessly pursued the idea of keeping aloof from the Marathas and the British.

When war seemed imminent the Jaipur and Jodhpur Darbars sent their agents, Bakshi Mitha Lal[26] and Vyas Fateh Ram,[27] respectively, to General Lake. After long and protracted negotiations, Maharaja Jagat Singh signed the treaty on December 12, 1803, at Sirhind and the same was ratified by the governor General in Council on January 15, 1804. Fateh Ram Vyas also concluded his engagement with Lord Lake on December 22, 1803.[28]

It was also ratified by Lord Wellesley[29] but the Maharaja withheld his signature and proposed[30] a new set of terms more in keeping with his position as a sovereign. The changed circumstances had left this as the only alternative.

The onus of the violation of this treaty was thrown on the weak shoulders of Maharaja Man Singh. But being thoroughly acquainted with the Maratha character, he could act in no other way. Vast hordes of Holkar were lying close to Jodhpur, but the forces of the Company were stationed at a distance and could not be easily procured for the protection of the Raj. On the other hand, the very news for the conclusion of such a defensive alliance would have provided an ample reason to Holkar to attack Jodhpur. Soon after the retreat of Holkar, the Maharaja expressed a desire to conclude a treaty.[31] and even sent the original treaty ratified to the British Commander-in-Chief.[32] By this time, much water had flowed under the bridges and the repeated requests did not fit in with British policy. Maharja Man Singh was held responsible for it by taking sides with Jaswant Rao Holkar.

The treaty with Jaipur was based on the same proposals which were communicated to the Maharaja in July, 1803. It established a firm and permanent friendship between the two signatories. The most important articles were the fourth and fifth by which the Maharaja was committed to lend the whole of his forces to the Company in the event of an enemy evincing a disposition not invade the country lately taken possession of by the Company in Hindustan. The Company guaranteed the security of the Maharaja against all external enemies for which the Maharaja was to pay. The clauses were directed particularly against Scindhia and Holkar.

The treaty had far-reaching repercussions in the relations between the Marathas and the Rajputs. It was now the responsibility of the Company to protect the state from the attack of any hostile power. The fear of facing the English, if the Marathas cast their covetous eye on Jaipur, made their plight miserable.[38] Holkar, who was mostly feeding his armies on Jaipur money, found himself hard-pressed. He was not prepared to acquiesce in changes which had been wrought so speedily.

On the other hand, Jaipur was relieved of the yearly exactions which she had been paying to Scindhia. She could make use of it in bearing the expenses of the forces of the Company when called in to maintain the state against enemy attack. She had to aid the Company with the forces, if an attack was launched on the British dominions.

A similar treaty was signed between Alwar and the Company as a reward for the services rendered by that state during the campaigns against Scindhia. The treaty was ratified on December 19, 1803. Hearing of such an alliance with the Company, Jaswant Rao addressed a letter to the Rao Raja to detach him from it.[34] But the Rao Raja did not care for the requests and threats of Jaswant Rao and the treaty remained intact.

Alwar was also provided with the same protection that was offered to Jaipur which saved this small state from the day-to-day encroachments of the Marathas. While the treaty with Jaipur was thrown to the winds in July 1806,[35] Alwar continued enjoying the Company's protection because of her faithful services during the second Anglo-Maratha war.

When Scindhia was busy fighting the English, Jaswant Rao turned towards Rajputana. He did his utmost to win over the Rajput Rajas to his side. When his attempts failed he took to rapine and made a move towards Mewar.[36] He reached Udaipur and wrought havoc. The powerless Rana deputed Bakshi Bhaskar Bhau to negotiate the tribute.[37] The agent agreed to a tribute of forty lakhs of rupees.[38] It was decided that the money already taken was to be deducted as well as a compensation for the damage done to the several villages would be taken into account. A sum of ten lakhs of rupees was to be paid immediately and the rest by instalments.[39] Holkar promised help in realising the dues from the tributaries of Mewar. Marching from Mewar en route to Lawa, he reached Bhanpura. He proceeded towards Ajmer and was busy levying contributions from the Chief of Kishangarh and creating disturbances at Ajmer. The fort of Ajmer had been re-taken by Maharja Man Singh when Daulat Ram Scindhia was busy fighting the Company.[40] Holkar levied considerable contributions in Ajmer and unsuccessfully attempted to possess the fort.[41] Scindhia feeling that the fort might fall into his hands informed Sawai Jagat Singh that the administration of Ajmer had been ceded to Bala Rao Inglia. He requested him to help him in quelling the disturbances caused by Jaswant Rao Holkar.[42] The Jaipur Darbar had just concluded the treaty with the Company and so nothing was done which might prejudice the English interests. Daulat Rao Scindhia also kept Raja Man Singh of Jodhpur informed of the activities of Holkar and begged for his help.[43] The Maharaja in his letter dated first Chaitra Sudi 2, 1860 V.S., assured Scindhia of it.[44] Holkar being frightened by the likely aid that Scindhia might be getting from Jodhpur, thought it well to give up his pursuits at Ajmer.

On the other hand, with the suppression of Scindhia, Holkar aloe remained outside the pale of the subsidiary system. Holkar's freedom of action was injurious to the interests of the Company. So letters were sent to Jaswant Rao Holkar to make peace as the Chiefs and Princes of all factions had done. To gain time Jaswant Rao deputed Sultan Baksh and Nauroj Ali as his envoys to the Company to arrange the terms of the treaty, but the peace project failed.[45]

The British intentions of deciding the issue by a battle made Jaswant Rao open negotiations with Jaipur, Udaipur and Jodhpur to lodge his family. Sawai Jagat Singh did not like to offend the Company. Udaipur had still afresh the memory of humiliations inflicted upon her at his hands. Only Maharaja Man Singh showed his willingness.[46] Jaswant Rao deputed Bhasker Bhau and Tantia Alikar, his agents for the purpose. An agreement was reached between the deputies of the two Darbars on Magh Sudi 5, 1860 V.S.[47] (17.1.1804) by which Jaswant Rao recognised the rights of Maharaja Man Singh on the fort of Ajmer and promised not to create any disturbances in the territory of Sambhar. Man Singh agreed to lodge his family[48] at a place of safety in his kingdom on being paid the expenses.[49] Jaswant Rao then sent his family to Jodhpur.[50] He also tried to detach the Macherey Raja from his alliance with the Company, but miserably failed in his attempt.[51]

Having done this, he arrived near Jaipur and threatened it.[52] As Jaipur had been an ally of the Company, General Lake on April 18, 1804,[53] left for the assistance of Jaipur and asked the Maharaja to join against Jaswant Rao. The two other armies from the Deccan and Gujrat under Arthur Wellesley and Colonel Monson also converged upon him. It was not a charitable disposition of the Company to launch upon a campaign for the purpose of redeeming one of their allies, but they were motivated by considerations of security to the British Empire.[54]

Jaswant Rao Holkar, watching the advance of the armies, proceeded southward and besieged Aligarh. He was driven away by another battalion headed by Colonel Liatinicho. Aligarh was captured by the forces of Company on May 16, 1804. Lord Lake, leaving Colonel Monson with special instructions not to let Jaswant Rao Holkar advance to northern India, returned to Kanpur. Colonel Monson, without weighing the consequences, crossed the Chambal and encamped near Kota. He deputed his agent Faiz Talab Khan to Kota to seek the help of Zalim Singh.[55] Trusting in the invincibility of the British arms and his policy of appeasing all parties, he did not hesitate to help. He sent seven hundred men under Bakshi Sheo Lal to cooperate with Colonel Monson.[56] He extended all cordiality to Monson during his stay at Kota for four days.[57] Sawai Jagat Singh also sent his army under Jeewan Ram to help the Company against Jaswant Rao Holkar.[58] As soon as Jaswant Rao knew of it, he addressed a very strong letter to him to face consequences if he failed to recall his forces.[59] He reminded Jeewan Ram of his unbecoming act in joining the Company against him.[60] But all these protests failed to make any impression.

When nothing was done Jaswant Rao encamped near Garot.[61] Monson also marched towards the South, crossed the Mukandra pass and encamped at Garot. He was informed that Holkar was lying nearby preparing for a battle. Therefore, Monson hurried back to Mukandra. A horrible engagement took place, in which Monson was roundly trounced by Holkar. Monson escaped, and was hotly pursued by Holkar.[62] Monson reached Kota.[63] He solemnly asked Zalim Singh for shelter. Zalim Singh was in a fix. He neither wanted to antagonise the Company, for his keen reading of the times had convinced him that the Company would ultimately come out successful against Holkar, nor was he ambitious to quarrel with Holkar as he was still a formidable force to reckon with. Zalim Singh, therefore, followed the policy of blowing hot and cold in the same breath towards the Company and Holkar. He supplied restricted provisions, medical aid[64] to Monson and sent his troops to ensure the safety of the retreating army until it left the Mukandra pass in its rear. He addressed an apologetic letter to Lord Lake[65] for his inability to do more. Thus he neither completely offended Holkar nor gave the Company a cause of complaint. Monson left his surplus baggage at Kota, lightened his forces and pressed forward. Monson, taking the road of Hindon and Bayana, reached Agra on August 31, 1804. Under these circumstances Monson's charge of treachery against Zalim Singh is hardly justifiable.

The troops of Kota, who had joined the war on Monson's side, were scattered in ruin—their Bakshi, Akhay Ram Pancholi, was taken prisoner, Afzal Khan[66] was slain and large numbers were either left wounded or dead on the battle-field.[67] Zalim Singh asked his son, Madho Singh, to distribute Rs. 5,000 to the wounded and bereaved families as "Zakhmana."[68]

Holkar reached Kota in pursuit of Colonel Monson and reprimanded Zalim Singh for such a treacherous act. He plundered the parganas of Suket and Chechat and caused a huge plunder. The village, which were most affected were Alopa, Barakhui and Ganeshpura.[69] Zalim Singh who was worried at the attitude of Jaswant Rao, wanted to get rid of him by making some payment. A meeting was arranged between the two and much of the ill-feeling was removed.[70] Zalim Singh agreed to pay him three lakhs of rupees for his expenses.[71] Jaswant Rao moved towards Bundi[72] and then hurriedly left for Mathura. For the next six months his absence from Rajputna was a period of peace there.

The disorderly retreat of Monson emboldened Holkar to besiege Delhi. When he was busy there, his capital of Indore fell into the hands of Colonel Murray. Lake's advance to the relief of Delhi led Holkar to abdandon the siege and move down the Doab. A part of his army faced humilation at Deeg on November 13, 1804, and he himself was defeated at Farrukhabad four days later. The defeat of Holkar did not subdue him completely and he devised another plan to fight the Company. Lake's failure to capture the fort of Bharatpur, whose Jat Raja giving up the English alliance had joined Hoklar, was of little help to him.

The failure of Lake before Bharatpur and Monson's retreat had created doubts in the minds of the authorities about the desirability of their policy followed towards the Marathas and the Rajputs. It had also shattered the fiction of British invincibility from the mind of Scindhia. Scindhia, who had helped Lord Lake with a force 10,000 strong under Bapooji Scindhia, showed signs of discontent. Jaswant Rao took it as a favourable time to come to terms with him against the Company.

Jaswant Rao proceeded to Sabalgarh where Daulat Rao Scindhia lay encamped and agreed to work out a plan for their joint action against the Company with the co-operation of the Rajputs. Letters of encouragement were sent to the Rajput chiefs who were dependent upon Scindhia and Holkar before the war between the Company and the Marathas.[73] Roop Chand[74] unsuccessfully attempted to enlist Sawai Jagat Singh against the Company.[75] An agent was also sent to Jodhpur.[76] Man Singh was willing to join the confederacy.[77] Jaswant Rao Holkar also tried to take Rao Raja into confidence. He offered to defend him against the Company.[78] But Rao Raja who was in treaty with the Company refused to side with him.[79] The proposals met the same fate at Udaipur where the Rana did not deem it advisable to side with the Marathas whose loyalties were shifting with the passage of time. Such was the bad harvest reaped by the Marathas for their deeds in Rajputana. When apprehensions for a renewal of hostilities between the two Imperial powers became apparent, Jaswant Rao Holkar and Daulat Rao Scindhia again requested Maharana Bhim singh to hand over the fort of Kamalmir in order to provide shelter for their families.[80] The Maharana not only refused the proposal but sent his Vakil Bhairon Bakash to Lord Lake, who was then at Mathura, to solicit the aid of the Company against the Marathas.[81] This was a sufficient indication of the Maharana's attitude towards the Marathas, for though the latter were lying near Mewar and the troops of the Company were at a long distance, yet the Maharana sought to win the Company against the Marathas.[82] But under Lord Wellesley's orders Rana was informed that the British Government had no intention of concluding defensive alliances with the native states any more.[83] As such, Maharana Bhim Singh could neither win over the Company to his side nor pacify the Marathas.

Jaswant Rao and Surjee Rao Ghatge still favoured the continuance of war against the English. Scindhia did not deem it with favour. Ambaji Inglia, Scindhia's chief adviser, prevailed upon the two chiefs to divide the Kingdom of Mewar among themselves instead of fighting against the English. The prospect of ready money appealed to both of them and they reached Badnor. Ambaji reached Rayala.[84] He attacked Lambia and captured it. The Maharana was very puzzled as to the action to be taken against the invaders. He deputed Krishna Pancholi and Rawat Sangram Singh to Holkar. They made a piteous appeal to Jaswant Rao Holkar saying, "Do you want to sell Mewar to Ambaji Inglia?" Holkar was moved by this appeal and even pressed upon Scindhia to give up the design of partitioning Mewar.[85] He even returned the district of Nimbahera to the Maharana.

Tantia Alikar, a minister of Jaswant Rao, proposed that Ambaji should be appointed as the *Subedar* of Mewar. Every one excepting Bhaskar Bhau favoured it. But the position of Ambaji was far from happy. Holkar, with the connivance of Scindhia, placed Ambaji under surveillance and demanded 65 lakhs of rupees from him.[86] Ambaji, at his own request, was allowed to go to Kota with Amir Khan and Bapuji Scindhia to make arrangements for the payment. He succeeded in paying nearly half of the demand made upon him.[87] After this the short-lived sanity between Scindhia and Holkar came to an abrupt end.

The tussle between Jaswant Rao and the Company had not yet come to an end. With the end of the rainy season, Jaswant Rao became restless and worried as Lord Lake intended resuming his campaign in pursuit of him, so he once again sent his family to Jodhpur,[88] and hurriedly marched towards the Punjab via Ajmer and Sambhar.[89] He arrived at Sambhar on September 15, 1805. He was hotly pursued by the forces of the Company. So, he left Sambhar earlier. He reached Kandela, a town fifteen miles North of Jaipur, and leaving there a major part of his army under Amir Khan[90] left Rajputana for Punjab.[91]

In the meantime, Daulat Rao Scindhia made preparations for sending an army against Mewar, but so long as Jaswant

Rao was in the vicinity of Ajmer these forces could not march. Soon after his departure, Ambaji Inglia and Sadashiv Rao invaded Mewar. They were satisfied when the Maharana agreed to pay them 16,00,000 lakhs of rupees.[92] It was indeed pitiful that the Maharana had nothing in his coffers to pay the Maratha chiefs and, therefore, Sada Sheo Rao was kept with Ambaji as a security for the payment.[93] Shah Vardhaman, from Udaipur, asked Raja Hamir Singh of Banera, who was only a noble of the Maharana, to help him with some money in paying the dues of Ambaji.

On the other hand, the British authorities who were already suspicious of the advantages likely to follow from the continuance of war against the Marathas, deemed the tussle with the Marathas unfavourable at the moment in view of the renewed Anglo-French struggle and the intention of Napoleon to invade England. So they recalled their war-loving Governor-General, Lord Wellesley. Lord Cornwallis was appointed in his place to take up the task of pacifying the Marathas. But his death in October, 1805, left it to Sir George Barlow who followed in his foot-steps.

A new treaty was signed with Daulat Rao Scindhia in November, 1805, which confirmed the treaty of Surjee-Arjungaon with some modifications in favour of Scindhia. The river Chambal was declared to be the boundary between the possessions of Scindhia and the Company. The Company undertook not to enter into any treaties with the Rajput chiefs of Jaipur, Jodhpur, Udaipur and other teritonies of Scindhia in Malwa, Mewar and Marwar. A similar treaty was signed with Holkar on the 25th of December, 1805, at Rajpurghat on the banks of the Beas by which Holkar gave up his rights north of the Chambal. The Company in turn promised not to interfere with his possessions south of the Chambal. It was inconceivable for the Company now to maintain relations with the tributary states of the Marathas in view of the treaties signed with Holkar and Scindhia.[94]

The treaty with Jodhpur had not come into effect and no encouragement was given by the Company to renew it.

The treaty with Jaipur was dissolved as the Maharaja had not exerted to oppose Holkar when the latter was proceeding towards the territory of the Company, after humiliating Colonel Monson.[95]

It was a vague charge laid on Sawai Jagat Singh as the Maharaja could not help due to the absence of explicit instructions from Major General Jones. But as he was weak and the Company had determined to free herself from all undertakings, so though he persisted in maintaining cordial relations with the Company, yet all proved futile.[96]

The Rajput States had aided the Company against the Marathas in the hope of Company's protection but now they were abandoned to the vendetta and fury of the Marathas. The short spell under the protection of the British umbrella, ended. Rajputana again became the hunting-ground not only for the Marathas alone but also the ravenous hordes of Amir Khan who, having tasted blood, had his appetite for it whetted.

REFERENCES

1. N. A. O. I. : GG. to the Court of Directors vide letters to the Court of Directors, 1805, Vol. 20, dated May 20, 1803.
2. Martin, M.: *Despatches, Minutes and Correspondence of Marquess Wellesley*, Vol. III, pp. 228-29.
3. Martin, *op. cit.*, III, 427-28.
4. Martin, *op. cit.*, III, 240-42.
5. N.A.O.I., translation of a Persian letter from Maharaja of Jaipur to Lord Wellesley, Vol. 49, Jan.-Dec., 1803, No. 154. Persian Correspondence.
6. Martin, *op. cit.*, Vol. III, pp. 224-25.
7. N.A.O.I.: Translation of a Persian letter from Lord Wellesley to Maharaja Sawai Pratap Singh, dated July 22, 1803. Copies of issues, Vol. 38, Folio 83, Persian Correspondence.
8. N.A.O.I.: *Foreign-Political and Secret*, July 22, 1803, Cons. No. 20, dated March 2, 1804. From Lord Wellesley to Maharaja Bhim Singh.

9. (a) D.O.A.B.: *Jodhpur Records,* Arzi Bahi No. 5, Folio 2A, dated Phalgun Budi 13, 1860 V.S. (9.2.1804). From Jodhpur to Daulat Rao Scindhia.

 (b) Pustak Prakash: Vividh Sangrahaya Gutka No. 2, Folio 32B.

10. Fadnavis means a public officer—Keeper of the Ragisters.

11. D.O.A.B.: From Jaswant Rao Holkar to Dewan Rai Chand, dated Kartik Sudi 3, 1859 V.S. (29.10.1802), Kharita section, Indore Bundle No. 113.

12. Brother of Jaswant Rao Holkar.

13. D.O.A.B.: From Jaswant Rao Holkar to Maharaja Sawai Pratap Singh, dated Kartik Sudi 3, 1859 V.S. Kharita Section, Indore Bundle No. 116.

14. Holkar made Warnak Rao as the Peshwa.

15. According to this treaty six battalions of infantry and proportionate field artillery were to be stationed at Poona: Peshwa agreed to give 26 lakhs of Rupees to the Company. The Peshwa agreed to refer all claims upon Gaikwar and Nizam for arbitration before the English.

16. D.O.A.B.: From Maharaja Man Singh to Maharaja Sawai Pratap Singh, dated Ashoj Sudi 1, 1859 V.S. (27.9.1802).

17. D.O.A.B.: From Jaswant Rao Holkar to Dewan Rai Chand, dated Kartik Sudi 3, 1859 V.S. (29.10.1802), Kharita Section, No. 113.

18. D.O.A.B.: From Maharaja Sawai Pratap Singh to Dualat Rao Scindhia, dated Magsar Sudi 13, 1859 V.S. (7.12.1802), Kharita Section, No. 22.

19. Martin, *op. cit.,* Vol. III, 427-28.

20. D.O.A.B.: From Jaswant Rao Holkar to Rai Ratan Lal, dated 1860 V.S. (9.3.1803 to 24.2.1804). Mutaffarik Kagazat, Hindi, Bundle No. 2, No. 14.

21. D.O.A.B.: From Jaswant Rao Holkar to Maharaja Sawai Jagat Singh, dated Ashoj Sudi 9, 1860 V.S. (29.9.1803). Kharita Section.

22. D.O.A.B.: From Jaswant Rao Holkar to Dewan Rai Chand, Mutaffarik Kagazat, Hindi, Bundle No. 2, No. 33.

23. D.O.A.B.: From Jaswant Rao Holkar to Sawai Jagat Singh, dated Posh Sudi 2, 1860 V.S. (30.11.1803). Kharita Section, Indore Bundle.

24. D.O.A.B.: From Jaswant Rao Holkar to Maharaja Sawai Jagat Singh, dated Magsar Budi 11, 1860 V.S. (9.11.1803), Kharita Section, Indore Bundle.

25. D.O.A.B.: From Maharaja Man Singh to Sawai Jagat Singh, dated Posh Sudi 10, 1860 V.S. (23.12.1803), Kharita Section.
26. Martin, *op. cit.*, III, 453-54.; Ojha, Jodhpur, 2, p. 780.
27. N.A.O.I.: Translation of Persian letter received December 8, 1803, Vol. 49, No. 259. From Maharaja Man Singh to Lord Wellesley.
28. N.A.O.I.: Treaty with Jodhpur, Cons. March 2, 1804, No. 215 A.
29. N.A.O.I.: Foreign Political and Secret Cons. No. 217, March 2, 1804, From Lord Wellesley to General Lake, dated January 13, 1804.
30. N.A.O.I.: Foreign Political and Secret Cons. No. 56A, June 14, 1804.
31. Martin, *op. cit.*, IV, 150-51.
32. N.A.O.I.: Foreign Political and Secret Cons. No. 4, September 6, 1804. From General Lake to Lord Wellesley, dated May 1, 1804.
33. Martin, *op. cit.*, IV, 115-16.
34. Martin, *op. cit.*, IV, 100.
35. Banerjee, *op. cit.*, p. 364.
36. D.O.A.B.: From Shah Kishor Das of Udaipur to Shambhu Singh, dated Magh Sudi 3, 1860 V.S. (15.1.1804), Muttafarika Kagazat, Bundle No. 2, No. 16.
37. Sitamow: English translation of Mohan Singh's Waqai-i-Holkar, Folio 121 B.
38. *Ibid.*
39. Martin, *op. cit.*, III, 470-71.
40. Sarda, *op. cit.*, p. 200.
41. Martin, *op. cit.*, IV, 108.
42. (a) D.O.A.B.: From Daulat Rao Scindhia to Maharaja Sawai Jagat Singh, dated Posh Sudi 12, 1860 V.S. (25.12.1803), Kharita Section, GB.

    (b) D.O.A.B.: From Daulat Rao Scindhia to Maharaja Sawai Jagat Singh dated Phalgun Sudi 12, 1860 V.S. (12.2.1804). Kharita Section, GB.
43. D.O.A.B.: Jodhpur records, Arzi Bahi No. 5, Folio 2A, dated Phalgun Budi 13, 1860, V.S. (19.2.1804). From Maharaja Man Singh to Daulat Rao Scindhia.

44. D.O.A.B.: Jodhpur records, Arzi Bahi No. 5, Folio 2A, dated Phalgun Budi 13, 1860, V.S. (13.3.1804). From Maharaja Man Sigh to Daulat Rao Scindhia.

45. Sitamow: English translation of Mohan Singh's Waqai-i-Holkar, Folio 128B and 129A.

46. Sitamow: English translation of Mohan Singh's Waqai-i-Holkar, Folio 127A.

47. D.O.A.B.: Jodhpur Records, Arzi Bahi No. 5, Folio 107A, dated Magh Sudi 5, 1860 V.S. (17.1.1804). Copy of agreement between the agents of Jaswant Rao Holkar and Raja Man Singh.

48. D.O.A.B.: Jodhpur Records, Arzi Bahi No. 5, Folio 108A, dated first Chaitra Budi 14, 1860 V.S. (10.3.1804). Jodhpur Rajya ki Khayat 4, p. 20.

49. Sitamow: English translation of Mohan Singh's Waqai-i-Holkar, Folio 128B. It mentions that Jaswant Rao Holkar agreed to pay Rs. 40,000 and fodder worth Rs. 10,000 per mensem.

50. (a) Pustak Prakash: Vividh Sangrahayva Gutka No. 2, Folio 32B.
(b) *Ibid*. Folios 179B and 180A.

51. Martin: *Wellesley's Despatches,* Vol. IV, p. 100.

52. Sardesia, New History...*op. cit.,* III, 423.

53. Martin, *op. cit.,* IV, 121. Jaswant Rao had murdered three British officers—Capt. Vickres, Dodd and Ryanin—on the protext that they were carrying on treacherous corespondence with Lord Lake. Malcolm, Memoir of C.I., Vol. 2, p. 326. They were murdered at Nahar Magrah about 22 kilometres from Udaipur. Fraser mentions that seven officers were murdered. Fraser, Memoir of Skinner, Vol. I, p. 303.

54. The power of Holkar was at once menacing to The Company as is evident when Lord Wellesley wrote to Lake, "In fact we cannot trust him with any power. Experience has manifested his treachery, rapacity and arrogant pretensions, and if we cannot reduce him, we have lost our ascendancy in India," Martin, *Wellesley's Despatches,* Vol. IV,p. 100, letter from GG. in Council to the Secret Committee, June 15, 1804.

55. A.O.K.: Bhandar No. 3, Basta No. 3/1, Talikon ka Bhandar, dated Shrawan Sudi 12, 1860-61 V.S.

56. A.O.K.: Bhandar No. 3, Basta No. 3/1, Talikon ka Bhandar, dated Shrawan Sudi 15, 1861-61 V.S.(21.8.1804). Zalim Singh sent a contingent of troopers under Amar Singh, the chief of Palait. *Bengal Past and Present,* Vol. LXXIV, Part II, July-December, 1955.

57. A.O.K.: Bhandar No. 1, Basta No. 13, Samvat 1861 V.S.
58. D.O.A.B.: From Jaswant Rao Holkar to Maharaja Sawai Jagat Singh, dated Shrawan Sudi 12, 1861 V.S. (18.8.1804).
59. *Ibid.*
60. D.O.A.B.: From Jaswant Rao Holkar to Jeewan Ram, dated Shrawan Sudi 12, 1861 V.S. (18.8.1804).
61. A railway station on the Kota-Ratlam line of the Western Railway.
62. A.O.K.: Bhandar No. 3, Basta No. 3/1, Talikon ka Bhandar, dated Shrawan Budi 9, 1861 V.S. (31.7.1804).
63. Sitamow: English translation of Mohan Singh's Waqai-i-Holkar, Folio 135A.
64. A.O.K.: Bhandar No. 1, Basta No. 13, Samvat 1861.
65. *Ibid.* Zalim did not allow Monson's troops into Kota on the plea that he was unable to provide them provisions, Basawan Lal, Tr., p. 217.
66. Brother of Anwar Khan, a Minister of the Kota Raja. Waqai-Holkar, f, 134b.
67. Nearly 400 to 500 of Kota troopers were either killed or taken prisoner, Sharma, M.L. Kota Rajya ka Itihasa, Vol. II, p. 491.
68. A.O.K.: Bhandar No. 3, Basta No. 3/1, Talikon Ka Bhandar, dated Shrawan Sudi 1861, V.S.
69. A.O.K.: Bhandar No. 3, Hukmon ki Talikon ka Khata, Samvat 1861.
70. D.O.A.B.: From Jaswant Rao Holkar to Maharaja Sawai Jagat Singh, dated Shrawan Sudi 3, 1861 V.S. (9.8.1804), Kharita Section, Indore Bundle.
71. N.A.O.I.: F & S, June 7, 1804, Cons. No. 76. From J. Malcolm to GG. Jaswant Rao realised the last year's tribute from Kota, two years' tribute in advance and a lakh of rupees as fine for the help afforded to Col. Monson by Kota. Waqai-Holkar, f, 135B.
72. Jaswant Rao moved towards Bundi as Monson had recommended his guns which were struck hard in mud to the care of the Raja of Bundi who remained attached to him. Fraser, Military Memoir of J. Skinner, Vol. II, p. 9.
73. N.A.O.I.: F & S, July 4, 1805, Cons. No. 24. From Jenkin's Camp to Lord Lake, dated June 7, 1805.
74. Vakil of Daulat Rao Scindhia.

75. N.A.O.I.: F & S, Aug. 23, 1805. From W. Sturrock to Col. Malcolm.
76. Duff: *History of the Marathas,* Vol. II, p. 362.
77. D.O.A.B.: Jodhpur Records, Arzi Bahi No. 5, Folio 3-A, dated Kartik Budi 1, 1862 V.S. (9.10.1805). From Jodhpur to Daulat Rao Scindhia.
78. N.A.O.I.: F & S, Oct. 4, 1805, Cons. No. 18. Translation of a letter from Jaswant Rao Holkar to Rao Raja of Macheri.
79. N.A.O.I.: F & S, Oct. 4, 1805, Cons. No. 19. Translation of a letter from Rao Raja of Macheri to Jaswant Rao Holkar.
80. N.A.O.I.: F & S, July 1, 1805, Cons. No. 11, From W. Sturrock to Col. Malcolm, dated June 19,1805.
81. N.A.O.I.: F & S,July 4, 1805, Cons. No. 21. From Jenkin's Camp to Lord Lake.
82. N.A.O.I.: F & S,July 4, 1805, Cons. No. 22. From Jenkin's Camp to Lord Lake.
83. *Ibid.*
84. Banera: From Maharaja Bhim Singh to Maharana Bhim Singh, dated Jaisath Budi 1, 1862 V.S. (27.4.1805).
85. Jaswant Rao was jealous of the growing power of Scindhia and he realised that the scheme of partition would give the lion's share to his rival, Scindhia. He was also aware of the strategic importance of Mewar's strongholds. He as such prevailed upon Ambaji not to harry the Rana. The unusual signs of unity between the Saktawuts and Chundawats sealed the project.
86. Waqai-Holkar, f. 177b.
87. *Ibid.,* f, 177b. According to Tod, Rs. 55 Lakhs were extorted from Ambaji (Vol. 2. p. 535). Malcolm says that Ambaji paid 56 lakhs (Memoirs I, p. 239).
88. N.A.O.I.: F & S., Sept. 12, 1805, Cons. No. 95. Translation of a letter for Talik Chand from Hurry Pandit, dated Aug. 17, 1805.
89. N.A.O.I.: F & S Oct. 17, 1805, Cons. No. 48, From W. Sturrock to Col. Malcolm, dated Sept. 16, 1805.
90. N.A.O.I.: F & S, Oct. 17, 1805, Cons. No. 77. Translation of a letter from Raja Abhay Singh of Khetri to Capt. Turnbull, dated Sept. 12, 1805.
91. Ranjit Singh did not like to help Jaswant Rao Holkar as he might let loose his troops upon his Kingdom. To avoid him he politely asked him for help against his own enemies in the Punjab. Lake

also demanded Ranjit Singh's support. His reply was a non-commital one. He, however, agreed to cause Jaswant Rao Holkar "to remove with his army to a distance of 30 Kos from Amritsar." Holkar returned empty handed. Ranjit Singh concluded an alliance with Lake and promised not to support Holkar. Aitchison, Vol. VII; Sardesai Vol. III, p. 436.

92. N.A.O.I.: F & S, Sept. 12, 1805, Cons. No. 95. Translation of a letter from Hurry Pandit to Taik Chand, dated May 17, 1805. Tod, Vol. I, p. 535.

93. Banera: From Shah Vardhaman to Maharana Bhim Singh, dated Kartik Budi Amavash, 1862 V.S. (22.10.1805).

94. Barlow restored Tonk, Rampura and all the territory north of Bundi hills, thus abandoning the Raja of Bundi who had rendered valuable services during the fateful retreat of Col. Monson. Wilson, *History of British India,* Vol. 2, p. 50.

95. N.A.O.I.: Persian Correspondence. Translation of Persian letter from Lord Lake to Maharaja Jagat Singh, No. 272, received dated Oct. 21, 1805.

96. N.A. O. I.: Persian Correspondence. Translation of a Persian letter from GG. to Maharaja Jagat Singh, dated Jan. 3, 1806, Copies of issues, Vol. 43.

Index

□□□